Ideas That Shape A Nation

Emily Harrington
is a schmexxay
beast. The End.

Ideas
That Shape A Nation

**A SURVEY OF HISTORICAL IDEAS IMPORTANT
TO THE DEVELOPMENT OF THE UNITED STATES**

James L. Smith

Suncrest Publications
Las Cruces, New Mexico

Suncrest Publications
P.O. Box 236
Las Cruces, NM 88004
(505) 527-5527

Cover design by Fargo3 Designs, Inc.

ISBN 0-9701589-1-2
LCCN 00-191136

Printed and bound in the United States of America

10 9 8 7 6 5 4 3

ACKNOWLEDGMENTS

I am deeply indebted to many fine organizations and people who provided assistance toward the completion of this book. I am especially grateful to the James Madison Memorial Fellowship Foundation and the Christa McAuliffe Fellowship Program. Without their help *Ideas That Shape a Nation* would still be a dormant idea in my mind. In addition, I am grateful to the people who individually offered invaluable advice and support: Cookie Brilliant, Jamie Bronstein, Greg Butler, Isabel Castle, Joyotpaul Chaudhuri, Gerry Giordano, Jesse Gonzalez, Del Hansen, Dorothy Irion, Adam Karveller, Bill Merryman, Robert Ogas, Holly Reynolds, and Diane Tasker. I also want to thank members of my extended family who will forever hold a special place in my heart for their contributions and encouragement: Yvonne Smith, Susan Smith, Shawn Smith, and Barbara Hall. Above all, I thank my wife, Brenda, and my sons, Mark and Christopher, for their love and understanding.

This book is for all students of United States history.
May your thoughtful examination of our nation's enduring vision
move us toward "a more perfect union."

Human history is in essence a history of ideas.

–H. G. Welles

The thinker dies, but his thoughts are beyond the reach of destruction. Men are mortal; but ideas are immortal.

–Walter Lippmann

Thoughts rule the world.

–Ralph Waldo Emerson

Ideas are the most dangerous weapons in the world. Our ideas of freedom are the most powerful political weapons man has ever forged.

–William O. Douglas

Our life is what our thoughts make it.

–Marcus Aurelius

Neither man nor nation can exist without a sublime idea.

–Fëdor Dostoevski

The ideas of economists and political philosophers, both when they are right and when they are wrong, are more powerful than is commonly understood. Indeed, the world is ruled by little else. Practical men, who believe themselves to be quite exempt from any intellectual influences, are usually the slaves of some defunct economist. Madmen in authority, who hear voices in the air, are distilling their frenzy from some academic scribblers of a few years back. I am sure that the power of vested interest is vastly exaggerated compared with the gradual encroachment of ideas.

–John Maynard Keynes

Great minds discuss ideas, average minds discuss events, small minds discuss people.

–Unknown

TABLE OF CONTENTS

Introduction: A History Worth Studying 1

PART 1: A FOUNDATION FOR A NEW NATION

1. **Aristotle** 5
   In framing an ideal we may assume what we wish, but should avoid impossibilities.

2. **Thomas Hobbes** 15
   Covenants without the sword are but words.

3. **John Locke** 25
   The liberty of man . . . is to be under no other legislative power, but that established, by consent, in the commonwealth.

4. **Jean Jacques Rousseau** 35
   [The people] have given themselves leaders in order to defend their liberty and not to enslave themselves.

5. **New England Puritans** 45
   We shall be as a city upon a hill, the eyes of all people are upon us.

6. **Roger Williams** 55
   The civil state is bound before God to take off that bond and yoke of soul oppression, and to proclaim free and impartial liberty to all people.

PART 2: BUILDING A NATION

7. **Thomas Paine** 67
   There is something exceedingly ridiculous in the composition of monarchy.

8. **The Federalist** 77
   If men were angels, no government would be necessary. If angels were to govern men, neither external nor internal controls on government would be necessary.

9. **The Anti-Federalists** 87
   What right had they to say, "We the People"? . . . instead of "We the States"?

10. **George Washington** 97
    I am sure the mass of citizens in these United States mean well, and I firmly believe they will always act well, whenever they can obtain a right understanding of matters.

11. **James Madison** 107
In a large Society, the people are broken into so many interests and parties, that a common sentiment is less likely to be felt . . . by a majority of the whole.

12. **Thomas Jefferson** 117
If there be any among us who would wish to dissolve this Union or to change its republican form, let them stand undisturbed as monuments of the safety with which error of opinion may be tolerated where reason is left free to combat it.

13. **Alexander Hamilton** 127
The voice of the people has been said to be the voice of God; and however generally this maxim has been quoted and believed, it is not true in fact. The people are turbulent and changing; they seldom judge or determine right.

14. **John Marshall** 137
The peculiar circumstances of the moment may render a measure more or less wise, but cannot render it more or less constitutional.

PART 3: EQUALITY AND THE RIGHTS OF THE MINORITY

15. **Alexis de Tocqueville** 149
Americans are so enamored of equality that they would rather be equal in slavery than unequal in freedom.

16. **Henry David Thoreau** 159
A government in which the majority rule in all cases cannot be based on justice.

17. **Elizabeth Cady Stanton** 169
We hold these truths to be self-evident: that all men and women are created equal.

18. **John C. Calhoun** 179
When not efficiently checked, [the government of the absolute majority] is the most tyrannical and oppressive that can be devised.

19. **Frederick Douglass** 189
Right is of no sex—truth is of no color—God is the Father of us all and we are all brethren.

PART 4: A NEW BIRTH OF FREEDOM

20. **Abraham Lincoln** 201
Its authors meant [the Declaration of Independence] to be . . . a stumbling block to those who . . . might seek to turn a free people back into the hateful paths of despotism.

PART 5: THE INDUSTRIAL REVOLUTION

21. **Adam Smith** 213
Every man, as long as he does not violate the laws of justice, is left perfectly free to pursue his own interest in his own way.

22. **Karl Marx** 223
The rich will do everything for the poor except get off their backs.

23. **William Graham Sumner** 233
The aggregation of large fortunes is not at all a thing to be regretted.

24. **Henry George** 243
We must make land common property.

25. **Thorstein Veblen** 253
It is for this [leisure] class to determine, in general outline, what scheme of life the community shall accept as decent or honorific.

26. **Eugene Debs** 263
The working class must get rid of the whole brood of masters and exploiters, and put themselves in possession and control of the means of production.

PART 6: THE END OF THE FRONTIER

27. **Frederick Jackson Turner** 275
The advance of the frontier has meant a steady movement away from the influence of Europe, a steady growth of independence on American lines.

PART 7: ECONOMIC AND POLITICAL DEVELOPMENTS OF THE TWENTIETH CENTURY

28. **Woodrow Wilson** 287
Big business is not dangerous because it is big, but because its bigness is an unwholesome inflation created by privileges and exemptions which it ought not to enjoy.

29. **Franklin Roosevelt** 297
The test of our progress is not whether we add more to the abundance of those who have much; it is whether we provide enough for those who have too little.

30. **John Maynard Keynes** 307
The central controls necessary to ensure full employment will, of course, involve a large extension of the traditional functions of government.

31. **Ronald Reagan** 317
Government exists to protect us from each other. Where Government has gone beyond its limits is in deciding to protect us from ourselves.

PART 8: A NEW SENSE OF JUSTICE

32. **William O. Douglas** 329
A symbol of our health is the respect we show to First Amendment values.

33. **Martin Luther King, Jr.** 339
[America] is a dream of a land where men of all races, of all nationalities and of all creeds can live together as brothers.

34. **Malcolm X** 349
Nobody can give you freedom. Nobody can give you equality or justice or anything. If you're a man, you take it.

35. **Betty Friedan** 359
Our culture does not permit women to accept or gratify their basic need to grow and fulfill their potentialities as human beings.

36. **The American Indian** 369
We believe in the future of a greater America, an America which we were the first to love, where life liberty, and the pursuit of happiness will be a reality.

37. **César Chávez** 379
If you're outraged at conditions, then you can't possibly be free or happy until you devote all your time to changing them and do nothing but that.

PART 9: PREPARING FOR A NEW ERA

38. **Rachel Carson** 391
The most alarming of all man's assaults upon the environment is the contamination of air, earth, rivers, and sea with dangerous and even lethal materials.

39. **Alvin Toffler** 401
With intelligence and a modicum of luck—the emergent civilization can be made more sane, sensible, and sustainable, more decent and more democratic than any we have ever known.

Glossary 411

Bibliography 421

Ideas That Shape A Nation

A History Worth Studying

Ideas That Shape a Nation presents historical ideas in the original words of persons who influenced the development of the United States government, its laws, economic system, and social movements. The book is based on the premise that history is more than a mere chronicle of what people did; it is also an examination of what people thought. If history students examine the *idea* of liberty and how it can cause a revolution or the *idea* of equality and how it can overturn entrenched social traditions, they can better appreciate the power of ideas to change people's lives. Indeed, a study of history is incomplete without evaluating the ideas motivating people and shaping events.

Without a convincing patron an idea may lie dormant for generations and never move beyond the realm of conjecture. For example, the republican idea that the people were sovereign and capable of ruling themselves without a king was not new in 1776. However, with a proponent like George Washington, the idea of a republic became more than academic scribbling; it became a practical philosophy for creating a new nation. Washington's determination to win the American Revolution was shaped in large part by his commitment to republican ideas.

After the American Revolution ideas about forming a new nation were plentiful. Some Americans, including Alexander Hamilton, believed Washington should use his army to overthrow civilian authority; others proposed that Washington become king. Washington, however, remained true to the idea of a people ruling themselves without a king and decided to give up command of his army and retire to his farm as a private citizen. The world was astonished, and even the king of England proclaimed Washington "the greatest character of the age." Washington's retirement from the pinnacle of power demonstrated to the world that the new American nation would not have a king and the idea of a republic would move from dream to reality.

Determining the merits of an idea, as well as judging whether it will improve conditions or lead to misery and chaos, can be problematic. When the federal government passed the Alien and Sedition Acts in 1798, Thomas Jefferson and James Madison voiced their opposition with an idea that would cause great division and anguish in the United States. The Alien and Sedition Acts subjected persons to arrest and imprisonment for making "malicious" statements against the government. Jefferson and Madison considered such laws to be unconstitutional and tyrannical—which they were. However, in an attempt to rid the nation of unjust legislation, Jefferson and Madison hatched an idea that led to unintended consequences. In the Kentucky and Virginia Resolutions they wrote that states should be able to nullify unconstitutional federal laws. Regardless of Jefferson's and Madison's good intention—the preservation of free speech—they gave credibility to the state sovereignty proclamations that led to the Civil War and the deaths of over 600,000 Americans.

Occasionally, ideas advocated by seemingly powerless individuals can be more influential than ideas backed by ballots or bullets. Frederick Douglass, an escaped slave, and Elizabeth Cady Stanton, a disenfranchised woman, could not vote, run for office, or lead great armies. However, with the logic of their ideas and the persuasiveness of their presentations, they profoundly influenced the course of American history. Using the idea of equality expressed in the Declaration of Independence, they protested the conditions of slavery and discrimination that were contrary to the declared ideals of the nation. Their dedication to a fight for justice, based on their commitment to equality, transformed American society.

An idea might inspire people for several generations as it is used to drive a variety of reform movements. After the Declaration of Independence proclaimed "all men are created equal," an almost century-long struggle preceded Abraham Lincoln's Emancipation Proclamation. In turn, for almost a century after slavery ended, Americans endured institutional and social prejudice before such people as Martin Luther King, Jr., Betty Friedan, and César Chávez helped move the nation a step closer to justice defined by equality. Despite the long struggle, inequality has yet to be eliminated from American society and prejudice still infects the American psyche. Who next will lead the nation a step closer to the idea that a free people governing themselves can completely embrace the idea that all *persons* are created equal?

Whether an idea is admirable or contemptible it can alter the course of history. A good idea might influence people because it reveals eternal and universal truths about the human condition. A bad idea might be persuasive because human beings are blind to its consequences. Due to the persistence of some ideas, whether they are good or bad, Americans of the twenty-first century will inevitably confront age-old questions, questions that are dealt with throughout the course of this book:

1. Should federal power override state and local power?
2. Should the needs of the community outweigh the rights of the individual?
3. To what extent should minority rights be protected in a system based on majority rule?
4. To what extent are all people created equal?
5. What limits, if any, should be placed on private property?
6. What idea best defines the United States?

A history of ideas is a history worth studying. When a child stands on the shoulders of its parent, the child can see farther than the parent. When we stand on the shoulders of great thinkers we are able to see farther into the mysteries of our existence. Understanding the ideas that define our world makes us a little wiser and, as a result, makes our world a little better.

PART 1

A FOUNDATION
FOR A NEW NATION

CHAPTER 1

ARISTOTLE

BACKGROUND

Aristotle (384-322 B.C.) was a Greek philosopher who had a far-reaching influence on Western thought. At the age of seventeen he enrolled in Plato's Academy in Athens where he remained for twenty years. After Plato died Aristotle left Athens and gained employment with King Philip of Macedon. Aristotle tutored the king's son Alexander who, as Alexander the Great, became master of the Persian Empire. Aristotle eventually returned to Athens and established his own school. Since he was Alexander's teacher, Aristotle was associated with the Macedonians, the conquerors of Athens. Fearing for his safety, Aristotle was forced to leave Athens after Alexander's death. Aristotle died of natural causes a year after leaving Athens.

Although much of what Aristotle wrote is lost, the lecture notes taken by his students reveal his enormous intellectual output. He commented extensively on astronomy, biology, anatomy, logic, rhetoric, physics, ethics, politics, and the arts. His interests were so diverse because he felt that a search for knowledge allowed an individual to achieve the good life.

For over two thousand years Aristotle's ideas profoundly influenced the work of scientists and philosophers. He promoted the idea of the pursuit of happiness and championed the idea of the Golden Mean which encouraged "moderation in all things." In addition, he established the study of logic that is associated with modern ideas of scientific analysis. Although many of his scientific conclusions were later proved incorrect, his systematic study of all fields of human interest places him as one of the world's most influential philosophers.

Western civilization owes much to the work of Aristotle. His description of the six types of government, as well as his ideas on mixed government, are noticeable in the ideas of America's founding fathers. In addition, his ideas on the importance of community, a strong middle class, and obedience to law are evident in modern political discourse. Unfortunately, his views on slavery and the inferiority of women also permeated Western thinking for thousands of years.

ARISTOTLE – IN HIS OWN WORDS

Politics, Book I

Every state is a community of some kind, and every community is established with a view to some good; for mankind always act in order to obtain that which they think good. But, if all communities aim at some good, the state or political community, which is the highest of all, and which embraces all the rest, aims at good in a greater degree than any other, and at the highest good.

Some people think that the qualifications of a statesman, king, house-holder, and master are the same, and that they differ, not in kind, but only in the number of their subjects. For example, the ruler over a few is called a master; over more, the manager of a household; over a still larger number, a statesman or king, as if there were no difference between a great household and a small state. The distinction which is made between the king and the statesman is as follows: When the government is personal, the ruler is a king; when according to the rules of the political science, the citizens rule and are ruled in turn, then he is called a statesman.

But all this is a mistake; for governments differ in kind, as will be evident to any who considers the matter according to the method which has hitherto guided us. . . .

. . . In the first place there must be a union of those who cannot exist without each other; namely, of male and female, that the race may continue (and this is a union which is formed, not of deliberate purpose, but because in common with other animals and with plants, mankind have a natural desire to leave behind them an image of themselves), and of natural ruler and subject, that both may be preserved. . . .

. . . The family is the association established by nature for the supply of men's everyday wants. . . . But when several families are united, and the association aims at something more than the supply of daily needs, the first society to be formed is the village. . . .

When several villages are united in a single complete community, large enough to be nearly or quite self-sufficing, the state comes into existence, originating in the bare needs of life, and continuing in existence for the sake of a good life. And therefore, if the earlier forms of society are natural, so is the state, for it is the end of them, and the nature of a thing is its end. For what each thing is when fully developed, we call its nature, whether we are speaking of a man, a horse, or a family. Besides, the final cause and end of a thing is the best, and to be self-sufficing is the end and the best.

Hence it is evident that the state is a creation of nature, and that man is by nature a political animal. And he who by nature and not by mere accident is without a state, is either a bad man or above humanity; he is like the "Tribeless, lawless, hearthless one." . . .

Further, the state is by nature clearly prior to the family and to the individual, since the whole is of necessity prior to the part; for example, if the whole body be destroyed, there will be no foot or hand, except in an equivocal sense, as we might speak of a stone hand; for when destroyed the hand will be no better than that. . . . The proof that the state is a creation of nature and prior to the individual is that the individual, when isolated, is not self-sufficing; and therefore his is like a part in relation to the whole. But he who is unable to live in society, or who has no need because he is sufficient for himself, must be either a beast or a god: he is no part of a state. A social instinct is implanted in all men by nature, and yet he who first founded the state was the greatest of benefactors. For man, when perfected, is the best of animals, but, when separated from law and justice, he is the worst of all. . . . Wherefore, if he have not virtue, he is the most unholy and the most savage of animals, and the most full of lust and gluttony. But justice is the bond of men in states, for the administration of justice, which is the determination of what is just, is the principle of order in political society. . . .

But is there any one thus intended by nature to be a slave, and for whom such a condition is expedient and right, or rather is not all slavery a violation of nature?

There is no difficulty in answering this question, on grounds both of reason and of fact. For that some should rule and others be ruled is a thing not only necessary, but expedient; from the hour of their birth, some are marked out for subjection, others for rule.

. . . The male is by nature superior, and the female inferior; and the one rules, and the other is ruled; this principle, of necessity, extends to all mankind. Where then there is such a difference as that between soul and body, or between men and animals, the lower sort are by nature slaves, and it is better for them as for all inferiors that they should be under the rule of a master. For he who can be, and therefore is, another's, and he who participates in rational principle enough to apprehend, but not to have, such a principle, is a slave by nature. Whereas the lower animals cannot even apprehend a principle; they obey their instincts. And indeed the use made of slaves and of tame animals is not very different; for both with their bodies minister to the needs of life. Nature would like to distinguish between the bodies of freemen and slaves, making the one strong for servile labour, the other upright, and although useless for such services, useful for political life in the arts both of war and peace. But the opposite often happens—that some have the souls and others have the bodies of freemen. And doubtless if men differed from one another in the mere forms of their bodies as much as the statues of the Gods do from men, all would acknowledge that the inferior class should be slaves of the superior. And if this is true of the body, how much more just that a similar distinction should exist in the soul? but the beauty of the body is seen, whereas the Beauty of the soul is not seen. It is clear, then, that some men are by nature free, and others slaves, and that for these latter slavery is both expedient and right.

Politics, **Book III**

Having determined these points, we have next to consider how many forms of government there are, and what they are; and in the first place what are the true forms, for when they are determined the perversions of them will at once be apparent. The words constitution and government have the same meaning, and the government which is the supreme authority in states, must be in the hands of one, or of a few, or of the many. The true forms of government, therefore, are those in which the one, or the few, or the many, govern with a view to the common interest; but governments which rule with a view to the private interest, whether of the one, or of the few, or of the many, are perversions. For the members of a state, if they are truly citizens, ought to participate in its advantages. Of forms of government in which one rules, we call that which regards the common interests, kingship or royalty; that in which more than one, but not many, rule, aristocracy; and it is so called, either because the rulers are the best men, or because they have at heart the best interests of the state and of the citizens. But when the citizens at large administer the state for the common interest, the government is called by the generic name—a constitution. And there is a reason for this use of language. One man or a few may excel in virtue; but as the number increases it becomes more difficult for them to attain perfection in every kind of virtue, though they may in military virtue, for this is found in the masses. Hence in a constitutional government the fighting-men have the supreme power, and those who possess arms are the citizens.

Of the above-mentioned forms, the perversions are as follows: of royalty, tyranny; of aristocracy, oligarchy; of constitutional government, democracy. For tyranny is a kind of monarchy which has in view the interest of the monarch only; oligarchy has in view the interest of the wealthy; democracy, of the needy: none of them the common good of all. . . .

. . . The true forms of government are three, and that the best must be that which is administered by the best, and in which there is one man, or a whole family, or many persons, excelling all the others together in virtue, and both rulers and subjects are fitted, the one to rule, the others to be ruled, in such a manner as to attain the most eligible life. We showed at the commencement of our inquiry that the virtue of the good man is necessarily the same as the virtue of the citizen of the perfect state. Clearly then in the same manner, and by the same means through which a man becomes truly good, he will frame a state that is to be ruled by an aristocracy or by a king, and the same education and the same habits will be found to make a good man and a man fit to be a statesman or king.

Politics, **Book IV**

Hence it is obvious that government too is the subject of a single science, which has to consider what government is best and of what sort it must be, to be most in accordance with our aspirations, if there were no external impediment, and also what kind of government is adapted to particular states. For the best is often unattainable, and therefore the true legislator and the statesman ought to be acquainted, not only with (1) that which is best in the abstract, but also with (2) that which is best relatively to circumstances. We should be able further to say how a state may be constituted under any given conditions; (3) both how it is originally formed and, when formed, how it may be longest preserved; the supposed state being so far from having the best constitution that it is unprovided even with the conditions necessary for the best; neither is it the best under the circumstances, but of an inferior type.

He ought, moreover, to know (4) the form of government which is best suited to states in general; for political writers, although they have excellent ideas, are often unpractical. We should consider, not only what form of government is best, but also what is possible and what is easily attainable by all. . . .

In our original discussion about governments we divided them into three true forms: kingly rule, aristocracy, and constitutional government, and three corresponding perversions—tyranny, oligarchy, and democracy. . . .

It is obvious which of the three perversions is the worst, and which is the next in badness. That which is the perversion of the first and most divine is necessarily the worst. And just as a royal rule, if not a mere name, must exist by virtue of some great personal superiority in the king, so tyranny, which is the worst of governments, is necessarily the farthest removed from a well-constituted form; oligarchy is little better, for it is a long way from aristocracy, and democracy is the most tolerable of the three. . . .

The reason why there are many forms of government is that every state contains many elements. In the first place we see that all states are made up of families, and in the multitude of citizens there must be some rich and some poor, and some in a middle condition; the rich are heavy-armed, and the poor are not. . . .

Now in all states there are three elements: one class is very rich, another very poor, and a third in a mean. It is admitted that moderation and the mean are best, and therefore it will clearly be best to possess the gifts of fortune in moderation; for in that condition of life men are most ready to follow rational principle. But he who greatly excels in beauty, strength, birth, or wealth, or on the other hand who is very poor, or very weak, or very much disgraced, finds it difficult to follow rational principle. Of these two the one sort grow into violent and great criminals, the others into rogues and petty rascals. . . . Again, the middle class is least likely to shrink from rule, or to be over-ambitious for it; both of which are injuries to the state. . . .

Thus it is manifest that the best political community is formed by citizens of the middle class, and that those states are likely to be well-administered, in which the middle class is large, and stronger if possible than both the other classes, or at any rate than either singly; for the addition of the middle class turns the scale, and prevents either of the extremes from being dominant. . . .

These considerations will help us to understand why most governments are either democratic or oligarchical. The reason is that the middle class is seldom numerous in them, and whichever party, whether the rich or the common people, transgresses the mean and predominates, draws the constitution its own way, and thus arises either oligarchy or democracy. There is another reason—the poor and the rich quarrel with one another, and whichever side gets the better, instead of establishing a just or popular government regards political supremacy as the prize of victory, and the one party sets up a democracy and the other an oligarchy. . . .

We have now to consider what and what kind of government is suitable to what and what kind of men. I may begin by assuming, as a general principle common to all governments, that the portion of the state which desires the permanence of the constitution ought to be stronger than that which desires the reverse.

Politics, Book V

In all well-attempted governments there is nothing which should be more jealously maintained than the spirit of obedience to law, more especially in small matters; for transgression creeps in unperceived and at last ruins the state, just as the constant recurrence of small expenses in time eats up a fortune. The expense does not take place all at once, and therefore is not observed; the mind is deceived, as in the fallacy which says that "if each part is little, then the whole is little."

Nicomachean Ethics, Book VIII

One may find resemblances to the constitutions and, as it were, patterns of them even in households. For the association of a father with his sons bears the form of monarchy, since the father cares for his children . . . it is the ideal of monarchy to be paternal rule. But among the Persians the rule of the father is tyrannical; they use their sons as slaves. Tyrannical too is the rule of a master over slaves; for it is the advantage of the master that is brought about in it. Now this seems to be a correct form of government, but the Persian type is perverted; for the modes of rule appropriate to different relations are diverse. The association of man and wife seems to be aristocratic; for the man rules in accordance with his worth, and in those matters in which a man should rule, but the matters that befit a woman he hands over to her. If the man rules in everything the relation passes over into oligarchy; for in doing so he is not acting in accordance with their respective worth, and not ruling in virtue of his superiority. Sometimes, however, women rule, because they are heiresses; so their rule is not in virtue of excellence but due to wealth and power, as in oligarchies. The association of brothers is like [democracy]; for they are equal, except in so far as they differ in age; hence if they differ *much* in age, the friendship is no longer of the fraternal type. Democracy is found chiefly in masterless dwellings (for here every one is on an equality), and in those in which the ruler is weak and every one has license to do as he pleases.

ARISTOTLE – A SIMULATED INTERVIEW

1. **Do human beings naturally live in communities?**
   A. All forms of community are natural. Human beings are by nature political animals.
   B. An individual unable to live in society is either a beast or a god.

2. **What are the different types of community?**
   A. The three levels of community are the family, the village, and the state.
   B. The *family* is a form of community that supplies everyday needs. Communal life begins with the family.
   C. The *village* is a form of community that stems from the union of many families seeking more than their daily needs.
   D. The *state* stems from several villages united in a single community.

3. **What is the most important type of community?**
   A. Since the state incorporates all types of communities, the state is the most important community.
   B. The state is the highest political organization; it is superior to the family or the village. The state is a creation of nature.

4. **What are the characteristics of a good society?**
   A. A good society demands obedience to the law. Human beings are the best of all animals. When separated from the rule of law human beings are the worst of all animals.
   B. The best political community is formed by citizens of the middle class. A large middle class prevents either the very rich or the very poor from dominating society.
   C. Human beings fulfill themselves by living as part of a state. Only in a perfect state can human beings achieve the highest level of virtue. Individuals are unfulfilled until they become part of a political organization.

5. **What are the different types of government?**
   A. Governments are classified according to two factors:
      1. *Who holds power?* This question has three possible answers: one, few, or many.
      2. *In whose interest is power exercised?* This question has two possible answers: private interest or the common interest.
   B. Government in its *true form* operates for the common interest. Government in its *deviation form* operates for private interest.

ARISTOTLE'S FORMS OF GOVERNMENT	
TRUE FORMS	**DEVIATION FORMS**
monarchy one person rules for the common interest	**tyranny** one person rules for his own benefit
aristocracy a few people rule for the common interest	**oligarchy** the wealthy rule for their own benefit
constitutional republic the masses rule for the common interest	**democracy** the poor rule for their own benefit

6. **What are the best and worst forms of government?**
    A. The ideal form of government is an aristocracy in which the best people, who are few in number, exercise power in the interests of the community.
    B. Since the ideal form of government is hard to achieve, and even harder to sustain, society should have a form of mixed government in which power is monopolized by no particular group.
    C. The worst form of government is tyranny. The second worst is oligarchy. The third worst is democracy.

7. **Is slavery natural?**
    A. Some people are born to rule; others are born to be ruled.
    B. Some people are naturally suited to slavery. Some people are by nature free and others are by nature slaves.
    C. Males are superior to females. Superior people should rule; inferior people should be slaves. Males should be the masters of the house.

8. **Should government remain the same from generation to generation?**
    A. The part of society that wants a permanent constitution should be stronger than the part that wants change.
    B. Government should be given a character that endures from generation to generation despite changes in officeholders.

STUDENT ACTIVITIES

Vocabulary
Define the following terms before reading the lesson on Aristotle.

1. apprehend	8. impediment	15. predominate
2. equivocal	9. latter	16. subjection
3. expedient	10. lust	17. transgression
4. fallacy	11. mean	18. tyranny
5. fraternal	12. oligarchical	19. virtue
6. generic	13. paternal	
7. gluttony	14. perversion	

Review
1. Who was Aristotle's famous teacher?
2. Who was Aristotle's famous student?
3. Why were Aristotle's intellectual pursuits so diverse?
4. Aristotle championed the idea of the Golden Mean. What was the Golden Mean?
5. How did Aristotle affect modern scientific analysis?
6. In what way did Aristotle influence America's founding fathers?
7. Aristotle pointed out that governments can be classified according to two questions. What are the two questions, and how might they be answered?
8. List and define the three true forms of government identified by Aristotle.
9. List and define the three deviation forms of government identified by Aristotle.
10. What is the primary difference between a true form of government and a deviation form of government?
11. What were the three levels of community identified by Aristotle?
12. Decide whether the following statements are **True** or **False** according to Aristotle.
    A. Community is natural to human existence.
    B. The state is a creation of nature.
    C. A person's connection with family is more important than a connection with the state.
    D. Human beings are the worst of all animals when they live in a system without laws.
    E. The best political community is formed by citizens of the middle class.
    F. Some people are born to rule.
    G. Slavery is natural to human existence.
    H. Men and women should be proclaimed equal in social status.
    I. Each generation has the right to form its own government.

What do you think?
On a scale of one through five, rate your opinion of the following quotations by Aristotle. Write a short statement explaining your rating.

1 – You **strongly agree** with the statement *or* you feel the statement is **admirable** considering the historical circumstances surrounding it.
5 – You **strongly disagree** with the statement *or* you feel the statement is **contemptible** considering the historical circumstances surrounding it.

A. *The state is a creation of nature.*
B. *Man is by nature a political animal.*
C. *The state is by nature clearly prior to the family and to the individual, since the whole is of necessity prior to the part.*
D. *The individual, when isolated, is not self-sufficing.*
E. *He who is unable to live in society . . . must be either a beast or a god.*
F. *Man when perfected, is the best of animals, but, when separated from law and justice, he is the worst of all.*
G. *From the hour of their birth, some are marked out for subjection, others for rule.*
H. *The best political community is formed by citizens of the middle class.*
I. *In all well-attempted governments there is nothing which should be more jealously maintained than the spirit of obedience to law.*
J. *The only stable state is the one in which all men are equal before the law.*
K. *Wealthy men are insolent and arrogant; their possession of wealth affects their understanding; they feel as if they had every good thing that exists; wealth becomes a standard of value for everything else, and therefore they imagine there is nothing they cannot buy.*
L. *A democracy is a government in the hands of men of low birth, no property, and unskilled labor.*
M. *The fate of empires depends on the education of youth.*
N. *Good laws if they are not obeyed, do not constitute good government.*
O. *Those who think that all virtue is to be found in their own party principles push matters to extremes; they do not consider that disproportion destroys a state.*
P. *Political society exists for the sake of noble actions, and not of mere companionship.*
Q. *In framing an ideal we may assume what we wish, but should avoid impossibilities.*

CHAPTER 2

THOMAS HOBBES

BACKGROUND

Thomas Hobbes (1588-1679) was born prematurely after his mother heard the Spanish Armada was threatening England. As an adult Hobbes described his birth by writing "my mother gave birth to twins, myself and fear." Although his comment illustrates a clever sense of humor, it also offers insight into Hobbes' political philosophy, a philosophy based on a human desire to avoid violent death.

Hobbes' father was a poor English clergyman who abandoned his family. Hobbes was therefore raised and educated by his uncle, a man who taught him an appreciation for classical languages and poetry. As a student at Oxford University, Hobbes grew bored with an intellectual culture based upon classical philosophies. He yearned for a new way of understanding the world and began rejecting his classical education.

In 1608 Hobbes secured employment as a tutor with the family of Lord William Cavendish. Traveling with the Cavendish family, Hobbes spent several years on the European continent meeting the leading scientific philosophers of the time. Inspired by such thinkers as Galileo and Descartes, Hobbes hoped to create what he called a "science of politics." He wanted to show how science could be used to create a society that allowed government to successfully maintain peace and security.

Hobbes eventually returned to England, but after civil war broke out in the 1640s he decided to move to France. Hobbes supported monarchy and feared he would be killed if he did not leave England. He did not return home for seven years.

In his old age Hobbes became somewhat of an English institution. Although he once wrote that life was "solitary, poor, nasty, brutish and short," he lived a long life and was admired by the English public and his numerous friends.

In his ninety-one years Hobbes produced several works of political theory. *Leviathan*, his most famous book, was published in 1651. Today *Leviathan* is recognized as a masterpiece of political theory. For students of United States history *Leviathan* is important because it examines the nature of security and the question of whether security should be gained at the expense of individual liberty—an issue that is still a topic of debate.

THOMAS HOBBES – IN HIS OWN WORDS

Leviathan, Chapter 11

I put for a general inclination of all mankind, a perpetual and restless desire of power after power, that ceaseth only in death. And the cause of this, is not always that a man hopes for a more intensive delight, than he has already attained to; or that he cannot be content with a moderate power: but because he cannot assure the power and means to live well, which he hath present, without the acquisition of more. And from hence it is, that kings, whose power is greatest, turn their endeavours to the assuring it at home by laws, or abroad by wars: and when that is done, there succeedeth a new desire; in some, of fame from new conquest; in others, of ease and sensual pleasure; in others, of admiration, or being flattered for excellence in some art, or other ability of the mind.

Competition of riches, honour, command, or other power, inclineth to contention, enmity, and war: because the way of one competitor, to the attaining of his desire, is to kill, subdue, supplant, or repel the other. Particularly, competition of praise, inclineth to a reverence of antiquity. For men contend with the living, not with the dead; to these ascribing more than due, that they may obscure the glory of the other.

Desire of ease, and sensual delight, disposeth men to obey a common power: because by such desires, a man doth abandon the protection might be hoped for from his own industry, and labour. Fear of death, and wounds disposeth to the same; and for the same reason.

Leviathan, Chapter 13

Nature hath made men so equal, in the faculties of body, and mind; as that though there be found one man sometimes manifestly stronger in body, or of quicker mind than another; yet when all is reckoned together, the difference between man, and man, is not so considerable, as that one man can thereupon claim to himself any benefit, to which another may not pretend, as well as he. For as to the strength of body, the weakest has strength enough to kill the strongest, either by secret machination, or by confederacy with others, that are in the same danger with himself. . . .

And as to the faculties of the mind . . . I find yet a greater equality amongst men, than that of strength. For prudence, is but experience; which equal time, equally bestows on all men, in those things they equally apply themselves unto. That which may perhaps make such equality incredible is but a vain conceit of one's own wisdom, which almost all men think they have in a greater degree, than the vulgar; that is, than all men but themselves, and a few others, whom by fame, or for concurring with themselves, they approve. For such is the nature of men, that howsoever they may acknowledge many others to be more witty, or more eloquent, or more learned; yet they will hardly believe there be many so wise as themselves: For they see their own wit at hand, and other men's at a distance. But this proveth rather that men are in that point equal, than unequal. For there is not ordinarily a greater sign of the equal distribution of any thing, than that every man is contented with his share.

From this equality of ability, ariseth equality of hope in the attaining of our ends. And therefore if any two men desire the same thing, which nevertheless they cannot both enjoy, they become enemies; and in the way to their end, (which is principally their own conservation, and sometimes their delectation only,) endeavour to destroy, or subdue one another. . . .

Again, men have no pleasure . . . in keeping company, where there is no power able to over-awe them all. For every man looketh that his companion should value him, at the same rate he sets upon himself: and upon all signs of contempt, or undervaluing, naturally endeavours, as far as he dares (which amongst them that have no common power to keep them in quiet, is far enough to make them destroy each other), to extort a greater value from his contemners, by damage; and from others, by the example.

So that in the nature of man, we find three principal causes of quarrel. First, competition; secondly, diffidence; thirdly, glory.

The first, maketh men invade for gain; the second, for safety; and the third, for reputation. The first use violence, to make themselves masters of other men's persons, wives, children, and cattle; the second, to defend them; the third, for trifles, as a word, a smile, a different opinion, and any other sign of undervalue, either direct in their person, or by reflection in their kindred, their friends, their nation, their profession, or their name.

Hereby it is manifest, that during the time men live without a common power to keep them all in awe, they are in that condition which is called war; and such a war, as is of every man, against every man. . . .

. . . In such condition, there is no place for industry; because the fruit thereof is uncertain: and consequently no culture of the earth; no navigation, nor use of the commodities that may be imported by sea; no commodious building; no instruments of moving, and removing such things as require much force; no knowledge of the face of the earth; no account of time; no arts; no letters; no society; and which is worst of all, continual fear, and danger of violent death; and the life of man, solitary, poor, nasty, brutish, and short. . . .

To this war of every man against every man, this also is consequent; that nothing can be unjust. The notions of right and wrong, justice and injustice have there no place. Where there is no common power, there is no law: where no law, no injustice. Force, and fraud, are in war the two cardinal virtues. Justice, and injustice are none of the faculties neither of the body, nor mind. . . .

The passions that incline men to peace, are fear of death; desire of such things as are necessary to commodious living; and a hope by their industry to obtain them. And reason suggesteth convenient articles of peace, upon which men may be drawn to agreement. These articles, are they, which otherwise are called the Laws of Nature.

Leviathan, **Chapter 15**

The laws of nature are immutable and eternal; for injustice, ingratitude, arrogance, pride, iniquity, acception of persons, and the rest, can never be made lawful. For it can never be that war shall preserve life, and peace destroy it.

Leviathan, **Chapter 17**

The final cause, end, or design of men, (who naturally love liberty, and dominion over others,) in the introduction of that restraint upon themselves, (in which we see them live in commonwealths,) is the foresight of their own preservation, and of a more contented life thereby; that is to say, of getting themselves out from that miserable condition of war, which is necessarily consequent . . . to, the natural passions of men, when there is no visible power to keep them in awe, and tie them by fear of punishment to the performance of their covenants, and observation of those laws of nature . . . .

For the laws of nature (as *justice, equity, modesty, mercy,* and (in sum) *doing to others, as we would be done to,*) of themselves, without the terror of some power, to cause them to be observed, are contrary to our natural passions, that carry us to partiality, pride, revenge, and the like. And covenants, without the sword, are but words, and of no strength to secure a man at all. Therefore notwithstanding the laws of nature, . . . if there be no power erected, or not great enough for our security; every man will, and may lawfully rely on his own strength and art, for caution against all other men. . . .

It is true, that certain living creatures, as bees, and ants, live sociably one with another, (which are therefore by Aristotle numbered amongst political creatures;) and yet have no other direction, than their particular judgments and appetites; nor speech, whereby one of them can signify to another, what he thinks expedient for the common benefit: and therefore some man may perhaps desire to know, why mankind cannot do the same. To which I answer,

First, that men are continually in competition for honour and dignity, which these creatures are not; and consequently amongst men there ariseth on that ground, envy and hatred, and finally war; but amongst these not so.

Secondly, that amongst these creatures, the common good differeth not from the private; and being by nature inclined to their private, they procure thereby the common benefit. But man, whose joy consisteth in comparing himself with other men, can relish nothing but what is eminent.

Thirdly, that these creatures, having not, (as man) the use of reason, do not see, nor think they see any fault, in the administration of their common business; whereas amongst men, there are very many, that think themselves wiser, and abler to govern the public, better than the rest; and these strive to reform and innovate, one this way, another that way; and thereby bring it into distraction and civil war.

Fourthly, that these creatures, though they have some use of voice, in making known to one another their desires, and other affections; yet they want that art of words, by which some men can represent to others, that which is good, in the likeness of evil; and evil, in the likeness of good; and augment, or diminish the apparent greatness of good and evil; discontenting men, and troubling their peace at their pleasure.

Fifthly, irrational creatures cannot distinguish between *injury*, and *damage*; and therefore as long as they be at ease, they are not offended with their fellows: whereas man is then most troublesome, when he is most at ease: for then it is that he loves to shew his wisdom, and control the actions of them that govern the commonwealth.

Lastly, the agreement of these creatures is natural; that of men, is by covenant only, which is artificial: and therefore it is no wonder if there be somewhat else required (besides covenant) to make their agreement constant and lasting; which is a common power, to keep them in awe, and to direct their action to the common benefit.

The only way to erect such a common power, as may be able to defend them from the invasion of foreigners, and the injuries of one another, and thereby to secure them in such sort, as that by their own industry, and by the fruits of the earth they may nourish themselves and live contentedly; is, to confer all their power and strength upon one man, or upon one assembly of men, that may reduce all their wills, by plurality of voices, unto one will: which is as much as to say, to appoint one man, or assembly of men, to bear their person; and every one to own, and acknowledge himself to be author of whatsoever he that so beareth their person, shall act, and therein to submit their wills, every one to his will, and their judgments, to his judgment. This is more than consent, or concord; it is a real unity of them all, in one and the same person, made by covenant of every man with every man, in such manner, as if every man should say to every man, *I authorise and give up my right of governing myself, to this man, or to this assembly of men, on this condition, that thou give up thy right to him, and authorize all his actions in like manner*. This done, the multitude so united in one person, is called a COMMONWEALTH, in Latin CIVITAS. This is the generation of that great LEVIATHAN, or rather (to speak more reverently) of that *mortal god*, to which we owe under the *immortal God*, our peace and defence. For by this authority, given him by every particular man in the commonwealth, he hath the use of so much power and strength conferred on him, that by terror thereof, he is enabled to form the wills of them all, to peace at home, and mutual aid against their enemies abroad. And in him consisteth the essence of the commonwealth; which (to define it,) is *one person, of whose acts a great multitude, by mutual covenants one with another, have made themselves every one the author, to the end he may use the strength and means of them all, as he shall think expedient, for their peace and common defence*.

And he that carrieth this person, is called SOVEREIGN, and said to have sovereign power; and every one besides, his SUBJECT.

The attaining to this sovereign power, is by two ways. One, by natural force; as when a man maketh his children, to submit themselves, and their children to his government, as being able to destroy them if they refuse; or by war subdueth his enemies to his will, giving them their lives on that condition. The other, is when men agree amongst themselves, to submit to some man, or assembly of men, voluntarily, on confidence to be protected by him against all others. This latter, may be called a political commonwealth, or commonwealth by *institution*; and the former, a commonwealth by *acquisition*.

Leviathan, Chapter 19

The difference of commonwealths, consisteth in the difference of the sovereign, or the person representative of all and every one of the multitude. And because the sovereignty is either in one man, or in an assembly of more than one; and into that assembly either every man hath right to enter, or not every one, but certain men distinguished from the rest; it is manifest, there can be but three kinds of commonwealth. For the representative must needs be one man, or more: and if more, then it is the assembly of all, or but of a part. When the representative is one man, then is the commonwealth a MONARCHY: when an assembly of all that will come together, then it is a DEMOCRACY, or popular commonwealth: when an assembly of a part only, then it is called an ARISTOCRACY. Other kind of commonwealth there can be none: for either one, or more, or all, must have the sovereign power (which I have shown to be indivisible) entire.

There be other names of government, in the histories, and books of policy; as *tyranny*, and *oligarchy*: But they are not the names of other forms of government, but of the same forms misliked. For they that are discontented under *monarchy*, call it *tyranny*; and they that are displeased with *aristocracy*, call it *oligarchy*: so also, they which find themselves grieved under a *democracy*, call it *anarchy*, (which signifies want of government;) and yet I think no man believes, that want of government, is any new kind of government: nor by the same reason ought they to believe, that the government is of one kind, when they like it, and another, when they mislike it, or are oppressed by the governors.

Leviathan, Chapter 21

The obligation of subjects to the sovereign, is understood to last as long, and no longer, than the power lasteth, by which he is able to protect them. For the right men have by nature to protect themselves, when none else can protect them, can by no covenant be relinquished. The sovereignty is the soul of the commonwealth; which once departed from the body, the members do no more receive their motion from it. The end of obedience is protection; which, wheresoever a man seeth it, either in his own, or in another's sword, nature applieth his obedience to it, and his endeavour to maintain it. And though sovereignty, in the intention of them that make it, be immortal; yet is it in its own nature, not only subject to violent death, by foreign war; but also through the ignorance, and passions of men, it hath in it, from the very institution, many seeds of a natural mortality, by intestine discord.

THOMAS HOBBES – A SIMULATED INTERVIEW

1. **What is human nature?**
    A. Human beings are motivated primarily by self-interest.
    B. In their hearts human beings are murderers and thieves.
    C. Emotion dominates human behavior more than rational thinking.
    D. Human beings naturally desire power. Even after people obtain power, they desire more power.

2. **What characteristics are evident in human beings who live in a state of nature?**
    A. In a state of nature there is no powerful authority to keep human beings under control. In a state of nature human beings are in a state of war.
    B. When two people desire the same object they both have a natural right to the object. However, only one person can possess the object, and a struggle for ownership is inevitable. In a state of nature there is a "war of every man against every man."
    C. All people are created equal in a state of nature. The weak can even destroy the strong through individual shrewdness and through alliances with others. In a state of war all ideas of right and wrong are irrelevant. Violence and deception are used to gain power.
    D. In a state of nature individuals are prevented from doing harm to themselves by their self-interest as well as their instinct for survival. However, because of self-interest, individuals might do harm to other people.

3. **Why do human beings desire an escape from the state of nature?**
    A. People dislike the state of nature and its unavoidable conflicts because people fear violent death.
    B. A human desire to escape the state of nature is evident in the laws of nature:
        1. Human beings have a natural instinct for self-preservation.
        2. Human beings will do everything they can to defend themselves.
        3. Human beings will grant complete obedience to an all-powerful government in order that they might live with peace and security.

4. **How can human beings escape the state of nature?**
    A. Government is the weapon that human beings use to protect themselves.
    B. The fear of violent death that results from living in a state of nature produces a desire for self-preservation. The desire for self-preservation leads to the creation of a government that will provide security.

C. People will abandon their rights to bring about security; they will voluntarily abide by the law of an absolute sovereign. People understand that complete obedience to an all-powerful sovereign—a *Leviathan*—will bring about peace and security.
D. Human beings must use science and rational thinking to escape the state of nature. Political ideas based upon scientific law can be proven conclusively and accepted universally. Science and rational thinking provide solutions to the problems of human existence.

5. What is the function of government?
A. Government provides society with peace and security. Accordingly, people should not be allowed to change their government, to judge their government, or to protest against their government. People should be granted freedom of thought, but not freedom of action.
B. Government must protect itself; government cannot allow itself to be abolished. An absence of government thrusts human beings into a state of nature where the state of war creates a possibility of violent death. Government should never give up its power.

STUDENT ACTIVITIES

Vocabulary
Define the following terms before reading the lesson on Hobbes.

1. acquisition	10. democracy	19. iniquity
2. anarchy	11. diffidence	20. intestine
3. aristocracy	12. diminish	21. machination
4. augment	13. discord	22. monarchy
5. commodity	14. eloquent	23. oligarchy
6. commonwealth	15. eminent	24. partiality
7. confederacy	16. endeavor	25. prudence
8. contemner	17. immutable	26. sovereignty
9. covenant	18. indivisible	27. tyranny

Review
1. What happened to Hobbes during the English civil war?
2. What was the title of Hobbes' most famous book on political theory?
3. According to Hobbes, what motivates human action?
4. According to Hobbes, what are the characteristics of life in a state of nature?
5. Why did Hobbes believe that an individual would not harm himself in a state of nature?
6. Why did Hobbes believe human beings desired an escape from the state of nature?
7. What is a Leviathan?

8. Why did Hobbes believe that government should protect itself from revolution?
9. Decide whether the following statements are **True** or **False** according to Thomas Hobbes.
   A. The principles of science should be used to describe political philosophy.
   B. Human beings are dominated by their passions more than rational thinking.
   C. All human beings are created equal.
   D. The power of government should be limited.
   E. Human beings can escape the state of nature through rational thought.
   F. The people should have the right to change their government.
   G. Human beings naturally desire power.
   H. Human beings have a natural instinct for self-preservation and will do everything they can to defend themselves.
   I. The desire for freedom prevents human beings from granting complete obedience to an all-powerful government.
   J. People should be granted freedom of thought, but not freedom of action.

What do you think?
On a scale of one through five, rate your opinion of the following quotations by Hobbes. Write a short statement explaining your rating.

1 – You **strongly agree** with the statement *or* you feel the statement is **admirable** considering the historical circumstances surrounding it.
5 – You **strongly disagree** with the statement *or* you feel the statement is **contemptible** considering the historical circumstances surrounding it.

A. *I put for a general inclination of all mankind, a perpetual and restless desire of power after power, that ceaseth only in death.*
B. *If any two men desire the same thing, which nevertheless they cannot both enjoy, they become enemies; and in the way to their end . . . endeavour to destroy, or subdue one another.*
C. *Men have no pleasure . . . in keeping company, where there is no power able to over-awe them all.*
D. *During the time men live without a common power to keep them all in awe, they are in that condition which is called war.*
E. *The life of man [is] solitary, poor, nasty, brutish, and short.*
F. *The passions that incline men to peace, are fear of death.*

G. *Men are continually in competition for honour and dignity . . . and consequently amongst men there ariseth on that ground, envy and hatred, and finally war.*

H. *I authorize and give up my right of governing myself, to this man, or to this assembly of men, on this condition, that thou give up thy right to him, and authorize all his actions in like manner.*

I. *Covenants without the sword are but words.*

J. *The condition of man . . . is a condition of war of everyone against everyone.*

K. *How could a state be governed . . . if every individual remained free to obey or not to obey the law according to his private gain?*

L. *A democracy is no more than an aristocracy of orators. The people are so readily moved by demagogues that control must be exercised by the government over speech and press.*

M. *Government is necessary, not because man is naturally bad . . . but because man is by nature more individualistic than social.*

N. *Corporations are many lesser commonwealths in the bowels of a greater, like worms in the entrails of a natural man.*

O. *Intemperance is naturally punished with diseases; rashness, with mischance; injustice, with violence of enemies; pride, with ruin; cowardice, with oppression; and rebellion, with slaughter.*

CHAPTER 3

JOHN LOCKE

BACKGROUND

Because John Locke's (1632-1704) mother died while he was still an infant, he was raised by his father, an English lawyer. After receiving his primary education at Westminster, an excellent school near London, Locke studied philosophy and medicine at Oxford University. Upon graduation he was employed as a physician by the wealthy and radical Earl of Shaftsbury.

Locke soon became active in the same revolutionary politics as his employer. Like his employer, Locke encouraged criticism of the king and rebellion against the government. Due to the controversial nature of his political ideas, he was forced to leave England and move to Holland where he joined a community of exiled English radicals. After the English Parliament installed a new king and queen during the Glorious Revolution of 1688, Locke returned to England.

During the last years of his life Locke served with distinction in the British government. He also became well known for his political philosophy, gaining wide recognition for his ideas even though he was sixty years old before many of his writings were published. By the time he died at age seventy-two he was considered one of England's greatest philosophers.

Locke's political ideas were found primarily in *The Second Treatise of Government*. This was not only his most famous work, but remains a classic work of political theory. He used the book to argue against the divine right of kings and defend a form of constitutional government that could protect natural rights. Many people today see his writings as some of the most enduring and influential descriptions of individual liberty ever published.

John Locke is often recognized as one of history's most thoughtful defenders of freedom. Unlike Thomas Hobbes, who expressed little concern for individual liberty, Locke's political interests centered around protecting individual rights. His ideas had a tremendous influence on Americans during the American Revolution and are evident in the constitutional traditions of the United States.

JOHN LOCKE – IN HIS OWN WORDS

The Second Treatise of Government, Chapter II

To understand political power, right, and derive it from its original, we must consider what state all men are naturally in, and that is, a *state of perfect freedom* to order their actions, and dispose of their possessions and persons, as they think fit, within the bounds of the law of nature; without asking leave, or depending upon the will of any other man.

A *state* also of *equality*, wherein all the power and jurisdiction is reciprocal, no one having more than another; there being nothing more evident, than that creatures of the same species and rank, promiscuously born to all the same advantages of nature, and the use of the same faculties, should also be equal one amongst another without subordination or subjection; unless the lord and master of them all should, by any manifest declaration of his will, set one above another, and confer on him, by an evident and clear appointment, an undoubted right to dominion and sovereignty. . . .

But though this be *a state of liberty*, yet *it is not a state of license*: though man in that state have an uncontrollable liberty to dispose of his person or possessions, yet he has not liberty to destroy himself, or so much as any creature in his possession, but where some nobler use than its bare preservation calls for it. The *state of nature* has a law of nature to govern it, which obliges every one: And reason, which is that law, teaches all mankind, who will but consult it, that being all *equal and independent*, no one ought to harm another in his life, health, liberty, or possessions. . . .

And that all men may be restrained from invading other's rights, and from doing hurt to one another, and the law of nature be observed, which willeth the peace and *preservation of all mankind*, the *execution* of the law of nature is, in that state, put into every man's hands, whereby every one has a right to punish the transgressors of that law to such a degree as may hinder its violation. For the *law of nature* would, as all other laws that concern men in this world, be in vain, if there were no body that in the state of nature had a *power to execute* that law, and thereby preserve the innocent and restrain offenders. And if any one in the state of nature may punish another for any evil he has done, every one may do so. For in that *state of perfect equality*, where naturally there is no superiority or jurisdiction of one over another, what any may do in prosecution of that law, every one must needs have a right to do. . . .

To this strange doctrine, viz. That *in the state of nature every one has the executive power* of the law of nature, I doubt not but it will be objected, that it is unreasonable for men to be judges in their own cases, that self-love will make men partial to themselves and their friends: And on the other side, that ill nature, passion and revenge will carry them too far in punishing others; and hence nothing but confusion and disorder will follow, and that therefore God hath certainly appointed government to restrain the partiality and violence of men. I easily grant, that civil government is the proper remedy for the inconveniences of the state of nature, which must certainly be great, where men may be judges in their own case, since it is easy to be imagined, that he who was so unjust as to do his brother an injury, will scarce be so just as to condemn himself for it: but I shall desire those who make this objection, to remember, that *absolute monarchs* are but men, and if government is to be the remedy of those evils, which necessarily follow from men's being judges in their own cases, and the state of nature is therefore not to be endured, I desire to know what kind of government that is, and how much better it is than the state of nature, where one man commanding a multitude, has the liberty to be judge in his own case, and may do to all his subjects whatever he pleases, without the least liberty to any one to question or control those who execute his pleasure? and in whatsoever he doth, whether led by reason, mistake or passion, must be submitted to? Much better it is in the state of nature, wherein men are not bound to submit to the unjust will of another: And if he that judges, judges amiss in his own, or any other case, he is answerable for it to the rest of mankind.

The Second Treatise of Government, Chapter IV

The *natural liberty* of man is to be free from any superior power on earth, and not to be under the will or legislative authority of man, but to have only the law of nature for his rule. The *liberty of man,* in society, is to be under no other legislative power, but that established, by consent, in the commonwealth; nor under the dominion of any will, or restraint of any law, but what the legislative shall enact, according to the trust put in it. . . . But *freedom of men under government,* is, to have a standing rule to live by, common to every one of that society, and made by the legislative power erected in it; a liberty to follow my own will in all things, where the rule prescribes not; and not to be subject to the inconstant, uncertain, unknown, arbitrary will of another man: As *freedom of nature* is, to be under no other restraint but the law of nature.

This freedom from absolute, arbitrary power, is so necessary to, and closely joined with a man's preservation, that he cannot part with it, but by what forfeits his preservation and life together. For a man, not having the power of his own life, cannot, by compact, or his own consent, enslave himself to any one, nor put himself under the absolute, arbitrary power of another, to take away his life, when he pleases. No body can give more power than he has himself; and he that cannot take away his own life, cannot give another power over it.

The Second Treatise of Government, Chapter V

Though the earth, and all inferior creatures, be common to all men, yet every man has a property in his own person: this no body has any right to but himself. The labour of his body, and the work of his hands, we may say, are properly his. Whatsoever then he removes out of the state that nature hath provided, and left it in, he hath mixed his labour with, and joined to it something that is his own, and thereby makes it his property. It being by him removed from the common state nature hath placed it in, it hath by this labour something annexed to it, that excludes the common right of other men. For this labour being the unquestionable property of the labourer, no man but he can have a right to what that is once joined to, at least where there is enough, and as good, left in common for others. . . .

. . . God, when he gave the world in common to all mankind, commanded man also to labour, and the penury of his condition required it of him. God and his reason commanded him to subdue the earth, i.e. improve it for the benefit of life, and therein lay out something upon it that was his own, his labour. He that, in obedience to this command of God, subdued, tilled, and sowed any part of it, thereby annexed to it something that was his *property*, which another had no title to, nor could without injury take from him.

The Second Treatise of Government, Chapter VIII

Men being, as has been said, by nature, all free, equal, and independent, no one can be put out of this estate, and subjected to the political power of another, without his own consent. The only way, whereby any one divests himself of his natural liberty, and puts on the *bonds of civil society*, is by agreeing with other men to join and unite into a community, for their comfortable, safe, and peaceable living one amongst another, in a secure enjoyment of their properties, and a greater security against any, that are not of it. This any number of men may do, because it injures not the freedom of the rest; they are left as they were in the liberty of the state of nature. When any number of men have so *consented to make one community or government*, they are thereby presently incorporated, and make *one body politic*, wherein the majority have a right to act and conclude the rest.

For when any number of men have, by the consent of every individual, made a *community*, they have thereby made that *community* one body, with a power to act as one body, which is only by the will and determination of the majority. For that which acts any community, being only the *consent* of the individuals of it, and it being necessary to that which is one body to move one way; it is necessary the body should move that way whither the greater force carries it, which is the *consent of the majority*: or else it is impossible it should act or continue one body, one community, which the consent of every individual that united into it, agreed that it should; and so every one is bound by that consent to be concluded by the majority. And therefore we see, that in assemblies, impowered to act by positive laws, where no number is set by that positive law which impowers them, the *act of the majority* passes for the act of the whole, and of course determines, as having by the law of nature and reason, the power of the whole.

And thus every man, by consenting with others to make one body politic under one government, puts himself under an obligation, to every one of that society, to submit to the determination of the majority, and to be concluded by it; or else this *original compact*, whereby he with others incorporate into one society, would signify nothing, and be no compact, if he be left free, and under no other ties than he was in before in the state of nature. For what appearance would there be of any compact? What new engagement if he were no farther tied by any decrees of the society, than he himself thought fit, and did actually consent to? This would be still as great a liberty, as he himself had before his compact, or any one else in the state of nature hath, who may submit himself, and consent to any acts of it if he thinks fit.

The Second Treatise of Government, **Chapter IX**

If man in the state of nature be so free, as has been said; if he be absolute lord of his own person and possessions, equal to the greatest, and subject to no body, why will he part with his freedom? why will he give up this empire, and subject himself to the dominion and control of any other power? To which it is obvious to answer, that though in the state of nature he hath such a right, yet the enjoyment of it is very uncertain, and constantly exposed to the invasion of others. For all being kings as much as he, every man his equal, and the greater part no strict observers of equity and justice, the enjoyment of their property he has in this state is very unsafe, very unsecure. This makes him willing to quit this condition which, however free, is full of fears and continual dangers: and it is not without reason, that he seeks out, and is willing to join in society with others, who are already united, or have a mind to unite, for the mutual preservation of their lives, liberties, and estates, which I call by the general name, property.

The great and *chief end*, therefore, of men's uniting into commonwealths, and placing themselves under government, *is the preservation of their property*. To which in the state of nature there are many things wanting.

First, There wants an established, settled, known law, received and allowed by common consent to be the standard of right and wrong, and the common measure to decide all controversies between them. For though the law of nature be plain and intelligible to all rational creatures; yet men being biased by their interest, as well as ignorant for want of studying it, are not apt to allow of it as a law binding to them in the application of it to their particular cases.

Secondly, In the state of nature there wants *a known and indifferent judge*, with authority to determine all differences according to the established law. For every one in that state being both judge and executioner of the law of nature, men being partial to themselves, passion and revenge is very apt to carry them too far, and with too much heat, in their own cases; as were as negligence, and unconcernedness, to make them too remiss in other men's.

Thirdly, In the state of nature, there often wants power to back and support the sentence when right, and to give it due execution. They who by any injustice offended, will seldom fail, where they are able, by force to make good their injustice such resistance many times makes the punishment dangerous, and frequently destructive, to those who attempt it.

Thus mankind, notwithstanding all the privileges of the state of nature, being but in an ill condition, while they remain in it, are quickly driven into society. Hence it comes to pass that we seldom find any number of men live any time together in this state. The inconveniencies that they are therein exposed to, by the irregular and uncertain exercise of the power every man has of punishing the transgressions of others, make them take sanctuary under the established laws of government, and therein seek *the preservation of their property*. It is this makes them so willingly give up every one his single power of punishing, to be exercised by such alone, as shall be appointed to it amongst them; and by such rules as the community, or those authorized by them to that purpose, shall agree on. And in this we have the original *right and rise of both the legislative and executive power*, as well as of the governments and societies themselves. . . .

But though men, when they enter into society, give up the equality, liberty, and executive power they had in the state of nature, in the hands of the society, to be so far disposed of by the legislative, as the good of the society shall require; yet it being only with an intention in every one the better to preserve himself, his liberty and property; (for no rational creature can be supposed to change his condition with an intention to be worse) the power of the society, or legislative constituted by them, *can never be supposed to extend farther, than the common good*; but is obliged to secure every one's property, by providing against those three defects above mentioned, that made the state of nature so unsafe and uneasy. And so whoever has the legislative or supreme power of any commonwealth, is bound to govern by established standing laws, promulgated and known to the people, and not by extemporary decrees; by indifferent and upright judges, who are to decide controversies by those laws; and to employ the force of the community at home, *only in the execution of such laws*; or abroad to prevent or redress foreign injuries, and secure the community from inroads and invasion. And all this to be directed to no other *end*, but the *peace*, *safety*, and *public good* of the people.

The Second Treatise of Government, Chapter XIX
The reason why men enter into society, is the preservation of their property; and the end why they choose and authorize a legislative, is, that there may be laws made, and rules set, as guards and fences to the properties of all the members of the society: to limit the power, and moderate the dominion, of every part and member of the society. . . . Whensoever therefore the *legislative* shall transgress this fundamental rule of society; and either by ambition, fear, folly or corruption, *endeavour to grasp* themselves, *or put into the hands of any other and absolute power* over the lives, liberties, and estates of the people; by this breach of trust they *forfeit the power*, the people had put into their hands.

JOHN LOCKE – A SIMULATED INTERVIEW

1. **What does nature grant to human beings?**
    A. The human mind at birth is a *tabula rasa*—a blank tablet. Through-out an individual's life ideas are imprinted on the tablet.
    B. The human mind at birth is imprinted with nothing except the ability to reason.
    C. Human beings are born with only the ability to reason; they are not born with innate ideas. The human mind is a container that can receive knowledge. The human mind cannot create knowledge on its own.

2. **What characteristics are evident in human beings who live in a state of nature?**
    A. Individuals possess perfect freedom in a state of nature; they live under no superior power.
    B. All people are born equal in a state of nature. No single person is given more than any other person.
    C. In a state of nature individuals possess their own labor. Since property is the product of labor, individuals possess their own property. Property includes not only an individual's material possessions, but also his life and his liberty.
    D. In a state of nature human beings are governed by natural law. Reason is the law of nature, and reason dictates that human beings should not be denied life, liberty, or property.
    E. Freedom in a state of nature is not a license to do whatever one pleases—no individual should deny others their natural rights.

3. **Why did human beings leave the state of nature to form a society?**
    A. The state of nature does not provide an impartial third party judge to settle disagreements.
    B. In a state of nature an individual who is harmed by others may not always be strong enough to bring about justice on his own.
    C. The state of nature provides insufficient means to protect property.

4. **What factors affect the creation of society?**
    A. Although human beings enjoy perfect freedom in a state of nature, they will "put on the bonds of civil society" to protect their property. The main reason human beings unite and form a government is for the preservation of their property.
    B. An individual must choose to enter a social contract. An individual will give up the freedom of living in a state of nature only when he decides for himself to join others in forming a community.

5. **What are the terms of the social contract?**
    A. Since government has the power to limit freedom, the government must obtain its power from the consent of the governed.
    B. Once a community is formed the majority shall rule. Human beings living under the social contract are obligated to obey the majority.
    C. A separation of powers in government is essential to protect the liberty of the people.

6. **What are the responsibilities of government under the social contract?**
    A. Government has obligations, not rights; only the people have rights. Government cannot do as it pleases.
    B. Taxes should not be raised without the consent of the people. No individual should have property taken away without consent.
    C. Property, which includes life and liberty, is a natural right. Government is obligated to protect life, liberty, and property.

7. **Do the people have the right to change their government?**
    A. The people have the right to alter or abolish the government if the government violates the trust of the people or does not protect the rights of the people.
    B. The people can revolt against any type of government. However, there is least likely to be a revolution against a government based on the consent of a population that has the right to rebel.

STUDENT ACTIVITIES

Vocabulary
Define the following terms before reading the lesson on Locke.

1.	annex	9.	extemporary	17.	promulgate
2.	commonwealth	10.	incorporate	18.	reciprocal
3.	compact	11.	jurisdiction	19.	sanctuary
4.	consent	12.	manifest	20.	sovereignty
5.	decree	13.	multitude	21.	subjection
6.	dominion	14.	negligence	22.	subordination
7.	endeavor	15.	penury	23.	transgressor
8.	engagement	16.	promiscuous		

Review
1. Why did Locke move from his homeland in England to Holland?
2. What was the title of Locke's most important book on political theory?
3. What was the significance of the *tabula rasa* in Locke's political philosophy?

4. What did Locke believe was the only thing given to the human mind at birth?
5. According to Locke, what are the characteristics of life in a state of nature?
6. Why did Locke believe human beings possessed a natural right to their property?
7. Why did Locke believe that freedom did not grant individuals the license to do whatever they pleased?
8. According to Locke, why did human beings leave the state of nature?
9. Why did Locke believe the people had to consent to raising taxes?
10. What three rights did Locke believe government was obligated to protect?
11. What did Locke believe was the best way to prevent revolution against the government?
12. Decide whether the following statements are **True** or **False** according to John Locke.
    A. The main reason human beings unite and form a government is to maintain their property.
    B. Government must obtain its power from the consent of the governed.
    C. Majority rule should be replaced by the rule of a single sovereign.
    D. The people have a right to alter or abolish their government.
    E. Individuals possess perfect freedom in a state of nature.
    F. Human beings are born equal in a state of nature.
    G. Property is the product of labor.
    H. The minority is not obligated to obey the majority.
    I. Government has obligations, not rights; only the people have rights.

What do you think?
On a scale of one through five, rate your opinion of the following quotations by Locke. Write a short statement explaining your rating.

1 – You **strongly agree** with the statement *or* you feel the statement is **admirable** considering the historical circumstances surrounding it.
5 – You **strongly disagree** with the statement *or* you feel the statement is **contemptible** considering the historical circumstances surrounding it.

A. *Reason . . . teaches all mankind . . . that being all equal and independent, no one ought to harm another in his life, health, liberty, or possessions.*
B. *It is unreasonable for men to be judges in their own cases. Self-love will make men partial to themselves and their friends.*
C. *The liberty of man, in society, is to be under no other legislative power, but that established, by consent, in the commonwealth.*

D. *Every man has a property in his own person: this no body has any right to but himself.*

E. *Men . . . being by nature, all free, equal and independent, no one can be put out of this estate, and subjected to the political power of another, without his own consent.*

F. *The act of the majority passes for the act of the whole, and of course determines, as having by the law of nature and reason, the power of the whole.*

G. *Every man, by consenting with others to make one body politic under one government, puts himself under an obligation, to every one of that society, to submit to the determination of the majority.*

H. *The great and chief end of men's uniting into commonwealths, and placing themselves under government, is the preservation of their property.*

I. *The power of the society, or legislative constituted by them, can never be supposed to extend farther, than the common good.*

J. *Wherever law ends, tyranny begins.*

K. *Good and evil, reward and punishment, are the only motives to a rational creature; these are the spur and reins whereby all mankind are set on work and guided.*

L. *Where there is no property there is no injustice.*

M. *New opinions are always suspected, and usually opposed, without any other reason but because they are not already common.*

N. *Reading furnishes the mind only with materials for knowledge; it is thinking [that] makes what we read ours.*

O. *The discipline of desire is the background of character.*

CHAPTER 4

JEAN JACQUES ROUSSEAU

BACKGROUND

Jean Jacques Rousseau (1712-1778) presents a dilemma for anyone searching for consistency in Rousseau's life or his ideas. He was an extreme moralist who lived a "loose," some may say immoral, life. He loved humanity, but hated people. He was a playwright who hated the theater. He knew he would not make a good father and consequently gave away his own children. In short, he was a sensitive, half-crazed genius whose ideas had tremendous influence.

His mother died nine days after he was born. When he was ten his father faced imprisonment and left him with his aunt and uncle in Geneva. Although Rousseau could read when he was only three years old, his formal education ended when he was thirteen. After a short apprenticeship to an engraver whom he hated, Rousseau ran away from Geneva at the age of sixteen. He left with no money and no skills to gain employment.

After leaving Geneva, Rousseau embraced and later abandoned both Roman Catholicism and a twenty-nine year old woman. While living with the woman, he read and studied with an insatiable desire to learn. He also made a living teaching music until 1742 when he moved to Paris where he gained employment as a secretary to a French ambassador.

In 1750 Rousseau won a prize for an essay which attacked modern civilization and defended the arts and sciences. The success of the essay allowed him to begin a new life as a celebrated intellectual. Although he wrote extensively, he is best remembered for *The Social Contract*, *Confessions*, and *Emile*. He also wrote operas and invented a new system of musical notation.

Rousseau arouses much debate among students of philosophy. His critics find too many contradictions and emotional outbursts. His supporters disagree over the content of his ideas. He has been described as the founder of Romanticism, a defender of individual freedom, a socialist, a totalitarian, and a utopian. Just as John Locke is often considered the intellectual father of the American Revolution, Rousseau is often considered the intellectual father of the French Revolution. His descriptions of liberty, equality, and democracy should be of vital interest to modern Americans.

JEAN JACQUES ROUSSEAU – IN HIS OWN WORDS

Discourse on the Origin of Inequality

I conceive of two kinds of inequality in the human species: one which I call natural or physical, because it is established by nature and consists in the difference of age, health, bodily strength, and qualities of mind or soul. The other may be called moral or political inequality, because it depends on a kind of convention and is established, or at least authorized, by the consent of men. This latter type of inequality consists in the different privileges enjoyed by some at the expense of others, such as being richer, more honored, more powerful than they, or even causing themselves to be obeyed by them.

There is no point in asking what the source of natural inequality is, because the answer would be found enunciated in the simple definition of the word. There is still less of a point in asking whether there would not be some essential connection between the two inequalities, for that would amount to asking whether those who command are necessarily better than those who obey, and whether strength of body or mind, wisdom or virtue are always found in the same individuals in proportion to power or wealth. Perhaps this is a good question for slaves to discuss within earshot of their master, but it is not suitable for reasonable and free men who seek the truth. . . .

The first person who, having enclosed a plot of land, took it into his head to say *this is mine* and found people simple enough to believe him, was the true founder of civil society. What crimes, wars, murders, what miseries and horrors would the human race have been spared, had someone pulled up the stakes or filled in the ditch and cried out to his fellow men: "Do not listen to this impostor. You are lost if you forget that the fruits of the earth belong to all and the earth to no one!" But it is quite likely that by then things had already reached the point where they could no longer continue as they were. For this idea of property, depending on many prior ideas which could only have arisen successively, was not formed all at once in the human mind. It was necessary to make great progress, to acquire much industry and enlightenment, and to transmit and augment them from one age to another, before arriving at this final stage in the state of nature. . . .

It would be no more reasonable to believe that initially the peoples threw themselves unconditionally and for all time into the arms of an absolute master, and that the first means of providing for the common security dreamed up by proud and unruly men was to rush headlong into slavery. In fact, why did they give themselves over to superiors, if not to defend themselves against oppression and to protect their goods, their liberties and their lives, which are, as it were, the constitutive elements of their being? Now, since in relations between men, the worst that can happen to someone is for him to see himself at the discretion of someone else, would it not have been contrary to good sense to begin by surrendering into the hands of a leader the only things for whose preservation they needed his help? What equivalent could he have offered them for the concession of so fine a right? And if he had dared to demand it on the pretext of defending them, would he not have immediately received the reply given in the fable: "what more will the enemy do to us?" It is therefore incontestable, and it is a fundamental maxim of all political right, that peoples have given themselves leaders in order to defend their liberty and not to enslave themselves. *If we have a prince*, Pliny said to Trajan, *it is so that he may preserve us from having a master.*

[Our] political theorists produce the same sophisms about the love of liberty that [our] philosophers have made about the state of nature. By the things they see they render judgments about very different things they have not seen; and they attribute to men a natural inclination to servitude owing to the patience with which those who are before their eyes endure their servitude, without giving a thought to the fact that it is the same for liberty as it is for innocence and virtue: their value is felt only as long as one has them oneself, and the taste for them is lost as soon as one has lost them. "I know the delights of your country," said Brasidas to a satrap who compared the life of Sparta to that of Persepolis, "but you cannot know the pleasures of mine."

As an unbroken steed bristles his mane, paws the ground with his hoof, and struggles violently at the mere approach of the bit, while a trained horse patiently endures the whip and the spur, barbarous man does not bow his head for the yoke that civilized man wears without a murmur, and he prefers the most stormy liberty to tranquil subjection. Thus it is not by the degradation of enslaved peoples that man's natural dispositions for or against servitude are to be judged, but by the wonders that all free peoples have accomplished to safeguard themselves from oppression. I know that enslaved peoples do nothing but boast of the peace and tranquillity they enjoy in their chains and that *they give the name 'peace' to the most miserable slavery*. But when I see free peoples sacrificing pleasures, tranquillity, wealth, power, and life itself for the preservation of this sole good which is regarded so disdainfully by those who have lost it; when I see animals born free and abhorring captivity break their heads against the bars of their prison; when I see multitudes of utterly naked savages scorn European pleasures and brave hunger, fire, sword and death, simply to preserve their independence, I sense that it is inappropriate for slaves to reason about liberty.

As for paternal authority, from which several have derived absolute government and all society, it is enough, without having recourse to the contrary proofs of Locke . . . to note that nothing in the world is farther from the ferocious spirit of despotism than the gentleness of that authority which looks more to the advantage of nature, the father is master of the child as long as his help is necessary for him; that beyond this point they become equals, and the son, completely independent of the father, then owes him merely respect and not obedience; for gratitude is clearly a duty that must be rendered, but not a right that can be demanded. Instead of saying that civil society derives from paternal power, on the contrary it must be said that it is from civil society that this power draws its principal force. An individual was not recognized as the father of several children until the children remained gathered about him. The goods of the father, of which he is truly the master, are the goods that keep his children in a state of dependence toward him, and he can cause their receiving a share in his estate to be consequent upon the extent to which they will have merited it from him by continuous deference to his wishes. Now, far from having some similar favor to expect from their despot (since they belong to him as personal possessions—they and all they possess—or at least he claims this to be the case), subjects are reduced to receiving as a favor what he leaves them of their goods. He does what is just when he despoils them; he does them a favor when he allows them to live.

In continuing thus to examine facts from the viewpoint of right, no more solidity than truth would be found in the belief that the establishment of tyranny was voluntary; and it would be difficult to show the validity of a contract that would obligate only one of the parties, where all the commitments would be placed on one side with none on the other, and that it would turn exclusively to the disadvantage of the one making the commitments. This odious system is quite far removed from being, even today, that of wise and good monarchs, and especially of the kind of France, as may be seen in various places in their edicts, and particularly in the following passage of a famous writing published in 1667 in the name of and by order of Louis XIV: *Let it not be said therefore that the sovereign is not subject to the laws of his state, for the contrary statement is a truth of the law of nations, which flattery has on occasion attacked, but which good princes have always defended as tutelary divinity of their states. How much more legitimate is it to say, with the wise Plato, that the perfect felicity of a kingdom is that a prince be obeyed by his subjects, that the prince obey the law, and that the law be right and always directed to the public good.* I will not stop to investigate whether, with liberty being the most noble of man's faculties, he degrades his nature, places himself on the level of animals enslaved by instinct, offends even his maker, when he unreservedly renounces the most precious of all his gifts, and allows himself to commit all the crimes he forbids us to commit, in order to please a ferocious or crazed master; nor whether this sublime workman should be more irritated at seeing his finest work destroyed rather than at seeing it dishonored. [I will disregard, if you will, the authority of Barbeyrac, who flatly declares, following Locke, that no one can sell his liberty to the point of submitting himself to an arbitrary power that treats him according to its fancy. *For,* he adds *this would be selling his own life, of which his is not the master.*] I will merely ask by what right those who have not been afraid of debasing themselves to this degree have been able to subject their posterity to the same ignominy and to renounce for it goods that do not depend on their liberality, and without which life itself is burdensome to all who are worthy of it.

Pufendorf says that just as one transfers his goods to another by conventions and contracts, one can also divest himself of his liberty in favor of someone. That, it seems to me, is very bad reasoning; for, in the first place, the goods I give away become something utterly foreign to me, and it is a matter of indifference to me whether or not these goods are abused; but it is important to me that my liberty is not abused, and I cannot expose myself to becoming the instrument of crime without making myself guilty of the evil I will be forced to commit. Moreover, since the right of property is merely the result of convention and human institution, every man can dispose of what he possesses as he sees fit. But it is not the same for the essential gifts of nature such as life and liberty, which everyone is allowed to enjoy, and of which it is at least doubtful that one has the right to divest himself. In giving up the one he degrades his being; in giving up the other he annihilates that being insofar as he can. And because no temporal goods can compensate for the one or the other, it would offend at the same time both nature and reason to renounce them, regardless of the price. But even if one could give away his liberty as he does his goods, the difference would be very great for the children who enjoy the father's goods only by virtue of a transmission of his right; whereas, since liberty is a gift they receive from nature in virtue of being men, their parents had no right to divest them of it. Thus, just as violence had to be done to nature in order to establish slavery, nature had to be changed in order to perpetuate this right. And the jurists, who have gravely pronounced that the child of a slave woman is born a slave, have decided, in other words, that a man is not born a man.

Thus it appears certain to men not only that governments did not begin with arbitrary power, which is but their corruption and extreme limit, and which finally brings them back simply to the law of the strongest, for which they were initially to have been the remedy; but also that even if they had begun thus, this power, being illegitimate by its nature, could not have served as a foundation for the rights of society, nor, as a consequence, for the inequality occasioned by social institutions. . . .

. . . It follows from this presentation that, since inequality is practically non-existent in the state of nature, it derives its force and growth from the development of our faculties and the progress of the human mind, and eventually becomes stable and legitimate through the establishment of property and laws. . . . It is obviously contrary to the law of nature, however it may be defined, for a child to command an old man, for an imbecile to lead a wise man, and for a handful of people to gorge themselves on superfluities while the starving multitude lacks necessities.

The Social Contract

Man is born free, and everywhere he is in chains. He who believes himself the master of others does not escape being more of a slave than they. How did this change take place? I have no idea. What can render it legitimate? I believe I can answer this question.

Were I to consider only force and the effect that flows from it, I would say that so long as a people is constrained to obey and does obey, it does well. As soon as it can shake off the yoke and does shake it off, it does even better. For by recovering its liberty by means of the same right that stole it, either the populace is justified in getting it back or else those who took it away were not justified in their actions. But the social order is a sacred right which serves as a foundation for all other rights. Nevertheless, this right does not come from nature. It is therefore founded upon convention. . . .

Since no man has a natural authority over his fellow man, and since force does not give rise to any right, conventions therefore remain the basis of all legitimate authority among men. . . .

Renouncing one's liberty is renouncing one's dignity as a man, the rights of humanity and even its duties. There is no possible compensation for anyone who renounces everything. Such a renunciation is incompatible with the nature of man. Removing all morality from his actions is tantamount to taking away all liberty from his will. Finally, it is a vain and contradictory convention to stipulate absolute authority on one side and a limitless obedience on the other. Is it not clear that no commitments are made to a person from whom one has the right to demand everything? And does this condition alone not bring with it, without equivalent or exchange, the nullity of the act? For what right would my slave have against me, given that all he has belongs to me, and that, since his right is my right, my having a right against myself makes no sense? . . .

If one enquires into precisely wherein the greatest good of all consists, which should be the purpose of every system of legislation, one will find that it boils down to the two principal objects, *liberty* and *equality*. Liberty, because all particular dependence is that much force taken from the body of the state; equality because liberty cannot subsist without it.

. . . Regarding equality, we need not mean by this word that degrees of power and wealth are to be absolutely the same, but rather that, with regard to power, it should transcend all violence and never be exercised except by virtue of rank and laws; and, with regard to wealth, no citizen should be so rich as to be capable of buying another citizen, and none so poor that he is forced to sell himself. This presupposes moderation in goods and credit on the part of the great, and moderation in avarice and covetousness on the part of the lowly.

This equality is said to be a speculative fiction that cannot exist in practice. But if abuse is inevitable, does it follow that it should not at least be regulated? It is precisely because the force of things tends always to destroy equality that the force of legislation should always tend to maintain it.

JEAN JACQUES ROUSSEAU – A SIMULATED INTERVIEW

1. **What characteristics are evident in human beings who live in a state of nature?**
    A. Human beings in a state of nature are *noble savages* living a happy and carefree existence.
    B. Human beings possess natural liberty in a state of nature. Leaders and rulers do not exist in a state of nature.
    C. Human beings do not possess private property in a state of nature. Private property is a characteristic of human society; private property is not found in nature.

2. **Are all human beings created equal?**
    A. Human beings are created equal in one respect—they possess natural liberty.
    B. Individual differences in physical strength, health, and intelligence are natural to human existence. Such differences are referred to as *natural inequality*.
    C. Individual differences in wealth and power do not exist in nature. Such differences are referred to as *political inequality*.
    D. Inequality is not a problem in a state of nature. Inequality presents numerous problems in society.

3. **How does society affect human beings?**
    A. Society takes away liberty and incites evil behavior. War, for example, does not exist in nature; war is a product of society.
    B. Due to the influence of society, modern human beings are unhappy, insecure, and selfish. "Civilization is a hopeless race to discover remedies for the evil it produces."
    C. In society human beings might be ruled by tyrants. Allowing tyrants to rule violates nature. A tyrant's power is an illegitimate power that takes away the natural liberty of the people.

4. **Why did human beings leave the state of nature?**
    A. Civil society began when the first person enclosed a plot of land and said, "This is mine."
    B. The existence of private property established a need to protect liberty. Human beings therefore turned to leaders who would protect liberty. Regrettably, leaders were often tyrants and took away liberty rather than protected it.
    C. Human beings cannot remain in a state of nature; they can never return to a state of nature. Human beings must consequently build a society that adequately preserves liberty and eliminates tyrants.

5. What are the characteristics of the best society?

    A. The best society protects liberty. The people enter a social contract to create a state that protects their liberty.

    B. In the best society the state acts in harmony with the *general will*. The general will is defined as the common good.

    C. In the best society the people are the lawmakers; they make political decisions directly rather than through representatives. This is known as *participatory* or *direct* democracy.

    D. In the best society each individual votes only for the common good. No person should ever vote according to individual self-interest.

    E. In the best society individuals participate in making the laws they obey. The best way to protect the liberty of the people is to require people to obey only those laws that the people have imposed upon themselves.

    F. In the best society schools teach good citizenship. Schools serve society best when they create *moral* individuals rather than *knowledgeable* individuals.

6. What are the disadvantages of participatory democracy?

    A. In a participatory democracy individuals might discover their self-interest is at odds with the general will. However, everyone must understand that living in a community requires the loss of some freedom.

    B. In society individuals lose their *natural liberty*, but they gain *civil liberty*. Civil liberty is defined as the responsibility that individuals owe to the common good.

    C. When an individual's self-interest conflicts with the general will he must be "forced to be free." He must be forced to conform to the common good.

7. If the people make the laws, what is the role of government?

    A. Government interprets and enforces the laws in a way that liberty and equality are properly maintained.

    B. Government exists to carry out the general will. A wise and powerful "lawgiver" should carry out the laws that create good citizens. The lawgiver's duty is to find the general will.

8. Is slavery natural?

    A. Many philosophers argue that slavery is natural. However, slavery is not natural because all human beings are born free. Slaves are denied liberty which is nature's most precious gift to human beings.

    B. Even slaves often defend slavery; slaves might argue that slavery allows them to live in peace. Slaves who make such an argument are misguided. Slaves cannot be trusted to think rationally when considering liberty.

STUDENT ACTIVITIES

Vocabulary

Define the following terms before reading the lesson on Rousseau.

1. arbitrary	10. ferocious	19. solidity
2. augment	11. gratitude	20. speculative
3. concession	12. ignominy	21. subjection
4. deference	13. imbecile	22. sublime
5. discretion	14. incontestable	23. successive
6. disposition	15. odious	24. superfluity
7. edict	16. paternal	25. tranquillity
8. enunciate	17. pretext	26. transmit
9. felicity	18. renunciation	27. tutelary

Review

1. Who is called the intellectual father of the French Revolution and the founder of Romanticism?
2. What are Rousseau's three most important books?
3. What is a noble savage?
4. How did Rousseau define the difference between natural inequality and political inequality?
5. In what respect were human beings created equal according to Rousseau?
6. What did Rousseau think happened when human beings left nature and entered society?
7. According to Rousseau, when did civil society begin?
8. What is the general will?
9. What is participatory democracy?
10. In the best society, how did Rousseau think individuals should vote?
11. According to Rousseau, what is the best way to protect the liberty of the people?
12. What did Rousseau think children should be taught in school?
13. How did Rousseau define *civil* liberty?
14. According to Rousseau, what is the purpose of government?
15. Decide whether the following statements are **True** or **False** according to Jean Jacques Rousseau.
    A. Government is natural to human existence.
    B. Property rights exist in a state of nature.
    C. Inequality is a problem whether human beings live in a state of nature or in civilization.
    D. The best society guarantees equality at the expense of liberty.
    E. Living in a community requires the loss of some freedom.
    F. Slavery is natural.
    G. Leaders do not exist in a state of nature.
    H. Society incites evil behavior.

What do you think?
On a scale of one through five, rate your opinion of the following quotations by Rousseau. Write a short statement explaining your rating.

1 – You **strongly agree** with the statement *or* you feel the statement is **admirable** considering the historical circumstances surrounding it.
5 – You **strongly disagree** with the statement *or* you feel the statement is **contemptible** considering the historical circumstances surrounding it.

A. *The first person who, having enclosed a plot of land, took it into his head to say this is mine and found people simple enough to believe him, was the true founder of civil society.*

B. *It is . . . incontestable, and it is a fundamental maxim of all political right, that peoples have given themselves leaders in order to defend their liberty and not to enslave themselves.*

C. *Since inequality is practically non-existent in the state of nature, it derives its force and growth from the development of the human mind, and eventually becomes stable and legitimate through the establishment of property and laws.*

D. *Man is born free, and everywhere he is in chains.*

E. *Renouncing one's liberty is renouncing one's dignity as a man, the rights of humanity and even its duties.*

F. *In the strict sense of the term, a true democracy has never existed and never will exist.*

G. *The strongest is never strong enough to be always the master, unless he transforms strength into right, and obedience into duty.*

H. *Those people who treat politics and morality separately will never understand either of them.*

I. *It should be remembered that the foundation of the social contract is property; and its first condition, that every one should be maintained in the peaceful possession of what belongs to him.*

J. *As soon as any man says of the affairs of state, "What does it matter to me?" the state may be given up as lost.*

K. *The people is never corrupted, but it is often deceived.*

L. *If we ask in what precisely consist the greatest good of all, which should be the end of every system of legislation, we shall find it reduces itself to two main objects, liberty and equality.*

M. *Laws are always useful to those who own, and injurious to those who do not.*

N. *Civilized man is born, lives, and dies in slavery; at his birth he is confined in swaddling clothes; at death he is nailed in a coffin.*

O. *Teach him to live a life rather than to avoid death; life is not breath but action.*

P. *One can buy anything with money except morality and citizens.*

CHAPTER 5

NEW ENGLAND PURITANS

BACKGROUND

During the sixteenth century a movement for religious reform started within the Church of England. This movement, known as Puritanism, based its philosophy primarily upon the teachings of John Calvin. Puritans received their name from a desire to "purify" the Church of England and strip it of all traces of Roman Catholic influence.

In the early seventeenth century a large number of Puritans migrated to Massachusetts Bay. Puritans hoped this "Great Migration" would allow them to build a model society based upon their strict moral code. By the 1640s the Puritan population of Massachusetts Bay had grown to about ten thousand. The Puritans soon outgrew their original settlements, and they looked for new areas to inhabit. Consequently, they formed new colonies in Connecticut, New Hampshire, and Maine.

John Winthrop (1588-1649), a well-educated English lawyer, served as governor or deputy governor of Massachusetts for almost twenty years. Administering the will of God as understood by church elders, Winthrop presided over the banishment of Quakers from Massachusetts. In 1639 he faced impeachment charges when his actions as deputy governor were challenged by elected town officials. He responded to the charges in his Little Speech. In the speech Winthrop did not advocate democracy as we know it. He argued that government by a select few acting in God's name should not be subject to popular control. Winthrop's speech helped convince church elders to clear him of all charges.

Although the literacy rate was high among Puritans, the religious leaders were generally intolerant of individuals and groups that disagreed with official thinking. In 1641 Puritan leaders adopted a Body of Liberties which reflected a belief that theirs was the only true religion. This policy of intolerance created divisions that led to the eventual fragmentation of the Puritan community.

Puritans not only played an important role in the development of New England, but their ideas were also evident in the revolutionary rhetoric of the 1770s. In modern times the Puritan tradition still exerts a significant influence on American culture and politics.

NEW ENGLAND PURITANS – IN THEIR OWN WORDS

John Winthrop, "A Modell of Christian Charity," 1630

God Almighty in his most holy and wise providence hath so disposed of the condition of mankind as in all times some must be rich, some poor, some high and eminent in power and dignity, others mean and in subjection. . . .

For the work we have in hand, it is by a mutual consent through a special overruling providence, and a more than ordinary approbation of the churches of Christ, to seek out a place of cohabitation and consortship under a due form of government, both civil and ecclesiastical. In such cases as this the care of the public must oversway all private respects, by which not only conscience, but mere civil policy doth bind us; for it is a true rule that particular estates cannot subsist in the ruin of the public.

The end is to improve our lives to do more service to the Lord, the comfort and increase of the body of Christ whereof preserved from the common corruptions of this evil world, to serve the Lord and work out our salvation under the power and purity of his holy ordinances. . . .

. . . We must love one another with a pure heart, fervently; we must bear one another's burdens; we must not look only on our own things, but also on the things of our brethren. Neither must we think that the Lord will bear with such failings at our hands as he doth from those among whome we have lived . . . .

. . . For we must consider that we shall be as a city upon a hill, the eyes of all people are upon us; so that if we shall deal falsely with our God in this work we have undertaken and so cause Him to withdraw His present help from us, we shall be made a story and a byword through the world.

John Winthrop, "Essay on the Power of the Church," 1637

1: The Scripture affords neither rule nor example of any such power in the Church, but divers ag^t it: for Christ disclameth it, where he asketh who made him a Judge of dividinge Inheritances. But if they should have this power, they must of necessity be Judges of such thinges: for putt Case, a Magistrate give sentence ag^t a member of a Church, upon a title of Inheritance, or in an Action of Debt or Trespasse, & he beinge offended wth the Magistrate for it (as supposinge it to be unjust) brings him to the Church for it, then must the Churche trye this title, & examine the matter of Debt or Trespasse, wth all the circumstances of it *de integro*; else how shall they be able to Judge whether the Magistrate hath given offence to his brother or not?

2: By occasion heerof the Church should become the Supreame Court in the Jurisdiction, & capable of all Appeales, & so in trueth meerly Antich^t, by beinge exalted aboue all that is called God, &c.

3: If this were allowed, then the Church should have power to Judge, where it wants meanes to finde out the Trueth: for the Churche cannot call in forrein witnesses: nor examine witnesses upon oath, or require the view of the records of the Court: all wh. may be needful for findinge out the trueth in many cases.

4: To examine a Civill businesse in a waye of Judicature (though it ayme not at outward punishment) is an exercise of such Aut^{ye}. as Christ forbidds his disciples: the Lords of the Gentiles exercise Aut^{ye}, etc.; but you shall not doe so.

5: Christ his kingdome is not of this world, therefore his officers in this kingdome cannot Juditially enquire into affaires of this world.

6: Such powers would confounde those Jurisdictions which Christ hath made distinct: for as he is Kinge of kinges & Lo^s: he hath sett up another kingdome in this worlde, wherein magistrates are his officers, and they are to be accountable to him for their miscarriages in the waye & order of this kingdome.

7: This would sett Christ ag^t himselfe in his owne Ordinances, without any ordinary meanes of redresse, & so there must needs be a defecte in his dispensations, wh. cant be; for if the Church (supposinge the Civill magistrates had intrenched upon Christs spirituall kingdome) should excommunicate them; & againe the magistrate (supposinge the Officers of the Church had vsurped upon his Civill authoritye) should imprison or banishe them: now is Christs kingdome divided, one ordinance ag^t another, not to moderation but to destruction: and heere is no menes to reconcile them: but if the Rule of Christ be observed, Resist not evill, & submit yo^{r}selves to the higher powers, now is the honor & safety of

[Here the paper is torn.]

It was Luthers Counsell to the Anabaptists . . . that thoughe their magistrates did oppresse & iniure them, yet they should praye for them, & comende them, & seeke to winne them by gentleness &c, & when the Churche shall binde kinges in chaines & nobles in fetters of iron (Ps: 149) (wh. cant be meant of Church censures, for it shalbe in vengeance & Judgment foretould af^t the heathen), then the meek shall be beautified wth salvation; then Kinges shalbe their nursing fathers &c; (Esay 49.23) they shall bowe downe to her & licke the duste of her feet; & none shall hurt or destroye in all the holy mountaine (Esay 65.25): So that the wisdome, pietye & meeknesse of the Church shall winne the hearts of kinges &c: & binde them so to her in the power of the Gospell, as they shall love the verye earth she treads on; they shall beare that reverence to her, as she shall need fear no hurt from them, no more than a child doth from the nurse: therefore no need to binde them by churche censures: they were other kinges whom he sayth the people should curse in the dayes of their calamitye; & yet when they should curse their kinges, he sayth, they should curse their God allso (Esay 8.21),—a man may not say to a king, thou art wicked; nor call princes ungodly (Job: 34. 18).

I denye not but that a private person may privately reproove a magistrate offendinge, but he may not doe it publicly: except he be publicly called to beare witnesse to the Trueth, as Stephen was.

I consent allso, that Magistrates should beare wth the faylinges of their Christian brethren, when in tender care of the public good & their honor &

comfort, they chance to excede the limitts of their lib^ty; but such breth: must then see, & not Justifie their faylings; for Christ bidds us not forgive o^r brother, till he saye, it repenteth him.

John Winthrop, "The Little Speech," 1639

The great questions that have troubled the country, are about the authority of the magistrates and the liberty of the people. It is yourselves who have called us to this office, and being called by you, we have our authority from God, in way of an ordinance, such as hath the image of God eminently stamped upon it, the contempt and violation whereof hath been vindicated with examples of divine vengeance. I entreat you to consider, that when you choose magistrates, you take them from among yourselves, men subject to like passions as you are. Therefore when you see infirmities in us, you should reflect upon your own and that would make you bear the more with us, and not be severe censurers of the failings of your magistrates, when you have continual experience of the like infirmities in yourselves and others. We account him a good servant, who breaks not his covenant. The covenant between you and us is the oath you have taken of us, which is to this purpose, that we shall govern you and judge your causes by the rules of God's laws and our own, according to our best skill. When you agree with a workman to build you a ship or house, etc., he undertakes as well for his skill as for his faithfulness, for it is his profession, and you pay him for both. But when you call one to be a magistrate, he doth not profess nor undertake to have sufficient skill for that office, nor can you furnish him with gifts, etc., therefore you must run the hazard of his skill and ability. But if he fail in faithfulness, which by his oath he is bound unto, that he must answer for. If it fall out that the case be clear to common apprehension, and the rule clear also, if he transgress here, the error is not in the skill, but in the evil of the will: it must be required of him. But if the case be doubtful, or the rule doubtful, to men of such understanding and parts as your magistrates are, if your magistrates should err here, yourselves must bear it.

For the other point concerning liberty, I observe a great mistake in the country about that. There is a two fold liberty, natural (I mean as our nature is now corrupt) and civil or federal. The first is common to man with beasts and other creatures. By this, man, as he stands in relation to man simply, hath liberty to do what he lists; it is a liberty to evil as well as to good. This liberty is incompatible and inconsistent with authority, and cannot endure the least restraint of the most just authority. The exercise and maintaining of this liberty makes men grow more evil, and in time to be worse than brute beasts . . . This is that great enemy of truth and peace, that wild beast, which all the ordinances of God are bent against, to restrain and subdue it. The other kind of liberty I call civil or federal, it may also be termed moral, in reference to the covenant between God and man, in the moral law, and the politic covenants and constitutions, amongst men themselves. This liberty is the proper end and object of authority, and cannot subsist without it; and it is a liberty to that only which is good, just, and honest. This liberty you are to stand for, with the hazard (not only of your goods, but) of your lives, if need be. Whatsoever crosseth this, is not authority, but a distemper thereof. This liberty is maintained and exercised in a way of subjection to authority; it is of the same kind of liberty wherewith Christ hath made us free. The woman's own choice makes such a man her husband; yet being so chosen, he is her lord, and she is to be subject to him, yet in a way of liberty, not of bondage; and a true wife accounts her subjection her honor and freedom, and would not think her condition safe and free, but in her subjection to her husband's authority. Such is the liberty of the church under the authority of Christ, her king and husband; his yoke is so easy and sweet to her as a bride's ornaments; and if through forwardness or wantonness, etc., she shake it off, at any time, she is at no rest in her spirit, until she take it up again; and whether her lord smiles upon her, and embraceth her in his arms, or whether he frowns, or rebukes, or smites her, she apprehends the sweetness of his love in all, and is refreshed, supported, and instructed by every such dispensation of his authority over her. On the other side, ye know who they are that complain of this yoke and say, let us break their bands, etc., we will not have this man to rule over us. Even so, brethren, it will be between you and your magistrates. If you stand for your natural corrupt liberties, and will do what is good in your own eyes, you will not endure the least weight of authority, but will murmur, and oppose, and be always striving to shake off that yoke; but if you will be satisfied to enjoy such civil and lawful liberties, such as Christ allows you, then you will quietly and cheerfully submit unto that authority which is set over you, in all the administrations of it, for your good. Wherein, if we fail at any time, we hope we shall be willing (by God's assistance) to hearken to good advice from any of you, or in any other way of God; so shall your liberties be preserved, in upholding the honor and power of authority amongst you.

Massachusetts Body of Liberties, 1641

No mans life shall be taken away, no mans honour or good name shall be stayned, no mans person shall be arested, restrayned, banished, dismembred, nor any wayes punished, no man shall be deprived of his wife or children, no mans goods or estaite shall be taken away from him, nor any way indammaged under coulor of law or Countenance of Authoritie, unlesse it be by vertue or equitie of some expresse law of the Country waranting the same, established by a generall Court and sufficiently published, or in case of the defect of a law in any parteculer case by the word of god. And in Capitall cases, or in cases concerning dismembring or banishment, according to that word to be judged by the Generall Court.

Every person within this Jurisdiction, whether Inhabitant or forreiner shall enjoy the same justice and law, that is generall for the plantation, which we constitute and execute one towards another without partialitie or delay.

Every man whether Inhabitant or forreiner, free or not free shall have libertie to come to any publique Court, Councel, or Town meeting, and either by speech or writeing to move any lawfull, seasonable, and materiall question, or to present any necessary motion, complaint, petition, Bill or information, whereof that meeting hath proper cognizance, so it be done in convenient time, due order, and respective manner. . . .

No Conveyance, Deede, or promise whatsoever shall be of validitie, If it be gotten by Illegal violence, imprisonment, threatenings, or any kinde of forcible compulsion called Dures. . . .

No man shall be twise sentenced by Civill Justice for one and the same Crime, offence, or Trespasse. . . .

All Jurors shall be chosen continuallie by the freemen of the Towne where they dwell. . . .

Any Shire or Towne shall have libertie to choose their Deputies whom and where they please for the General Court. So be it they be free men, and have taken there oath of fealtie, and Inhabiting in this Jurisdiction. . . .

The Freemen of every Towneship shall have power to make such by laws and constitutions as may concerne the wellfare of their Towne, provided they be not of a Criminall, but onely of a prudentiall nature. . . .

Everie marryed woeman shall be free from bodilie correction or stripes by her husband, unlesse it be in his owne defence upon her assalt. If there be any just cause of correction complaint shall be made to Authoritie assembled in some Court, from which onely she shall receive it. . . .

If any servants shall flee from the Tiranny and crueltie of their masters to the howse of any freeman of the same Towne, they shall be there protected and susteyned till due order be taken for their relife. Provided due notice thereof be speedily given to their maisters from whom they fled. And the next Assistant or Constable where the partie flying is harboured. . . .

If any man after legall conviction shall have or worship any other god, but the lord god, he shall be put to death.

If any man or woeman be a witch, (that is hath or consulteth with a familiar spirit,) They shall be put to death. . . .

If any man shall conspire and attempt any invasion, insurrection, or publique rebellion against our commonwealth, or shall indeavour to surprize any Towne or Townes, fort or forts therein, or shall treacherously and perfediouslie attempt the alteration and subversion of our frame of politie or Government fundamentallie, he shall be put to death.

All the people of god within this Jurisdiction who are not in a church way, and be orthodox in Judgement, and not scandalous in life, shall have full libertie to gather themselves into a Church Estaite. Provided they doe it in a Christian way, with due observation of the rules of Christ revealed in his word.

Every Church hath free libertie of Election and ordination of all their officers from time to time, provided they be able, pious and orthodox.

NEW ENGLAND PURITANS – A SIMULATED INTERVIEW

1. **What are the Five Points of Calvinism adopted by Puritans?**
   A. In the beginning God predetermined certain souls for salvation and others for damnation.
   B. Christ died only for the elect who were chosen for salvation.
   C. Human beings are corrupt and depraved.
   D. Human beings can do nothing on earth to earn salvation. Achieving grace and gaining salvation are entirely the work of God.
   E. The elect cannot fall away from grace. Once a soul achieves grace it has been granted salvation for eternity.

2. **How can human beings recognize those who are chosen for salvation?**
   A. Although good behavior cannot earn salvation, the ability to be good is evidence that an individual is one of the elect.
   B. The elect display virtues of hard work, thrift, moderation, and temperance.
   C. God helps those on earth who have been chosen for salvation. The elect are therefore recognized by the rewards granted by God.

3. **What is the function of the Puritan church?**
   A. God rules over human corruption and depravity. In serving God the Puritan church teaches Christian virtue and in the process provides a foundation for social order.
   B. Only the elect can be members of the church. Church leaders are chosen by members of the church.
   C. Church membership is required before an individual can participate in politics.

4. **What is the function of the state in a Puritan society?**
   A. Christ is the king of kings; an earthly kingdom in Christ's name is embodied in the state.
   B. Government stems from a voluntary agreement by church members.
   C. Although chosen by church members, government officials serve according to God's law. Government officials are accountable to Christ, not to the members of the church.
   D. The people should recognize that their chosen officials come from the people. When government officials make mistakes, the people should remember that officials are human. Only God is infallible.

5. **Should church and state be separate?**
   A. Christ's kingdom should not be divided against itself. Church and state should support each other, even if state officials are not members of the church.

    B. Church and state should remain united in function—they both serve God.

    C. Government officials gain their authority from God, not from the electorate.

6. Should church and state protect the liberty of the people?

    A. Human beings possess two types of liberty:

        1. *Natural liberty* allows human beings to act as they please whether they do evil or do good. If natural liberty continues too long, human beings are more likely to do evil.

        2. *Civil liberty* comes from the covenant between human beings and God. Civil liberty requires people to do only that which is good, just, and honest. Civil liberty demands that someone with authority control the actions of the people.

    B. Individuals who want to live in a Christian society must submit to a government that gains its authority from God.

7. What liberties should the state recognize?

    A. No person can be denied life, liberty, or property unless the denial is in accordance with the law.

    B. Although laws are made by the elect only, all people are equal under the law.

    C. The people have a right to petition the government on lawful issues.

    D. No person can be sentenced twice for the same crime.

    E. The people have the right to choose their own government.

    F. Any person who worships a false god, practices witchcraft, or attacks the government will be put to death.

8. What is the role of education in a Puritan society?

    A. An educated citizenry is necessary in order that individuals can interpret the meaning of Scripture. Education should be accompanied by an acknowledgment of the immensity of human ignorance.

    B. Children should learn obedience to both God and parents.

    C. Since God speaks primarily through the ministry, ministers should have a university education.

9. What role should American Puritans play in the world?

    A. Puritans in America can create a "city upon a hill." Puritans can create a community of saints living in the wilderness.

    B. In order that American Puritans set an example for the world, they must love one another; they must develop a strong sense of community; they must guard against moral errors.

    C. Puritans must show the world that the Puritans in America are God's chosen people.

STUDENT ACTIVITIES

Vocabulary
Define the following terms before reading the lesson on the Puritans.

1. approbation	8. dispose	15. providence
2. brethren	9. ecclesiastical	16. prudential
3. cognizance	10. eminent	17. rebuke
4. cohabitation	11. excommunicate	18. smite
5. consortship	12. fealty	19. transgress
6. *de integro*	13. judicature	20. wanton
7. dispensation	14. magistrate	21. yoke

Review
1. The Puritan philosophy was based upon the teachings of what person?
2. What was the Great Migration?
3. Who served as governor or deputy governor of Massachusetts for almost twenty years?
4. How did Puritans decide whether an individual had been chosen for salvation?
5. Why did Puritans believe that church and state should be united?
6. How did Puritans describe the difference between natural liberty and civil liberty?
7. Why did Puritans believe education was important?
8. What is the "city upon a hill"?
9. What did Puritans hope to show the world?
10. Decide whether the following statements are **True** or **False** according to New England Puritans
    A. The Puritan religion is the only true religion.
    B. Certain souls are predestined for salvation and others for damnation.
    C. Human beings are corrupt and depraved.
    D. Government officials are accountable primarily to church members.
    E. Human beings are equal under the law.
    F. No person should be denied life, liberty, or property without the due process of law.
    G. Church membership should be a requirement for participation in politics.
    H. Government officials gain their authority from the people who elect them.
    I. Ministers should have a university education.
    J. Puritans in America are God's chosen people.

What do you think?
On a scale of one through five, rate your opinion of the following quotations by New England Puritans. Write a short statement explaining your rating.

1 – You **strongly agree** with the statement *or* you feel the statement is **admirable** considering the historical circumstances surrounding it.
5 – You **strongly disagree** with the statement *or* you feel the statement is **contemptible** considering the historical circumstances surrounding it.

A. *God Almighty in his most holy and wise providence hath so disposed of the condition of mankind as in all times some must be rich, some poor, some high and eminent in power and dignity, others mean and in subjection.*
B. *We must love one another with a pure heart, fervently, we must bear one another's burdens; we must not look only on our own things, but also on the things of our brethren.*
C. *We shall be as a city upon a hill, the eyes of all people are upon us; so that if we shall deal falsely with our God in this work we have undertaken and so cause Him to withdraw His present help from us, we shall be made a story and a byword through the world.*
D. *Christ his kingdom is not of this world, therefore his officers in this kingdom cannot judicially inquire into affairs of this world.*
E. *I entreat you to consider, that when you choose magistrates, you take them from among yourselves, men subject to like passions as you are.*
F. *Every person within this jurisdiction whether inhabitant or foreigner shall enjoy the same justice and law . . . which we constitute and execute one towards another without partiality or delay.*
G. *Any . . . town shall have liberty to choose their deputies whom and where they please for the General Court.*
H. *God foreordained, for His own glory and the display of His attributes of mercy and justice, a part of the human race, without any merit of their own, to eternal salvation, and another part, in just punishment of their sin, to eternal damnation.* (John Calvin)
I. *God, who is perfect righteousness, cannot love the iniquity which He sees in all. All of us, therefore, have that within us which deserves the hatred of God.* (John Calvin)
J. *Having undertaken, for the glory of God, and advancements of the Christian faith and honor of our king and country, a voyage to plant the first colony in the northern parts of Virginia, do by these presents solemnly and mutually in the presence of God and one of another, covenant and combine ourselves together into a civil body politic, for our better ordering, and preservation and furtherance of the ends aforesaid; and by virtue hereof to enact, constitute and convenient for the general good of the colony, unto which we promise all due submission and obedience.* (William Bradford, The Mayflower Compact)

CHAPTER 6

ROGER WILLIAMS

BACKGROUND

Roger Williams (1603-83) sailed from London to New England in the Great Migration of the 1630s. After landing in Boston he served as a Puritan minister in Salem. His time in Massachusetts, however, was short. In 1635 the General Court found him guilty of heresy and banished him from Massachusetts.

Williams, a religious zealot, was banished because he attacked the idea of royal authority over the colonies. He also believed that land in America belonged to native inhabitants. This idea was in direct opposition to an English policy proclaiming that land belonged to the king. Governor John Winthrop stated that Williams was guilty of "great contempt for authority."

After leaving Massachusetts, Williams established a new colony in Providence, Rhode Island. He hoped to create a colony protecting liberty of conscience. Rhode Island therefore became the first colony in New England to grant religious freedom. Williams also established peace between English settlers and Indians. He even learned the language of the Indians and protected them from having their land taken away.

Williams believed that Rhode Island should protect an individual's religious freedom as long as civil laws were obeyed. In the 1670s, however, Williams found himself at odds with Rhode Island Quakers. He was disturbed by the Quaker assertion that they possessed the only means of salvation. By 1672 the Quakers were so numerous they gained control of the colonial government. Williams therefore felt compelled to challenge their religious doctrine. Deeply affected by the rightness of his religious beliefs, Williams was unable to admit that Quakers had a right to their convictions. Williams found himself contradicting his lifelong belief that there was no certain way of obtaining salvation.

Roger Williams is important as the founder of a colony based on religious freedom. He died impoverished and did not gain the recognition he deserved until almost one hundred years after his death. Not until the American Revolution did Americans begin to appreciate his legacy of religious freedom.

ROGER WILLIAMS – IN HIS OWN WORDS

Mr. Cotton's Letter Answered, 1644

After my public trial and answers at the General Court, one of the most eminent magistrates stood up and spake:

"Mr Williams," saith he, "holds forth these four particulars:

"First, that we have not our land by patent from the King but that the natives are the true owners of it, and that we ought to repent of such a receiving it by patent.

"Secondly, that it is not lawful to call a wicked person to swear, to pray, as being actions of God's worship.

"Thirdly, that it is not lawful to hear any of the ministers of the parish assemblies in England.

"Fourthly, that the civil magistrate's power extends only to the bodies and goods and outward state of men."

I acknowledge the particulars were rightly summed up, and I also hope that as I then maintained the rocky strength of them to my own and other consciences' satisfaction, so (through the Lord's assistance) I shall be ready for the same grounds not only to be bound and banished but to die also in New England as for most holy truths of God in Christ Jesus.

The Bloody Tenet of Persecution for the Cause of Conscience, 1644

While I plead the cause of truth and innocency against the bloody doctrine of persecution for the cause of conscience, I judge it not unfit to give alarm to myself and all men to prepare to be persecuted or hunted for cause of conscience.

Whether thou standest charged with ten or but two talents, if thou huntest any for cause of conscience, how canst thou say thou followest the Lamb of God who so abhorred that practice?

If Paul, if Jesus Christ were present here at London, and the question were proposed what religion they would approve of—the Papists', Prelatists', Presbyterians', Independents'—would each say, "Of mine, of mine"?

But put the second question: if one of the several sorts should by major vote attain the sword of steel, what weapons doth Christ Jesus authorize them to fight with in His cause? Do not all men hate the persecutor, and every conscience, true or false, complain of cruelty, tyranny? . . .

First, That the blood of so many hundred thousand souls of Protestants and Papists, spilt in the wars of present and former ages, . . . is not required nor accepted by Jesus Christ the Prince of Peace.

Secondly, pregnant scriptures and arguments are throughout the work proposed against the doctrine of persecution for cause of conscience. . . .

Fourthly, The doctrine of persecution for cause of conscience, is proved guilty of all the blood of the souls crying for vengeance under the altar.

Fifthly, All civil states with their officers of justice in their respective constitutions and administrations are proved essentially civil, and therefore not judges, governors or defenders of the spiritual or Christian state and worship.

Sixthly, It is the will and command of God, that (since the coming of his Sonne the Lord Jesus) a permission of the most Paganist, Jewish, Turkish, or antichristian consciences and worships, be granted to all men in all nations and countries: and they are onely to be fought against with that sword which is only (in soul matters) able to conquer, to wit, the sword of God's spirit, the word of God. . . .

Eighthly, God requireth not an uniformity of religion to be enacted and enforced in any civil state; which informed uniformity (sooner or later) is the greatest occasion of civil war . . . .

Ninthly, In holding an enforced uniformity of religion in a civil state, we must necessarily disclaim our desires and hopes of the Jews' conversion to Christ.

Tenthly, An enforced uniformity of religion throughout a nation or civil state, confounds the civil and religious, denies the principles of Christianity and civility, and that Jesus Christ is come in the flesh.

Eleventhly, The permission of other consciences and worships than a state professeth, only can (according to God) procure a firm and lasting peace, (good assurance being taken according to the wisdom of the civil state for uniformity of civil obedience from all sorts).

Twelfthly, lastly, true civility and Christianity may both flourish in a state or kingdom, notwithstanding the permission of diverse and contrary consciences, either of Jew or Gentile. . . .

When a kingdom or state, town or family, lies and lives in the guilt of a false God, false Christ, false worship, no wonder if sore eyes be troubled at the appearance of the light, be it never so sweet? No wonder if a body full of corrupt humors be troubled at strong (though wholesome) physic? . . . If the husbandmen were troubled when the Lord of the vineyard sent servant after servant, and at last His only son, and they beat and wounded and killed even the Son Himself, because they meant themselves to seize upon the inheritance unto which they had no right? Hence all those tumults about the Apostles in the Acts, whereas good eyes are not so troubled at light; vigilant and watchful persons, loyal and faithful, are not so troubled at the true, no, nor at a false religion of Jew or Gentile.

Breach of civil peace may arise when false and idolatrous practices are held forth, and yet no breach of civil peace from the doctrine or practice or the manner of holding forth, but from that wrong and preposterous way of suppressing, preventing, and extinguishing such doctrines or practices by weapons of wrath and blood—whips, stocks, imprisonment, banishment, death &c.—by which men commonly are persuaded to convert heretics and to cast out unclean spirits, which only the finger of God can do, that is, the mighty power of the Spirit in the Word.

Hence the town is in an uproar and the country takes the alarm to expel that fog or mist of error, heresy, blasphemy (as is supposed) with swords and guns; whereas 'tis light alone, even light from the bright shining sun of righteousness, which is able, in the souls and consciences of men, to dispel and scatter such fogs and darkness. . . .

The world lies in wickedness, is like a wilderness or a sea of wild beasts innumerable—fornicators, covetous, idolaters, &c., &c.—with whom God's people may lawfully converse and cohabit in cities, towns, &c., else must they not live in the world but go out of it. In which world—as soon as ever the Lord Jesus had sown the good seed, the children of the kingdom, true Christianity or the true church—the enemy Satan, presently in the night of security, ignorance, and error (whilst men slept), sowed also these tares, which are antichristians or false Christians. These strange professors of the name of Jesus, the ministers and prophets of God beholding, they are ready to run to heaven to fetch fiery judgments from thence to consume these strange Christians, and to pluck them by the roots out of the world. But the Son of Man, the meek lamb of God (for the elects' sake, which must be gathered out of Jew and Gentile, pagan, antichristian) commands a permission of them in the world until the time of the end of the world, when the goats and sheep, the tares and wheat, shall be eternally separated each from other.

. . . The Lord Jesus compared the kingdom of heaven to the sowing of seed. The true messengers of Christ are the sowers, who cast the seed of the Word of the kingdom upon four sorts of ground, which four sorts of ground or hearts of men cannot be supposed to be of the church; nor will it ever be proved that the church consisteth of any more sorts or natures of ground. And the proper work of the church concerns the flourishing and prosperity of this sort of ground, and the other unconverted three sorts, who it may be seldom or never come near the church unless they be forced by the civil sword (which the pattern or first sowers never used), and being forced, they are put into a way of religion by such a course. If not so, they are forced to live without a religion, for one of the two must necessarily follow. . . .

Now, after the Lord Jesus had propounded that great leading parable of the sower and the seed, He is pleased to propound this parable of the tares, with admirable coherence and sweet consolation to the honest and good ground, who with glad and honest hearts, having received the Word of the kingdom, may yet seem to be discouraged and troubled with so many antichristians and false professors of the name of Christ. The Lord Jesus therefore gives direction concerning these tares, that unto the end of the world, successively in all the sorts and generations of them, they must be (not approved or countenanced, but) let alone or permitted in the world.

The Bloody Tenet Yet More Bloody, 1652

Among the crying sins of our own or other sinful nations, those two are ever among the loudest—to wit, invented devotions to the God of heaven; secondly, violence and oppression on the sons of men (especially if His sons) for dissenting. And against both these, and that the impartial and dreadful hand of the most holy and jealous God (a consuming fire) tear and burn not up the roots of these plantations, but graciously discovering the plants which are not His, he may graciously fructify and cause to flourish what His right hand will own: I say this is the humble and unfeigned desire and cry (at the throne of grace) of your so long despised outcast. . . .

I confess in this plea for freedom to all consciences in matters (merely of worship), I have impartially pleaded for the freedom of the consciences of the Papists themselves, the greatest enemies and persecutors (in Europe) of the saints and truths of Jesus: yet I have pleaded for no more than is their due and right, and (whatever else shall be the consequent) it shall stand for a monument and testimony against them, and be an aggravation of their former, present, or future cruelties against Christ Jesus the head, and all that uprightly love Him, His true disciples and followers.

The Hireling Ministry, 1652

The civil sword cannot rightfully act either in restraining the souls of the people from worship, etc., or in constraining them to worship . . . .

If they please to take off the yokes, the soul yokes of binding all persons to such parochial or parish forms, permitting them to enjoy their own belief, whether within or without such parish worships, parish maintenance, parish marryings, parish buryings, by which the souls and consciences of so many have been inbondaged in life and death, and after death.

If they please so far to permit impartially all consciences, and especially the consciences, the meetings and assemblings of faithful and conscionable people (the volunteers in preaching Christ Jesus), so as that what tithes or otherwise, by the sword, or else cease preaching for want of such or such a maintenance, or can remove from bishoprics or benefices . . . for fatter and ranker pastures, or, wanting spiritual work and maintenance, are too fine to work with their hands as the first patterns, Christ's first ministers, did— how can they say, as Peter to Christ Jesus, "Lord, Thou knowest all things, Thou knowest I love Thee," etc.? . . .

The first grand design of Christ Jesus is to destroy and consume His mortal enemy, Antichrist. This must be done by the breath of His mouth in His prophets and witnesses. Now the nations of the world have impiously stopped this heavenly breath and stifled the Lord Jesus in His servants. Now if it shall please the civil state to remove the state bars set up to resist the holy Spirit of god in His servants (whom yet finally to resist is not in all the powers of the world), I humbly conceive that the civil state hath made a fair progress in promoting the Gospel of Jesus Christ.

The *summa totalis* of all the former particulars is this:

First, since the people of this nation have been forced into a national way of worship, both popish and Protestant (as the wheels of time's revolutions, by God's mighty Providence and permission, have turned about), the civil state is bound before God to take off that bond and yoke of soul oppression, and to proclaim free and impartial liberty to all the people . . . to choose and maintain what worship and ministry their souls and consciences are persuaded of; which act, as it will prove an act of mercy and righteousness to the enslaved nations, so is it of a binding force to engage the whole and every interest and conscience to preserve the common freedom and peace; however, an act most suiting with the piety and Christianity of the Holey Testament of Christ Jesus.

Second, the civil state is humbly to be implored to provide in their high wisdom for the security of all the respective consciences, in their respective meetings, assemblings, worshipings, preachings, disputings, etc., and that civil peace and the beauty of civility and humanity be maintained among the chief opposers and dissenters.

Third, it is the duty of all that are in authority, and of all that are able, to countenance, encourage, and supply such true volunteers as give and devote themselves to the service and ministry of Christ Jesus in any kind, although it be also the duty, and will be the practice, of all such whom the spirit of God sends upon any work of Christ's . . . than the work and service of their Lord and Master should be neglected.

Letter to the Town of Providence, 1655

That ever I should speak or write a tittle that tends to such an infinite liberty of conscience is a mistake, and which I have ever disclaimed and abhorred. To prevent such mistakes, I shall at present only propose this case: There goes many a ship to sea, with many hundred souls in one ship, whose weal and woe is common, and is a true picture of a commonwealth or a human combination or society. It hath fallen out sometimes that both Papists and Protestants, Jews and Turks, may be embarked in one ship; upon which supposal I affirm that all the liberty of conscience that ever I pleaded for turns upon these two hinges: that none of the Papists, Protestants, Jews, or Turks be forced to come to the ship's prayers or worship, if they practice any. I further add that I never denied that, notwithstanding this liberty, the commander of this ship ought to command the ship's course, yea, and also command that justice, peace, and sobriety be kept and practiced, both among the seamen and all the passengers. If any of the seamen refuse to perform their services, or passengers to pay their freight; if any refuse to help, in person or purse, towards the common charges or defense; if any refuse to obey the common laws and orders of the ship concerning their common peace or preservation; if any shall mutiny and rise up against their commanders and officers; if any should preach or write that there ought to be no commanders or officers because all are equal in Christ, therefore no masters nor officers, no laws nor order, nor corrections nor punishments—I say, I never denied but in such cases, whatever is pretended, the commander or commanders may judge, resist, compel, and punish such transgressors according to their deserts and merits. This, if seriously and honestly minded, may, if it so please the Father of lights, let in some light to such as willingly shut not their eyes.

ROGER WILLIAMS – A SIMULATED INTERVIEW

1. **What is the function of the church?**
   A. The church is a place where God's true religion can find pure and proper practice on earth.
   B. The church is a garden in which Christ separates His saints from the world. The garden is holy, and the church is not responsible for the sinners of the world. All worldly weeds must be excluded from Christ's garden. Christians should separate from the Church of England which is a false church.
   C. The church is holy and must not be shared with non-Christians. God withholds his presence from any group that includes non-Christians. Acts of worship must be performed only by true Christians when they are separated from the world. Ministers should not preach to non-Christians. Christians should not pray with non-Christians.

2. **How should Christians treat non-Christians?**
   A. The scriptures do not allow persecution; no one should be persecuted for remaining true to religious conscience. Christ used no weapons to fight for His cause.
   B. Christians should not use force to prohibit people from worshiping as they please. Persecution in the name of religion has caused too much bloodshed in history.
   C. Christians should not attempt to punish non-Christians. People who are not Christian should be punished by God, not by human beings.
   D. Christians must learn to live in the same world as those who are not Christians. Jesus gave instructions on how to survive in a world of wicked people.
   E. No person can be so sure of religious truth that he can impose his beliefs on others.

3. **Should people be granted religious freedom?**
   A. Liberty of conscience should be granted to everyone. Even pagan and anti-Christian groups should be allowed to worship as they please.
   B. Individual conscience must be respected even if it is wrong. When conscience is wrong it can be corrected by Scripture.
   C. God does not require uniformity of religion. Any attempt to force uniformity of religion leads to civil war. Peace can only be maintained by allowing freedom of religion.
   D. Christianity will flourish in a society of diverse religions. Freedom of thought is the only way to achieve true Christianity. Freedom of thought requires toleration of all groups.
   E. Liberty of conscience is necessary because no individual can know what God intends. No one group can determine religious truth with absolute certainty.

4. What is the function of government?
   A. Government is necessary to regulate the actions of people. Christians must join others in establishing a government and submitting to its authority.
   B. Government derives its power from the people. Government cannot exercise religious power because the people do not have religious power. Only God has religious power.

5. Should church and state be separate?
   A. Church and state should be separate. Government has no authority over the church or religion. The government should not involve itself in spiritual matters. Government has no business with the church.
   B. Government can only regulate the actions of people. Government cannot regulate thought or conscience. Just as government should not require an oath of loyalty, it should not support one religion over another.
   C. The true religion, which is known only to God, will flourish if the government does not force uniformity in religious practices. A government that believes it is on a special mission for God will drench the world in blood. People who use force in defense of religion are not true Christians. Force is used only to support a false, unchristian religion. Christ did not rule by the sword.
   D. Christians in this world must do business with people who are not true Christians. Christians must be completely separate from the world only when they are in the church.
   E. A true Christian would seldom become a government official. Christ advised Christians on how to conduct themselves as subjects of a government, not as leaders in the government. Government requires skills that have nothing to do with religion.
   F. The elimination of religion from government offers the world a prospect of peace.

6. What rights do Indians possess?
   A. Indians are true owners of American land. The King does not legitimately own the land.
   B. Contrary to the beliefs of some religious groups, Indians are not the agents of the devil. Indians are human beings who should be loved and respected.

STUDENT ACTIVITIES

Vocabulary
Define the following terms before reading the lesson on Williams.

1. benefice	10. fornicator	19. piety
2. bishopric	11. heretic	20. tare
3. blasphemy	12. idolater	21. tithe
4. breach	13. impious	22. transgress
5. civility	14. magistrate	23. unfeigned
6. cohabit	15. parable	24. tumult
7. conscience	16. parish	25. uniformity
8. covetous	17. parochial	26. vengeance
9. eminent	18. persecute	27. weal

Review
1. Why was Williams, a Puritan minister, banished from Massachusetts?
2. What new colony was founded by Williams?
3. What was the first colony in New England to grant religious freedom?
4. What religious group in Rhode Island did Williams fight against?
5. Why did Williams believe that non-Christians should not be allowed into the church?
6. Why did Williams believe that Christians should avoid persecuting non-Christians?
7. Why did Williams believe that Christians should learn to live in the same world with non-Christians?
8. What did Williams believe was the only way to maintain peace in society?
9. What did Williams think would happen to Christianity in a society of diverse religions?
10. Why did Williams believe in a separation of church and state?
11. Why did Williams believe that most Christians should avoid government service?
12. Decide whether the following statements are **True** or **False** according to Roger Williams.
    A. Ministers should reach out and preach to non-Christians.
    B. Non-Christians should be punished by God, not by human beings.
    C. Liberty of conscience should be granted to all persons except pagan and anti-Christian groups.
    D. God requires uniformity of religion.
    E. No individual can know what God intends.
    F. No human being can determine religious truth with absolute certainty.
    G. The elimination of religion from government threatens the morality of society.
    H. Indians are agents of the devil.

What do you think?

On a scale of one through five, rate your opinion of the following quotations by Williams. Write a short statement explaining your rating.

1 – You **strongly agree** with the statement *or* you feel the statement is **admirable** considering the historical circumstances surrounding it.

5 – You **strongly disagree** with the statement *or* you feel the statement is **contemptible** considering the historical circumstances surrounding it.

A. *The blood of so many hundred thousand souls of Protestants and Papists, spilt in the wars of present and former ages, . . . is not required nor accepted by Jesus Christ the Prince of Peace.*

B. *An enforced uniformity of religion throughout a nation or civil state, confounds the civil and religious, denies the principles of Christianity and civility, and that Jesus Christ is come in the flesh.*

C. *We have not our land by patent from the King, but that the natives are the true owners of it, and that we ought to repent of such a receiving it by patent.*

D. *The world lies in wickedness, is like a wilderness or a sea of wild beasts innumerable . . . with whom God's people may lawfully converse and cohabit in cities, towns, &c.*

E. *The civil sword cannot rightfully act either in restraining the souls of the people from worship, etc., or in constraining them to worship.*

F. *The civil state is bound before God to take off that bond and yoke of soul oppression, and to proclaim free and impartial liberty to all the people.*

G. *The civil state is humbly to be implored to provide in their high wisdom for the security of all the respective consciences, in their respective meetings, asssemblings, worshippings, preachings, disputings, etc.*

H. *Nature knows no difference between European and American in blood, birth, bodies, etc., God having of one blood made all mankind.*

I. *Boast not proud English of thy birth and blood. Thy brother Indian is by birth as good. Of one blood God made him, and thee and all, as wise, as fair, as strong, as personal.*

J. *All lawful magistrates in the world . . . have, and can have no more power, than fundamentally lies in the bodies of fountains themselves, which power, might, or authority, is not religious, Christian, etc., but natural, human, and civil.*

K. *It is unnecessary, unlawful, dishonorable, ungodly, unchristian in most cases in the world [to persecute people for their faith], for there is a possibility of keeping sweet peace in most cases, and if it be possible, it is the express command of God that peace be kept.*

PART 2

BUILDING A NATION

CHAPTER 7

THOMAS PAINE

BACKGROUND

Born into a poor Quaker family in England, Thomas Paine (1737-1809) became one of the most idealistic thinkers of the American Revolution. His influence on both European and American radical movements was immense. Paine, a genuine humanitarian, achieved fame for his hatred of any government based on hereditary privilege.

As a man of little formal education he worked at a variety of trades. After his radical ideas got him into trouble he decided to leave England. With the aid of Ben Franklin, Paine moved to Philadelphia in 1774 where he secured employment writing for newspapers.

In January 1776 Paine published *Common Sense*, a pamphlet that sold over 150,000 copies at a time when the non-slave colonial population was only 2.5 million. Advocating ideas similar to those expressed by John Locke, Paine used *Common Sense* to argue for American independence from England. He stressed that Americans were on a mission of greatness when he wrote, "We have it in our power to begin the world over again."

While serving as a soldier in the revolutionary army he wrote *The American Crisis*, a series of papers designed to rally support for the cause of independence. He also took part in writing a new constitution for Pennsylvania, a constitution that became the era's most democratic state constitution.

In 1787 Paine returned to Europe where he became actively involved in the debates surrounding the French Revolution. In France he wrote *The Rights of Man* to defend the ideals of the French Revolution. In *The Rights of Man* he presented a vision of a republican system that promoted social welfare through a redistribution of wealth.

As a result of his activities during the French Revolution, Paine was arrested in 1793 and confined in the Bastille. While awaiting execution he wrote *The Age of Reason* to defend deism and to attack many fundamental principles of Christianity. Although he was eventually released from prison, he left with a reputation as an atheist.

In 1807 he returned to America where he was vilified by orthodox Christians. He spent the last years of his life in poverty. Only six people attended his funeral.

THOMAS PAINE – IN HIS OWN WORDS

Common Sense, 1776

Some writers have so confounded society with government as to leave little or no distinction between them, whereas they are not only different but have different origins. Society is produced by our wants, and government by our wickedness; the former promotes our happiness *positively* by uniting our affections, the latter *negatively* by restraining our vices. The one encourages intercourse, the other creates distinctions. The first is a patron, the last a punisher.

Society in every state is a blessing, but government even in its best state is but a necessary evil, in its worst state an intolerable one; for when we suffer or are exposed to the same miseries *by a government* which we might expect in a country *without government*, our calamity is heightened by reflecting that we furnish the means by which we suffer. Government, like dress, is the badge of lost innocence; the palaces of kings are built on the ruins of the bowers of paradise. For were the impulses of conscience clear, uniform, and irresistibly obeyed, man would need no other lawgiver; but that not being the case, he finds it necessary to surrender up a part of his property to furnish means for the protection of the rest, and this he is induced to do by the same prudence which in every other case advises him out of two evils to choose the least. . . .

Here then is the origin and rise of government, namely, a mode rendered necessary by the inability of moral virtue to govern the world; here too is the design and end of government, viz., freedom and security. And however our eyes may be dazzled with show or our ears deceived by sound, however prejudice may warp our wills or interest darken our understanding, the simple voice of nature and reason will say it is right.

I draw my idea of the form of government from a principle in nature which no art can overturn, viz., that the more simple anything is, the less liable it is to be disordered and the easier repaired when disordered; and with this maxim in view I offer a few remarks on the so much boasted constitution of England. That it was noble for the dark and slavish times in which it was erected is granted. When the world was overrun with tyranny, the least remove therefrom was a glorious rescue. But that it is imperfect, subject to convulsions, and incapable of producing what it seems to promise is easily demonstrated.

Absolute governments (though the disgrace of human nature) have this advantage with them: that they are simple; if the people suffer, they know the head from which their suffering springs, know likewise the remedy, and are not bewildered by a variety of causes and cures. But the constitution of England is so exceedingly complex that the nation may suffer for years together without being able to discover in which part the fault lies; some will say in one and some in another, and every political physician will advise a different medicine. . . .

The same constitution which gives the Commons a power to check the king by withholding the supplies gives afterward the king a power to check the Commons by empowering him to reject their other bills, it again supposes that the king is wiser than those whom it has already supposed to be wiser than him. A mere absurdity!

There is something exceedingly ridiculous in the composition of monarchy; it first excludes a man from the means of information, yet empowers him to act in cases where the highest judgment is required. The state of a king shuts him from the world, yet the business of a king requires him to know it thoroughly; wherefore the different parts, by unnaturally opposing and destroying each other, prove the whole character to be absurd and useless. . . .

But it is not so much the absurdity as the evil of hereditary succession which concerns mankind. Did it insure a race of good and wise men, it would have the seal of divine authority, but as it opens a door to the *foolish* and *wicked*, and the *improper*, it has in it the nature of oppression. Men who look upon themselves born to reign and others to obey soon grow insolent. Selected from the rest of mankind, their minds are early poisoned by importance; and the world they act in differs so materially from the world at large that they have but little opportunity of knowing its true interests and, when they succeed to the government, are frequently the most ignorant and unfit of any throughout the dominions. . . .

. . . I offer nothing more than simple facts, plain arguments, and common sense; and have no other preliminaries to settle with the reader than that he will divest himself of prejudice and prepossession, and suffer his reason and his feelings to determine for themselves; that he will put on, or rather that he will not put off, the true character of a man, and generously enlarge his views beyond the present day.

Volumes have been written on the subject of the struggle between England and America. Men of all ranks have embarked in the controversy, from different motives and with various designs; but all have been ineffectual, and the period of debate is closed. Arms as the last resource decide the contest; the appeal was the choice of the king, and the continent has accepted the challenge. . . .

The sun never shined on a cause of greater worth. 'Tis not the affair of a city, a county, a province, or a kingdom, but of a continent—of at least one-eighth part of the habitable globe. 'Tis not the concern of a day, a year, or an age; posterity are virtually involved in the contest, and will be more or less affected even to the end time by the proceedings now. Now is the seedtime of continental union, faith, and honor. The least fracture now will be like a name engraved with the point of a pin on the tender rind of a young oak; the wound would enlarge with the tree, and posterity read it in fullgrown characters. . . .

I challenge the warmest advocate for reconciliation to show a single advantage that this continent can reap by being connected with Great Britain. I repeat the challenge; not a single advantage is derived. Our corn will fetch its price in any market in Europe, and our imported goods must be paid for, buy them where we will.

But the injuries and disadvantages we sustain by that connection are without number, and our duty to mankind at large, as well as to ourselves, instruct us to renounce the alliance; because any submission to or dependence on Great Britain tends directly to involve this continent in European wars and quarrels and sets us at variance with nations who would otherwise seek our friendship and against who we have neither anger nor complaint. As Europe is our market for trade, we ought to form no partial connection with any part of it. It is the true interest of America to steer clear of European connections, which she never can do while by her dependence on Britain, she is made the makeweight in the scale of British politics. . . .

A government of our own is our natural right; and when a man seriously reflects on the precariousness of human affairs, he will become convinced that it is infinitely wiser and safer to form a Constitution of our own in a cool, deliberate manner while we have it in our power than to trust such an interesting event to time and chance. If we omit it now, some[one] may hereafter arise, who laying hold of popular disquietudes, may collect together the desperate and the discontented, and by assuming to themselves the power of government may sweep away the liberties of the continent like a deluge. Should the government of America return again into the hands of Britain, the tottering situation of things will be a temptation for some desperate adventurer to try his fortune, and in such a case what relief can Britain give? Ere she could hear the news, the fatal business might be done, and ourselves suffering like the wretched Britons under the oppression of the conqueror. Ye that oppose independence now, ye know not what ye do; ye are opening a door to eternal tyranny by keeping vacant the seat of government. . . .

Ye that tell us of harmony and reconciliation, can ye restore to us the time that is past? Can ye give to prostitution its former innocence? Neither can ye reconcile Britain and America. The last cord now is broken, the people of England are presenting addresses against us. There are injuries which nature cannot forgive; she would cease to be nature if she did. As well can the lover forgive the ravisher of his mistress as the continent forgive the murderers of Britain. The Almighty has implanted in us these unextinguishable feelings for good and wise purposes. They are the guardians of his image in our hearts. They distinguish us from the herd of common animals. The social compact would dissolve and justice be extirpated [from] the earth, or have only a casual existence, were we callous to the touches of affection. The robber and the murderer would often escape unpunished did not the injuries which our tempers sustain provoke us into justice.

O ye that love mankind! Ye that dare oppose not only the tyranny but the tyrant, stand forth! Every spot of the Old World is overrun with oppression. Freedom has been hunted round the globe. Asia and Africa have long expelled her. Europe regards her like a stranger, and England has given her warning to depart. O! receive the fugitive, and prepare in time an asylum for mankind.

The American Crisis I, 1777

These are the times that try men's souls. The summer soldier and the sunshine patriot will, in this crisis, shrink from the service of their country, but he that stands it *now* deserves the love and thanks of man and woman. Tyranny, like hell, is not easily conquered; yet we have this consolation with us that, the harder the conflict, the more glorious the triumph. What we obtain too cheap, we esteem too lightly; it is dearness only that gives everything its value. Heaven knows how to put a proper price upon its goods, and it would be strange indeed if so celestial an article as freedom should not be highly rated. Britain, with an army to enforce her tyranny, has declared that she has a right (*not only to tax*) but *to bind us in all cases whatsoever*; and if being *bound in that manner* is not slavery, then is there not such a thing as slavery upon earth. Even the expression is impious, for so unlimited a power can belong only to God.

The American Crisis XIII, 1777

It was the cause of America that made me an author. The force with which it struck my mind and the dangerous condition the country appeared to be in, by courting an impossible and an unnatural reconciliation with those who were determined to reduce her, instead of striking out into the only line that could cement and save her—*a declaration of independence*—made it impossible for me, feeling as I did, to be silent; and if, in the course of more than seven years, I have rendered her any service, I have likewise added something to the reputation of literature by freely and disinterestedly employing it in the great cause of mankind and showing that there may be genius without prostitution.

Rights of Man, Part One, 1791

There never did, there never will, and there never can exist a Parliament, or any description of men, or any generation of men, in any country, possessed of the right or the power of binding and controlling posterity to the "end of time," or of commanding forever how the world shall be governed or who shall govern it; and therefore all such clauses, acts, or declarations by which the makers of them attempt to do what they have neither the right nor the power to do, nor the power to execute, are in themselves null and void.

Every age and generation must be as free to act for itself, *in all cases*, as the ages and generation which preceded it. The vanity and presumption of governing beyond the grave is the most ridiculous and insolent of all tyrannies.

Man has no property in man; neither has any generation a property in the generations which are to follow. The Parliament or the people of 1688, or of any other period, had no more right to dispose of the people of the present day, or to bind or to control them *in any shape whatever*, than the Parliament or the people of the present day have to dispose of, bind, or control those who are to live a hundred or a thousand years hence.

Every generation is and must be competent to all the purposes which its occasions require. It is the living, and not the dead, that are to be accommodated. When man ceases to be, his power and his wants cease with him; and having no longer any participation in the concerns of this world, he has no longer any authority in directing who shall be its governors, or how its government shall be organized or how administered. . . .

The illuminating and divine principle of the equal rights of man (for it has its origin from the Maker of man) relates not only to the living individuals, but to generations of men succeeding each other. Every generation is equal in rights to the generations which preceded it, by the same rule that every individual is born equal in rights with his contemporary. . . .

Hitherto we have spoken only (and that but in part) of the natural rights of man. We have now to consider the civil rights of man and to show how the one originates from the other. Man did not enter into society to become *worse* than he was before, nor to have fewer rights than he had before, but to have those rights better secured. His natural rights are the foundations of all his civil rights. But in order to pursue this distinction with more precision, it is necessary to make the different qualities of natural and civil rights.

A few words will explain this. Natural rights are those which appertain to man in right of his existence. Of this kind are all the intellectual rights, or rights of the mind, and also all those rights of acting as an individual for his own comfort and happiness which are not injurious to the natural rights of others. Civil rights are those which appertain to man in right of his being a member of society. . . .

A constitution is not a thing in name only, but in fact. It has not an ideal, but a real existence; and wherever it cannot be produced in a visible form, there is none. A constitution is a thing *antecedent* to a government, and a government is only the creature of a constitution. The constitution of a country is not the act of its government, but of the people constituting a government.

It is the body of elements to which you can refer and quote article by article, and which contains the principles on which the government shall be established, the manner in which it shall be organized, the powers it shall have, the mode of elections, the duration of parliaments or by what other name such bodies may be called, the powers which the executive part of the government shall have, and, in fine, everything that relates to the complete organization of a civil government and the principles on which it shall act and by which it shall be bound.

A constitution, therefore, is to a government what the laws made afterward by that government are to a court of judicature. The court of judicature does not make the laws, neither can it alter them; it only acts in conformity to the laws made, and the government is in like manner governed by the constitution.

THOMAS PAINE – A SIMULATED INTERVIEW

1. **What is the function of government?**
   A. Government is a necessary evil. Government is a result of the failure of depending on moral virtue to control human behavior.
   B. Government should protect freedom and security.
   C. Government should not adopt an official state religion. An official state religion is unnatural, unnecessary, inefficient, and corrupt.
   D. Government should use its tax money for helping the poor, educating children, and providing pensions for the elderly.

2. **What is wrong with monarchy?**
   A. Monarchy is a ridiculous system of government. A king needs to understand the world thoroughly, but the life of a monarch separates him from the world. Kings shut themselves out of the lives of common people.
   B. Monarchy is based on hereditary succession to power. This does not insure good and wise rulers. In fact, foolish and wicked rulers may easily take power.

3. **What is the best type of government?**
   A. A republican form of government is superior to monarchy. No government is legitimate that does not rest on the consent of the people. Unlike monarchy, a republican form of government rests on the consent of the people.
   B. In a republican form of government the people must express their consent directly and as often as possible.
   C. Government should be simple. A simple government does not easily become confused and disorderly. In addition, a simple government is easier to repair.

4. **What rights do the people possess?**
   A. All citizens are equal in their natural rights and civil rights:
      1. *Natural rights* include freedom of thought as well as the right to pursue comfort and happiness. Natural rights, however, do not allow people to injure each other.
      2. *Civil rights* are determined by society.
   B. Natural rights must be the basis of civil rights. Civil rights are defined by society and protected by the government.

5. **Do the people have a right to change their government?**
   A. The people have a natural right to live under a government of their own choosing.
   B. People who are living under the wrong kind of government have the right to change their government.

6. **What principles must guide the writing of a constitution?**
   A. The writing of a constitution comes before the creation of a government. Constitutions create governments; governments do not create constitutions.
   B. A constitution is to a government what the law is to a court. Just as a court's decisions are restricted by the law, a government's actions are restricted by a constitution.
   C. No people have the right to bind future generations to past decisions. Every generation must be free to act for itself in all cases. No generation has the right to govern future generations.
   D. A constitution should be short and simple.
   E. A constitution should apply universally to all people.

7. **What role should America play in the world?**
   A. The world has never seen a greater and more noble cause than the American Revolution. Americans must never reconcile with the British; Americans must persevere and win a victory for humanity.
   B. In a world "overrun with oppression," America is an "asylum for mankind."

STUDENT ACTIVITIES

Vocabulary
Define the following terms before reading the lesson on Paine.

1. absurd	10. extirpate	19. prepossession
2. advocate	11. hereditary	20. presumption
3. antecedent	12. induce	21. prostitution
4. asylum	13. insolent	22. prudence
5. calamity	14. intercourse	23. reconciliation
6. confound	15. judicature	24. republican
7. contemporary	16. null and void	25. succession
8. deluge	17. posterity	26. vanity
9. disquietude	18. precariousness	27. wretched

Review
1. Where was Thomas Paine born?
2. Who helped Paine move to Philadelphia and secure employment writing for newspapers?
3. What pamphlet written by Paine argued for American independence from England?
4. What title was given to the papers Paine wrote to rally support for the American Revolution?
5. What book did Paine write to defend the ideals of the French Revolution?

6. What religion was attacked by Paine in *The Age of Reason*?
7. Why did Paine feel monarchy was a ridiculous form of government?
8. Why did Paine feel that a republican form of government was superior to monarchy?
9. How did Paine describe the difference between natural rights and civil rights?
10. What role did Paine feel America should play in the world?
11. Why did Paine think government should remain simple?
12. Decide whether the following statements are **True** or **False** according to Thomas Paine.
    A. Government is a necessary evil.
    B. Government should adopt an official state religion.
    C. Government should use its tax money to support the poor and the elderly.
    D. The people have a right to alter or abolish their government.
    E. Every government should establish a constitution.
    F. Each generation has the right to create its own constitution.
    G. No government is legitimate that does not rest on the consent of the people.
    H. A constitution should apply universally to all people.

What do you think?
On a scale of one through five, rate your opinion of the following quotations by Paine. Write a short statement explaining your rating.

1 – You **strongly agree** with the statement *or* you feel the statement is **admirable** considering the historical circumstances surrounding it.
5 – You **strongly disagree** with the statement *or* you feel the statement is **contemptible** considering the historical circumstances surrounding it.

A. *Society is produced by our wants, and government by our wickedness; the former promotes our happiness positively by uniting our affections, the latter negatively by restraining our vice.*
B. *Society in every state is a blessing, but government, even in its best state is but a necessary evil; in its worst state, an intolerable one.*
C. *Here then is the origin and rise of government, namely, a mode rendered necessary by the inability of moral virtue to govern the world; here too is the design and end of government, viz., freedom and security.*
D. *I draw my ideas of the form of government from a principle in nature which no art can overturn, viz., that the more simple anything is, the less liable it is to be disordered and the easier repaired when disordered.*
E. *Every generation is equal in rights to the generations which preceded it, by the same rule that every individual is born equal in rights with his contemporary.*

F. *Every age and generation must be as free to act for itself, in all cases, as the ages and generation which preceded it. The vanity and presumption of governing beyond the grave is the most ridiculous and insolent of all tyrannies.*

G. *A constitution of a country is not the act of its government, but of the people constituting a government.*

H. *The right of voting for representatives is the primary right by which other rights are protected. To take away this right is to reduce a man to slavery.*

I. *Those who expect to reap the blessing of freedom must, like men, undergo the fatigue of supporting it.*

J. *It is the object only of war that makes it honorable. And if there was ever a just war since the world began, it is this [Revolution] in which America is now engaged.*

K. *The cause of America is the cause of all mankind.*

L. *Moderation in temper is always a virtue, but moderation in principle is always a vice.*

M. *The more perfect civilization is, the less occasion it has for government, because the more does it regulate its own affairs, and govern itself. . . . All the great laws of society are laws of nature.*

N. *No extraordinary power should be lodged in any one individual.*

CHAPTER 8

THE FEDERALIST

BACKGROUND

The convention which brought about the U.S. Constitution met in 1787 from May through September. Fifty-five delegates from twelve states—Rhode Island boycotted the convention—gathered to revise the Articles of Confederation. However, once the delegates were in Philadelphia they decided to establish an entirely new national government. After the convention a new Constitution was submitted to specially-elected state conventions for debate and possible ratification.

Ratification of the Constitution was not guaranteed. Supporters of the Constitution, known as Federalists, hoped the weak national government created by the Articles of Confederation would be replaced by a strong and energetic government. Opponents of the Constitution, known as Anti-Federalists, felt that a stronger national government would destroy state authority and threaten liberty.

The debate was intense. Even though nine of thirteen states were needed for ratification, a vote against the Constitution in any one of four key states—Pennsylvania, Massachusetts, Virginia, or New York—would raise serious doubts about whether the Constitution was workable. Alexander Hamilton, a New York politician who supported the Constitution, persuaded James Madison of Virginia and John Jay of New York to write essays urging ratification.

Hamilton wrote fifty-one essays; Madison wrote twenty-nine; and Jay, who became ill, wrote five. First published in New York newspapers under the pen name "Publius," the eighty-five essays eventually formed a book known as *The Federalist Papers.* Although originally written to convince New York politicians to vote for ratification, the essays are today highly respected for their superb analysis and interpretation of the Constitution. *The Federalist Papers* give modern readers an excellent description of the fundamental principles upon which the United States established a "new order of the ages" (*novus ordo seclorum*).

THE FEDERALIST – IN THE WORDS OF "PUBLIUS"

Number 2 (Jay)

Nothing is more certain than the indispensable necessity of government; and it is equally undeniable that whenever and however it is instituted, the people must cede to it some of their natural rights, in order to vest it with requisite powers. It is well worthy of consideration, therefore, whether it would conduce more to the interest of the people of America that they should, to all general purposes, be one nation, under one federal government, than that they should divide themselves into separate confederacies and give to the head of each the same kind of powers which they are advised to place in one national government.

Number 10 (Madison)

Among the numerous advantages promised by a well-constructed Union, none deserves to be more accurately developed than its tendency to break and control the violence of faction. . . . The instability, injustice, and confusion introduced into the public councils have, in truth, been the mortal diseases under which popular governments have everywhere perished, as they continue to be the favorite and fruitful topics from which the adversaries to liberty derive their most specious declamations. . . . Complaints are everywhere heard from our most considerate and virtuous citizens, equally the friends of public and private faith and of public and personal liberty, that our governments are too unstable, that the public good is disregarded in the conflicts of rival parties, and that measures are too often decided, not according to the rules of justice and the rights of the minor party, but by the superior force of an interested and overbearing majority. . . .

By a faction I understand a number of citizens, whether amounting to a majority or minority of the whole, who are united and actuated by some common impulse of passion, or of interest, adverse to the rights of other citizens, or to the permanent and aggregate interests of the community.

There are two methods of curing the mischiefs of faction: the one, by removing its causes; the other, by controlling its effects.

There are again two methods of removing the causes of faction: the one, by destroying the liberty which is essential to its existence; the other by giving to every citizen the same opinions, the same passions, and the same interests.

It could never be more truly said than of the first remedy that it was worse than the disease. Liberty is to faction what air is to fire, an aliment without which it instantly expires. But it could not be a less folly to abolish liberty, which is essential to political life, because it nourishes faction than it would be to wish the annihilation of air, which is essential to animal life, because it imparts to fire its destructive agency.

The second expedient is as impracticable as the first would be unwise. As long as the reason of man continues fallible, and he is at liberty to exercise it, different opinions will be formed. As long as the connection subsists between his reason and his self-love, his opinions and his passions will have a reciprocal influence on each other; and the former will be objects to which the latter will attach themselves. . . .

The latent causes of faction are thus sown in the nature of man; and we see them everywhere brought into different degrees of activity, according to the different circumstances of civil society. A zeal for different opinions concerning religion, concerning government, and many other points, as well of speculation as of practice; an attachment to different leaders ambitiously contending for pre-eminence and power; or to persons of other descriptions whose fortunes have been interesting to the human passions, have, in turn, divided mankind into parties, inflamed them with mutual animosity, and rendered them much more disposed to vex and oppress each other than to co-operate for their common good. . . . But the most common and durable source of factions has been the various and unequal distribution of property. Those who hold and those who are without property have ever formed distinct interests in society. Those who are creditors, and those who are debtors, fall under a like discrimination. . . .

No man is allowed to be a judge in his own cause, because his interest would certainly bias his judgment, and, not improbably, corrupt his integrity. . . .

It is vain to say that enlightened statesmen will be able to adjust these clashing interests and render them all subservient to the public good. . . .

The inference to which we are brought is that the causes of faction cannot be removed and that relief is only to be sought in the means of controlling its *effects*.

If a faction consists of less than a majority, relief is supplied by the republican principle, which enables the majority to defeat its sinister views by regular vote. It may clog the administration, it may convulse the society; but it will be unable to execute and mask its violence under the forms of the Constitution. When a majority is included in a faction, the form of popular government, on the other hand, enables it to sacrifice to its ruling passion or interest both the public good and the rights of other citizens. To secure the public good and private rights against the danger of such a faction, and at the same time to preserve the spirit and the form of popular government, is then the great object to which our inquiries are directed. . . .

By what means is the object attainable? Evidently by one of two only. Either the existence of the same passion or interest in a majority at the same time must be prevented, or the majority, having such coexistent passion or interest, must be rendered, by their number and local situation, unable to concert and carry into effect schemes of oppression. . . .

From this view of the subject it may be concluded that a pure democracy, by which I mean a society consisting of a small number of citizens, who assemble and administer the government in person, can admit of no cure for the mischiefs of faction. A common passion or interest will, in almost every case, be felt by a majority of the whole; a communication and concert results from the form of government itself; and there is nothing to check the inducements to sacrifice the weaker party or an obnoxious individual. Hence it is that such democracies have ever been spectacles of turbulence and contention; have ever been found incompatible with personal security or the rights of property; and have in general been as short in their lives as they have been violent in their deaths. . . .

A republic, by which I mean a government in which the scheme of representation takes place, opens a different prospect, and promises the cure for which we are seeking. Let us examine the points in which it varies from pure democracy, and we shall comprehend both the nature of the cure and the efficacy which it must derive from the Union.

The two great points of difference between a democracy and a republic are: first, the delegation of the government, in the latter, to a small number of citizens elected by the rest; secondly, the greater number of citizens, and greater sphere of country, over which the latter may be extended.

The effect of the first difference is, on the one hand, to refine and enlarge the public views, by passing them through the medium of a chosen body of citizens, whose wisdom may best discern the true interest of their country, and whose patriotism and love of justice will be least likely to sacrifice it to temporary or partial considerations. Under such a regulation it may well happen that the public voice, pronounced by the representatives of the people, will be more consonant to the public good than if pronounced by the people themselves, convened for the purpose. On the other hand, the effect may be inverted. Men of factious tempers, of local prejudices, or of sinister designs, may, by intrigue, by corruption, or by other means, first obtain the suffrages, and then betray the interests of the people. The question resulting is, whether small or extensive republics are most favorable to the election of proper guardians of the public weal; and it is clearly decided in favor of the latter by two obvious considerations.

In the first place it is to be remarked that however small the republic may be the representatives must be raised to a certain number in order to guard against the cabals of a few; and that however large it may be they must be limited to a certain number in order to guard against the confusion of a multitude. . . .

In the next place, as each representative will be chosen by a greater number of citizens in the large than in the small republic, it will be more difficult for unworthy candidates to practice with success the vicious arts by which elections are too often carried; and the suffrages of the people being more free, will be more likely to center in men who possess the most attractive merit and the most diffusive and established characters. . . .

The other point of difference is, the greater number of citizens and extent of territory which may be brought within the compass of republican than of democratic government; and it is this circumstance principally which renders factious combinations less to be dreaded in the former than in the latter. The smaller the society, the fewer probably will be the distinct parties and interests composing it; the fewer the distinct parties and interest, the more frequently will a majority be found of the same party; and the smaller the number of individuals composing a majority, and the smaller the compass within which they are placed, the more easily will they concert and execute their plans of oppression. Extend the sphere and you take in a greater variety of parties and interests; you make it less probable that a majority of the whole will have a common motive to invade the rights of other citizens; or if such a common motive exists, it will be more difficult for all who feel it to discover their own strength, and to act in unison with each other. . . .

Hence, it clearly appears, that the same advantage which a republic has over a democracy, in controlling the effects of faction, is enjoyed by a large over a small republic—is enjoyed by the Union over the States composing it. . . .

The influence of factious leaders may kindle a flame within their particular States, but will be unable to spread a general conflagration through the other States. A religious sect may degenerate into a political faction in a part of the Confederacy; but the variety of sects dispersed over the entire face of it must secure the national councils against any danger from that source. A rage for paper money, for an abolition of debts, for an equal division of property, or for any other improper or wicked project, will be less apt to pervade the whole body of the Union than a particular member of it; in the same proportion as such a malady is more likely to taint a particular county or district, than an entire State.

In the extent and proper structure of the Union, therefore, we behold a republican remedy for the diseases most incident to republican government. And according to the degree of pleasure and pride we feel in being republicans ought to be our zeal in cherishing the spirit and supporting the character of federalists.

Number 14 (Madison)

We have seen the necessity of the Union as our bulwark against foreign danger, as the conservator of peace among ourselves, as the guardian of our commerce and other common interests, as the only substitute for those military establishments which have subverted the liberties of the old world, and as the proper antidote for the diseases of faction. . . .

. . . It is that in a democracy the people meet and exercise the government in person; in a republic they assemble and administer it by their representatives and agents. A democracy, consequently, must be confined to a small spot. A republic may be extended over a large region. . . .

. . . the immediate object of the federal Constitution is to secure the union of the thirteen primitive States, which we know to be practicable.

Number 51 (Madison)

The great security against a gradual concentration of the several powers in the same department consists in giving to those who administer each department the necessary constitutional means and personal motives to resist encroachments of the others. . . . Ambition must be made to counteract ambition. The interest of the man must be connected with the constitutional rights of the place. It may be a reflection on human nature that such devices should be necessary to control the abuses of government. But what is government itself but the greatest of all reflections on human nature? If men were angels, no government would be necessary. If angels were to govern men, neither external nor internal controls on government would be necessary. In framing a government which is to be administered by men over men, the great difficulty lies in this: you must first enable the government to control the governed; and in the next place oblige it to control itself. A dependence on the people is, no doubt, the primary control on the government; but experience has taught mankind the necessity of auxiliary precautions.

Number 70 (Hamilton)

Men often oppose a thing merely because they have had no agency in planning it, or because it may have been planned by those whom they dislike. But if they have been consulted, and have happened to disapprove, opposition then becomes, in their estimation, an indispensable duty of self-love. They seem to think themselves bound in honor, and by all the motives of personal infallibility, to defeat the success of what has been resolved upon contrary to their sentiments. Men of upright, benevolent tempers have too many opportunities of remarking, with horror, to what desperate lengths this disposition is sometimes carried, and how often the great interests of society are sacrificed to the vanity, to the conceit, and to the obstinacy of individuals, who have credit enough to make their passions and their caprices interesting to mankind. Perhaps the question now before the public may, in its consequences, afford melancholy proofs of the effects of this despicable frailty, or rather detestable vice, in the human character.

Number 78 (Hamilton)

Whoever attentively considers the different departments of power must perceive that, in a government in which they are separated from each other, the judiciary, from the nature of its functions, will always be the least dangerous to the political rights of the Constitution; because it will be the least in a capacity to annoy or injure them. The executive not only dispenses the honors but holds the sword of the community. The legislature not only commands the purse but prescribes the rules by which the duties and rights of every citizen are to be regulated. The judiciary, on the contrary, has no influence over either the sword or the purse; no direction either of the strength or of the wealth of the society, and can take no active resolution whatever. It may truly be said to have neither FORCE nor WILL but merely judgement; and must ultimately depend upon the aid of the executive arm even for the efficacy of its judgements.

THE FEDERALIST – A SIMULATED INTERVIEW

1. **What is the function of government?**
    A. Human beings are imperfect and easily corrupted. Government is necessary to control the actions of human beings.
    B. In spite of imperfections, human beings enjoy a capacity for reason and justice that makes freedom possible. Government must control the people without violating their rights.

2. **What are the advantages of a republican form of government?**
    A. In a republican system the people are governed by elected representatives. Republicanism allows the people to protect their rights through the control of elected officials.
    B. In a democracy the people meet in one place to make political decisions directly. In a republic elected representatives meet to make decisions in the name of the people. Democracy is more suited to a small society. Republicanism is more suited to a large society such as the United States.
    C. Republicanism allows public opinion to be filtered through debating representatives who make decisions based upon their wisdom, patriotism, and love of justice. Elected representatives should protect the nation from the sometimes irrational demands of the people.

3. **What are the advantages of a federal system of government?**
    A. In a federal system a central government exists side by side with state governments. Federalism is the natural outcome of a desire to unify the American states.
    B. A federal system of government will protect the liberty of the people by guarding state governments from centralization.
    C. A federal system will strengthen the nation and keep it safe from foreign danger.
    D. A well-constructed federal system can control political factions.

4. **What causes the formation of political factions?**
    A. Human beings forever voice differences of opinion concerning such issues as religion and government. Factions are natural.
    B. Factions most likely develop from an unequal distribution of property. Those who have property will always be in conflict with those who do not have property.

5. **How do political factions threaten society?**
    A. Factions of a majority possess political power in a republican system. An electoral majority might threaten the rights of the minority.

   B. Factions of less than a majority can cause mischief and threaten the public interest.

   C. Factions can lead to instability in government and a neglect of the public interest. A weak system of government in a divided society is dangerous.

6. How can political factions be controlled?

   A. There are two methods of dealing with factions: remove the causes or control the harmful effects. There are two methods of removing the causes: deny freedom or give everyone the same opinions. Removing the causes of factions is impossible and undesirable. Society must therefore control the effects of factions.

   B. Minority factions are best controlled in a republican system in which the majority rules.

   C. Majority factions are eliminated in a large nation in which a diversity of interests prevents a single faction from gaining a majority.

   D. The ambition of political factions can best be regulated by dividing power in the government. "Ambition must be made to counteract ambition."

7. What are the advantages of the U.S. Constitution?

   A. Instability and anarchy are dangerous. The U.S. Constitution allows for a stable, orderly system of government without excessive centralization.

   B. The Constitution allows the federal government to act directly upon the people. Since the Constitution creates a republican government with limited power, the people's rights cannot be violated.

   C. The Constitution creates a strong union with an energetic central government. The nation has the stability and the strength to prevent foreign domination and domestic rebellion.

   D. In order that governmental power be restrained, the Constitution separates powers between three branches of the federal government as well as between the federal government and state governments. Among the three federal branches the judicial branch of government is least likely to threaten political rights. The president controls the army; the legislature controls the finances; the judiciary holds only the power of its reasoned opinions.

   E. The Constitution clearly defines the powers of a limited government. The Constitution grants the federal government supremacy over the states only in areas assigned to the federal government.

8. Why was a bill of rights not included in the Constitution?

   A. A bill of rights is designed to protect the people from a monarch. In a republican system of government a bill of rights is unnecessary.

B. The Constitution itself is a bill of rights. The Constitution creates a republican government with limited powers. The Constitution contains safeguards against the abuse of power.

C. A bill of rights in the Constitution would be dangerous. A bill of rights would indicate there are exceptions to the powers granted to the federal government, and the federal government might therefore claim more powers than specifically delegated. With extended powers, the rights of the people could easily be violated.

STUDENT ACTIVITIES

Vocabulary

Define the following terms before reading the lesson on the Federalist.

1. aliment	10. consonant	19. melancholy
2. antidote	11. declamation	20. mutual
3. auxiliary	12. efficacy	21. obstinacy
4. benevolent	13. faction	22. passion
5. bulwark	14. fallible	23. preeminence
6. commensurate	15. indispensable	24. requisite
7. conduce	16. inducement	25. taint
8. confederacy	17. latent	26. weal
9. conflagration	18. malady	27. zeal

Review

1. What state boycotted the Constitutional Convention?
2. To whom was the Constitution submitted for ratification?
3. How many of the thirteen states were needed to ratify the Constitution?
4. What term was used to describe supporters of the Constitution?
5. What four states were integral to the ratification of the Constitution?
6. Who were the authors of *The Federalist Papers*?
7. *The Federalist Papers* were published under what pen name?
8. How did the Federalist define the difference between a republic and a democracy?
9. What did the Federalist believe was the most likely cause of political factions?
10. Why did the Federalist believe factions of a majority were dangerous?
11. Why did the Federalist believe factions of less than a majority were dangerous?
12. What did the Federalist think was the best way to control majority factions?
13. What did the Federalist think was the best way to control minority factions?
14. In what way did the Federalist think the Constitution was itself a bill of rights?
15. Why did the Federalist think a bill of rights would be dangerous?

16. Decide whether the following statements are **True** or **False** according to the Federalist.
   A. Human beings are imperfect and easily corrupted.
   B. Government must control the people without violating their rights.
   C. Elected representatives should protect the nation from the some-times irrational demands of the people.
   D. Human beings have a capacity for reason and justice that makes freedom possible.
   E. Factions are natural to human existence.
   F. In a federal system a central government exists side by side with state governments.

What do you think?
On a scale of one through five, rate your opinion of the following quotations by the Federalist. Write a short statement explaining your rating.

1 – You **strongly agree** with the statement *or* you feel the statement is **admirable** considering the historical circumstances surrounding it.
5 – You **strongly disagree** with the statement *or* you feel the statement is **contemptible** considering the historical circumstances surrounding it.

A. *As long as the reason of man continues fallible, and he is at liberty to exercise it, different opinions will be formed.*
B. *The most common and durable source of factions has been the various and unequal distribution of property.*
C. *If a faction consists of less than a majority, relief is supplied by the republican principle, which enables the majority to defeat its sinister views by regular vote.*
D. *When a majority is included in a faction, the form of popular govern-ment . . . enables it to sacrifice to its ruling passion or interest both the public good and the rights of other citizens.*
E. *A pure democracy, by which I mean a society consisting of a small number of citizens, who assemble and administer the government in person, can admit of no cure for the mischiefs of faction.*
F. *It may well happen that the public voice, pronounced by the representa-tives of the people, will be more consonant to the public good than if pronounced by the people themselves, convened for the purpose.*
G. *If men were angels, no government would be necessary. If angels were to govern men, neither external nor internal controls on government would be necessary.*
H. *Men often oppose a thing merely because they have had no agency in planning it, or because it may have been planned by those whom they dislike.*

CHAPTER 9

THE ANTI-FEDERALISTS

BACKGROUND

During the debate over ratification of the U.S. Constitution (1787-88) persons who opposed ratification were known as Anti-Federalists. Men such as Patrick Henry, Richard Henry Lee, George Mason, James Monroe, John Hancock, and Samuel Adams were some of the most prominent leaders of the time; they were also Anti-Federalists. In spite of their notable leadership, Anti-Federalists were not an organized group and did not speak with one voice. Opposition to the Constitution therefore stemmed from a variety of viewpoints.

On the whole, Anti-Federalists acknowledged that the Articles of Confederation needed reform; they also felt the Constitution went too far in strengthening the central government. They argued that the president was too strong and the judiciary held too much power. They argued that the federal legislature was too small, and representatives would find it difficult to serve large numbers of people in congressional districts. The Anti-Federalists feared the vagueness of the "elastic clause" which allowed Congress to make any law "necessary and proper."

In several states the supporters of the Constitution met great opposition and ratification was not guaranteed. In Massachusetts, the sixth state to vote for ratification, Federalists had to compromise in order to win support. Massachusetts Federalists promised that amendments to the Constitution would be considered by the new Congress. Following the "Massachusetts Compromise" the states of South Carolina, New Hampshire, Virginia, and New York voted for ratification on the condition that amendments would be adopted. In the end only two states—Rhode Island and North Carolina—did not vote for ratification.

The Constitution might never have been ratified without the agreements made in the ratifying conventions. Accordingly, Representative James Madison of Virginia introduced several amendments in the First Congress. These amendments came to be known as the Bill of Rights and were ratified in 1791. The Bill of Rights, an integral part of America's political tradition, is an important legacy of the Anti-Federalist opposition to the Constitution.

THE ANTI-FEDERALISTS – IN THEIR OWN WORDS

Letters from the Federal Farmer (Letter I)

[These letters were probably written by Melancton Smith.]

There are three different forms of free government under which the United States may exist as one nation; and now is, perhaps, the time to determine to which we will direct our views. 1. Distinct republics connected under a federal head. In this case the respective state governments must be the principal guardians of the peoples rights, and exclusively regulate their internal police: in them must rest the balance of government. The congress of the states, or federal head must consist of delegates amenable to, and removable by the respective states: This congress must have general directing powers; powers to require men and monies of the states; to make treaties: peace and war: to direct the operations of armies, etc. Under this federal modification of government, the powers of congress would be rather advisory or recommendatory than coercive. 2. We may do away with the several state governments, and form or consolidate all the states into one entire government, with one executive, one judiciary, and one legislature, consisting of senators and representatives collected from all parts of the union: In this case there would be a complete consolidation of the states. 3. We may consolidate the states as to certain national objects, and leave them severally distinct independent republics, as to internal police generally. Let the general government consist of an executive, a judiciary and balanced legislature, and its powers extend exclusively to all foreign concerns, causes arising on the seas to commerce, imports, armies, navies, Indian affairs, peace and war, and to a few internal concerns of the community; to the coin, post-offices, weights and measures, a general plan for the militia, to naturalization, *and, perhaps to bankruptcies*, leaving the internal police of the community, in other respects, exclusively to the state governments; as the administration of justice in all causes arising internally, the laying and collecting of internal taxes, and the forming of the militia according to a general plan prescribed. . . .

Touching the first, or federal plan, I do not think much can be said in its favor: The sovereignty of the nation, without coercive and efficient powers to collect the strength of it, cannot always be depended on to answer the purposes of government and in a congress of representatives of sovereign states, there must necessarily be an unreasonable mixture of powers in the same hands.

As to the second, or complete consolidating plan, it deserves to be carefully considered at this time, by every American: If it be impracticable, it is a fatal error to model our governments directing our views ultimately to it.

The third plan, or partial consolidation, is, in my opinion, the only one that can secure the freedom and happiness of this people. I once had some general ideas that the second plan was practicable, but from long attention, and the proceedings of the convention, I am fully satisfied, that this third plan is the only one we can with safety and propriety proceed upon. Making this the standard to point out, with candor and fairness, the parts of the new constitution which appear to be improper, is my object. The convention appears to have proposed the partial consolidation evidently with a view to collect all powers ultimately, in the United States into one entire government; and from its views in this respect, and from the tenacity of the small states to have an equal vote in the senate, probably originated the greatest defects in the proposed plan.

Independent of the opinions of many great authors, that a free elective government cannot be extended over large territories, a few reflections must evince, that one government and general legislation alone, never can extend equal benefits to all parts of the United States: Different laws, customs, and opinions exist in the different states, which by a uniform system of laws would be unreasonably invaded. The United States contain about a million of square miles, and in half a century will, probably, contain ten millions of people; and from the center to the extremes is about 800 miles.

Before we do away the state governments, or adopt measures that will tend to abolish them, and to consolidate the states into one entire government, several principles should be considered and facts ascertained.

Letters from the Federal Farmer (Letter II)

There are certain unalienable and fundamental rights, which in forming the social compact, ought to be explicitly ascertained and fixed—a free and enlightened people, in forming this compact, will not resign all their rights to those who govern, and they will fix limits to their legislators and rulers, which will soon be plainly seen by those who are governed, as well as by those who govern; and the latter will know they cannot be passed unperceived by the former, and without giving a general alarm—these rights should be made the basis of every constitution: and if a people be so situated, or have such different opinions that they cannot agree in ascertaining and fixing them, it is a very strong argument against their attempting to form one entire society, to live under one system of laws only.—I confess, I never thought the people of these states differed essentially in these respects; they having derived all these rights from one common source, the British systems; and having in the formation of their state constitutions, discovered that their ideas relative to these rights are very similar. However, it is now said that the states differ so essentially in these respects, and even in the important article of the trial by jury, that when assembled in convention, they can agree to no words by which to establish that trial, or by which to ascertain and establish many other of these rights, as fundamental articles in the social compact. If so, we proceed to consolidate the states on no solid basis whatever.

Letters from the Federal Farmer (Letter IV)

The general presumption being, that men who govern, will, in doubtful cases, construe laws and constitutions most favorably for increasing their own powers; all wise and prudent people, in forming constitutions, have drawn the line, and carefully described the powers parted with and the powers reserved. . . . The state legislatures are obliged to take notice of the bills of rights of their respective states. The bills of rights, and the state constitutions, are fundamental compacts only between those who govern, and the people of the same state.

On the whole, the position appears to me to be undeniable, that this bill of rights ought to be carried farther, and some other principles established, as a part of this fundamental compact between the people of the United States and their federal rulers.

Letters from the Federal Farmer (Letter V)

This subject of consolidating the states is new; and because forty or fifty men have agreed in a system, to suppose the good sense of this country, an enlightened nation, must adopt it without examination, and though in a state of profound peace, without endeavoring to amend those parts they perceive are defective, dangerous to freedom, and destructive of the valuable principles of republican government—is truly humiliating. It is true there may be danger in delay; but there is danger in adopting the system in its present form.

Letters from the Federal Farmer (Letter XVI)

We do not by declarations change the nature of things, or create new truths, but we give existence, or at least establish in the minds of the people truths and principles which they might never otherwise have thought of, or soon forgot. If a nation means its systems, religious or political, shall have duration, it ought to recognize the leading principles of them in the front page of every family book. What is the usefulness of a truth in theory, unless it exists constantly in the minds of the people, and has their assent . . . . Men, in some countries do not remain free, merely because they are entitled to natural and unalienable rights; men in all countries are entitled to them, not because their ancestors once got together and enumerated them on paper, but because, by repeated negotiations and declarations, all parties are brought to realize them, and of course to believe them to be sacred. Were it necessary, I might shew the wisdom of our past conduct, as a people in not merely comforting ourselves that we were entitled to freedom, but in constantly keeping in view, in addresses, bills of rights, in newspapers, the particular principles on which our freedom must always depend.

Patrick Henry, Speech, June 1788

[This speech was delivered to the Virginia Ratifying Convention.]
This Constitution is said to have beautiful features; but when I come to examine these features, Sir, they appear to me horridly frightful: Among other deformities, it has an awful squinting; it squints towards monarchy: And does not this raise indignation in the breast of every American? Your President may easily become King: Your Senate is so imperfectly con-structed that your dearest rights may be sacrificed by what may be a small

minority; and a very small minority may continue forever unchangeably this Government, although horribly defective: Where are your checks in this Government?

Address of the Pennsylvania Minority, December 1787
[After the Pennsylvania Convention ratified the Constitution, members of the minority signed a dissenting statement written by Samuel Bryan.]

The first consideration that this review suggests, is the omission of a BILL OF RIGHTS, ascertaining and fundamentally establishing those unalienable and personal rights of men, without the full, free, and secure enjoyment of which there can be no liberty, and over which it is not necessary for a good government to have the control. The principal of which are the rights of conscience, personal liberty by the clear and unequivocal establishment of the writ of *habeas corpus*, jury trial in criminal and civil cases, by an impartial jury of the vicinage or country, with the common-law proceedings, for the safety of the accused in criminal prosecutions; and the liberty of the press, that scourge of tyrants, and the grand bulwark of every other liberty and privilege; the stipulations heretofore made in favor of them in the state constitutions, are entirely superseded by this constitution.

The legislature of a free country should be so formed as to have a competent knowledge of its constituents, and enjoy their confidence. To produce these essential requisites, the representation ought to be fair, equal, and sufficiently numerous, to possess the same interests, feelings, opinions, and views, which the people themselves would possess, were they all assembled; and so numerous as to prevent bribery and undue influence, and so responsible to the people, by frequent and fair elections, as to prevent their neglecting or sacrificing the views and interests of their constituents, to their own pursuits. . . .

As this government will not enjoy the confidence of the people, but be executed by force, it will be a very expensive and burthensome government. The standing army must be numerous, and as a further support, it will be the policy of this government to multiply officers in every department: judges, collectors, tax gatherers, excisemen and the whole host of revenue officers will swarm over the land, devouring the hard earnings of the industrious. Like the locusts of old, impoverishing and desolating all before them. . . .

We have not confined our views to the interests of the welfare of this state. . . . We have overlooked all local circumstances—we have considered this subject on the broad scale of the general good; we have asserted the cause of the present and future ages; the cause of liberty and mankind.

"Brutus," Essay I
[Essays signed by "Brutus" were published in New York to counter the arguments in *The Federalist*. "Brutus" was Robert Yates, a New York judge.]

The territory of the United States is of vast extent; it now contains near three millions of souls, and is capable of containing much more than ten times that number. Is it practicable for a country, so large and so numerous as they will soon become, to elect a representation, that will speak their sentiments, without their becoming so numerous as to be incapable of transacting public business? It certainly is not.

In a republic, the manners, sentiments, and interests of the people should be similar. If this be not the case, there will be a constant clashing of opinions; and the representatives of one part will be continually striving against those of the other. This will retard the operations of government, and prevent such conclusions as will promote the public good. If we apply this remark to the condition of the United States, we shall be convinced that it forbids that we should be one government. The United States includes a variety of climates. The productions of the different parts of the union are very variant, and their interests, of consequence, diverse. Their manners and habits differ as much as their climates and productions; and their sentiments are by no means coincident. The laws and customs of the several states are, in many respects, very diverse, and in some opposite; each would be in favor of its own interests and customs, and, of consequence, a legislature, formed of representatives from the respective parts, would not only be too numerous to act with any care or decision, but would be composed of such heterogeneous and discordant principles, as would constantly be contending with each other. The laws cannot be executed in a republic, of an extent equal to that of the United States, with promptitude.

"Brutus," Essay X
The liberties of a people are in danger from a large standing army, not only because the rulers may employ them for the purposes of supporting themselves in any usurpations of power, which they may see proper to exercise, but there is great hazard, that an army will subvert the forms of the government, under whose authority they are raised, and establish one according to the pleasure of their leader.

"Cato," Letter V
["Cato" was New York Governor George Clinton.]
It is a very important objection to this government, that the representation consists of so few; too few to resist the influence of corruption, and the temptation to treachery, against which all governments ought to take precautions—how guarded you have been on this head, in your own state constitution, and yet the number of senators and representatives proposed for this vast continent, does not equal those of your own state; how great the disparity, if you compare them with the aggregate numbers in the United States.

THE ANTI-FEDERALISTS – A SIMULATED INTERVIEW

1. **Under what different types of government could the United States exist as one nation?**
   A. The United States could exist as one nation under three possible types of government:
      1. The United States could be a collection of independent states held together by a central government. The central government would serve as an advisor to the states. The central government would not possess coercive power over the states.
      2. The United States could abolish state governments and form a single centralized government.
      3. The United States could allow the states to remain independent republics. Power would be delegated to a central government on issues related to foreign affairs, trade, and a few domestic concerns.
   B. The third option stated above is best for the United States. The states should remain independent with select powers delegated to a central government. The Constitution, however, goes too far in denying power to the states. The Constitution allows for the ultimate consolidation of all power in the central government. The Constitution threatens to create a single nation that will destroy the power of the states.

2. **Why are small republics better than large republics?**
   A. The people are more likely to have a voice in government.
   B. The people are more likely to participate actively in government.
   C. The people are more likely to obey the laws of the government.
   D. The people are more likely to know their elected officials.
   E. Elected officials are more likely to know and understand their constituents.

3. **Is the United States too large for an effective republican form of government?**
   A. The opinions of the people should be similar in a republic. If not, constant disagreements will slow down the operations of government and endanger the public interest. The United States is too large and the people are too diverse for a republican form of government to work effectively. Republicanism is more likely to work at the state level.
   B. Power cannot be trusted, especially a distant and impersonal power such as that created by the Constitution. In the United States the people are too far removed from the central government; the people sense little connection with the central government. Corruption in the central government is likely to be a constant problem for the nation.

4. **Does the Constitution protect the rights of the people?**
    A. Human beings in all nations are entitled to freedom and a protection of their rights. The Constitution does not provide for this basic entitlement.
    B. No republican constitution is safe unless it provides for the protection of rights. The U.S. Constitution contains a significant flaw—it does not provide a bill of rights.
    C. A protection of rights should be the basis of all constitutions. However, when the people cannot agree on the specific nature of rights no attempt should be made to form *one* society with *one* system of laws. Rights are protected better by state governments where there is greater uniformity of opinion. In a large nation the rights of the people are less likely to be protected.

5. **What are the fundamental defects in the Constitution?**
    A. The Constitution does not provide a bill of rights. Under the Constitution the rights of the people could be violated by the government.
    B. The Constitution does not provide for enough representatives. Corruption is less likely when government is made up of a larger number of representatives.
    C. The Constitution does not adequately separate powers. Each branch of the government should be more independent and not share power with the other branches.
    D. Under the Constitution the judiciary is too far removed from the people. Judges who are appointed for life will become agents of arbitrary power.
    E. The Constitution comes dangerously close to creating a monarchy. The president may easily become a king.
    F. The people are too far removed from the central government. The central government cannot gain the support of the people. The government will have to be maintained by force.
    G. A large standing army threatens the interests of the people. The Constitution allows for a standing army that can undermine the rights of the people. Providing funds for a standing army could bankrupt the nation.
    H. Under the Constitution the government is likely to burden the people with taxes.

STUDENT ACTIVITIES

Vocabulary
Define the following terms before reading the lesson on the Anti-Federalists.

1. aggregate	9. defective	17. requisite
2. amend	10. discordant	18. respective
3. ascertain	11. endeavor	19. retard
4. bulwark	12. *habeas corpus*	20. stipulation
5. coercive	13. heterogeneous	21. treachery
6. coincident	14. militia	22. unalienable
7. consolidation	15. naturalization	23. usurpation
8. construe	16. promptitude	24. vicinage

Review
1. Who were some of the leading Anti-Federalists?
2. Why is it difficult to focus on a single Anti-Federalist philosophy?
3. What is the elastic clause?
4. Why did Anti-Federalists fear the elastic clause?
5. What was the Massachusetts Compromise?
6. What two states did not vote for ratification of the Constitution?
7. What is an important legacy of the Anti-Federalists?
8. What did the Anti-Federalists believe was the best way to allow the United States to exist as one government?
9. Why did the Anti-Federalists think a republican form of government was unsuitable at the national level?
10. Why did the Anti-Federalists think rights were better protected by state governments?
11. Decide whether the following statements are **True** or **False** according to the Anti-Federalists.
    A. The Constitution does not go far enough in strengthening the federal government.
    B. The Constitution should create a stronger presidency and a stronger judiciary.
    C. The Constitution creates a federal legislature that is too small.
    D. Small republics are better than large republics.
    E. Corruption will be a constant problem for the United States government.
    F. The Constitution creates a judiciary that is too far removed from the people.
    G. The Constitution comes dangerously close to creating a monarchy.
    H. The Constitution should grant more power to a standing army.
    I. The Constitution creates a government that will burden the people with taxes.

What do you think?
On a scale of one through five, rate your opinion of the following quotations by the Anti-Federalists. Write a short statement explaining your rating.

1 – You **strongly agree** with the statement *or* you feel the statement is **admirable** considering the historical circumstances surrounding it.
5 – You **strongly disagree** with the statement *or* you feel the statement is **contemptible** considering the historical circumstances surrounding it.

A. *One government and general legislation alone, never can extend equal benefits to all parts of the United States.*

B. *Among other deformities, it [the Constitution] has an awful squinting towards monarchy . . . Your President may easily become King.*

C. *The legislature of a free country should be so formed as to have a competent knowledge of its constituents, and enjoy their confidence. To produce these essential requisites, the representation ought to be fair, equal, and sufficiently numerous, to possess the same interests, feelings, opinion, and views, which the people themselves would possess, were they assembled.*

D. *As this government [under the Constitution] will not enjoy the confidence of the people, but be executed by force, it will be a very expensive and burthensome government. The standing army must be numerous.*

E. *In a republic, the manners, sentiments, and interest of the people should be similar.*

F. *The laws cannot be executed in a republic, of an extent equal to that of the United States, with promptitude.*

G. *The liberties of a people are in danger from a large standing army, not only because the rulers may employ them for the purposes of supporting themselves in any usurpations of power, which they may see proper to exercise, but there is great hazard, that an army will subvert the forms of the government, under whose authority they are raised, and establish one according to the pleasure of their leader.*

H. *What right had they to say, "We the People"? . . . instead of "We the States"? States are the characteristics, and the soul of a confederation.* (Patrick Henry)

I. *Shall we imitate the example of those nations who have gone from a simple to a splendid Government? Are those nations more worthy of our imitation? What can make an adequate satisfaction to them for the loss they have suffered in attaining such a Government—for the loss of their liberty?* (Patrick Henry)

J. *The truth is, that the rights of individuals are frequently opposed to the apparent interest of the majority—for this reason the greater the portion of political freedom in a form of government the greater the necessity of a bill of rights.* (A Maryland Farmer)

CHAPTER 10

GEORGE WASHINGTON

BACKGROUND

If George Washington (1732-99) had died in his twenties, he would be remembered as a daring frontiersman. Enduring many hardships in the American wilderness and in the West Indies, he escaped death by pulling himself out of an icy river, suffering through a near-fatal case of smallpox, and heroically surviving a battle after his horse was twice shot out from under him. When a bad cold killed him at age sixty-seven his tremendous accomplishments as a general and nation-builder led Henry Lee to eulogize him as "first in war, first in peace, and first in the hearts of his countrymen."

A man of little formal education, Washington worked as a surveyor until he was chosen to lead Virginia's militia during the French and Indian War. After four years in the English army he retired to his estate at Mount Vernon, Virginia. Washington lived the life of a gentleman farmer until 1775 when he was chosen to command the continental army during the American Revolution. To show his commitment to the American cause he refused pay for his services. He also did not return home for eight years.

As commander in chief, Washington molded a disorganized, dirty, undisciplined mob into an army that outlasted the world's greatest military power. Although he won important victories at Trenton and Princeton, he persevered through several military defeats, holding together a revolutionary army that continually faced disintegration. After the British defeat at Yorktown and a treaty recognizing American independence he resigned his military commission and retired to Mount Vernon in 1783.

In 1787 he returned to the service of his nation and presided at the Constitutional Convention. In 1789 he was unanimously elected first president of the United States. During two terms he guided the nation through troublesome times. He not only created a new government, but also ensured its survival. As president he played an indispensable role in securing the success of a revolution he led. In the final analysis, Washington may not only be America's most influential leader, but also one of the most influential persons who ever lived.

GEORGE WASHINGTON – IN HIS OWN WORDS

Letter to the Committee of Congress, January 1778

A small knowledge of human nature will convince us, that, with far the greatest part of mankind, interest is the governing principle; and that almost every man is more or less under its influence. Motives of public virtue may for a time or in particular instances, actuate men to the observance of conduct purely disinterested; but they are not of themselves sufficient to produce a persevering conformity to the refined dictates and obligations of social duty. . . . No institution, not built on the presumptive truth of these maxims can succeed.

Circular to the States, June 1783

There are four things, which I humbly conceive, are essential to the well being, I may even venture to say, to the existence of the United States as an Independent Power:

1st. An indissoluble Union of the States under one Federal Head.

2dly. A Sacred regard to Public Justice.

3dly. The adoption of a proper Peace Establishment, and

4thly. The prevalence of that pacific and friendly Disposition, among the People of the United States, which will induce them to forget their local prejudices and policies, to make those mutual concessions which are requisite to the general prosperity, and in some instances, to sacrifice their individual advantages to the interest of the Community.

These are the Pillars on which the glorious Fabrick of our Independency and National Character must be supported.

Letter to Reverend William Gordon, July 1783

It now rests with the Confederated Powers, by the line of conduct they mean to adopt, to make this Country great, happy, and respectable; or to sink it into littleness; worse perhaps, into Anarchy and Confusion; for certain I am, that unless adequate Powers are given to Congress for the *general* purposes of the Federal Union that we shall soon moulder into dust and become contemptable in the Eyes of Europe, if we are not made the sport of their politicks . . . .

. . . A hundd. thousand men coming one after another cannot move a Ton weight; but the united strength of 50 would transport it with ease.

Letter to Robert Morris, April 1786

I can only say that there is not a man living who wishes more sincerely than I do, to see a plan adopted for the abolition of slavery; but there is only one proper and effectual mode by which it can be accomplished, and that is by Legislative authority.

Letter to Bushrod Washington, November 1787

The warmest friends and the best supporters the Constitution has, do not contend that it is free from imperfections; but they found them unavoidable and are sensible, if evil is likely to arise there from, the remedy must come hereafter; for in the present moment, it is not to be obtained; and, as there is a Constitutional door open for it, I think the People (for it is with them to Judge) can as they will have the advantage of experience on their Side, decide with as much propriety on the alterations and amendments which are necessary [as] ourselves. I do not think we are more inspired, have more wisdom, or possess more virtue, than those who will come after us.

The power under the Constitution will always be in the People. It is entrusted for certain defined purposes, and for a certain limited period, to representatives of their own chusing; and whenever it is executed contrary to their Interest, or not agreeable to their wishes, their Servants can, and undoubtedly will be, recalled.

Letter to Marquis de Lafayette, February 1788

As to my sentiments with respect to the merits of the new Constitution . . . . It appears to me, then little short of a miracle, that the Delegates from so many different States . . . should unite in forming a system of national Government, so little liable to well founded objections. . . . With regard to the two great points (the pivots upon which the whole machine must move,) my Creed is simply,

1st. That the general Government is not invested with more Powers than are indispensably necessary to perform the functions of a good Government; and, consequently, that no objection ought to be made against the quantity of Power delegated to it.

2dly. That these Powers . . . are so distributed among the Legislative, Executive, and Judicial Branches, into which the general Government is arranged, that it can never be in danger of degenerating into a monarchy, an Oligarchy, an Aristocracy, or any other despotic or oppressive form, so long as there shall remain any virtue in the body of the People.

. . . We are not to expect perfection in this world; but mankind, in modern times, have apparently made some progress in the science of government. Should that which is now offered to the People of America, be found on experiment less perfect than it can be made, a Constitutional door is left open for its amelioration.

Letter to Reverend Francis Adrian Vanderkemp, May 1788

I had always hoped that this land might become a safe and agreeable Asylum to the virtuous and persecuted part of mankind, to whatever nation they might belong . . . .

. . . Under a good government (which I have no doubt we shall establish) this Country certainly promises greater advantages, than almost any other, to persons of moderate property, who are determined to be sober, industrious and virtuous members of Society.

Address to the Pennsylvania Legislature, September 1789

It should be the highest ambition of every American to extend his views beyond himself, and to bear in mind that his conduct will not only affect himself, his country, and his immediate posterity; but that its influence may be co-extensive with the world, and stamp political happiness or misery on ages yet unborn. To establish this desirable end; and to establish the government of *laws*, the union of these States is absolutely necessary; therefore in every proceeding, this great, this important object should ever be kept in view; and so long as our measures tend to this; and are marked with the wisdom of a well-informed and enlightened people, we may reasonably hope, under the smiles of Heaven, to convince the world that the happiness of nations can be accomplished by pacific revolutions in their political systems without the destructive intervention of the sword.

To the Roman Catholics in the United States of America, March 1790

As mankind becomes more liberal they will be more apt to allow that all those who conduct themselves as worthy members of the community are equally entitled to the protection of civil government. I hope ever to see America among the foremost nations in examples of justice and liberality.

Letter to John Jay, May, 1796

I am *Sure* the Mass of Citizens in these United States *mean well*, and I firmly believe they will always *act well*, whenever they can obtain a right understanding of matters; but in some parts of the Union, where the sentiments of their delegates and leaders are adverse to the Government and great pains are taken to inculcate a belief that their rights are assailed, and their liberties endangered, it is not easy to accomplish this; especially, as is the case invariably, when the Inventors, and abetters of pernicious measures use infinitely more industry in disseminating the poison, than the well disposed part of the Community to furnish the antidote. To this source all our discontents may be traced and from it our embarrassments proceed. Hence serious misfortunes originating in misrepresentation frequently flow and spread before they can be dissipated by truth.

Farewell Address, September 1796

The Unity of Government . . . is a main Pillar in the Edifice of your real independence, the support of your tranquility at home; your peace abroad; of your safety; of your prosperity; of that very Liberty which you so highly prize. . . .

In contemplating the causes wch. may disturb our Union it occurs as matter of serious concern, that any ground should have been furnished for characterizing parties by *Geographical* discriminations: *Northern* and *Southern*; *Atlantic* and *Western*; whence designing men may endeavour to excite a belief that there is a real difference of local interests and views. One of the expedients of Party to acquire influence, within particular districts, is to misrepresent the opinions and aims of other Districts. You cannot shield yourselves too much against the jealousies and heart burnings which spring from these misrepresentations. They tend to render Alien to each other those who ought to be bound together by fraternal affection. . . .

. . . Let me now take a more comprehensive view, and warn you in the most solemn manner against the baneful effects of the Spirit of Party, generally. . . .

The alternate domination of one faction over another, sharpened by the spirit of revenge natural to party dissention, which in different ages and countries has perpetrated the most horrid enormities, is itself a frightful despotism. But this leads at length to a more formal and permanent despotism. The disorders and miseries, which result, gradually incline the minds of men to seek security and repose in the absolute power of an Individual: and sooner or later the chief of some prevailing faction more able or more fortunate than his competitors, turns this disposition to the purposes of his own elevation, on the ruins of Public Liberty. . . .

It serves always to distract the Public Councils and enfeeble the Public Administration. It agitates the Community with ill founded Jealousies and false alarms, kindles the animosity of one part against another, foments occasionally riot and insurrection. It opens the door to foreign influence and corruption, which find a facilitated access to the government itself through the channels of party passions. Thus the policy and the will of one country, are subjected to the policy and will of another. . . .

Of all the dispositions and habits which lead to political prosperity, Religion and morality are indispensable supports. . . . The mere Politician, equally with the pious man ought to respect and to cherish them. . . .

Promote then as an object of primary importance, Institutions for the general diffusion of knowledge. In proportion as the structure of a government gives force to public opinion, it is essential that public opinion should be enlightened. . . .

Observe good faith and justice towards all Nations. Cultivate peace and harmony with all. Religion and morality enjoin this conduct; and can it be that good policy does not equally enjoin it? It will be worthy of a free, enlightened, and, at no distant period, a great Nation, to give to mankind the magnanimous and too novel example of a People always guided by an exalted justice and benevolence. Who can doubt that in the course of time and things the fruits of such a plan would richly repay any temporary advantages wch. might be lost by a steady adherence to it?. . . The experiment, at least, is recommended by every sentiment which ennobles human Nature. Alas! is it rendered impossible by its vices?

In the execution of such a plan nothing is more essential than that permanent inveterate antipathies against particular Nations and passionate attachments for others should be excluded; and that in place of them just and amicable feelings towards all should be cultivated. The Nation, which indulges towards another an habitual hatred, or an habitual fondness, is in some degree a slave. It is a slave to its animosity or to its affection, either of which is sufficient to lead it astray from its duty and its interest. Antipathy in one Nation against another, disposes each more readily to offer insult and injury, to lay hold of slight causes of umbrage, and to be haughty and intractable, when accidental or trifling occasions of dispute occur. Hence frequent collisions, obstinate envenomed and bloody contests. . . .

So likewise, a passionate attachment of one Nation for another produces a variety of evils. Sympathy for the favourite nation, facilitating the illusion of an imaginary common interest, in cases where no real common interest exists, and infusing into one the enmities of the other, betrays the former into a participation in the quarrels and Wars of the latter without adequate inducement or justification: It leads also to concessions to the favourite Nation of privileges denied to others, which is apt doubly to injure the Nation making the concessions; by unnecessarily parting with what ought to have been retained; and by exciting jealousy, ill will, and a disposition to retaliate, in the parties from whom equal privileges are withheld: And it gives to ambitious, corrupted, or deluded citizens (who devote themselves to the favourite Nation) facility to betray, or sacrifice the interests of their own country, without odium, sometimes even with popularity . . . .

Against the insidious wiles of foreign influence. . . the jealousy of a free people ought to be constantly awake; since history and experience prove that foreign influence is one of the most baneful foes of Republican Government. . . .

. . . I anticipate with pleasing expectation that retreat, in which I promise myself to realize, without alloy, the sweet enjoyment of partaking, in the midst of my fellow Citizens, the benign influence of good Laws under a free Government, the ever favourite object of my heart, and the happy reward, as I trust, of our mutual cares, labours and dangers.

Last Will and Testament, July 1799

Upon the decease of my wife, it is my Will and desire that all the Slaves which I hold in *my own right*, shall receive their freedom. . . . Whereas among those who will receive freedom . . . there may be some, who from old age or bodily infirmities, and others who on account of their infancy, that will be unable to support themselves; it is my Will and desire that all who come under the first and second description shall be comfortably cloathed and fed by my heirs while they live; and that such of the latter description as have no parents living, or if living are unable, or unwilling to provide for them, shall be bound by the Court until they shall arrive at the age of twenty five years . . . .The Negroes thus bound, are . . . to be taught to read and write; and to be brought up to some useful occupation, agreeably to the Laws of the Commonwealth of Virginia, providing for the support of Orphans and other poor Children. . . . And I do moreover most pointedly, and most solemnly enjoin it upon my Executors . . . to see that *this* clause respecting Slaves, and every part thereof be religiously fulfilled.

GEORGE WASHINGTON – A SIMULATED INTERVIEW

1. **What actions are essential for preserving American independence?**
    A. The American people should set aside local prejudices and promote the interests of the nation.
    B. The United States must establish a strong and permanent union of the states. With a strong federal union the United States can prevent two undesirable situations:
        1. The United States can avoid degenerating into a nation of petty local arguments and anarchy.
        2. The United States can avoid being used by European nations for their own selfish interests.

2. **Did the framers of the U.S. Constitution create an effective form of government?**
    A. The Constitution is not perfect because the men who wrote it are not perfect. The framers are not necessarily wiser, more inspired, or more virtuous than leaders of the future. Provisions have therefore been established for future generations to change the Constitution.
    B. The Constitution grants powers to the national government that are necessary for the operation of good government.
    C. The Constitution is commendable for its division of powers in the central government. Power is separated in a way that the United States should never sink into monarchy, oligarchy, or aristocracy as long as the people remain virtuous.
    D. Due to the separation of powers, the Constitution should be successful in preventing a single individual or political faction from having too much power.
    E. Human beings are motivated primarily by self interest. Government must therefore be formed upon the assumption that people will pursue their self-interest. The Constitution succeeds in forming a government based upon this assumption.

3. **Under what conditions, if any, should government be changed?**
    A. Experience is the standard for measuring the need for change. When the people discover through experience that change is necessary, changes should be made. Elected representatives should respond to the people and pass new legislation or amend the Constitution.
    B. Government officials are elected to govern in the interest of the people. If officials fail to act in the interests of the people, they should be recalled by the people.

4. Should the United States allow slavery?

A. Slavery violates the fundamental principles of the American revolution.

B. Slavery does not allow an efficient means of getting slaves to work. Seeing no profit in their labor, slaves cannot always be convinced to work. Punishment fails against people who have little to lose.

C. Slavery is financially unsound. Slaves may break machines, work slowly, and steal property. Since slaves cannot possess private property, they cannot be expected to respect the property of others.

D. Slavery is a sectional issue that threatens the unity of the nation.

E. Slavery should be abolished by legislative power.

5. What issues are fundamental to the long term success of the United States?

A. Americans should beware of demagogues who spread falsehoods. A lie can flow freely before truth has a chance to stop it. People intend to do right and will act properly when given accurate information.

B. Americans should beware of political parties. A dominant political faction can take away the people's liberty. Political parties also open the United States to foreign influence.

C. Americans should beware of geographical divisions. Demagogues can use geographical jealousies to divide the American people.

D. Religion and morality are necessary for the success of the nation. Politicians as well as ordinary citizens should be guided by morality.

E. Americans should support institutions of learning. An educated citizenry is essential in a government based upon public opinion.

F. The United States should cultivate peace and harmony with all nations. The United States should avoid "passionate attachments" to any nation. In addition, the United States should avoid permanent hatred toward any nation.

G. The United States should proclaim neutrality in regard to European conflicts.

6. What role should the United States play in the world?

A. The United States should serve as an asylum for persecuted people in all nations. The United States offers opportunities for anyone who is sober, industrious, and virtuous.

B. Americans should show the world that a free people can govern themselves peacefully without intervention of the military. Americans have a unique role in the world and should act in a way that will inspire human beings for generations.

C. The United States should set an example of a nation guided by justice, compassion, and liberality. Individual Americans should be aware that their conduct will influence "ages yet unborn."

STUDENT ACTIVITIES

Vocabulary
Define the following terms before reading the lesson on Washington.

1. actuate	10. confederated	19. magnanimous
2. agitate	11. despotic	20. obstinate
3. amelioration	12. disposition	21. odium
4. amicable	13. edifice	22. oligarchy
5. animosity	14. enfeeble	23. pacific
6. antipathy	15. envenom	24. persevere
7. asylum	16. induce	25. prevalence
8. baneful	17. insidious	26. propriety
9. benevolence	18. inveterate	27. umbrage

Review
1. Who referred to Washington as "first in war, first in peace, and first in the hearts of his countrymen"?
2. In what war did Washington command Virginia's militia?
3. What was Washington's title during the American Revolution?
4. What role did Washington play at the Constitutional Convention?
5. What were two reasons Washington wanted to strengthen the federal union?
6. What motivates human beings according to Washington?
7. What did Washington believe should happen to elected officials who failed to govern in the interests of the people?
8. Although Washington felt people had good intentions, what was essential to their acting appropriately in a political setting?
9. According to Washington, what is America's unique role in the world?
10. Decide whether the following statements are **True** or **False** according to George Washington.
    A. The Constitution is perfect, and future generations should not change it.
    B. The separation of powers will keep the United States from sinking into despotism as long as the people remain virtuous.
    C. Slavery should be abolished.
    D. A strong two party system offers people essential political options.
    E. An educated citizenry is essential to the success of the nation.
    F. The United States should cultivate peace and harmony with all nations.
    G. The United States should fight for republicanism whenever it is threatened in Europe.
    H. The United States should serve as an asylum for persecuted people in all nations.
    I. The United States should be guided by justice, compassion, and liberality.

What do you think?
On a scale of one through five, rate your opinion of the following quotations by Washington. Write a short statement explaining your rating.

1 – You **strongly agree** with the statement *or* you feel the statement is **admirable** considering the historical circumstances surrounding it.
5 – You **strongly disagree** with the statement *or* you feel the statement is **contemptible** considering the historical circumstances surrounding it.

A. *A small knowledge of human nature will convince us, that, with far the greatest part of mankind, interest is the governing principle; and that almost every man is more or less under its influence.*
B. *I can only say that there is not a man living who wishes more sincerely than I do, to see a plan adopted for the abolition of slavery; but there is only one proper and effectual mode by which it can be accomplished, and that is by legislative authority.*
C. *I had always hoped that this land might become a safe and agreeable Asylum to the virtuous and persecuted part of mankind, to whatever nation they might belong.*
D. *This country certainly promises greater advantages, than almost any other, to persons of moderate property, who are determined to be sober, industrious and virtuous members of society.*
E. *As mankind becomes more liberal they will be more apt to allow that all those who conduct themselves as worthy members of the community are equally entitled to the protection of civil government.*
F. *I am sure the mass of citizens in these United States mean well, and I firmly believe they will always act well, whenever they can obtain a right understanding of matters.*
G. *Let me . . . warn you in the most solemn manner against the baneful effects of the spirit of party.*
H. *Observe good faith and justice towards all nations. Cultivate peace and harmony with all.*
I. *There is nothing which can better deserve our patronage than the promotion of science and literature. Knowledge is in every country the surest basis of public happiness.*
J. *I have always given it as my decided opinion that no nation had a right to intermeddle in the internal concerns of another; that everyone had a right to form and adopt whatever government they liked best to live under themselves.*
K. *The very idea of the power and the right of the people to establish government, presupposes the duty of every individual to obey the established government.*
L. *Experience has taught us that men will not adopt and carry into execution measures the best calculated for their own good without the intervention of a coercive power.*

CHAPTER 11

JAMES MADISON

BACKGROUND

James Madison (1751-1836) served his nation in many capacities. His most important contribution was helping to create the U.S. Constitution and securing its ratification. He was also responsible for pushing the Bill of Rights through Congress. For good reason, Madison is known as the father of the Constitution.

A painfully shy man of only 5' 4" and 100 pounds, he made a poor first impression. However, as a scholar and politician he worked hard while others slept. He arrived at the Constitutional Convention in 1787 more prepared than other delegates. He consequently played a most influential role in gaining a new constitution for the nation.

Needing nine of thirteen states for ratification, supporters of the Constitution viewed New York as a key state. Alexander Hamilton, a New York lawyer, enlisted Madison and John Jay to help write essays defending the Constitution. Madison's contributions to the collection of essays, known as *The Federalist Papers*, are today recognized as superior works of political theory.

During the nation's early years Madison became fearful of Hamilton's political ideas, ideas that Madison felt were corruptive. Madison therefore joined Thomas Jefferson in helping create a new political party to oppose Hamilton. When Jefferson became president in 1801 Madison served as secretary of state. When Jefferson left the presidency Madison was elected president.

During Madison's first term the United States entered the War of 1812 against England. Madison's weak leadership did not serve the nation well in wartime, and many people blamed him for the British destruction of Washington, D.C. Nevertheless, after the war Americans felt they had twice defeated the world's most powerful nation; Madison's reputation survived the war.

After Madison retired from politics he lived almost twenty years at his home in Virginia. As an elder statesman he enjoyed studying and commenting on the development of the nation he helped construct. In 1836 he became the last delegate from the Constitutional Convention to die.

JAMES MADISON – IN HIS OWN WORDS

"A Memorial and Remonstrance Against Religious Assessments," 1785
The Religion then of every man must be left to the conviction and conscience of every man; and it is the right of every man to exercise it as these
may dictate. This right is in its nature an unalienable right. It is unalienable;
because the opinions of men, depending only on the evidence contemplated
by their own minds, cannot follow the dictates of other men . . . .

. . . Who does not see that the same authority which can establish
Christianity, in exclusion of all other Religions, may establish with the same
ease any particular sect of Christians, in exclusion of all other Sects? . . .

. . . Whilst we assert for ourselves a freedom to embrace, to profess and
to observe the Religion which we believe to be of divine origin, we cannot
deny an equal freedom to those whose minds have not yet yielded to the
evidence which has convinced us. If this freedom be abused, it is an offence
against God, not against man . . . .

Experience witnesseth that ecclesiastical establishments, instead of
maintaining the purity and efficacy of Religion, have had a contrary
operation. During almost fifteen centuries, has the legal establishment of
Christianity been on trial. What have been its fruits? More or less in all
places, pride and indolence in the Clergy; ignorance and servility in the laity;
in both, superstition, bigotry and persecution. . . .

. . . If Religion be not within [the] cognizance of Civil Government, how
can its legal establishment be said to be necessary to civil Government?
What influences in fact have ecclesiastical establishments had on Civil
Society? In some instances they have been seen to erect a spiritual tyranny
on the ruins of Civil authority; in many instances they have been seen
upholding the thrones of political tyranny; in no instance have they been
seen the guardians of the liberties of the people. Rulers who wished to
subvert the public liberty, may have found an established clergy convenient
auxiliaries. A just government, instituted to secure & perpetuate it, needs
them not. Such a government will be best supported by protecting every
citizen in the enjoyment of his Religion with the same equal hand which
protects his person and his property; by neither invading the equal rights of
any Sect, nor suffering any Sect to invade those of another. . . .

. . . Torrents of blood have been spilt in the old world, by vain attempts
of the secular arm to extinguish Religious discord, by proscribing all
difference in Religious opinions. Time has at length revealed the true
remedy. Every relaxation of narrow and rigorous policy, wherever it has
been tried, has been found to assuage the disease. The American Theatre has
exhibited proofs, that equal and compleat liberty, if it does not wholly
eradicate it, sufficiently destroys its malignant influence on the health and
prosperity of the State.

Speech to Constitutional Convention, June 1787
All civilized societies would be divided into different sects, factions, and

interests, as they happened to consist of rich and poor, debtors and creditors, the landed, the manufacturing, the commercial interests, the inhabitants of this district, or that district, the followers of this political leader or that political leader, the disciples of this religious sect or that religious sect. In all cases where a majority are united by a common interest or passion, the rights of the minority are in danger. What motives are to restrain them? A prudent regard to the maxim that honesty is the best policy is found by experience to be as little regarded by bodies of men as by individuals. Respect for character is always diminished in proportion to the number among whom the blame or praise is to be divided. Conscience, the only remaining tie, is known to be inadequate in individuals: In large numbers, little is to be expected from it. Besides, religion itself may become a motive to persecution and oppression. These observations are verified by the histories of every country ancient and modern. In Greece and Rome the rich and poor, the creditors and debtors, as well as the patricians and plebeians alternately oppressed each other with equal unmercifulness. . . . The lesson we are to draw from the whole is that where a majority are united by common sentiment and have an opportunity, the rights of the minor party become insecure. In a republican government the majority if united have always an opportunity. The only remedy is to enlarge the sphere, and thereby divide the community into so great a number of interests and parties, that in the first place a majority will not be likely at the same moment to have a common interest separate from that of the whole or of the minority; and in the second place, that in case they should have such an interest, they may not be apt to unite in the pursuit of it.

Letter to Thomas Jefferson, October 1787
Those who contend for a simple Democracy, or a pure republic, actuated by the sense of the majority, and operating within narrow limits, assume or suppose a case which is altogether fictitious. They found their reasoning on the idea, that the people composing the Society, enjoy not only an equality of political rights; but that they have all precisely the same interests, and the same feelings in every respect. Were this in reality the case, their reasoning would be conclusive. The interest of the majority would be that of the minority also; the decisions could only turn on mere opinion concerning the good of the whole, of which the major voice would be the safest criterion; and within a small sphere, this voice could be most easily collected, and the public affairs most accurately managed. We know however that no society ever did or can consist of so homogeneous a mass of Citizens. . . . It remains then to be enquired whether a majority having any common interest, or feeling any common passion, will find sufficient motives to restrain them from oppressing the minority. . . . In a large Society, the people are broken into so many interests and parties, that a common sentiment is less likely to be felt, and the requisite concert less likely to be formed, by a majority of the whole.

Letter to Thomas Jefferson, October 1788

My own opinion has always been in favor of a bill of rights; provided it be so framed as not to imply powers not meant to be included in the enumeration. At the same time I have never thought the omission a material defect, nor been anxious to supply it even by *subsequent* amendment, for any other reason than that it is anxiously desired by others. I have favored it because I supposed it might be of use, and if properly executed could not be of disservice. . . .

It has been remarked that there is a tendency in all Governments to an augmentation of power at the expense of liberty. But the remark as usually understood does not appear to me well founded. Power when it has attained a certain degree of energy and independence goes on generally to further degrees. But when below that degree, the direct tendency is to further degrees of relaxation, until the abuses of liberty beget a sudden transition to an undue degree of power. With this explanation the remark may be true; and . . . is . . . applicable to the Governments in America. It is a melancholy reflection that liberty should be equally exposed to danger whether the Government have too much or too little power, and that the line which divides these extremes should be so inaccurately defined by experience.

To the *National Gazette*, December 1791

Public opinion sets bounds to every government, and is the real sovereign in every free one.

As there are cases where the public opinion must be obeyed by the government; so there are cases, where not being fixed, it may be influenced by the government. . . .

The larger a country, the less easy for its real opinion to be ascertained, and the less difficult to be counterfeited; when ascertained or presumed, the more respectable it is in the eyes of individuals. This is favorable to the authority of government. For the same reason, the more extensive a country, the more insignificant is each individual in his own eyes. This may be unfavorable to liberty.

Whatever facilitates a general intercourse of sentiments, as good roads, domestic commerce, a free press, and particularly a *circulation of newspapers through the entire body of the people*, and *Representatives going from, and returning among every part of them*, is equivalent to a contraction of territorial limits, and is favorable to liberty, where these may be too extensive.

To the *National Gazette*, February 20, 1792

No Government is perhaps reducible to a sole principle of operation . . . It is useful, nevertheless, to analyze the several kinds of government, and to characterize them by the spirit which predominates in each. . . .

First. A government operating by a permanent military force, which at once maintains the government, and is maintained by it; which is at once the cause of burdens on the people, and of submission in the people to their burdens. Such have been the governments under which human nature has groaned through every age. . . .

Secondly. A government operating by corrupt influence; substituting the motive of private interest in place of public duty; converting its pecuniary dispensations into bounties to favorites, or bribes to opponents; accommodating its measures to the avidity of a part of the nation instead of the benefit of the whole; in a word, enlisting an army of interested partizans whose tongues, whose pens, whose intrigues, and whose active combinations, by supplying the terror of the sword, may support a real domination of the few, under an apparent liberty of the many. Such a government, wherever to be found, is an imposter. . . .

Thirdly. A government deriving its energy from the will of the society, and operating by the reason of its measures, on the understanding and interest of the society. Such is the government for which philosophy has been searching, and humanity been fighting, from the most remote ages. Such are republican governments which it is the glory of America to have invented, and her unrivalled happiness to possess.

Response to "Pacificus," April 1793

If there be a principle that ought not be questioned within the United States, it is that every nation has a right to abolish an old government and establish a new one. This principle is not only recorded in every public archive, written in every American heart, and sealed with the blood of a host of American martyrs, but is the only lawful tenure by which the United States hold their existence as a nation.

Notes for Speech on the Right of Suffrage, 1821

The right of suffrage is a fundamental article in Republican Constitutions. The regulation of it is, at the same time, a task of peculiar delicacy. Allow the right exclusively to property, and the rights of persons may be oppressed. . . . Extend it equally to all, and the rights to property or the claims of justice may be overruled by a majority without property, or interested in measures of injustice. . . .

In a just & free Government, therefore, the rights both of property & of persons ought to be effectually guarded. Will the former be so in case of a universal & equal suffrage. Will the latter be so in case of a suffrage confined to the holders of property. . . .

In all Govts there is a power which is capable of oppressive exercise. In Monarchies and Aristocracies oppression proceeds from a want of sympathy & responsibility in the Govt. towards the people. In popular Governments the danger lies in an undue sympathy among individuals composing a majority, and a want of responsibility in the majority to the minority. The characteristic excellence of the political System of the U.S. arises from a distribution and organization of its powers, which . . . provides better guards than are found in any other popular Govt. against interested combinations of a Majority against the rights of a Minority.

Letter to Edward Livingston, July 1822

It was the belief of all sects at one time that the establishment of Religion by law, was right and necessary; that the true religion ought to be established in exclusion of every other; and that the only question to be decided was which was the true religion. . . . The example of the Colonies, now States, which rejected religious establishments altogether, proved that all Sects, might be safely & advantageously put on a footing of equal & entire freedom. . . . We are teaching the world the great truth that Gov^t do better without Kings & Nobles than with them. The merit will be doubled by the other lesson that Religion flourishes in greater purity, without than with the aid of Gov^t.

Letter to W.T. Barry, August 1822

Learned institutions ought to be favorite objects with every free people. They throw that light over the public mind which is the best security against crafty and dangerous encroachments on the public liberty. . . . They are themselves schools for the particular talents required for some of the public trusts, on the able execution of which the welfare of the people depends. They multiply the educated individuals, from among whom the people may elect a due portion of their public agents of every description . . . .

Without such institutions . . . none but the few whose wealth enables them to support their sons abroad can give them the fullest education; and in proportion as this is done, the influence is monopolized which superior information every where possesses. At cheaper and nearer seats of learning, parents with slender incomes may place their sons in a course of education, putting them on a level with the sons of the richest. . . .

. . . A popular Government, without popular information, or the means of acquiring it, is but a Prologue to a Farce or a Tragedy or, perhaps both. Knowledge will forever govern ignorance: And a people who mean to be their own Governors, must arm themselves with the power which knowledge gives.

Letter to N.P. Trist, April 1828

Those who see erroneous statements of facts without ever seeing a contradiction of them, and specious comments without any exposure of their fallacies, will, of course, be generally under the delusions so strongly painted by Mr. Jefferson. It has been said, that any country might be governed at the will of one who had the exclusive privilege of furnishing its popular songs. The result would be far more certain from a monopoly of the politics of the press. Could it be so arranged that every newspaper, when printed on one side, should be handed over to the press of an adversary, to be printed on the other, thus presenting to every reader both sides of every question, truth would always have a fair chance.

But such a remedy is ideal.

JAMES MADISON – A SIMULATED INTERVIEW

1. **Why should the United States adopt a republican form of government?**
    A. The best form of government is one that bases its power on the will of the people. In other words, the best form of government is a republican form of government.
    B. In a republican society public opinion decides the limits to government power and government must obey public opinion.
    C. Every nation possesses the right to abolish an old government and establish a new one. This is the essence of republicanism as well as all American political thought.

2. **What dangers are inherent in a republican form of government?**
    A. The danger of republicanism does not necessarily come from the arbitrary power of government. It arises from united majorities using government to protect their interests.
    B. All societies naturally divide into groups with different interests. In a republican form of government a united majority possesses political power and may take away the rights of the minority. For example, if only property owners vote, the rights of non-property owners are in danger. If everyone votes, property owners are in a minority and may consequently lose their property.
    C. People in a minority cannot expect a united majority to protect their rights. People in a minority cannot depend solely on the good character and morals of the rulers for protection. Automatic protection of minorities must be instituted.

3. **Are the problems of republicanism more evident at the state or national level?**
    A. Small societies present easier opportunities for united majorities to oppress minorities. State governments therefore cannot be trusted to protect the rights of minorities and individuals.
    B. In a large society the people divide into numerous interest groups, and a united majority is less likely to be formed. The national government is therefore less likely to take away rights than state and local governments.

4. **What are the solutions to the problems found in republican societies?**
    A. Contrary to the belief that small societies are most suitable for a republican form of government, a national government can work well under republican principles. The United States can find a republican remedy for the problems of a republican society.

B. Rights can be protected by distributing power in a way that the power of united majorities is controlled. This can be accomplished best within a large nation.

C. A national veto over state laws is necessary to keep states from abusing their power. The national government should be given a veto over the acts of the states "in all cases whatsoever." [Madison expressed this idea in a letter to George Washington in April 1787. However, in the 1790s Madison supported more state power on the grounds that excessive nationalism might corrupt the United States government.]

5. Should the United States adopt a bill of rights?

A. A bill of rights is not enough to protect people from the government. A united majority that is determined to take away people's rights will not be stopped by a bill of rights.

B. A bill of rights limits the power of government. However, individual rights can be threatened whether the government has too much power or whether it has too little power.

C. Although leaving a bill of rights out of the Constitution was not a mistake, including a bill of rights would do no harm.

D. Because some people fear the power of the United States government, a bill of rights should be added to calm their fears. A bill of rights is necessary for political reasons.

6. What should define the relationship between religion and government?

A. Church and State should remain separate. The same government that can make Christianity the official religion over all other religions might also choose to establish a single denomination over all other denominations.

B. When religion becomes involved in government the liberty of the people is threatened. History provides no examples of government-supported religion serving as a defender of freedom. In fact, religion might be used to justify persecution and oppression.

C. Each person possesses a natural right to individual religious beliefs. Government should not deny religious freedom.

D. Religion flourishes more without the help of government than with the help of government.

7. What actions are essential for the success of the United States?

A. The welfare of society depends upon the education of the people. Since people with knowledge will rule people who are ignorant, education protects society against those who threaten liberty. In addition, education multiplies the number of talented individuals available to the people when they elect a government.

B. A monopoly of the press is a threat to the nation. People should not live under delusions resulting from printed misinformation. Ideas printed in a newspaper should be open to opposing arguments in order that people may determine the truth.

STUDENT ACTIVITIES

Vocabulary
Define the following terms before reading the lesson on Madison.

1. ascertain	10. efficacy	19. martyr
2. assuage	11. encroachment	20. maxim
3. augmentation	12. enumeration	21. patrician
4. avidity	13. eradicate	22. perpetuate
5. beget	14. erroneous	23. plebeian
6. bigotry	15. fallacy	24. predominate
7. cognizance	16. homogeneous	25. subsequent
8. dispensation	17. indolence	26. subvert
9. ecclesiastical	18. laity	27. unalienable

Review
1. Why is Madison considered the "father of the Constitution"?
2. Madison served as secretary of state under which president?
3. Madison served as president during what war?
4. Who was the last delegate from the Constitutional Convention to die?
5. Why did Madison feel that a republican form of government was the best form of government?
6. According to Madison, what limits the power of government in a republican society?
7. What did Madison think was the greatest danger of republicanism?
8. Why did Madison want automatic protection of minorities instituted in the government?
9. What did Madison think was the problem with small societies?
10. What did Madison think was the advantage of a large society?
11. In what situations did Madison believe the national government should be given a veto over state actions?
12. Why did Madison think that a bill of rights was not enough to protect the people from the government?
13. Why did Madison want a bill of rights added to the Constitution?
14. Why did Madison believe that church and state should remain separate?
15. Why did Madison think education was important?
16. Why did Madison fear a monopoly in the press?
17. Decide whether the following statements are **True** or **False** according to James Madison.
    A. All nations possess the right to abolish their government.

B. History provides no examples of government-supported religion defending freedom.
C. Religion flourishes more without government's help than with it.
D. A bill of rights should be added to the Constitution to calm the fears of the people.

What do you think?
On a scale of one through five, rate your opinion of the following quotations by Madison. Write a short statement explaining your rating.

1 – You **strongly agree** with the statement *or* you feel the statement is **admirable** considering the historical circumstances surrounding it.
5 – You **strongly disagree** with the statement *or* you feel the statement is **contemptible** considering the historical circumstances surrounding it.

A. *The Religion then of every man must be left to the conviction and conscience of every man; and it is the right of every man to exercise it as these may dictate.*
B. *Who does not see that the same authority which can establish Christianity, in exclusion of all other Religions, may establish with the same ease any particular sect of Christians, in exclusion of all other Sects?*
C. *In all cases where a majority are united by a common interest or passion, the rights of the minority are in danger.*
D. *In a large Society, the people are broken into so many interests and parties, that a common sentiment is less likely to be felt . . . by a majority of the whole.*
E. *It is a melancholy reflection that liberty should be equally exposed to danger whether the Government have too much or too little power.*
F. *Public opinion sets bounds to every government, and is the real sovereign in every free one.*
G. *Religion flourishes in greater purity, without than with the aid of Government.*
H. *Knowledge will forever govern ignorance: And a people who mean to be their own Governors, must arm themselves with the power which knowledge gives.*
I. *Learned institutions ought to be favorite objects with every free people. They throw that light over the public mind which is the best security against crafty & dangerous encroachments on the public liberty.*
J. *Could it be so arranged that every newspaper, when printed on one side, should be handed over to the press of an adversary, to be printed on the other, thus presenting to every reader both sides of every question, truth would always have a fair chance.*
K. *Perhaps it is a universal truth that the loss of liberty at home is to be charged to provisions against danger, real or pretended, from abroad.*

CHAPTER 12

THOMAS JEFFERSON

BACKGROUND

In the early days of United States history Thomas Jefferson (1743-1826) was not only an important political leader, he was also one of the nation's most influential political philosophers. Although he was a man of several contradictions, he was also a man of great vision, and his role in the creation of the United States should not be underrated. His ideas played a prominent role in shaping the new nation. In fact, many people still use his ideas to define America's political character.

Jefferson was a man of tremendous intellectual curiosity. He studied science, natural history, classical literature, philosophy, music, art, logic, ethics, law, and Latin. In addition to his intellectual pursuits, he was a farmer, an architect, an inventor, and a politician.

Throughout his long public career he served as a member of the Virginia House of Burgesses, governor of Virginia, minister to France, secretary of state, vice president, and president of the United States. As a member of the Second Continental Congress he was the chief author of the Declaration of Independence. Few Americans contributed as much to the creation of the United States as Thomas Jefferson.

Jefferson lived a life of privilege. He loved good books, fine wine, and French cuisine. He was also infatuated with gadgets. His home at Monticello contained many of his favorite creations such as a dumbwaiter, special serving shelves, and an eight-day clock.

Many of Jefferson's contemporaries referred to him as thin-skinned, touchy, and humorless. He was also criticized for his inability to confront people with whom he disagreed; he hated face-to-face confrontations. Today he is sometimes denounced for his less-than-enlightened attitude regarding African-Americans and women.

A modern visitor to Jefferson's home at Monticello can view his grave and read the epitaph he wrote for himself. The words on his tombstone describe him simply as the author of the Declaration of Independence, the author of the Virginia Statute of Religious Freedom, and the father of the University of Virginia.

THOMAS JEFFERSON – IN HIS OWN WORDS

The Declaration of Independence, July 1776

We hold these truths to be self-evident, that all men are created equal, that they are endowed by their Creator with certain unalienable Rights, that among these are Life, Liberty, and the pursuit of Happiness. That to secure these rights, Governments are instituted among Men, deriving their just powers from the consent of the governed. That whenever any Form of Government becomes destructive of these ends, it is the Right of the People to alter or to abolish it, and to institute new Government, laying its foundation on such principles and organizing its powers in such form, as to them shall seem most likely to effect their Safety and Happiness. Prudence, indeed, will dictate that Governments long established should not be changed for light and transient causes; and accordingly all experience hath shown, that mankind are more disposed to suffer, while evils are sufferable, than to right themselves by abolishing the forms to which they are accustomed. But when a long train of abuses and usurpations, pursuing invariably the same Object evinces a design to reduce them under absolute Despotism, it is their right, it is their duty, to throw off such Government, and to provide new Guards for their future security.

Notes on Virginia (Query XVII), 1781

The legitimate powers of government extend to such acts only as are injurious to others. But it does me no injury for my neighbor to say there are twenty gods, or no God. It neither picks my pocket nor breaks my leg. If it be said, his testimony in a court of justice cannot be relied on, reject it then, and be the stigma on him. Constraint may make him worse by making him a hypocrite, but it will never make him a truer man. It may fix him obstinately in his errors, but will not cure them. Reason and free inquiry are the only effectual agents against error. Give a loose to them, they will support the true religion by bringing every false one to their tribunal, to the test of their investigation. They are the natural enemies of error, and of error only. Had not the Roman government permitted free inquiry, Christianity could never have been introduced. Had not free inquiry been indulged at the era of the Reformation, the corruptions of Christianity could not have been purged away. If it be restrained now, the present corruptions will be protected, and new ones encouraged. . . . It is error alone which needs the support of government. Truth can stand by itself. . . . Difference of opinion is advantageous in religion. The several sects perform the office of a *censor morum* over such other. Is uniformity attainable? Millions of innocent men, women, and children, since the introduction of Christianity, have been burnt, tortured, fined, imprisoned; yet we have not advanced one inch towards uniformity. What has been the effect of coercion? To make one half the world fools, and the other half hypocrites. To support roguery and error all over the earth. Let us reflect that it is inhabited by a thousand millions of people. That these profess probably a thousand different systems of religion.

That ours is but one of that thousand. That if there be but one right, and ours that one, we should wish to see the nine hundred and ninety-nine wandering sects gathered into the fold of truth. But against such a majority we cannot effect this by force. Reason and persuasion are the only practicable instruments. To make way for these, free inquiry must be indulged.

Notes on Virginia (Query XVIII), 1781

Our children see this, and learn to imitate it; for man is an imitative animal. This quality is the germ of all education in him. From his cradle to his grave he is learning to do what he sees others do. If a parent could find no motive either in his philanthropy or his self-love, for restraining the intemperance of passion towards his slave, it should always be a sufficient one that his child is present. But generally it is not sufficient. The parent storms, the child looks on, catches the lineaments of wrath, puts on the same airs in the circle of smaller slaves, gives a loose to the worst of passions, and thus nursed, educated, and daily exercised in tyranny, cannot but be stamped by it with odious peculiarities. The man must be a prodigy who can retain his manners and morals undepraved by such circumstances. And with what execration should the statesman be loaded, who, permitting one half the citizens thus to trample on the rights of the other, transforms those into despots, and these into enemies, destroys the morals of the one part, and the *amor patriae* of the other. . . . Indeed I tremble for my country when I reflect that God is just; that his justice cannot sleep forever; that considering numbers, nature and natural means only, a revolution of the wheel of fortune, an exchange of situation is among possible events; that it may become probably by supernatural interference!

Notes on Virginia (Query XIX), 1781

Those who labor in the earth are the chosen people of God, if ever He had a chosen people, whose breasts He has made his peculiar deposit for substantial and genuine virtue. It is the focus in which he keeps alive that sacred fire, which otherwise might escape from the face of the earth. Corruption of morals in the mass of cultivators is a phenomenon of which no age nor nation has furnished an example. . . . While we have land to labor then, let us never wish to see our citizens occupied at a workbench, or twirling a distaff. Carpenters, masons, smiths, are wanting in husbandry; but, for the general operations of manufacture, let our workshops remain in Europe. It is better to carry provisions and materials to workmen there, than bring them to the provisions and materials, and with them their manners and principles. The loss by the transportation of commodities across the Atlantic will be made up in happiness and permanence of government. The mobs of great cities add just so much to the support of pure government, as sores do to the strength of the human body. It is the manners and spirit of a people which preserve a republic in vigor. A degeneracy in these is a canker which soon eats to the heart of its laws and constitution.

Letter to George Wythe, August 1786
I think by far the most important bill in our whole code is that for the diffusion of knowledge, among the people. No other sure foundation can be devised for the preservation of freedom, and happiness. . . . Preach my dear Sir, a crusade against ignorance; establish and improve the law for educating the common people. Let our countrymen know that the people alone can protect us against these evils, and that the tax which will be paid for this purpose is not more than the thousandth part of what will be paid to kings, priests and nobles who will rise up among us if we leave the people in ignorance.

Letter to Colonel Edward Carrington, January 1787
The tumults in America, I expected would have produced in Europe an unfavorable opinion of our political state. But it has not. On the contrary, the small effect of these tumults seems to have given more confidence in the firmness of our governments. The interposition of the people themselves on the side of government has had a great effect on the opinion here. I am persuaded myself that the good sense of the people will always be found to be the best army. They may be led astray for a moment, but will soon correct themselves. The people are the only censors of their governors; and even their errors will tend to keep these to the true principles of their institution. To punish these errors too severely would be to suppress the only safeguard of the public liberty. The way to prevent these irregular interpositions of the people, is to give them full information of their affairs through the channel of the public papers, and to contrive that those papers should penetrate the whole mass of the people. The basis of our governments being the opinion of the people, the very first subject should be to keep that right; and were it left to me to decide whether we should have a government without newspapers, or newspapers without a government, I should not hesitate a moment to prefer the latter. But I should mean that every man should receive those papers, and be capable of reading them.

Letter to Colonel William Smith, November 1787
God forbid we should ever be twenty years without such a rebellion. The people cannot be all, and always, well informed. The part which is wrong will be discontented, in proportion to the importance of the facts they misconceive. If they remain quiet under such misconceptions, it is a lethargy, the forerunner of death to the public liberty. We have had thirteen States independent for eleven years. There has been one rebellion. That comes to one rebellion in a century and a half, for each State. What country before, ever existed a century and a half without a rebellion? And what country can preserve its liberties, if its rulers are not warned from time to time, that this people preserve the spirit of resistance? Let them take arms. The remedy is to see them right as to facts, pardon and pacify them. What signify a few lives lost in a century or two? The tree of liberty must be refreshed from time

to time, with the blood of patriots and tyrants. It is its natural manure.

Letter to James Madison, September 1789
The question whether one generation of men has a right to bind another, seems never to have been started either on this or our side of the water. Yet it is a question of such consequences as not only to merit decision, but place also among the fundamental principles of every government. The course of reflection in which we are immersed here, on the elementary principles of society, has presented this question to my mind; and that no such obligation can be transmitted, I think very capable of proof. I set out on this ground, which I suppose to be self-evident, that the *earth belongs in usufruct to the living*; that the dead have neither powers nor rights over it. The portion occupied by any individual ceases to be his when himself ceases to be, and reverts to the society. If the society has formed no rules for the appropriation of its lands in severality, it will be taken by the first occupants, and these will generally be the wife and children of the decedent. If they have formed rules of appropriation, those rules may give it to the wife and children, or to some one of them, or to the legatee of the deceased. So they may give it to its creditor. But the child, the legatee or creditor, takes it, not by natural right, but by a law of the society of which he is a member, and to which he is subject. Then, no man can, by *natural right*, oblige the lands he occupied, or the persons who succeed him in that occupation, to the payment of debts contracted by him. For if he could, he might during his own life, eat up the usufruct of the lands for several generations to come; and then the lands would belong to the dead, and not to the living, which is the reverse of our principle.

What is true of every member of the society, individually, is true of them all collectively; since the rights of the whole can be no more than the sum of the rights of the individuals. . . .

On similar ground it may be proved that no society can make a perpetual constitution, or even a perpetual law. The earth belongs always to the living generation. They may manage it then, and what proceeds from it, as they please, during their usufruct. They are masters too of their own persons, and consequently may govern them as they please. But persons and property make the sum of the objects of government. The constitution and the laws of their predecessors [are] extinguished then in their natural course with those who gave them being. This could preserve that being till it ceased to be itself, and no longer. Every constitution then, and every law, naturally expires at the end of 19 years. If it be enforced longer, it is an act of force, and not of right.

First Inaugural Address, 1801
All too, will bear in mind this sacred principle, that though the will of the majority is in all cases to prevail, that will, to be rightful, must be reasonable; that the minority possess their equal rights, which equal laws must protect,

and to violate which would be oppression. Let us, then, fellow citizens, unite with one heart and one mind. Let us restore to social intercourse that harmony and affection without which liberty and even life itself are but dreary things. And let us reflect that having banished from our land that religious intolerance under which mankind so long bled and suffered, we have yet gained little if we countenance a political intolerance as despotic, as wicked, and capable of as bitter and bloody persecutions. During the throes and convulsions of the ancient world, during the agonizing spasms of infuriated man, seeking through blood and slaughter his long-lost liberty, it was not wonderful that the agitations of the billows should reach even this distant and peaceful shore; that this should be more felt and feared by some and less by others; that this should divide opinions as to measures of safety. But every difference of opinion is not a difference of principle. We have called by different names brethren of the same principle. We are all republicans—we are all federalists. If there be any among us who would wish to dissolve this Union or to change its republican form, let them stand undisturbed as monuments of the safety with which error of opinion may be tolerated where reason is left free to combat it.

Letter to John Adams, October 1813

I agree with you that there is a natural aristocracy among men. The grounds of this are virtue and talents. Formerly, bodily powers gave place among the aristoi. But since the invention of gunpowder has armed the weak as well as the strong with missile death, bodily strength, like beauty, good humor, politeness and accomplishments, has become but an auxiliary ground of distinction. There is also an artificial aristocracy, founded on wealth and birth, without either virtue or talents; for with these it would belong to the first class. The natural aristocracy I consider as the most precious gift of nature, for the instruction, the trusts, and government of society. And indeed, it would have been inconsistent in creation to have formed man for the social state, and not to have provided virtue and wisdom enough to manage the concerns of the society. May we not even say, that the form of government is the best, which provides the most effectually for a pure selection of these natural aristoi into the offices of government?

Letter to Roger Weightman, June 1826

All eyes are opened, or opening to the rights of man. The general spread of the light of science has already laid open to every view the palpable truth, that the mass of mankind has not been born with saddles on their backs, nor a favored few booted and spurred, ready to ride them legitimately, by the grace of God. These are grounds of hope for others. For ourselves, let the annual return of this day forever refresh our recollections of these rights, and an undiminished devotion to them.

THOMAS JEFFERSON – A SIMULATED INTERVIEW

1. **What fundamental ideas should shape the power of government?**
   A. Government's powers should originate from the consent of the people. The United States should adopt a republican form of government.
   B. The people are the best instrument to judge the actions of government. Even when the people are wrong they should not be punished. Liberty is threatened whenever the people are punished.
   C. The government should follow the will of the majority in all cases.
   D. Government should protect rights to life, liberty, and the pursuit of happiness.
   E. Government has the legitimate power to regulate people who are injuring others. However, no one is injured when one person disagrees with another. Government should not regulate the expression of ideas.
   F. Government should be simple and frugal.
   G. Civilian authority should be superior to military authority.

2. **What principles should guide the writing of a constitution?**
   A. No generation should bind future generations to decisions of the past. A constitution should terminate when the persons who wrote it are dead. The world belongs to the living, and constitutions should expire after nineteen years.
   B. Since the states granted powers to the central government, the national constitution should allow the states to be the final judge of federal laws.
   C. Although the majority should rule, the minority should never be denied their rights. The United States should adopt a bill of rights to protect the rights of the minority.

3. **Should the government allow freedom of expression?**
   A. All people should be allowed freedom of expression. Society should be intolerant of intolerance.
   B. Rational people must be left free to expose false beliefs. Freedom of expression is the best way to destroy errors of opinion. A search for truth is helped by difference of opinion.

4. **Do the people have a right to rebel against the government?**
   A. A periodic rebellion is a good thing; political leaders should be reminded that the people still possess their spirit of resistance. In fact, the nation should not go twenty years without a rebellion.
   B. When the government does not protect rights the people have a right to alter or abolish the government.

    C. Government should not be changed because of a short-term abuse of power. Only a long-term misuse of power justifies change.

5. What role should slavery play in the United States?
    A. Slavery denies freedom and allows human beings to be treated as property. Slavery should be gradually abolished. Slavery threatens the long term success of the United States.
    B. After slavery is abolished slaves should be deported to Santo Domingo or Africa.

6. What role should education play in the United States?
    A. The freedom and happiness of the people depend on their level of education. The nation must crusade against ignorance.
    B. The people must be given honest information to assist them in carrying out civic duties. Freedom of the press is essential to the education of the people.

7. Should the United States have an aristocracy?
    A. Society has a natural aristocracy, an aristocracy of the virtuous and the talented. Society should turn to virtuous and talented individuals for leadership in government.
    B. The United States should develop an intellectual aristocracy, instead of an aristocracy based on birth and wealth. An educational system based upon free public education would produce a pool of talented individuals from which the people could select their leaders.

8. Should the United States promote an agricultural or a manufacturing economy?
    A. Farmers are God's chosen people. Agricultural societies are not easily corrupted.
    B. Manufacturing creates large cities. In turn, the mobs of large cities are a threat to good government. Cities unleash social forces that corrupt the morals of the people.
    C. The United States should preserve its agricultural society and resist the development of manufacturing. Manufactured goods can be purchased from Europe.
    D. For the United States to remain an agricultural society, the people must have access to land. The accumulation of large estates should therefore be prevented. Land should be made available to as many people as possible, and the requirement that inheritance be limited to the oldest male child should be abolished.
    E. The United States should expand and acquire new land for agrarian pursuits.

9. **What policy should the United States apply toward people in frontier regions?**
   A. People on the frontier should be given no reason to resent the federal government. Self-government should be permitted from the earliest days of territorial development.
   B. New states should be admitted to the United States on an equal basis with old states. The people of the new states should be granted first class citizenship.
   C. The United States should not allow slavery in the frontier regions.

STUDENT ACTIVITIES

Vocabulary
Define the following terms before reading the lesson on Jefferson.

1. *amor patriae*	10. distaff	19. prudence
2. aristoi	11. execration	20. roguery
3. billow	12. hypocrite	21. stigma
4. canker	13. intemperance	22. tribunal
5. *censor morum*	14. legatee	23. unalienable
6. contemporary	15. lethargy	24. usufruct
7. countenance	16. lineaments	25. usurpation
8. degeneracy	17. philanthropy	26. wrath
9. despotism	18. practicable	

Review Questions
1. What public offices were held by Thomas Jefferson?
2. What three accomplishments did Jefferson want listed on his tombstone?
3. Who should be the final judge of federal laws according to Jefferson?
4. How did Jefferson think minority rights should be protected?
5. According to Jefferson, what is the best way to fight errors of opinion?
6. According to Jefferson, what justifies a change of government?
7. What natural aristocracy did Jefferson think should govern society?
8. Why did Jefferson think that a farming society was superior to an industrial society?
9. Why did Jefferson want the United States to expand in geographic size?
10. Decide whether the following statements are **True** or **False** according to Thomas Jefferson.
    A. The United States should adopt a republican form of government.
    B. Government should follow the will of the majority in all cases.
    C. The government should regulate ideas that threaten the security of the community.
    D. Civilian authority should be superior to military authority.

    E. Government should be simple and frugal.
    F. Each generation should be free to write its own constitution.
    G. A periodic rebellion is a good thing.
    H. Freed slaves should be deported to Santo Domingo or Africa.
    I. Slavery should be allowed in frontier territories.
    J. New states should be admitted to the United States on an equal basis with old states.

What do you think?
On a scale of one through five, rate your opinion of the following quotations by Jefferson. Write a short statement explaining your rating.

1 – You **strongly agree** with the statement *or* you feel the statement is **admirable** considering the historical circumstances surrounding it.
5 – You **strongly disagree** with the statement *or* you feel the statement is **contemptible** considering the historical circumstances surrounding it.

A. *It does me no injury for my neighbor to say there are twenty gods, or no God. It neither picks my pocket nor breaks my leg.*
B. *[Reason and free inquiry] will support the true religion by bringing every false one to their tribunal.*
C. *Those who labor in the earth are the chosen people of God.*
D. *The tax which will be paid for the purpose of education is not more than the thousandth part of what will be paid to kings, priests and nobles who will rise up among us if we leave the people in ignorance.*
E. *Were it left to me to decide whether we should have a government without newspapers, or newspapers without a government, I should not hesitate a moment to prefer the latter.*
F. *The tree of liberty must be refreshed from time to time, with the blood of patriots and tyrants. It is its natural manure.*
G. *The earth belongs always to the living generation. . . . Every constitution then, and every law, naturally expires at the end of 19 years. If it be enforced longer, it is an act of force, and not of right.*
H. *If there be any among us who would wish to dissolve this Union or to change its republican form, let them stand undisturbed as monuments of the safety with which error of opinion may be tolerated where reason is left free to combat it.*
I. *There is a natural aristocracy among men. The grounds of this are virtue and talent.*
J. *The merchant has no country.*
K. *I hold it, that a little rebellion, now and then, is a good thing, and as necessary in the political world as storms in the physical.*
L. *When a man assumes a public trust, he should consider himself public property.*

CHAPTER 13

ALEXANDER HAMILTON

BACKGROUND

Alexander Hamilton (1755-1804) grew up as an illegitimate child in the West Indies. As an obviously bright young man he caught the attention of wealthy patrons who offered to finance his education. Agreeing to their offer, Hamilton left the West Indies when he was seventeen and moved to New York. His life after moving to New York is evidence that men of humble ancestry could succeed in early America.

By the time he was nineteen he had gained recognition as a writer of anti-British pamphlets and as a soldier in the Revolutionary Army. He caught the attention of General George Washington and joined Washington's staff where he served with distinction. However, his impulsiveness and short temper eventually led to a separation from Washington. Hamilton left the army in 1781.

After the war Hamilton joined a campaign to strengthen the national government. He played a key role in the movement that led to the Constitutional Convention. However, as a delegate to the convention he played a relatively minor role. Although he was privately critical of the work done at the convention, he publicly supported the Constitution and devoted all his energies to its ratification. To win support of the Constitution he enlisted James Madison and John Jay to help write a series of essays. These essays were later combined into a book known as *The Federalist Papers,* a book that became the era's best-known analysis of the Constitution.

In 1789 President Washington asked Hamilton to serve as secretary of the treasury. In that position Hamilton successfully strengthened the nation's finances. In spite of his success, many prominent leaders, such as Thomas Jefferson, emphatically disagreed with Hamilton's policies. From this disagreement the nation's first two political parties emerged. Supporters of Hamilton were known as Federalists; supporters of Jefferson were known as Democratic-Republicans.

After Hamilton left the cabinet in 1795 he practiced law and promoted the Federalist party in New York. His lifelong service to the nation ended prematurely in 1804 when he was killed in a duel with Vice President Aaron Burr.

ALEXANDER HAMILTON – IN HIS OWN WORDS

"A Full Vindication of the Measures of Congress," 1774

The only distinction between freedom and slavery consists in this: In the former state, a man is governed by the laws to which he has given his consent, either in person, or by his representative: in the latter, he is governed by the will of another. In the one case his life and property are his own, in the other, they depend upon the pleasure of a master. It is easy to discern which of these two states is preferable. No man in his senses can hesitate in choosing to be free, rather than a slave.

That Americans are entitled to freedom, is incontestible upon every rational principle. All men have one common original: they participate in one common nature, and consequently have one common right. No reason can be assigned why one man should exercise any power, or preeminence over his fellow creatures more than another; unless they have voluntarily vested him with it.

"The Farmer Refuted," 1775

Upon this [natural] law, depend the natural rights of mankind, the Supreme Being gave existence to man, together with the means of preserving and beautifying that existence. He endowed him with rational faculties, by the help of which, to discern and pursue such things, as were consistent with his duty and interest, and invested him with an inviolable right to personal liberty, and personal safety.

Hence, in a state of nature, no man had any *moral* power to deprive another of his life, limbs, property or liberty; nor the least authority to command, or exact obedience from him; except that which arose from the ties of consanguinity.

Hence also, the origin of all civil government, justly established, must be a voluntary compact, between the rulers and the ruled; and must be liable to such limitations, as are necessary for the security of the *absolute rights* of the latter; for what original title can any man or set of men have, to govern others, except their own consent? To usurp dominion over a people, in their own despite, or to grasp at a more extensive power than they are willing to intrust, is to violate that law of nature, which gives every man a right to his personal liberty; and can, therefore, confer no obligation to obedience.

Letter to James Duane, September 1780

The fundamental defect [of the Articles of Confederation] is a want of power in Congress. . . . It may however be said that it has originated from three causes—an excess of the spirit of liberty which has made the particular states show a jealousy of all power not in their own hands . . . this jealousy has led them to exercise a right of judging in the last resort of the measures recommended by Congress . . . a want of sufficient means at their disposal to answer the public exigencies and of vigor to draw forth those means . . . .

. . . Congress had never any definitive powers granted them and of course could exercise none—could do nothing more than recommend. The manner in which Congress was appointed would warrant, and the public good required, that they should have considered themselves as vested with full power *to preserve the republic from harm*. They have done many of the highest acts of sovereignty, which were always cheerfully submitted to . . . all these implications of a complete sovereignty were never disputed, and ought to have been a standard for the whole conduct of Administration. Undefined powers are discretionary powers, limited only by the object for which they were given—in the present case, the independence and freedom of America. The confederation made no difference; for as it has not been generally adopted, it had no operation. . . .

But the confederation itself is defective and requires to be altered, it is neither fit for war, nor peace. The idea of an uncontrollable sovereignty in each state, over its internal police, will defeat the other powers given to Congress, and make our union feeble and precarious. There are instances without number, where acts necessary for the general good, and which rise out of the powers given to Congress must interfere with the internal police of the states, and there are as many instances in which the particular states by arrangements of internal police can effectually though indirectly counteract the arrangements of Congress.

The Continentalist II, 1781

In a single state, where the sovereign power is exercised by delegation, whether it be a limited monarchy or a republic, the danger most commonly is, that the sovereign will become too powerful for his constituents; in federal governments, where states are represented in a general council, the danger is on the other side—that the members will be an overmatch for his common head, or in other words, that it will not have sufficient influence and authority to secure the obedience of the several parts of the confederacy. . . .

From the plainest principles of human nature, two inferences are to be drawn, one, that each member of a political confederacy, will be more disposed to advance its own authority upon the ruins of that of the confederacy, than to make any improper concessions in its favour, or support it in unreasonable pretensions; the other, that the subjects of each member, will be more devoted in the attachments and obedience to their own particular governments, than to that of the union. . . .

The particular governments will have more empire over the minds of their subjects, than the general one, because their agency will be more direct, more uniform, and more apparent.

The Continentalist VI, 1782

A mere regard to the interests of the confederacy will never be a principle sufficiently active to crush the ambition and intrigues of different members.

Force cannot effect it. A contest of arms will seldom be between the common sovereign and a single refractory member, but between distinct combinations of the several parts against each other. A sympathy of situations will be apt to produce associates to the disobedient. The application of force is always disagreeable—the issue uncertain. It will be wise to obviate the necessity of it by interesting such a number of individuals in each state, in support of the federal government, as will be counterpoised to the ambition of others, and will make it difficult for them to unite the people in opposition to the first and necessary measures of the Union.

There is something noble and magnificent in the perspective of a great federal republic, closely linked in the pursuit of a common interest—tranquil and prosperous at home, respectable abroad. But there is something proportionably diminutive and contemptible in the prospect of a number of petty states, with the appearance only of union, jarring, jealous, and perverse, without any determined direction, fluctuating and unhappy at home, weak and insignificant by their dissensions in the eyes of other nations.

Happy America, if those to whom thou has entrusted the guardianship of thy infancy know how to provide for thy future repose, but miserable and undone if their negligence or ignorance permits the spirit of discord to erect her banner on the ruins of thy tranquility!

"On the Treatment of Loyalists," 1784

It is, however, a common observation that men bent upon mischief are more active in the pursuit of their object than those who aim at doing good. Hence it is, in the present moment, we see the most industrious efforts made to violate the constitution of this state, to trample upon the rights of the subject . . . while dispassionate and upright men almost totally neglect the means of counteracting these dangerous attempts. . . .

Nothing is more common than for a free people, in times of heat and violence, to gratify momentary passions by letting into the government principles and precedents which afterwards prove fatal to themselves. Of this kind is the doctrine of disqualification, disfranchisement, and banishment, by acts of legislature. The dangerous consequences of this power are manifest. If the legislature can disfranchise any number of citizens at pleasure by general descriptions, it may soon confine all the votes to a small number of partisans, and establish an aristocracy or an oligarchy. If it may banish at discretion all those whom particular circumstances render obnoxious without hearing or trial, no man can be safe nor know when he may be the innocent victim of a prevailing faction. The name of liberty applied to such a government would be a mockery of common sense. . . .

. . . No citizen can be deprived of any right which the citizens in general are entitled to, unless forfeited by some offense. It has been seen that the regular and constitutional mode of ascertaining whether this forfeiture has been incurred is by legal process, trial, and conviction. . . .

Viewing the subject in every possible light, there is not a single interest of the community but dictates moderation rather than violence. That honesty is still the best policy; that justice and moderation are the surest supports of every government—are maxims which, however they may be called trite, are at all times true: though too seldom regarded, but rarely neglected with impunity. Were the people of America, with one voice, to ask, "What shall we do to perpetuate our liberties and secure our happiness?" the answer would be, "Govern well," and you have nothing to fear, either from internal disaffection or external hostility. Abuse not the power you possess, and you need never apprehend its diminution or loss. But if you make a wanton use of it; if you furnish another example, that despotism may debase the government of the many as well as the few; you, like all others that have acted the same part, will experience that licentiousness is the forerunner to slavery.

Speech at the Constitutional Convention, 1787 (From James Madison's Notes)

The English model was the only good one on this subject [of forming a government]. The hereditary interest of the king was so interwoven with that of the nation, and his personal emoluments so great, that he was placed above the danger of being corrupted from abroad—and at the same time was both sufficiently independent and sufficiently controlled, to answer the purpose of the institution at home. One of the weak sides of republics was their being liable to foreign influence & corruption. Men of little character, acquiring great power become easily the tools of intermeddling neighbors . . . What is the inference from all these observations? That we ought to go as far in order to attain stability and permanence, as republican principles will admit. Let one branch of the Legislature hold their places for life or at least during good behavior. Let the Executive also be for life.

Report on Credit, 1790

In a country, which, like this, is possessed of little active wealth, or in other words, little monied capital, the necessity for the resource, must, in such emergencies, be proportionably urgent.

And as on the one hand, the necessity for borrowing in particular emergencies cannot be doubted, so on the other, it is equally evident, that to be able to borrow upon *good terms*, it is essential that the credit of a nation should be well established. . . .

. . . A general belief, accordingly, prevails, that the credit of the United States will quickly be established on the firm foundation of an effectual provision for the existing debt.

Report on Manufactures, 1791

It ought to be conceded that the cultivation of the earth—as the primary and most certain source of national supply—as the immediate and chief source of subsistence to man—as the principal source of those materials which constitute the nutriment of other kinds of labor—as including a state most favourable to the freedom and independence of the human mind—one, perhaps, most conducive to the multiplication of the human species—has *intrinsically a strong claim to pre-eminence over every other kind of industry.* . . .

. . . Tillage ought to be no obstacle to listening to any substantial inducements to the encouragement of manufactures, which may be otherwise perceived to exist, through an apprehension; that they may have a tendency to divert labour from a more to a less profitable employment. . . .

To affirm, that the labour of the Manufacturer is unproductive, because he consumes as much of the produce of land, as he adds value to the raw materials which he manufactures, is not better founded, than it would be to affirm, that the labour of the farmer, which furnishes materials to the manufacturer is unproductive, *because he consumes an equal value of manufactured articles.* Each furnishes a certain portion of the produce of his labor to the other, and each destroys a correspondent portion of the produce of the labour of the other. In the mean time the maintenance of two Citizens, instead of one, is going on; the State has two members instead of one; and they together consume twice the value of what is produced from the land.

"Opinion on the Constitutionality of the Bank," 1791

It may be truly said of every government, as well as of that of the United States, that it has only a right to pass such laws as are necessary & proper to accomplish the objects entrusted to it. For no government has a right to do *merely what it pleases.* . . .

It is no valid objection to the doctrine to say, that it is calculated to extend the powers of the general government throughout the entire sphere of State legislation. The same thing has been said, and may be said with regard to every exercise of power by *implication* or *construction.* The moment the literal meaning is departed from, there is a chance of error and abuse. And yet an adherence to the letter of its powers would at once arrest the motions of the government. It is not only agreed, on all hands, that the exercise of constructive powers is indispensable, but every act which has been passed is more or less an exemplification of it.

But the doctrine which is contended for is not chargeable with the consequence imputed to it. It does not affirm that the National government is sovereign in all respects, but that it is sovereign to a certain extent: that is, to the extent of the objects of its specified powers.

It leaves therefore a criterion of what is constitutional, and what is not so. This criterion is the *end* to which the measure relates as a *mean.* If the end be clearly comprehended within any of the specified powers, & if the measure have an obvious relation to that end, and is not forbidden by any particular provision of the constitution—it may safely be deemed to come within the compass of the national authority. There is also this further criterion which may materially assist the decision. Does the proposed measure abridge a pre-existing right of any State, or of any individual? If it does not, there is a strong presumption in favour of its constitutionality.

ALEXANDER HAMILTON – A SIMULATED INTERVIEW

1. **What is human nature?**
   A. Human beings possess the ability to think rationally.
   B. Human beings do not think rationally when they are part of a mob.
   C. Human beings who wish to do evil are more active than those who wish to do good.
   D. Human beings naturally desire freedom.

2. **What are the best and worst types of government?**
   A. Democracy is an undesirable form of government. Democracy creates an ungovernable mob that is incapable of rational deliberation. Aristocracy is preferable to democracy.
   B. Republican government is often unstable. Stability is essential to protect the nation from corruption and foreign influence.
   C. The best government is a republican government that does not allow the people to influence elected officials directly. Government officials should form public policy for the common good without having to satisfy the passions of the people.

3. **The powers of government should be based upon what fundamental ideas?**
   A. The purpose of government is to protect the rights of the governed. All human beings possess the right to personal freedom and safety. No individual should be denied his rights unless he commits a crime against society.
   B. Government must be based upon a voluntary contract between the rulers and the ruled.
   C. Government should act for the common good and benefit society as a whole. All classes of people benefit from good government.

4. **What basic ideas should Americans consider when writing a constitution?**
   A. The federal government should be more powerful than state governments for several reasons:
      1. If too much power is granted to the states, each state will have a tendency to promote its own interests over the interests of the nation.
      2. A strong federal government will promote peace within the nation. A weak federal government will allow pettiness and jealousy between the states.
      3. A strong union of the states will win the respect of other nations. All Americans will benefit when the federal government protects national security.

    B. The federal government should be granted clear-cut, centralized powers:
1. Presidents and Senators should be elected for life.
2. The President should appoint state governors.
3. State laws contrary to the laws of the federal government should be invalid.

5. What laws of the federal government are constitutional?
    A. The congressional power to make laws that are "necessary and proper" does not give the government the power to do what it pleases. Only the laws that are "necessary and proper" within areas delegated to federal jurisdiction are constitutional. Issues under federal jurisdiction are those relating to war, peace, trade, finances, and foreign affairs.
    B. No law is constitutional that limits the pre-existing rights of any state or individual.

6. How should the United States strengthen its financial situation?
    A. A nation should be able to borrow money in an emergency. All nations therefore need to establish good credit, and the best way to establish credit is to pay toward existing debts.
    B. A national bank is needed to stabilize the nation's currency. The national bank should not only control the currency of the nation, but also extend financial credit to the federal government.

7. Should the United States promote an agricultural economy or a manufacturing economy?
    A. Agriculture is essential to human existence as well as the economic health of the nation. The United States should work to enrich its farming economy.
    B. Manufacturing would strengthen the American economy. Manufacturing should be encouraged with government aid.
    C. A diverse economy best serves the national interest. The United States should promote both agricultural production and manufacturing.

8. What is essential to the long term success of the United States?
    A. Stability in government is vital to the success of any nation. Wealthy people most likely desire stability. Wealthy people must therefore be given a strong voice in shaping public policy.
    B. Individual Americans should learn to sacrifice self-interest for the national interest. Each individual is better off when obeying the commands of the community as a whole.

STUDENT ACTIVITIES

Vocabulary
Define the following terms before reading the lesson on Hamilton.

1.	compact	10.	disfranchise	19.	obviate
2.	conducive	11.	dispassionate	20.	preeminence
3.	confederation	12.	dominion	21.	pretension
4.	consanguinity	13.	exigency	22.	refractory
5.	consent	14.	inference	23.	repose
6.	criterion	15.	intermeddle	24.	sovereignty
7.	debase	16.	intrigue	25.	tillage
8.	despotism	17.	licentiousness	26.	trite
9.	discretionary	18.	maxim	27.	usurp

Review

1. Why did Hamilton leave the West Indies, where he was born, and go to New York?
2. What role did Hamilton play during the American Revolution?
3. What role did Hamilton play in the Constitutional Convention?
4. Who did Hamilton enlist to help write *The Federalist Papers*?
5. What role did Hamilton play in Washington's presidency?
6. What political party supported Hamilton?
7. What political party opposed Hamilton?
8. How did Hamilton view human nature?
9. Why did Hamilton think that both democracies and republics were undesirable?
10. According to Hamilton, what is the best form of government?
11. What powers should be granted to the federal government?
12. What issues should be under federal jurisdiction?
13. Why should wealthy persons have a strong voice in shaping public policy?
14. Decide whether the following statements are **True** or **False** according to Alexander Hamilton.
    A. A powerful state government is likely to promote its own interests over the nation's interests.
    B. A strong federal government will promote peace within the nation.
    C. A strong national union will win the respect of other nations.
    D. The United States should avoid a national debt in all situations.
    E. A national bank is needed to stabilize the nation's currency.
    F. Manufacturing should be encouraged with government aid.
    G. The United States should promote industry at the expense of agriculture.
    H. Each individual is better off when obeying the commands of the community as a whole.

What do you think?
On a scale of one through five, rate your opinion of the following quotations by Hamilton. Write a short statement explaining your rating.

1 – You **strongly agree** with the statement *or* you feel the statement is **admirable** considering the historical circumstances surrounding it.
5 – You **strongly disagree** with the statement *or* you feel the statement is **contemptible** considering the historical circumstances surrounding it.

A. *No reason can be assigned why one man should exercise any power, or preeminence over his fellow creatures more than another; unless they have voluntarily vested him with it.*

B. *The particular governments* [state governments] *will have more empire over the minds of their subjects, than the general one* [national government], *because their agency will be more direct, more uniform, and more apparent.*

C. *It is, however, a common observation that men bent upon mischief are more active in the pursuit of their object than those who aim at doing good.*

D. *Nothing is more common than for a free people, in times of heat and violence, to gratify momentary passions by letting into the government principles and precedents which afterwards prove fatal to themselves.*

E. *That honesty is still the best policy; that justice and moderation are the surest supports of every government—are maxims which, however they may be called trite, are at all times true.*

F. *Were the people of America, with one voice, to ask, "What shall we do to perpetuate our liberties and secure our happiness?" the answer would be, "Govern well," and you have nothing to fear, either from internal disaffection or external hostility.*

G. *It may be truly said of every government . . . that it has only a right to pass such laws as are necessary and proper to accomplish the objects entrusted to it. For no government has a right to do merely what it pleases.*

H. *Self-preservation is the first principle of our nature.*

I. *Constitutions should consist only of general provisions; the reason is that they must necessarily be permanent, and that they cannot possibly calculate for the possible change of things.*

J. *Your people sir, is a great beast.*

K. *The process of election (by the electoral college) affords a moral certainty that the office of President will never fall to the lot of any man who is not in an eminent degree endowed with the requisite qualifications.*

L. *Take mankind in general; they are vicious, their passions may be operated upon.*

CHAPTER 14

JOHN MARSHALL

BACKGROUND

After President John Adams lost the election of 1800 he worked with members of the Federalist Party to pack the judicial branch with Federalist judges. Making appointments during literally the last hours of his presidency, Adams chose John Marshall (1755-1835) to serve as chief justice. Marshall therefore obtained his appointment to the Supreme Court in 1801 as a "midnight judge." He served on the Supreme Court until his death thirty-four years later.

Before joining the Supreme Court, Marshall had served as a soldier in the American Revolution, a member of the Virginia assembly, a minister to France during the XYZ affair, a member of the House of Representatives, and as secretary of state under John Adams. In spite of Marshall's years of public service there was little indication he would play such an important role in shaping the American legal system. He had almost no formal education, and although he was licensed to practice law, he had studied law for only six weeks.

Shaped in his youth by the Virginia frontier, Marshall reportedly displayed a plain, but dignified, manner. In describing Marshall a colleague once said, "I love his laugh—it is too hearty for an intriguer; and his good temper and unwearied patience are equally agreeable on the bench and in the study." All told, Marshall was an intelligent, amiable, and good-hearted man who exhibited only one deep-rooted prejudice—he detested his cousin Thomas Jefferson.

Before Marshall became chief justice, the Supreme Court was considered lacking in "weight" and "respect." Marshall, however, used his powers effectively to advance his beliefs in national supremacy, private property, and judicial review. He helped clarify the areas of the Constitution that were vague. He also played a key role in adding to the powers of the Constitution as well as to the powers of the Supreme Court. Under Marshall's leadership the Supreme Court asserted its right to decide ultimately whether the acts of government were constitutional. After his long tenure no one would ever again doubt the importance of the Supreme Court.

JOHN MARSHALL – IN HIS OWN WORDS

Speech on the Fairness and Jurisdiction of the Federal Courts, June 1788

How disgraceful is it that the State Courts cannot be trusted, says the Honorable Gentleman! What is the language of the constitution? Does it take away their jurisdiction? Is it not necessary that the Federal Courts should have cognizance of cases arising under the constitution, and the laws of the United States? What is the service or purpose of a Judiciary, but to execute the laws in a peaceable orderly manner, without shedding blood, or creating a contest, or availing yourselves of force? If this be the case, where can its jurisdiction be more necessary than here? To what quarter will you look for protection from an infringement on the constitution, if you will not give the power to the Judiciary? There is no other body that can afford such a protection.

Marbury v. Madison, 1803

The constitution vests the whole judicial power of the United States in one supreme court, and such inferior courts as congress shall, from time to time, ordain and establish. . . .

The question, whether an act, repugnant to the constitution, can become the law of the land, is a question deeply interesting to the United States; but, happily, not of an intricacy proportioned to its interest. It seems only necessary to recognize certain principles, supposed to have been long and well established, to decide it. That the people have an original right to establish, for their future government, such principles as, in their opinion, shall most conduce to their own happiness, is the basis on which the whole American fabric has been erected. The exercise of this original right is a very great exertion; nor can it, nor ought it, to be frequently repeated. The principles, therefore, so established, are deemed fundamental. And as the authority from which they proceed is supreme, and can seldom act, they are designed to be permanent.

This original and supreme will organizes the government, and assigns to different departments their respective powers. It may either stop here, or establish certain limits not to be transcended by those departments. The government of the United States is of the latter description. The powers of the legislature are defined and limited; and that those limits may not be mistaken, or forgotten, the constitution is written. To what purpose are powers limited, and to what purpose is that limitation committed to writing, if these limits may, at any time, be passed by those intended to be restrained? The distinction between a government with limited and unlimited powers is abolished, if those limits do not confine the persons on whom they are imposed, and if acts prohibited and acts allowed, are of equal obligation. It is a proposition too plain to be contested, that the constitution controls any legislative act repugnant to it; or, that the legislature may alter the constitution by an ordinary act. . . .

Certainly, all those who have framed written constitutions contemplate them as forming the fundamental and paramount law of the nation, and consequently, the theory of every such government must be, that an act of the legislature, repugnant to the constitution, is void. This theory is essentially attached to a written constitution, and is, consequently, to be considered, by this court, as one of the fundamental principles of our society. It is not, therefore, to be lost sight of, in the further consideration of this subject. . . .

It is, emphatically, the province and duty of the judicial department, to say what the law is. Those who apply the rule to particular cases, must of necessity expound and interpret that rule. If two laws conflict with each other, the courts must decide on the operation of each. So, if a law be in opposition to the constitution; if both the law and the constitution apply to a particular case, so that the court must either decide that case, conformably to the law, disregarding the constitution; or conformably to the constitution, disregarding the law; the court must determine which of these conflicting rules governs the case. This is of the very essence of judicial duty. If then, the courts are to regard the constitution, and the constitution is superior to any ordinary act of the legislature, the constitution, and not such ordinary act, must govern the case to which they both apply.

Those, then, who controvert the principle that the constitution is to be considered in court as a paramount law, are reduced to the necessity of maintaining that courts must close their eyes on the constitution, and see only the law. This doctrine would subvert the very foundation of all written constitutions. It would declare that an act which, according to the principles and theory of our government, is entirely void, is yet, in practice, completely obligatory. It would declare, that if the legislature shall do what is expressly forbidden, such act notwithstanding the express prohibition, is in reality effectual. It would be giving to the legislature a practical and real omnipotence, with the same breath which professes to restrict their powers within narrow limits. It is prescribing limits, and declaring that those limits may be passed at pleasure. . . .

The judicial power of the United States is extended to all cases arising under the constitution. . . .

It is also not entirely unworthy of observation, that in declaring what shall be the supreme law of the land, the constitution itself is first mentioned; and not the laws of the United States generally, but those only which shall be made in pursuance of the constitution, have that rank.

Thus, the particular phraseology of the constitution of the United States confirms and strengthens the principle, supposed to be essential to all written constitutions, that a law repugnant to the constitution is void; and that courts, as well as other departments, are bound by that instrument.

McCulloch v. Maryland, 1819

This government is acknowledged by all, to be one of enumerated powers. The principle, that it can exercise only the powers granted to it, would seem too apparent, to have required to be enforced by all those arguments, which its enlightened friends, while it was depending before the people, found it necessary to urge. That principle is now universally admitted. But the question respecting the extent of the powers actually granted, is perpetually arising, and will probably continue to arise, so long as our system shall exist. . . .

If any one proposition could command the universal assent of mankind, we might expect it would be this—that the government of the Union, though limited in its powers, is supreme within its sphere of action. This would seem to result, necessarily, from its nature. It is the government of all; its powers are delegated by all; it represents all, and acts for all. Though any one state may be willing to control its operations, no state is willing to allow others to control them. The nation, on those subjects on which it can act, must necessarily bind its component parts. . . . The government of the United States, then, though limited in its powers, is supreme; and its laws, when made in pursuance of the constitution, form the supreme law of the land, "anything in the constitution or laws of any state to the contrary notwithstanding." . . .

But the Constitution of the United States has not left the right of Congress to employ the necessary means, for the execution of the powers conferred on the government, to general reasoning. To its enumeration of powers is added, that of making "all laws which shall be necessary and proper, for carrying into execution the foregoing powers, and all the other powers vested by this constitution, in the government of the United States, or in any department thereof." . . .

Congress is not empowered by it to make laws, which may have relation to the powers conferred on the government, but such only as may be *"necessary and proper"* for carrying them into execution. The word *"necessary"* is considered as controlling the whole sentence, and as limiting the right to pass laws for the execution of the granted powers, to such as are indispensable, and without which the power would be nugatory. That it excludes the choice of means, and leaves to Congress, in each case, that only which is most direct and simple. . . .

It being the opinion of the Court, that the act incorporating the bank is constitutional; and that the power of establishing a branch in the State of Maryland might be properly exercised by the bank itself, we proceed to inquire—

Whether the state of Maryland may, without violating the constitution, tax that branch? . . .

That the power to tax involves the power to destroy; that the power to destroy may defeat and render useless the power to create; that there is a plain repugnance in conferring on one government a power to control the constitutional measures of another, which other, with respect to those very measures, is declared to be supreme over that which exerts the control, are propositions not to be denied. But all inconsistencies are to be reconciled by the magic of the word *confidence.* Taxation, it is said, does not necessarily and unavoidably destroy. To carry it to the excess of destruction, would be an abuse, to presume which, would banish that confidence which is essential to all government. But is this a case of confidence? Would the people of any one State trust those of another with a power to control the most insignificant operations of their State government? We know they would not. Why, then, should we suppose that the people of any one State should be willing to trust those of another with a power to control the operations of a government to which they have confided their most important and most valuable interests? In the legislature of the Union alone, are all represented. The legislature of the Union alone, therefore, can be trusted by the people with the power of controlling measures which concern all, in the confidence that it will not be abused. This, then, is not a case of confidence, and we must consider it as it really is.

Cohens v. Virginia, 1821

The American States, as well as the American people, have believed a close and firm Union to be essential to their liberty and to their happiness. They have been taught by experience that this Union cannot exist without a government for the whole; and they have been taught by the same experience that this government would be a mere shadow, that must disappoint all their hopes, unless invested with large portions of that sovereignty which belongs to independent States. Under the influence of this opinion, and thus instructed by experience, the American people, in the conventions of their respective States, adopted the present constitution. . . .

But a constitution is framed for ages to come, and is designed to approach immortality as nearly as human institutions can approach it. Its course cannot always be tranquil. It is exposed to storms and tempests, and its framers must be unwise statesmen, indeed, if they have not provided it, as far as its nature will permit, with the means of self-preservation from the perils it may be destined to encounter. No government ought to be so defective in its organization, as not to contain within itself the means of securing the execution of its own laws against other dangers than those which occur every day. Courts of justice are the means most usually employed; and it is reasonable to expect that a government should repose on its own Courts, rather than on others. There is certainly nothing in the circumstances under which our constitution was formed; nothing in the history of the times, which would justify the opinion that the confidence reposed in the States was so implicit as to leave in them and their tribunals the power of resisting or defeating, in the form of law, the legitimate measures of the Union. . . . We are told, and we are truly told, that the great change which is to give efficacy to the present system, is its ability to act on individuals directly, instead of acting through the instrumentality of state governments. But, ought not this ability, in reason and sound policy, to be applied directly to the protection of individuals employed in the execution of the laws, as well as to their coercion? . . .

It is very true that, whenever hostility to the existing system shall become universal, it will be also irresistible. The people made the constitution, and the people can unmake it. It is the creature of their will, and lives only by their will. But this supreme and irresistible power to make or to unmake resides only in the whole body of the people; not in any subdivision of them. The attempt of any of the parts to exercise it is usurpation, and ought to be repelled by those to whom the people have delegated their power of repelling it. . . .

That the United States form, for many, and for most important purposes, a single nation, has not yet been denied. In war, we are one people. In making peace, we are one people. In all commercial regulations, we are one and the same people. In many other respects, the American people are one; and the government which is alone capable of controlling and managing their interests, in all these respects, is the government of the Union. It is their government, and in that character they have no other. America has chosen to be, in many respects, and to many purposes, a nation; and for all these purposes her government is complete; to all these objects, it is competent. The people have declared, that in the exercise of all powers given for these objects, it is supreme. It can, then, in effecting these objects, legitimately control all individuals or governments within the American territory. The constitution and laws of a State, so far as they are repugnant to the constitution and laws of the United States, are absolutely void. These States are constituent parts of the United States. They are members of one great empire—for some purposes sovereign, for some purposes subordinate.

Barron v. Baltimore, 1833

The 5th amendment must be understood as restraining the power of the general government, not as applicable to the States. In their several constitutions they have imposed such restrictions on their respective governments as their own wisdom suggested; such as they deemed most proper for themselves. It is a subject on which they judge exclusively, and with which others interfere no further than they are supposed to have a common interest. . . .

Had the people of the several States, or any of them required changes in their constitutions; had they required additional safeguards to liberty from the apprehended encroachments of their particular governments; the remedy was in their own hands, and would have been applied by themselves. . . . Had the framers of these amendments intended them to be limitations on the powers of the state governments, they would have imitated the framers of the original constitution, and have expressed that intention. Had congress engaged in the extraordinary occupation of improving the constitutions of the several States by affording the people additional protection from the exercise of power by their own governments in matters which concerned themselves alone, they would have declared this purpose in plain and intelligible language.

JOHN MARSHALL – A SIMULATED INTERVIEW

1. **What principles should guide the writing of a constitution?**
   A. The people of a nation possess the right to make a constitution according to fundamental and permanent principles favorable to human happiness.
   B. A constitution should not be created just for the generation that writes it; a constitution should also serve future generations. A constitution is designed to be permanent.
   C. The people of a nation make a constitution, and they have the right to get rid of it. The U.S. Constitution, however, can only be replaced by the people of the entire nation. It cannot be replaced by "subdivisions" of the people.

2. **How much power does the U.S. Constitution grant the federal government?**
   A. The framers of any constitution must provide the means of preserving their constitution when it is exposed to the "storms and tempests" of history. Accordingly, the Constitution grants Congress the power to make laws that are "necessary and proper."
   B. Congress does not have the right to make *any* law. Congress may only make laws necessary to executing its assigned powers.
   C. Since the Constitution is the supreme law of the nation, Congress does not have the power to change the Constitution's meaning with ordinary legislation. Only an amendment can change the Constitution.
   D. Any act of the federal government contrary to the Constitution should not be allowed.

3. **What role does the federal judiciary play in the United States government?**
   A. The judicial branch of the federal government was created to decide national questions. The federal judiciary does not have the power to decide all issues.
   B. Congress should not pass laws to accomplish objectives not under its jurisdiction. In cases where Congress goes beyond its delegated powers, the judicial branch should rule that such laws are unconstitutional.
   C. The judicial branch should decide the law according to the Constitution. The Constitution is superior to any ordinary act of the legislature. The judiciary has the duty of preserving federal law as the supreme law of the land.
   D. Acts of government should be decided primarily through the legislative process. The judicial branch must practice restraint in deciding limits on the acts of government.

E.   The duty of a judge is to exercise objective judgement based on the legal standard of the Constitution. A judge should not impose personal views into the law.

4.   **How much power does the federal government have over the actions of state governments?**
A.   When the American people ratified the Constitution they rejected a confederation of independent states in favor of a general government creating one nation.
B.   The federal government binds the states together. A strong federal government that unites the states is essential to the liberty and the happiness of the people.
C.   The federal government has the power to act upon individuals directly without involving state governments.
D.   The federal government is supreme within the sphere of powers granted to it.
E.   The federal government does not have the power to restrict the constitutional acts of a state government. A state government does not have the power to restrict the constitutional acts of the federal government.
F.   Federal courts must abide by state court decisions on questions of local statutes. For example, slavery is almost exclusively a local issue; few cases dealing with slavery should come before the Supreme Court.

5.   **Does the U.S. Constitution protect private property?**
A.   Private property is an important right. One of the fundamental principles of the Constitution is the protection of private property.
B.   A strong constitutional protection of property rights, as well as investment capital, will promote national prosperity.
C.   The Supreme Court should protect private property from the actions of both federal and state legislatures.

6.   **Does the Bill of Rights protect individuals from both federal and state governments?**
A.   The Bill of Rights restricts the power of the federal government and protects the rights of individuals. However, the Bill of Rights only restricts the powers of the federal government. The Bill of Rights does not restrict the powers of state governments.
B.   Each state must adopt its own safeguards for individual rights. If the framers of the Bill of Rights had intended to protect individuals from the power of a state government, they would have stated that intention in plain language.

STUDENT ACTIVITIES

Vocabulary
Define the following terms before reading the lesson on Marshall.

1. avail	8. enumerated	15. omnipotence
2. cognizance	9. indispensable	16. paramount
3. competent	10. intricacy	17. phraseology
4. conduce	11. judicial	18. pursuance
5. confidence	12. jurisdiction	19. repugnant
6. contrary	13. nugatory	20. sovereignty
7. efficacy	14. obligatory	21. usurpation

Review
1. Who appointed Marshall to the Supreme Court?
2. What were "midnight judges"?
3. What public offices were held by Marshall before he became chief justice?
4. Who was Marshall's cousin?
5. What three beliefs did Marshall advance as chief justice?
6. Why did Marshall believe Congress should have the power to make laws that were "necessary and proper"?
7. Did Marshall think Congress should be able to make *any* law? Explain.
8. In what cases should the judicial branch of government declare laws unconstitutional?
9. How did Marshall think individual rights should be protected from the power of state government?
10. Decide whether the following statements are **True** or **False** according to John Marshall.
    A. Each generation should write its own constitution.
    B. As a representative of the people, Congress has the power to change the Constitution with ordinary acts of legislation.
    C. Acts of government should be decided primarily through the legislative process.
    D. Judges cannot be expected to keep their personal politics separate from legal rulings.
    E. The federal government has the power to act directly upon the American people.
    F. The federal government has the power to restrict the constitutional acts of state governments.
    G. The Supreme Court should declare slavery unconstitutional.
    H. Private property is an important right that should be protected by the Supreme Court.
    I. The federal Bill of Rights does not apply to the actions of state governments.

What do you think?
On a scale of one through five, rate your opinion of the following quotations by Marshall. Write a short statement explaining your rating.

1 – You **strongly agree** with the statement *or* you feel the statement is **admirable** considering the historical circumstances surrounding it.
5 – You **strongly disagree** with the statement *or* you feel the statement is **contemptible** considering the historical circumstances surrounding it.

A. *That the people have an original right to establish, for their future government, such principles as, in their opinion, shall most conduce to their own happiness, is the basis on which the whole American fabric has been erected.*

B. *It is a proposition too plain to be contested, that the constitution controls any legislative act repugnant to it; or, that the legislature may alter the constitution by an ordinary act.*

C. *It is, emphatically, the province and duty of the judicial department, to say what the law is.*

D. *The judicial power of the United States is extended to all cases arising under the constitution.*

E. *The government of the United States, then, though limited in its powers, is supreme; and its laws, when made in pursuance of the constitution, form the supreme law of the land, "anything in the constitution or laws of any state to the contrary notwithstanding."*

F. *Congress is not empowered by it* [the Constitution] *to make laws, which may have relation to the powers conferred on the government, but such only as may be "necessary and proper."*

G. *The power to tax involves the power to destroy.*

H. *A constitution is framed for ages to come, and is designed to approach immortality as nearly as human institutions can approach it.*

I. *The people made the constitution, and the people can unmake it. It is the creature of their will, and lives only by their will.*

J. *The constitution and laws of a State, so far as they are repugnant to the constitution and laws of the United States, are absolutely void.*

K. *The 5th amendment must be understood as restraining the power of the general government, not as applicable to the States.*

L. *The peculiar circumstances of the moment may render a measure more or less wise, but cannot render it more or less constitutional.*

M. *The government of the United States has been emphatically termed a government of laws, and not of men.*

PART 3

EQUALITY AND
THE RIGHTS
OF THE MINORITY

CHAPTER 15

ALEXIS DE TOCQUEVILLE

BACKGROUND

Alexis de Tocqueville (1805-59), a French aristocrat, studied law in Paris and hoped for a career in politics. As a twenty-six year old magistrate he and fellow aristocrat Gustave de Beaumont received an appointment from the French government to report on the American prison system. Beginning in 1831 they toured the United States for nine months. Starting in New York they traveled as far west as Green Bay on Lake Michigan and as far south as New Orleans. After they returned to France and submitted their report Tocqueville began writing his observations on the society he had visited.

His observations were recorded in the book *Democracy in America*. Published in two volumes in 1835 and 1840, *Democracy in America* met with critical acclaim and was widely read in Europe. The book provided personal commentary on such issues as equality, liberty, religion, the press, racism, the role of government, the importance of the judiciary, and the problems of majority rule. Since revolutions were sweeping the Western world during the nineteenth century, Europeans looked upon the United States with more than academic interest. Throughout Europe people questioned whether democracy could provide a stable form of government. Tocqueville's book therefore supplied Europeans with insight about the workability of a democratic form of government.

In 1848 Tocqueville was elected to a committee chosen to write a new French constitution. Although his advice was largely rejected, he became a member of the Legislative Assembly and served with distinction until 1851 when Napoleon III became the emperor of France. Tocqueville refused to take part in public life under Napoleon III. In fact, Tocqueville even refused to swear an oath of allegiance to the French government. Tocqueville died of tuberculosis in 1859.

Tocqueville's *Democracy in America* remains his most important legacy. The book is considered a classic work of political theory as well as an important study of American society under Jacksonian democracy. For several generations the book has remained standard reading for anyone studying political science or United States history.

ALEXIS DE TOCQUEVILLE – IN HIS OWN WORDS

Democracy in America, Volume One, 1835

Among the novel objects that attracted my attention during my stay in the United States, nothing struck me more forcibly than the general equality of conditions. I readily discovered the prodigious influence which this primary fact exercises on the whole course of society, by giving a certain direction to public opinion, and a certain tenor to the laws; by imparting new maxims to the governing powers, and peculiar habits to the governed. I speedily perceived that the influence of this fact extends far beyond the political character and the laws of the country, and that it has no less empire over civil society than over the Government; it creates opinions, engenders sentiments, suggests the ordinary practices of life, and modifies whatever it does not produce. The more I advanced in the study of American society, the more I perceived that the equality of conditions is the fundamental fact from which all others seem to be derived, and the central point at which all my observations constantly terminated. . . .

I do not mean that there is any deficiency of wealthy individuals in the United States; I know of no country, indeed where the love of money has taken stronger hold upon the affections of men, and where profounder contempt is expressed for the theory of the permanent equality of property. . . .

. . . In America most of the rich men were formerly poor; most of those who now enjoy leisure were absorbed in business during their youth; the consequence of which is, that when they might have had a taste for study they had no time for it, and when time is at their disposal they have no longer the inclination

There is no class, then, in America in which the taste for intellectual pleasures is transmitted with hereditary fortune and leisure, and by which the labours of the intellect are held in honour. Accordingly, there is an equal want of the desire and the power of application to these objects.

A middle standard is fixed in America for human knowledge. All approach as near to it as they can; some as they rise, others as they descend. Of course, an immense multitude of persons are to be found who entertain the same number of ideas on religion, history, science, political economy, legislation, and government. . . .

America, then, exhibits in her social state a most extraordinary phenomenon. Men are there seen on a greater equality in point of fortune and intellect, or, in other words, more equal in their strength, than in any other country of the world, or in any age of which history has preserved the remembrance. . . .

The very essence of democratic government consists in the absolute sovereignty of the majority; for there is nothing in democratic States which is capable of resisting it. . . .

. . . The majority therefore in that country exercises a prodigious actual authority, and a moral influence which is scarcely less preponderant; no obstacles exist which can impede or so much as retard its progress, or which can induce it to heed the complaints of those whom it crushes upon its path. This state of things is fatal in itself and dangerous for the future. . . .

It is in the examination of the display of public opinion in the United States that we clearly perceive how far the power of the majority surpasses all the powers with which we are acquainted in Europe. Intellectual principles exercise an influence which is so invisible, and often so inappreciable, that they baffle the toils of oppression. At the present time the most absolute monarchs in Europe are unable to prevent certain notions, which are opposed to their authority, from circulating in secret throughout their dominions, and even in their courts. Such is not the case in America; as long as the majority is still undecided, discussion is carried on; but as soon as its decision is irrevocably pronounced, a submissive silence is observed, and the friends, as well as the opponents, of the measure unite in assenting to its propriety. The reason of this is perfectly clear: no monarch is so absolute as to combine all the powers of society in his own hands, and to conquer all opposition with the energy of a majority which is invested with the right of making and of executing the laws.

The authority of a king is purely physical, and it controls the actions of the subject without subduing his private will; but the majority possesses a power which is physical and moral at the same time; it acts upon the will as well as upon the actions of men, and it represses not only all contest, but all controversy.

I know no country in which there is so little true independence of mind and freedom of discussion as in America. . . .

In America, the majority raises very formidable barriers to the liberty of opinion: within these barriers an author may write whatever he pleases, but he will repent it if he ever step beyond them. . . . Every sort of compensation, even that of celebrity, is refused to him. Before he published his opinions he imagined that he held them in common with many others; but no sooner has he declared them openly than he is loudly censured by his overbearing opponents, while those who think like him, without having the courage to speak, abandon him in silence. He yields at length, oppressed by the daily efforts he has been making, and he subsides into silence, as if he was tormented by remorse for having spoken the truth.

Fetters and headsmen were the coarse instruments which tyranny formerly employed; but the civilization of our age has refined the arts of despotism, which seemed, however, to have been sufficiently perfected before. The excesses of monarchical power had devised a variety of physical means of oppression: the democratic republics of the present day have rendered it as entirely an affair of the mind as that will which it is intended to coerce. Under the absolute sway of an individual despot the body was attacked in order to subdue the soul, and the soul escaped the blows which were directed against it and rose superior to the attempt; but such is not the course adopted by tyranny in democratic republics; there the body is left free, and the soul is enslaved. The sovereign can no longer say, "You shall think as I do on pain of death"; but he says: "You are free to think differently from me, and to retain your life, your property, and all that you possess; but if such be your determination, you are henceforth an alien among your people. You may retain your civil rights, but they will be useless to you, for you will never be chosen by your fellow-citizens if you solicit their suffrages, and they will affect to scorn you if you solicit their esteem. You will remain among men, but you will be deprived of the rights of mankind. Your fellow-creatures will shun you like an impure being, and those who are most persuaded of your innocence will abandon you too, lest they should be shunned in their turn. Go in peace! I have given you your life, but it is an existence incomparably worse than death."

Democracy in America, Volume Two, 1840

In the United States the majority undertakes to supply a multitude of ready-made opinions for the use of individuals, who are thus relieved from the necessity of forming opinions of their own. Everybody there adopts great numbers of theories, on philosophy, morals, and politics, without inquiry, upon public trust; and if we look to it very narrowly, it will be perceived that religion herself holds her sway there, much less as a doctrine of revelation than as a commonly received opinion. The fact that the political laws of the Americans are such that the majority rules the community with sovereign sway, materially increases the power which that majority naturally exercises over the mind. For nothing is more customary in man than to recognize superior wisdom in the person of his oppressor. . . .

. . . It must be acknowledged that equality, which brings great benefits into the world, nevertheless suggests to men . . . some very dangerous propensities. It tends to isolate them from each other, to concentrate every man's attention upon himself. . . .

I think that democratic communities have a natural taste for freedom: left to themselves, they will seek it, cherish it, and view any privation of it with regret. But for equality, their passion is ardent, insatiable, incessant, invincible: they call for equality in freedom; and if they can not obtain that, they still call for equality in slavery. They will endure poverty, servitude, barbarism—but they will not endure aristocracy. . . .

. . . As social conditions become more equal, the number of persons increases who, although they are neither rich enough nor powerful enough to exercise any great influence over their fellow-creatures, have nevertheless acquired or retained sufficient education and fortune to satisfy their own wants. They owe nothing to any man, they expect nothing from any man; they acquire the habit of always considering themselves as standing alone, and they are apt to imagine that their whole destiny is in their own hands. Thus not only does democracy make every man forget his ancestors, but it hides his descendants, and separates his contemporaries from him; it throws him back forever upon himself alone, and threatens in the end to confine him entirely within the solitude of his own heart. . . .

The principle of equality, which makes men independent of each other, gives them a habit and a taste for following, in their private actions, no other guide but their own will. This complete independence, which they constantly enjoy toward their equals and in the intercourse of private life, tends to make them look upon all authority with a jealous eye, and speedily suggests to them the notion and the love of political freedom. Men living at such times have a natural bias to free institutions. Take any one of them at a venture, and search if you can his most deep-seated instincts; you will find that of all governments he will soonest conceive and most highly value that government whose head he has himself elected, and whose administration he may control. Of all the political effects produced by the equality of conditions, this love of independence is the first to strike the observing, and to alarm the timid; nor can it be said that their alarm is wholly misplaced, for anarchy has a more formidable aspect in democratic countries than elsewhere. As the citizens have no direct influence on each other, as soon as the supreme power of the nation fails, which kept them all in their several stations, it would seem that disorder must instantly reach its utmost pitch, and that, every man drawing aside in a different direction, the fabric of society must at once crumble away.

I am, however, persuaded that anarchy is not the principal evil that democratic ages have to fear, but the least. . . .

I think . . . that the species of oppression by which democratic nations are menaced is unlike anything which ever before existed in the world. . . . I am trying myself to choose an expression which will accurately convey the whole of the idea I have formed of it, but in vain; the old words despotism and tyranny are inappropriate: the thing itself is new; and since I can not name it, I must attempt to define it.

I seek to trace the novel features under which despotism may appear in the world. The first thing that strikes the observation is an innumerable multitude of men all equal and alike, incessantly endeavouring to procure the petty and paltry pleasures with which they glut their lives. Each of them, living apart, is as a stranger to the fate of all the rest—his children and his private friends constitute to him the whole of mankind; as for the rest of his fellow-citizens, he is close to them, but he sees them not—he touches them, but he feels them not; he exists but in himself and for himself alone; and if his kindred still remain to him, he may be said at any rate to have lost his country. Above this race of men stands an immense and tutelary power, which takes upon itself alone to secure their gratifications, and to watch over their fate. That power is absolute, minute, regular, provident, and mild. It would be like the authority of a parent, if, like that authority, its object was to prepare men for manhood; but it seeks, on the contrary, to keep them in perpetual childhood: it is well content that the people should rejoice, provided they think of nothing but rejoicing. For their happiness such a government willingly labours, but it chooses to be the sole agent and the only arbiter of that happiness: it provides for their security, foresees and supplies their necessities, facilitates their pleasures, manages their principal concerns, directs their industry, regulates the descent of property, and subdivides their inheritances—what remains, but to spare them all the care of thinking and all the trouble of living? Thus it every day renders the exercise of the free agency of man less useful and less frequent; it circumscribes the will within a narrower range, and gradually robs a man of all the uses of himself. The principle of equality has prepared men for these things: it has predisposed men to endure them, and oftentimes to look on them as benefits.

After having thus successively taken each member of the community in its powerful grasp, and fashioned them at will, the supreme power then extends its arm over the whole community. It covers the surface of society with a network of small complicated rules, minute and uniform, through which the most original minds and the most energetic characters can not penetrate, to rise above the crowd. The will of man is not shattered, but softened, bent, and guided: men are seldom forced by it to act, but they are constantly restrained from acting: such a power does not destroy, but it prevents existence; it does not tyrannize, but it compresses, enervates, extinguishes, and stupefies a people, till each nation is reduced to be nothing better than a flock of timid and industrious animals, of which the government is the shepherd.

I have always thought that servitude of the regular, quiet, and gentle kind which I have just described might be combined more easily than is commonly believed with some of the outward forms of freedom; and that it might even establish itself under the wing of the sovereignty of the people. Our contemporaries are constantly excited by two conflicting passions; they want to be led, and they wish to remain free: as they can not destroy either one or the other of these contrary propensities, they strive to satisfy them both at once. They devise a sole, tutelary, and all-powerful form of government, but elected by the people. They combine the principle of centralization and that of popular sovereignty; this gives them a respite; they console themselves for being in tutelage by the reflection that they have chosen their own guardians. Every man allows himself to be put in leading-strings, because he sees that it is not a person or a class of persons, but the people at large, that holds the end of his chain. By this system the people shake off their state of dependence just long enough to select their master, and then relapse into it again. A great many persons at the present day are quite contented with this sort of compromise between administrative despotism and the sovereignty of the people; and they think they have done enough for the protection of individual freedom when they have surrendered it to the power of the nation at large. This does not satisfy me: the nature of him I am to obey signifies less to me than the fact of extorted obedience.

ALEXIS DE TOCQUEVILLE – A SIMULATED INTERVIEW

1. **What are the most important characteristics of American democracy?**
    A. The central idea shaping the United States is the idea of equality. A belief in equality shapes American politics, law, and social custom.
    B. The United States is ruled by the will of the majority. Institutions and customs reflect a belief that the people are sovereign.

2. **What are the positive aspects of American democracy?**
    A. Democratic laws may not be as well executed as aristocratic laws, but they are more just.
    B. Public officials are not always honorable, but they are controlled by the electorate. Corruption is temporary in a democracy.
    C. The right to vote creates a deeper patriotism than is found in an aristocracy. Individuals feel they have a personal interest in the success of the country.

3. **What are the negative aspects of American democracy?**
    A. Politicians can be bought. Democracy does not always enlist the best individuals into public service.
    B. Frequent elections bring forth frequent changes in government. Democracy cannot plan for the long term as well as aristocracy. For example, since democracy gets carried away by momentary passions, aristocracy provides a superior way to create foreign policy.
    C. Many believe that anarchy is the greatest danger confronting democracy. In fact, democracy is most threatened by the tyranny of the majority. The majority is dangerous.

4. **How is the majority dangerous?**
    A. The majority possesses enough power to control human thought. Even absolute sovereigns in Europe do not possess this power.
    B. Absolute governments punish by striking at a person's body; the soul is left untouched. The majority, however, leaves the body alone and controls the soul. The minority is punished by social exclusion.
    C. The majority imposes ideas on individuals. Individuals are supplied with ready-made opinions; individuals are relieved of having to form their own opinions.
    D. Rule by the majority makes free choice useless. The majority traps individuals in a form of slavery. Individuals are enslaved by society.
    E. Unaware that the majority is in control, individuals are consoled by thinking that at least they have chosen their own leaders.
    F. The tyranny of the majority is not the tyranny of a large group over a small group; this can happen in any society. The tyranny of the majority is an intellectual oppression.

5. **How does equality affect American society?**
   A. The desire for equality has caused Americans to adopt a mediocre standard for human knowledge. The mass of Americans possess roughly the same ideas.
   B. Although Americans desire liberty, the desire for equality is stronger. Americans prefer equality in slavery to inequality in freedom. Americans will not tolerate aristocracy.
   C. Social equality makes individuals feel independent of each other. Each individual takes care of his own affairs and begins to feel that his destiny is in his own hands. With his family and friends he creates a little society for himself and abandons the greater society.

6. **How does individualism affect American society?**
   A. Americans learn from birth to be independent. Americans are distrustful of authority and appeal to governmental power only when they cannot do without it. Americans are more likely to form voluntary associations than to ask government for help.
   B. Individualism creates the danger of anarchy. When individuals feel they have no direct influence on each other the central power holding society together starts to disintegrate.
   C. Individualism can turn into outright selfishness. Individuals lose a sense of belonging to the larger human family unless they are given well-defined social responsibilities.

7. **What is essential for the success of American democracy?**
   A. Government must be decentralized. This requires a minimal power in the federal government and maximum in local government.
   B. Government officials should be disciplined by frequent elections.
   C. Presidents should not be allowed to run for reelection. The opportunity for reelection dominates the mind of a president. The president therefore becomes subservient to public opinion.
   D. The majority should be protected from its own mistakes. This is best done through a separation of powers and an independent judiciary.
   E. The right to organize groups and petition the government should be protected. Free association is the essence of good citizenship.
   F. Freedom of the press is essential. Freedom of the press allows victims of oppression to appeal for justice.
   G. Due process of law must be respected. Due process of law prevents the strong from trampling on the rights of the weak.
   H. Every American political issue ends up a legal issue. An independent judiciary is therefore necessary to control the majority and check the power of elected officials.
   I. America must combine the ideas of liberty and equality. The problems of equality are best corrected with liberty. Liberty forces people to be citizens and to develop an enlightened self-interest.

STUDENT ACTIVITIES

Vocabulary

Define the following terms before reading the lesson on Tocqueville.

1. ardent	7. extort	13. maxim
2. barbarism	8. fetters	14. multitude
3. contemporaries	9. headsmen	15. predispose
4. dominion	10. insatiable	16. prodigious
5. enervate	11. irrevocably	17. propensity
6. esteem	12. kindred	18. tutelary

Review

1. What appointment did Tocqueville receive from the French government in 1831?
2. How long did Tocqueville travel in the United States?
3. What book contains Tocqueville's observations on the United States?
4. Why did Europeans look at the United States with more than academic interest in the 1830s?
5. According to Tocqueville, what central idea shapes the United States?
6. What did Tocqueville believe was a characteristic of corruption in a democracy?
7. Why did Tocqueville think the right to vote in a democracy created a deeper patriotism than was found in an aristocracy?
8. Although many people think anarchy is democracy's greatest danger, what did Tocqueville think was the greatest danger?
9. According to Tocqueville, why is a majority a greater danger than an absolute sovereign?
10. What did Tocqueville think was stronger than the American desire for liberty?
11. What did Tocqueville think was the greatest danger of individualism?
12. According to Tocqueville, what happens when people have no well-defined social responsibilities?
13. What did Tocqueville think was the best way to correct the problems of equality?
14. What effect does liberty have on citizenship according to Tocqueville?
15. Decide whether the following statements are **True** or **False** according to Alexis de Tocqueville.
    A. Democracy cannot plan for the long term as well as aristocracy.
    B. Majority rule makes free choice useless.
    C. The mass of Americans possess roughly the same ideas.
    D. Social equality makes individuals dependent on each other.
    E. Americans naturally distrust authority.
    F. The American government should be centralized at the federal level.
    G. Presidents should be allowed to run for reelection.
    H. In the United States every political issue ends up a legal issue.

What do you think?
On a scale of one through five, rate your opinion of the following quotations by Tocqueville. Write a short statement explaining your rating.

1 – You **strongly agree** with the statement *or* you feel the statement is **admirable** considering the historical circumstances surrounding it.
5 – You **strongly disagree** with the statement *or* you feel the statement is **contemptible** considering the historical circumstances surrounding it.

A. *I know of no country . . . where the love of money has taken stronger hold upon the affections of men, and where profounder contempt is expressed for the theory of the permanent equality of property.*
B. *A middle standard is fixed in America for human knowledge.*
C. *As long as the majority is still undecided, discussion is carried on; but as soon as its decision is irrevocably pronounced, a submissive silence is observed.*
D. *I know no country in which there is so little true independence of mind and freedom of discussion as in America.*
E. *In America the majority raises very formidable barriers to the liberty of opinion.*
F. *In the United States the majority undertakes to supply a multitude of ready-made opinions for the use of individuals, who are thus relieved from the necessity of forming opinions on their own.*
G. *Americans are so enamored of equality that they would rather be equal in slavery than unequal in freedom.*
H. *In America I saw the freest and most enlightened men, placed in the happiest circumstances which the world affords: it seemed to me as if a cloud habitually hung upon their brow, and I thought them serious and almost sad even in their pleasures . . . , forever brooding over advantages they do not possess.*
I. *In America the independence of woman is irrecoverably lost in the bonds of matrimony: if an unmarried woman is less constrained there than elsewhere, a wife is subjected to stricter obligations.*
J. *Nothing is so petty, so insipid, so crowded with paltry interests, in one word, so anti-poetic, as the life of man in the United States.*
K. *The American aristocracy can be found in the lawyer's bar and the judge's bench.*
L. *In the principle of equality I discern two tendencies: the one leading the mind of every man to untried thoughts; the other prohibiting him from thinking at all.*
M. *A man who raises himself by degrees to wealth and power, contracts, in the course of this protracted labor, habits of prudence and restraint which he cannot afterwards shake off. A man cannot gradually enlarge his mind as he does his house.*

CHAPTER 16

HENRY DAVID THOREAU

BACKGROUND

Henry David Thoreau (1817-1862) was born into a poor family in Concord, Massachusetts. As a child he was recognized as a good, although not outstanding, student. Nevertheless, in 1833 he was awarded a scholarship to attend Harvard. At Harvard, he gained a reputation as an individualist and rejected the values of his fellow students. He simply was not interested in the kind of material success sought by his peers.

After graduation he returned to his hometown and worked for a short time as a teacher. He eventually resigned his teaching position after arguing with the headmaster about the school's policy of flogging students. He never returned to teaching and spent the rest of his life at a variety of odd jobs. He also wrote extensively; his dream was to become a great poet.

Thoreau loved nature and enjoyed taking long walks in the woods. In 1845 he decided to learn more about nature and to confront "the essential facts of life." For almost two years he lived near Walden Pond on a piece of land owned by his friend Ralph Waldo Emerson. Thoreau's experience living with nature was described in his book *Walden*.

In addition to *Walden*, Thoreau wrote many philosophical and literary essays. His most famous essay, "Civil Disobedience," described his refusal to pay a tax of one dollar, a tax he felt would be used to support slavery. Little did Thoreau know that "Civil Disobedience" would have tremendous historical influence. The essay provided Mahatma Gandhi and Martin Luther King, Jr. with a philosophy that brought about profound change in the twentieth century.

Thoreau was part of an American intellectual movement known as transcendentalism, a term used to describe New England romantics and reformers in the early 1800s. Although Thoreau did not become a great poet, he did produce a body of written work that has inspired several generations. Thoreau has motivated many people to think about the morality of their government and the limits, if any, of individualism.

HENRY DAVID THOREAU – IN HIS OWN WORDS

"Civil Disobedience," 1848

I heartily accept the motto, "That government is best which governs least;" and I should like to see it acted up to more rapidly and systematically. Carried out, it finally amounts to this, which also I believe—"That government is best which governs not at all;" and when men are prepared for it that will be the kind of government which they will have. Government is at best but an expedient; but most governments are sometimes, inexpedient. The objections which have been brought against a standing army, and they are many and weighty, and deserve to prevail, may also at last be brought against a standing government. The standing army is only an arm of the standing government. The government itself, which is only the mode which the people have chosen to execute their will, is equally liable to be abused and perverted before the people can act through it. Witness the present Mexican war, the work of comparatively a few individuals using the standing government as their tool; for, in the outset, the people would not have consented to this measure.

This American government—what is it but a tradition, though a recent one, endeavoring to transmit itself unimpaired to posterity, but each instant losing some of its integrity? It has not the vitality and force of a single living man; for a single man can bend it to his will. It is a sort of wooden gun to the people themselves. But it is not the less necessary for this; for the people must have some complicated machinery or other, and hear its din, to satisfy that idea of government which they have. Governments show thus how successfully men can be imposed on, even impose on themselves, for their own advantage. It does not keep the country free. It does not settle the West. It does not educate. The character inherent in the American people has done all that has been accomplished; and it would have done somewhat more, if the government had not sometimes got in its way. . . .

. . . I ask for, not at once no government, but *at once* a better government. Let every man make known what kind of government would command his respect, and that will be one step toward obtaining it.

After all, the practical reason why, when the power is once in the hands of the people a majority are permitted, and for a long period continue, to rule is not because they are most likely to be in the right, nor because this seems fairest to the minority, but because they are physically the stronger. But a government in which the majority rule in all cases cannot be based on justice, even as far as men understand it. Can there not be a government in which majorities do not virtually decide right and wrong, but conscience?—in which majorities decide only those questions to which the rule of expediency is applicable? Must the citizen ever for a moment, or in the least degree, resign his conscience to the legislator? Why has every man a conscience, then? I think that we should be men first, and subjects afterward. It is not desirable to cultivate a respect for the law, so much as for the right. The only obligation which I have a right to assume is to do at any time what

I think right. It is truly enough said that a corporation has no conscience; but a corporation of conscientious men is a corporation with a conscience. Law never made men a whit more just; and, by means of their respect for it, even the well-disposed are daily made the agents of injustice. A common and natural result of an undue respect for law is, that you may see a file of soldiers, colonel, captain, corporal, privates, powder-monkeys, and all, marching in admirable order over hill and dale to the wars, against their wills, ay, against their common sense and consciences, which makes it very steep marching indeed, and produces a palpitation of the heart. They have no doubt that it is a damnable business in which they are concerned; they are all peaceably inclined. Now, what are they? Men at all? or small movable forts and magazines, at the service of some unscrupulous man in power? Visit the Navy-Yard, and behold a marine, such a man as an American government can make . . . a mere shadow and reminiscence of humanity, a man laid out alive and standing, and already, as one may say, buried, under arms with funeral accompaniments . . . .

The mass of men serve the state thus, not as men mainly, but as machines, with their bodies. They are the standing army; and the militia, jailers, constables, *posse comitatus*, etc. In most cases there is no free exercise whatever of the judgement or of the moral sense; but they put themselves on a level with wood and earth and stones; and wooden men can perhaps be manufactured that will serve the purpose as well. Such command no more respect than men of straw or a lump of dirt. They have the same sort of worth only as horses and dogs. Yet such as these even are commonly esteemed good citizens. Others—as most legislators, politicians, lawyers, ministers, and office-holders—serve the state chiefly with their heads; and, as they rarely make any moral distinctions, they are as likely to serve the devil, without *intending* it, as God. A very few—as heroes, patriots, martyrs, reformers in the great *sense*, and *men*—serve the state with their consciences also, and so necessarily resist it for the most part; and they are commonly treated as enemies by it. . . .

How does it become a man to behave toward this American government today? I answer that he cannot without disgrace be associated with it. I cannot for an instant recognize that political organization as *my* government which is the *slave's* government also. . . .

All voting is a sort of gaming, like checkers or backgammon, with a slight moral tinge to it, playing with right and wrong, with moral questions; and betting naturally accompanies it. The character of the voters is not staked. I cast my vote, perchance, as I think right; but I am not vitally concerned that the right should prevail. I am willing to leave it to the majority. Its obligation, therefore, never exceeds that of expediency. Even voting *for the right* is *doing* nothing for it. It is only expressing to men feebly your desire that it should prevail. A wise man will not leave the right to the mercy of chance, nor wish it to prevail through the power of the majority. There is but little virtue in the action of masses of men. When the majority shall at length vote for the abolition of slavery, it will be because they are indifferent to slavery, or because there is but little slavery left to be abolished by their vote. *They* will then be the only slaves. Only *his* vote can hasten the abolition of slavery who asserts his own freedom by his vote. . . .

It is not a man's duty, as a matter of course, to devote himself to the eradication of any, even the most enormous, wrong; he may still properly have other concerns to engage him; but it is his duty, at least, to wash his hands of it, and, if he gives it no thought longer, not to give it practically his support. If I devote myself to other pursuits and contemplations, I must first see, at least, that I do not pursue them sitting upon another man's shoulders. I must get off him first, that he may pursue his contemplations too. . . .

Unjust laws exist: shall we be content to obey them, or shall we endeavor to amend them, and obey them until we have succeeded, or shall we transgress them at once? Men generally, under such a government as this, think that they ought to wait until they have persuaded the majority to alter them. They think that, if they should resist, the remedy would be worse than the evil. But it is the fault of the government itself that the remedy *is* worse than the evil. *It* makes it worse. Why is it not more apt to anticipate and provide for reform? Why does it not cherish its wise minority? Why does it cry and resist before it is hurt? Why does it not encourage its citizens to be on the alert to point out its faults, and *do* better than it would have them? Why does it always crucify Christ and excommunicate Copernicus and Luther, and pronounce Washington and Franklin rebels? . . .

As for adopting the ways which the State has provided for remedying the evil, I know not of such ways. They take too much time, and a man's life will be gone. I have other affairs to attend to. I came into this world, not chiefly to make this a good place to live in, but to live in it, be it good or bad. A man has not everything to do, but something; and because he cannot do *everything*, it is not necessary that he should do *something* wrong. It is not my business to be petitioning the Governor or the Legislature any more than it is theirs to petition me; and if they should not hear my petition, what should I do then? . . .

Under a government which imprisons any unjustly, the true place for a just man is also a prison. . . .

. . . The rich man . . . is always sold to the institution which makes him rich. Absolutely speaking, the more money, the less virtue; for money comes between a man and his objects, and obtains them for him; and it was certainly no great virtue to obtain it. It puts to rest many questions which he would otherwise be taxed to answer; while the only new question which it puts is the hard but superfluous one, how to spend it. Thus his moral ground is taken from under his feet. The opportunities of living are diminished in proportion as what are called the "means" are increased. The best thing a man can do for his culture when he is rich is to endeavor to carry out those schemes which he entertained when he was poor. . . .

Thus the State never intentionally confronts a man's sense, intellectual or moral, but only his body, his senses. It is not armed with superior wit or honesty, but with superior physical strength. I was not born to be forced. I will breathe after my own fashion. . . .

I have never declined paying the highway tax, because I am as desirous of being a good neighbor as I am of being a bad subject; and as for supporting schools, I am doing my part to educate my fellow-countrymen now. It is for no particular item in the tax-bill that I refuse to pay it. I simply wish to refuse allegiance to the State, to withdraw and stand aloof from it effectually. I do not care to trace the course of my dollar, if I could, till it buys a man or a musket to shoot one with—the dollar is innocent—but I am concerned to trace the effects of my allegiance. In fact, I quietly declare war with the State, after my fashion, though I will still make what use and get what advantage of her I can, as is usual in such cases. . . .

. . . Seen from a lower point of view, the Constitution, with all its faults, is very good; the law and the courts are very respectable; even this State and this American government, are, in many respects, very admirable, and rare things, to be thankful for, such as a great many have described them; but seen from a point of view a little higher, they are what I have described them; seen from a higher still, and the highest, who shall say what they are, or that they are worth looking at or thinking of at all?

However, the government does not concern me much, and I shall bestow the fewest possible thoughts on it. It is not many moments that I live under a government, even in this world. If a man is thought-free, fancy-free, imagination-free, that which *is not* never for a long time appearing *to be* to him, unwise rulers or reformers cannot fatally interrupt him. . . .

. . . Is a democracy, such as we know it, the last improvement possible in government? Is it not possible to take a step further towards recognizing and organizing the rights of man? There will never be a really free and enlightened State until the state comes to recognize the individual as a higher and independent power, from which all its own power and authority are derived, and treats him accordingly. I please myself with imagining a state at least which can afford to be just to all men, and to treat the individual with respect as a neighbor; which even would not think it inconsistent with its own repose if a few were to live aloof from it, not meddling with it, nor embraced by it, who fulfilled all the duties of neighbors and fellow-men. A State which bore this kind of fruit, and suffered it to drop off as fast as it ripened, would prepare the way for a still more perfect and glorious State, which also I have imagined, but not yet anywhere seen.

Walden, 1854

The mass of men lead lives of quiet desperation. What is called resignation is confirmed desperation. From the desperate city you go into the desperate country, and have to console yourself with the bravery of minks and muskrats. A stereotyped but unconscious despair is concealed even under what are called the games and amusements of mankind. There is no play in them, for this comes after work. But it is a characteristic of wisdom not to do desperate things.

When we consider what, to use the words of the catechism, is the chief end of man, and what are the true necessaries and means of life, it appears as if men had deliberately chosen the common mode of living because they preferred it to any other. Yet they honestly think there is no choice left. But alert and healthy natures remember that the sun rose clear. It is never too late to give up our prejudices. No way of thinking or doing, however ancient, can be trusted without proof. What everybody echoes or in silence passes by as true today may turn out to be falsehood tomorrow, mere smoke of opinion, which some had trusted for a cloud that would sprinkle fertilizing rain on their fields. . . .

Still we live meanly, like ants; though the fable tells us that we were long ago changed into men; like pygmies we fight with cranes; it is error upon error, and clout upon clout, and our best virtue has for its occasion a superfluous and evitable wretchedness. Our life is frittered away by detail. An honest man has hardly need to count more than his ten fingers, or in extreme cases he may add his ten toes, and lump the rest. Simplicity, simplicity, simplicity! I say let your affairs be as two or three, and not a hundred or a thousand; instead of a million count half a dozen, and keep your accounts on your thumbnail. In the midst of this chopping sea of civilized life, such are the clouds and storms and quicksands and thousand-and-one items to be allowed for, that a man has to live, if he would not founder and go to the bottom and not make his port at all, by dead reckoning, and he must be a great calculator indeed who succeeds. Simplify, simplify. Instead of three meals a day, if it be necessary eat but one; instead of a hundred dishes, five; and reduce other things in proportion. . . .

Why should we live with such hurry and waste of life? We are determined to be starved before we are hungry. Men say that a stitch in time saves nine, and so they take a thousand stitches today to save nine tomorrow. As for *work*, we haven't any of any consequence.

"Walking," 1862

A man's ignorance sometimes is not only useful, but beautiful,—while his knowledge, so called, is oftentimes worse than useless, besides being ugly. Which is the best man to deal with,—he who knows nothing about a subject, and, what is extremely rare, knows that he knows nothing, or he who really knows something about it, but thinks that he knows all?

My desire for knowledge is intermittent, but my desire to bathe my head in atmospheres unknown to my feet is perennial and constant. The highest that we can attain to is not Knowledge, but Sympathy with Intelligence. I do not know that this higher knowledge amounts to anything more definite than a novel and grand surprise on a sudden revelation of the insufficiency of all that we called Knowledge before,—a discovery that there are more things in heaven and earth than are dreamed of in our philosophy.

HENRY DAVID THOREAU – A SIMULATED INTERVIEW

1. **What ideas are held by transcendentalists?**
   A. Human intuition is more important than reason; feelings are more important than facts.
   B. The universal truth of human existence transcends any particular place, time, individual, or institution.
   C. Human beings should have faith in themselves and the goodness of the universe.
   D. Nature is the greatest teacher human beings can find; human beings are divine because they are part of nature.
   E. Governments, churches, and all other institutions are insignificant; the individual is all that matters.

2. **What is human nature?**
   A. Human nature remains constant throughout history. A classical education composed of studying the great works of history provides insight into human nature.
   B. Human beings are naturally free. People in tune with their true nature go beyond what is called knowledge; they possess true freedom.

3. **How should people conduct their lives?**
   A. Too many people live shallow, unfulfilled lives. People should realize they can always change their lives.
   B. Too many people spend their lives coping with meaningless detail. People should learn to simplify their lives.
   C. Too many people look to government or church for guidance. The truth of human existence is found within each individual.
   D. Material possessions inhibit the development of the human spirit. Rich people are owned by the thing that makes them rich. People should live free and uncommitted.
   E. American society is competitive, wasteful, and extravagant. People should learn to be concerned not with how much they can consume, but how little.
   F. Individuals should concentrate on self-improvement. Personal reform is more important than social or political reform.

4. **Should individuals obey the laws of society?**
   A. Obeying the law is less important than remaining true to conscience and morality.
   B. Each person has a duty to resist what is wrong. Waiting for the government to take action is not good enough. Individuals should remain true to their conscience and actively defy evil.
   C. If the government imprisons anyone unjustly, people who care about justice should protest by also going to prison.

5. **What is the best type of government?**
   A. The best government is the one that governs least. Ideally, the best government is the one that governs not at all. However, in the short term the nation needs a *better* government rather than *no* government.
   B. The best state is the one that recognizes the supremacy and the independence of the individual.
   C. Government is useful only for educating children, building roads, preventing crime, and protecting wildlife.

6. **What is wrong with a government based upon the will of the people?**
   A. Even if government is based upon majority rule, the government is liable to be corrupted before the people can make it act in their interest.
   B. A government based on the will of the people does not necessarily produce good decisions. The majority is not always right.
   C. The masses of human beings will seldom do what is right. A wise individual should not allow moral issues of right and wrong to turn into a political game played by the masses.
   D. No government, even one based on the will of the people, rules with goodness and morality. All governments rule through physical force.

7. **Should individuals serve their country?**
   A. Whatever achievements have been made in America have been made by the people; the government achieves nothing of value.
   B. Men who serve in the military give up their humanity when they become soldiers. Soldiers are not free individuals; soldiers are machines.
   C. In serving their country, legislators, politicians, lawyers, and ministers are as likely to assist the devil as to assist God. Service to an institution does not allow an individual to act morally.
   D. People who make moral distinctions and stay true to their conscience are likely to find themselves at odds with the government.

8. **Should people vote?**
   A. Voting is a game where the players are gambling on issues of morality. Voting cannot decide what is right and what is wrong.
   B. Even if people vote for what is right, nothing has been done to make sure that right triumphs. All that has been achieved with voting is that people have expressed a desire for right to prevail.

STUDENT ACTIVITIES

Vocabulary
Define the following terms before reading the lesson on Thoreau.

1. conscientious	7. excommunicate	13. reminiscence
2. contemplations	8. expedient	14. stereotyped
3. din	9. integrity	15. superfluous
4. eradication	10. palpitation	16. transgress
5. esteemed	11. perverted	17. unscrupulous
6. evitable	12. *posse comitatus*	18. wretchedness

Review
1. What reputation did Thoreau acquire as a student at Harvard?
2. Where did Thoreau spend almost two years confronting "the essential facts of life"?
3. What is the name of Thoreau's book describing his experience living with nature?
4. Why did Thoreau refuse to pay a tax of one dollar?
5. What two men were influenced by Thoreau's essay on civil disobedience?
6. What did transcendentalists believe was the greatest teacher human beings could find?
7. According to Thoreau, why do some people feel their lives are shallow and unfulfilled?
8. Where did Thoreau think the truth of human existence was found?
9. Why did Thoreau think rich people were not free?
10. According to Thoreau, what is more important than social or political reform?
11. According to Thoreau, what is the best government?
12. What value did Thoreau see in government?
13. According to Thoreau, how do governments rule?
14. What did Thoreau think happened to people who made moral distinctions and stayed true to their conscience?
15. Decide whether the following statements are **True** or **False** according to Henry David Thoreau.
    A. Governments, churches, and all other institutions are insignificant; all that matters is the individual.
    B. What people call "human nature" actually changes according to historical circumstances.
    C. People should learn to simplify their lives.
    D. American society is competitive, wasteful, and extravagant.
    E. The majority should rule.
    F. Young men should join the military to defend freedom.
    G. All citizens should register to vote.
    H. Ministers are as likely to assist the devil as to assist God.

What do you think?
On a scale of one through five, rate your opinion of the following quotations by Thoreau. Write a short statement explaining your rating.

1 – You **strongly agree** with the statement *or* you feel the statement is **admirable** considering the historical circumstances surrounding it.
5 – You **strongly disagree** with the statement *or* you feel the statement is **contemptible** considering the historical circumstances surrounding it.

A. *If a man does not keep pace with his companions, perhaps it is because he hears a different drummer. Let him step to the music which he hears, however measured or far away.*

B. *I heartily accept the motto, "That government is best which governs least;" and I should like to see it acted up to more rapidly and systematically.*

C. *A government in which the majority rule in all cases cannot be based on justice, even as far as men understand it.*

D. *Most legislators, politicians, lawyers, ministers, and office-holders serve the state chiefly with their heads; and, as they rarely make any moral distinctions, they are as likely to serve the devil, without intending it, as God.*

E. *All voting is a sort of gaming, like checkers or backgammon, with a slight moral tinge to it, playing with right and wrong, with moral questions; and betting naturally accompanies it.*

F. *Under a government which imprisons any unjustly, the true place for a just man is also a prison.*

G. *The rich man . . . is always sold to the institution which makes him rich. Absolutely speaking, the more money, the less virtue.*

H. *Seen from a lower point of view, the Constitution, with all its faults, is very good . . . . However, the government does not concern me much, and I shall bestow the fewest possible thoughts on it.*

I. *Our life is frittered away by detail.*

J. *Simplicity, simplicity, simplicity. I say let your affairs be as two or three, and not a hundred or a thousand; instead of a million count half a dozen, and keep your accounts on your thumbnail.*

K. *A man's ignorance sometimes is not only useful, but beautiful,—while his knowledge, so called, is oftentimes worse than useless, besides being ugly.*

L. *Cultivate poverty like a garden herb . . . Do not trouble yourself to get new things, whether clothes or friends. . . . Sell your clothes and keep your thought. God will see that you do not want society.*

M. *Business! I think that there is nothing, not even crime, more opposed to poetry, to philosophy, ay, to life itself, than this incessant business.*

N. *Blessed are they who never read a newspaper, for they shall see Nature, and through her God.*

CHAPTER 17

ELIZABETH CADY STANTON

BACKGROUND

Elizabeth Cady (1815-1902) grew up as a spirited young woman who was often at odds with her father, a conservative judge. When her only brother died her father said, "Oh my daughter, I wish you were a boy!" He knew that opportunities for women were severely limited by social attitudes and legal obstacles. He felt that Elizabeth would never be able to live up to the high hopes he had for his son.

When Elizabeth decided to get married her father protested strongly because her fiancé was a radical abolitionist. However, Elizabeth ignored her father's protests and married Henry Stanton in a ceremony omitting the traditional bride's vow to obey her husband. After the wedding Henry pursued his career as a lawyer, businessman, and politician while Elizabeth took care of their seven children.

In 1840 she traveled to London for an international abolitionist convention. Women were not allowed to speak at the convention and were restricted to sitting in the balcony. Angered by the clear injustice of these restrictions, she decided to dedicate her life to promoting women's rights.

In 1848 Elizabeth Cady Stanton and Lucretia Mott helped organize a women's rights convention in Seneca Falls, New York. Stanton pushed the convention to support a woman's right to vote as a sacred right. With the help of Frederick Douglass a resolution demanding women's suffrage was adopted. In addition, the convention released a declaration of sentiments written by Stanton and patterned after the Declaration of Independence.

Stanton, often working with her friend Susan B. Anthony, continued her role as a staunch supporter of women's rights until her death. At times her views alienated those who might normally have agreed with her. She believed in sexual freedom, birth control, and liberal divorce laws. She also attacked organized religion by publishing a *Woman's Bible*. In reinterpreting the *Bible* from a woman's point of view she concluded that society used religion to justify the oppression of women. Even when her ideas aroused controversy, she stayed true to her convictions.

ELIZABETH CADY STANTON – IN HER OWN WORDS

Address Delivered at Seneca Falls, July 1848

We are assembled to protest against a form of government, existing without the consent of the governed—to declare our right to be free as man is free, to be represented in the government which we are taxed to support, to have such disgraceful laws as give man the power to chastise and imprison his wife, to take the wages which she earns, the property which she inherits, and, in case of separation, the children of her love; laws which make her the mere dependent of his bounty. It is to protest against such unjust laws as these that we are assembled today, and to have them, if possible, forever erased from our statute-books, deeming them a shame and a disgrace to a Christian republic in the nineteenth century. . . .

And, strange as it may seem to many, we now demand our right to vote according to the declaration of the government under which we live. . . . We have no objection to discuss the question of equality, for we feel that the weight of argument lies wholly with us, but we wish the question of equality kept distinct from the question of rights, for the proof of the one does not determine the truth of the other. All white men in this country have the same rights, however they may differ in mind, body or estate. . . . But to have drunkards, idiots, horse-racing, rum-selling rowdies, ignorant foreigners, and silly boys fully recognized, while we ourselves are thrust out from all the rights that belong to citizens, it is too grossly insulting to the dignity of woman to be longer quietly submitted to. The right is ours. Have it we must. Use it we will. The pens, the tongues, the fortunes, the indomitable wills of truth, that no just government can be formed without the consent of the governed, we shall echo and re-echo in the ears of the unjust judge, until by continual coming we shall weary him. . . .

One common objection to this movement is, that if the principles of freedom and equality which we advocate were put into practice, it would destroy all harmony in the domestic circle. Here let me ask, how many truly harmonious households have we now? . . . The only happy households we now see are those in which husband and wife share equally in counsel and government. There can be no true dignity or independence where there is subordination to the absolute will of another, no happiness without freedom. Let us then have no fears that the movement will disturb what is seldom found, a truly united and happy family.

The Seneca Falls Declaration and Resolutions, 1848

We hold these truths to be self-evident: that all men and women are created equal; that they are endowed by their Creator with certain inalienable rights; that among these are life, liberty, and the pursuit of happiness; that to secure these rights governments are instituted, deriving their just powers from the consent of the governed. . . .

The history of mankind is a history of repeated injuries and usurpations on the part of man toward woman, having in direct object the establishment of an absolute tyranny over her. To prove this, let facts be submitted to a candid world.

He has never permitted her to exercise her inalienable right to the elective franchise.

He has compelled her to submit to laws, in the formation of which she had no voice.

He has withheld from her rights which are given to the most ignorant and degraded men—both natives and foreigners. . . .

He has made her, if married, in the eye of the law, civilly dead.

He has taken from her all right in property, even to the wages she earns.

. . . In the covenant of marriage, she is compelled to promise obedience to her husband, he becoming, to all intents and purposes, her master—the law giving him power to deprive her of liberty, and to administer chastisement.

He has so framed the laws of divorce, as to what shall be the proper causes, and in case of separation, to whom the guardianship of the children shall be given, as to be wholly regardless of the happiness of women—the law, in all cases, going upon a false supposition of the supremacy of man, and giving all power into his hands. . . .

He has monopolized nearly all the profitable employments, and from those she is permitted to follow, she receives but a scanty remuneration. He closes against her all the avenues to wealth and distinction which he considers most honorable to himself. As a teacher of theology, medicine, or law, she is not known.

He has denied her the facilities for obtaining a thorough education, all colleges being closed against her. . . .

He has created a false public sentiment by giving to the world a different code of morals for men and women, by which moral delinquencies which exclude women from society, are not only tolerated, but deemed of little account in man. . . .

He has endeavored, in every way that he could, to destroy her confidence in her own powers, to lessen her self-respect, and to make her willing to lead a dependent and abject life.

Now, in view of this entire disfranchisement of one-half the people of this country, their social and religious degradation—in view of the unjust laws above-mentioned, and because women do feel themselves aggrieved, oppressed, and fraudulently deprived of their most sacred rights, we insist that they have immediate admission to all the rights and privileges which belong to them as citizens of the United States.

Address to the New York State Legislature, 1854

We have every qualification required by the Constitution, necessary to the legal voter, but the one of sex. We are moral, virtuous, and intelligent, and in all respects quite equal to the proud white man himself, and yet by your laws we are classed with idiots, lunatics, and negroes . . . in fact, our legal position is lower than that of either; for the negro can be raised to the dignity of a voter if he possess himself of $250; the lunatic can vote in his moments of sanity, and the idiot, too, if he be a male one, and not more than nine-tenths a fool; but we . . . are denied the most sacred rights of citizens, because, forsooth, we came not into this republic crowned with the dignity of manhood! . . .

There is nothing that an unruly wife might do against which the husband has not sufficient protection in the law. But not so with the wife. If she have a worthless husband, a confirmed drunkard, a villain, or a vagrant, he has still all the rights of a man, a husband, and a father. Though the whole support of the family be thrown upon the wife, if the wages she earns be paid to her by her employer, the husband can receive them again. . . .

. . . There is no human love so strong and steadfast as that of the mother for her child; yet behold how ruthless are your laws touching this most sacred relation. Nature has clearly made the mother the guardian of the child; but man, in his inordinate love of power, does continually set nature and nature's laws at open defiance. . . .

. . . Thus, by your laws, the child is the absolute property of the father, wholly at his disposal in life or at death. . . .

Many times and oft it has been asked us, with unaffected seriousness, "What do you women want? What are you aiming at?" . . .

. . . Would not one code answer for all of like needs and wants? Christ's golden rule is better than all the special legislation that the ingenuity of man can devise: "Do unto others as you would have others do unto you." This, men and brethren, is all we ask at your hands. We ask no better laws than those you have made for yourselves. We need no other protection than that which your present laws secure to you.

Address to the New York State Legislature, 1860
[This speech was written by Stanton and Susan B. Anthony.]

Allow me just here to call the attention of that party now so much interested in the slave of the Carolinas, to the similarity in his condition and that of the mothers, wives, and daughters of the Empire State. The negro has no name, He is Cuffy Douglas or Cuffy Brooks, just whose Cuffy he may chance to be. The woman has no name. She is Mrs. Richard Roe or Mrs. John Doe, just whose Mrs. she may chance to be. Cuffy has no right to his earnings; he can not buy or sell, or lay up anything that he can call his own. Mrs. Roe has no right to her earnings; she can neither buy nor sell, make contracts, nor lay up anything that she can call her own. Cuffy has no right to his children; they can be sold from him at any time. Mrs. Roe has no right to her children; they may be bound out to cancel a father's debts of honor. The unborn child, even, by the last will of the father, may be placed under the guardianship of a stranger and a foreigner. Cuffy has no legal existence; he is subject to restraint and moderate chastisement. Mrs. Roe has no legal existence; she has not the best right to her own person. The husband has the power to restrain, and administer moderate chastisement. . . .

The prejudice against color . . . is no stronger than that against sex. It is produced by the same cause, and manifested very much in the same way. The negro's skin and the woman's sex are both *prima facie* evidence that they were intended to be in subjection to the white Saxon man. The few social privileges which the man gives the woman, he makes up to the negro in civil rights. The woman may sit at the same table and eat with the white man; the free negro may hold property and vote. The woman may sit in the same pew with the white man in church; the free negro may enter the pulpit and preach. Now, with the black man's right to suffrage . . . it is evident that the prejudice against sex is more deeply rooted and more unreasonably maintained than that against color. . . .

Just imagine an inhabitant of another planet entertaining himself some pleasant evening in searching over our great national compact, our Declaration of Independence, our Constitutions, or some of our statute-books; what would he think of those "women and negroes" that must be so fenced in, so guarded against? Why, he would certainly suppose we were monsters, like those fabulous giants . . . of olden times, so dangerous to civilized man, from our size, ferocity, and power. . . .

Now do not think, gentlemen, we wish you to do a great many troublesome things for us. We do not ask our legislators to spend a whole session in fixing up a code of laws to satisfy a class of most unreasonable women. . . . In mercy, let us take care of ourselves, our property, our children, and our homes. . . . Undo what man did for us in the dark ages, and strike out all special legislation for us; strike the words "white male" from all your constitutions, and then, with fair sailing, let us sink or swim, live or die, survive or perish together.

"Home Life," 1875

Let us now glance at a few of the popular objections to liberal divorce laws. It is said that to make divorce respectable by laws, gospel and public sentiment is to break up all family relations. Which is to say that human affections are the result and not the foundation of the canons of the church and statutes of the state. . . . To open the doors of escape to those who dwell in continual antagonism, to the unhappy wives of drunkards, libertines, knaves, lunatics and tyrants, need not necessarily embitter the relations of those who *are* contented and happy, but on the contrary the very fact of freedom strengthens and purifies the bond of union. When husbands and wives . . . are bound together only by affection, marriage will be a life long friendship and not a heavy yoke, from which both may sometimes long for deliverance. The freer the relations are between human beings, the happier. . . .

It is said that the 10,000 libertines, letchers and egotists would take a new wife every Christmas if they could legally and reputably rid themselves in season of the old one. . . . [This] objection is based on the idea that woman will always remain the penniless, helpless, resistless victim of every man she meets, that she is today. But in the new regime, when she holds her place in the world of work, educated to self-support, with land under her feet and a shelter over her head, the results of her own toil, the social, civil and political equal of the man by her side, she will not clutch at every offer of marriage, like the drowning man at the floating straw. Though men should remain just what they are, the entire revolution in woman's position now inaugurated forces a new moral code in social life.

Address of Welcome to the International Council of Women, March 1888

Women have been the mere echoes of men. Our laws and constitutions, our creeds and codes, and the customs of social life are all of masculine origin. The true woman is as yet a dream of the future. A just government, a humane religion, a pure social life await her coming. Then, and not till then, will the golden age of peace and prosperity be ours. . . .

. . . In the Old World they have governments and people; here we have a government of the people, by the people, for the people—that is, we soon shall have when that important half, called women, are enfranchised, and the laboring masses know how to use the power they possess.

"The Solitude of Self," 1892

The strongest reason for giving woman all the opportunities for higher education . . . is the solitude and personal responsibility of her own individual life. . . . No matter how much women prefer to lean, to be protected and supported, nor how much men desire to have them do so, they must make the voyage of life alone, and for safety in an emergency, they must know something of the laws of navigation. To guide our own craft, we must be captain, pilot, engineer; with chart and compass to stand at the wheel; to watch the winds and waves, and know when to take in the sail, and to read the signs in the firmament over all. It matters not whether the solitary voyager is man or woman; nature, having endowed them equally, leaves them to their own skill and judgement in the hour of danger, and, if not equal to the occasion, alike they perish. . . .

We ask for the complete development of every individual, first, for his own benefit and happiness. In fitting out an army, we give each soldier his own knapsack, arms, powder, his blanket, cup, knife, fork and spoon. We provide alike for all their individual necessities; then each man bears his own burden.

Again, we ask complete individual development for the general good; for the consensus of the competent on the whole round of human interests, on all questions of national life; and here each man must bear his share of the general burden. It is sad to see how soon friendless children are left to bear their own burdens, before they can analyze their feelings; before they can even tell their joys and sorrows, they are thrown on their own resources. The great lesson that nature seems to teach us at all ages is self-dependence, self-protection, self-support.

ELIZABETH CADY STANTON – A SIMULATED INTERVIEW

1. **What conditions do women face in early nineteenth century America?**
   A. Women are denied the right to vote. Intelligent, moral women cannot vote. However, lunatics and idiots can vote if they are white males.
   B. Women must obey laws they have no voice in passing.
   C. Marriage is a contract of ownership; a wife must obey her husband.
   D. A woman has no legal recourse against the misbehavior of her husband. The law protects only the rights of the husband. If a husband is an alcoholic or brutalizes his family, the law protects him.
   E. A woman cannot divorce her husband.
   F. A woman has no legal control over her own children. The strongest human love comes from a mother for her child, and men interfere with nature by placing themselves between a mother and her child.
   G. Women are denied basic rights of property. If a woman does own property, her property comes under the legal control of her husband when she gets married.
   H. Men monopolize all the profitable fields of employment and opportunities for wealth.
   I. Men and women live under different moral standards. What is considered immoral behavior for a woman is acceptable behavior for a man.

2. **How is marriage for women similar to slavery in the South?**
   A. Neither wives nor slaves possess their own name.
   B. Neither wives nor slaves have a right to their own earnings.
   C. Neither wives nor slaves have a right to possess property.
   D. Neither wives nor slaves have control over their own children.
   E. Neither wives nor slaves have legal recourse against the actions of their husbands or masters.

3. **What rights should be granted to women?**
   A. Women should be allowed to vote.
   B. Women should be allowed to hold office.
   C. Marriage should be a contract of partnership; a woman should have a voice in her own marriage as well as a voice in society.
   D. Women should decide for themselves when they want to have children.
   E. Divorce laws should be changed to allow a woman to escape an intolerable marriage.
   F. Women should be given opportunities for higher education in order that they may become independent and self-sufficient.

G. Women should gain the same kind of independence and equal rights that abolitionists are trying to gain for slaves.

4. On what grounds should rights be granted to women?
A. Each individual should be allowed to pursue his or her potential. This is a basic human right.
B. Each individual should be allowed the opportunity for self-sufficiency and independence.
C. The U.S. Constitution created a republican form of government based upon the consent of the governed. Women should have a voice in making laws that they must obey.
D. According to the principles of the Declaration of Independence, women are entitled to equal rights including the right to vote. All people, men and women, should be equal under the law.

5. What effect will granting equal rights to women have on families?
A. Equality for women will not damage the institution of the family. The male desire to protect women often turns into tyranny. A truly happy family is made up of a husband and wife sharing equally in their relationship.
B. Women who are primarily wives and mothers are still capable of thinking and acting for themselves without the protection of men. The family will not be destroyed.
C. Motherhood is the most important of all professions. However, women can be mothers as well as active participants in society without threatening their families.

STUDENT ACTIVITIES

Vocabulary
Define the following terms before reading the lesson on Stanton.

1. antagonism	8. indomitable	15. remuneration
2. canon	9. inordinate	16. statute
3. chastisement	10. knave	17. theology
4. covenant	11. libertine	18. tyrant
5. delinquency	12. lunatic	19. usurpation
6. firmament	13. prerogative	20. vagrant
7. fraudulent	14. *prima facie*	

Review
1. Why did Elizabeth Cady's father protest her marriage?
2. Where was the women's rights convention that Stanton and Lucretia Mott organized in 1848?

3. What role did Frederick Douglass play at the 1848 women's rights convention?
4. Stanton patterned her declaration of sentiments after what document?
5. Who was Susan B. Anthony?
6. In what book did Stanton attack organized religion?
7. In what ways did Stanton think marriage was similar to slavery?
8. Why did Stanton believe that equality for women would not damage families?
9. What did Stanton think was characteristic of a truly happy family?
10. What did Stanton think was the most important of all professions?
11. Decide whether the following statements are **True** or **False** according to Elizabeth Cady Stanton.
    A. Women and men live under different moral standards.
    B. Women in the early 1800s are legally required to obey their husbands.
    C. Women in the early 1800s have no legal recourse against the misbehavior of their husbands.
    D. Women in the early 1800s have no legal control of their own children.
    E. Women in the early 1800s are denied basic rights of property.
    F. Men monopolize all profitable fields of employment.
    G. Women should be allowed to vote and hold office.
    H. Women should be given opportunities for higher education.
    I. Liberalized divorce laws will weaken the moral fabric of society.
    J. Women should have a voice in making the laws they must obey.
    K. Women cannot be active participants in society and fulfill the duties of motherhood at the same time.

What do you think?
On a scale of one through five, rate your opinion of the following quotations by Stanton. Write a short statement explaining your rating.

1 – You **strongly agree** with the statement *or* you feel the statement is **admirable** considering the historical circumstances surrounding it.
5 – You **strongly disagree** with the statement *or* you feel the statement is **contemptible** considering the historical circumstances surrounding it.

A. *The only happy households we now see are those in which husband and wife share equally in counsel and government.*
B. *There can be no true dignity or independence where there is subordination to the absolute will of another, no happiness without freedom.*
C. *We hold these truths to be self-evident: that all men and women are created equal.*
D. *There is no human love so strong and steadfast as that of the mother for her child.*

E. *We ask no better laws than those you have made for yourselves. We need no other protection than that which your present laws secure to you.*

F. *The prejudice against color . . . is no stronger than that against sex. It is produced by the same cause, and manifested very much in the same way.*

G. *To open the doors of escape [with liberal divorce laws] to those who dwell in continual antagonism, . . . need not necessarily embitter the relations of those who are contented and happy, but on the contrary the very fact of freedom strengthens and purifies the bond of union.*

H. *No matter how much women prefer to lean, to be protected and supported, nor how much men desire to have them do so, they must make the voyage of life alone, and for safety in an emergency, they must know something of the laws of navigation.*

I. *The more complete the despotism, the more smoothly all things move on the surface.*

J. *We still wonder at the stolid incapacity of all men to understand that woman feels the invidious distinctions of sex exactly as the black man does those of color, or the white man the more transient distinctions of wealth, family, position, place, and power; that she feels as keenly as man the injustice of disfranchisement.*

K. *I am weary seeing our laboring classes so wretchedly housed, fed, and clothed, while thousands of dollars are wasted every year over unsightly statues. If these great men must have outdoor memorials let them be in the form of handsome blocks of buildings for the poor.*

L. *If we were free and developed, healthy in body and mind, as we should be under natural conditions, our motherhood would be our glory. That function gives women such wisdom and power as no male can ever possess.*

CHAPTER 18

JOHN C. CALHOUN

BACKGROUND

John C. Calhoun (1782-1850), who came from a wealthy family in South Carolina, decided to seek a college degree in New England. After he graduated from Yale he began a legal career that led to a long career in politics. For forty years he played a major role in the United States government. He served as a U.S. representative, U.S. senator, secretary of war, secretary of state, and vice president. In addition, he was considered a serious candidate for president in every election from 1824 to 1848.

When Calhoun entered Congress in 1811 he was a leading War Hawk, helping to guide the United States into the War of 1812 with England. Following the war he played a key role in creating the Second Bank of the United States. He also wrote a bill to build a nationwide network of roads and canals, a bill that was vetoed by President Madison.

In 1824 Calhoun ran for vice president on the tickets of both John Quincy Adams and Andrew Jackson. After serving four years as vice president under Adams, Calhoun was elected vice president again in 1828, but this time under Jackson. While Calhoun was in his second term as vice president, he became a political enemy of Jackson. In a famous incident at a Jefferson birthday dinner President Jackson made a toast to "Our Federal Union: it must be preserved." Calhoun responded, "The Union—next to our Liberty most dear. May we all remember that it can be preserved only by respecting the rights of States." Calhoun left the vice presidency after Jackson's first term and was elected to the Senate.

Before he left the vice presidency Calhoun wrote "South Carolina Exposition and Protest" to advocate state nullification of any federal law that violated the rights of the minority. He later wrote *Disquisition on Government* in which he further developed his case for minority rights.

Calhoun, along with Daniel Webster, Henry Clay, and Andrew Jackson, dominated American political life in the first half of the nineteenth century. His contribution to the history of ideas stems primarily from his desire to protect the minority from the tyranny of the majority.

JOHN C. CALHOUN – IN HIS OWN WORDS

"South Carolina Exposition and Protest," 1828

Our system consists of two distinct and independent Governments. The general powers, expressly delegated to the General Government, are subject to its sole and separate control; and the States cannot, without violating the constitutional compact, interpose their authority to check, or in any manner to counteract its movements so long as they are confined to the proper sphere. So, also, the peculiar and local powers reserved to the States are subject to their exclusive control; nor can the General Government interfere, in any manner, with them, without violating the Constitution.

In order to have a full and clear conception of our institutions, it will be proper to remark that there is, in our system, a striking distinction between *Government* and *Sovereignty*. The separate governments of the several States are vested in their Legislative, Executive, and Judicial Departments; while the sovereignty resides in the people of the States respectively. The powers of the General Government are also vested in its Legislative, Executive, and Judicial Departments, while the sovereignty resides in the people of the several States who created it. But, by an express provision of the Constitution, it may be amended or changed by three-fourths of the States; and thus each State, by assenting to the Constitution with this provision, has modified its original right as a sovereign, of making its individual consent necessary to any change in its political condition; and, by becoming a member of the Union, has placed this important power in the hands of three-fourths of the States,—in whom the highest power known to the Constitution actually resides. Not the least portion of this high sovereign authority resides in Congress, or any of the departments of the General Government. They are but the creatures of the Constitution, and are appointed but to execute its provisions; and, therefore, any attempt by all, or any of these departments, to exercise any power which, in its consequences, may alter the nature of the instrument, or change the condition of the parties to it, would be an act of usurpation.

It is thus that our political system, resting on the great principle involved in the recognized diversity of geographical interests in the community, has, in theory, with admirable sagacity, provided the most efficient check against their dangers. Looking to facts, the Constitution has formed the States into a community only to the extent of their common interests; leaving them distinct and independent communities as to all other interests, and drawing the line of separation with consummate skill, as before stated.

Speech on the Reception of Abolition Petitions, 1837

I hold that in the present state of civilization, where two races of different origin, and distinguished by color, and other physical differences, as well as intellectual, are brought together, the relation now existing in the slaveholding States between the two, is, instead of an evil, a good—a positive good. I feel myself called upon to speak freely upon the subject where the honor and interests of those I represent are involved. I hold then, that there never has yet existed a wealthy and civilized society in which one portion of the community did not, in point of fact, live on the labor of the other. Broad and general as is this assertion, it is fully borne out by history.

A Disquisition on Government, 1849

I assume as an incontestable fact that man is so constituted as to be a social being. His inclinations and wants, physical and moral, irresistibly impel him to associate with his kind; and he has accordingly, never been found, in any age or country, in any state other than the social. In no other, indeed, could he exist, and in no other—were it possible for him to exist—could he attain to a full development of his moral and intellectual faculties or raise himself, in the scale of being, much above the level of the brute creation.

I next assume also as a fact not less incontestable that, while man is so constituted as to make the social state necessary to his existence and the full development of his faculties, this state itself cannot exist without government. The assumption rests on universal experience. In no age or country has any society or community ever been found, whether enlightened or savage, without government of some description. . . .

. . . While man is created for the social state and is accordingly so formed as to feel what affects others as well as what affects himself, he is, at the same time, so constituted as to feel more intensely what affects him directly than what affects him indirectly through others, or, to express it differently, he is so constituted that his direct or individual affections are stronger than his sympathetic or social feelings. I intentionally avoid the expression *"selfish* feelings" as applicable to the former, because, as commonly used, it implies an unusual excess of the individual over the social feelings in the person to whom it is applied and, consequently, something depraved and vicious. . . .

It follows, then that man is so constituted that government is necessary to the existence of society, and society to his existence and the perfection of his faculties. It follows also that government has its origin in this two-fold constitution of his nature: the sympathetic or social feelings constituting the remote, and the individual or direct the proximate, cause. . . .

Government, although intended to protect and preserve society, has itself a strong tendency to disorder and abuse of its powers, as all experience and almost every page of history testify. The cause is to be found in the same constitution of our nature which makes government indispensable. The powers which it is necessary for government to possess in order to repress violence and preserve order cannot execute themselves. They must be administered by men in whom, like others, the individual are stronger than the social feelings. And hence the powers vested in them to prevent injustice and oppression on the part of others will, if left unguarded, be by them converted into instruments to oppress the rest of the community. That by which this is prevented, by whatever name called, is what is meant by *constitution*, in its most comprehensive sense, when applied to *government*.

Having its origin in the same principle of our nature, *constitution* stands to *government* as *government* stands to *society*; and as the end for which society is ordained would be defeated without government, so that for which government is ordained would, in a great measure, be defeated without constitution. But they differ in this striking particular. There is no difficulty in forming government. It is not even a matter of choice whether there shall be one or not. Like breathing, it is not permitted to depend on our volition. Necessity will force it on all communities in some one form or another. Very different is the case as to constitution. Instead of a matter of necessity, it is one of the most difficult tasks imposed on man to form a constitution worthy of the name, while to form a perfect one—one that would completely counteract the tendency of government to oppression and abuse and hold it strictly to the great ends for which it is ordained—has thus far exceeded human wisdom, and possibly ever will. From this another striking difference results. Constitution is the contrivance of man, while government is of divine ordination. Man is left to perfect what the wisdom of the Infinite ordained as necessary to preserve the race.

With these remarks I proceed to the consideration of the important and difficult question, How is this tendency of government to be counteracted? Or, to express it more fully, How can those who are invested with the powers of government be prevented from employing them as the means of aggrandizing themselves instead of using them to protect and preserve society? . . .

There is but one way in which this can possibly be done, and that is by such an organism as will furnish the ruled with the means of resisting successfully this tendency on the part of the rulers to oppression and abuse. Power can only be resisted by power—and tendency by tendency. Those who exercise power and those subject to its exercise—the rulers and the ruled—stand in antagonistic relations to each other. The same constitution of our nature which leads rulers to oppress the ruled—regardless of the object for which government is ordained—will, with equal strength, lead the ruled to resist when possessed of the means of making peaceable and effective resistance. Such an organism, then, as will furnish the means by which resistance may be systematically and peaceably made on the part of the ruled to oppression and abuse of power on the part of the rulers is the first and indispensable step toward *forming* a constitutional government. And as this can only be effected by or through the right of suffrage—the right on the part of the ruled to choose their rulers at proper intervals and to hold them thereby responsible for their conduct—the responsibility of the rulers to the ruled, through the right of suffrage, is the indispensable and primary principle in the *foundation* of a constitutional government. When this right is properly guarded, and the people sufficiently enlightened to understand their own rights and the interests of the community and duly to appreciate the motives and conduct of those appointed to make and execute the laws, it is all-sufficient to give to those who elect effective control over those they have elected. . . .

. . . The sum total, then, of its effects, when most successful, is to make those elected the true and faithful representatives of those who elected them—instead of irresponsible rulers, as they would be without it; and thus, by converting it into an agency, and the rulers into agents, to divest government of all claims to sovereignty and to retain it unimpaired to the community. . . .

It necessarily results that the right of suffrage, by placing the control of the government in the community, must, from the same constitution of our nature which makes government necessary to preserve society, lead to conflict among its different interests—each striving to obtain possession of its powers as the means of protecting itself against the others or of advancing its respective interests regardless of the interests of others. For this purpose a struggle will take place between the various interests to obtain a majority in order to control the government. If no one interest be strong enough, of itself, to obtain it, a combination will be formed between those whose interests are most alike—each conceding something to the others until a sufficient number is obtained to make a majority. . . .

. . . The dominant majority, for the time, would have the same tendency to oppression and abuse of power which, without the right of suffrage, irresponsible rulers would have. No reason, indeed, can be assigned why the latter would abuse their power, which would not apply, with equal force, to the former. The dominant majority, for the time, would in reality, through the right of suffrage, be the rulers—the controlling, governing and irresponsible power; and those who make and execute the laws would, for the time, be in reality but *their* representatives and agents. . . .

As, then, the right of suffrage, without some other provision, cannot counteract the tendency of government, the next question for consideration is, What is that other provision? . . .

From what has been said, it is manifest that this provision must be of a character calculated to prevent any one interest or combination of interests from using the powers of government to aggrandize itself at the expense of the others. Here lies the evil; and just in proportion as it shall prevent, or fail to prevent it, in the same degree it will effect, or fail to effect, the end intended to be accomplished. There is but one certain mode in which this result can be secured, and that is by the adoption of some restriction or limitation, which shall so effectually prevent any one interest or combination of interests from obtaining the exclusive control of the government as to render hopeless all attempts directed to that end. There is, again, but one mode in which this can be effected, and that is by taking the sense of each interest or portion of the community which may be unequally and injuriously affected by the action of the government separately, through its own majority or in some other way by which its voice may be fairly expressed, and to require the consent of each interest either to put or to keep the government in action. This, too, can be accomplished only in one way, and that is by such an organism of the government—and, if necessary for the purpose of the community also—as will, by dividing and distributing the powers of government, give to each division or interest, through its appropriate organ, either a concurrent voice in making and executing the laws or a veto on their execution. It is only by such an organism that the assent of each can be made necessary to put the government in motion, or the power made effectual to arrest its action when put in motion; and it is only by the one or the other that the different interests, orders, classes, or portions into which the community may be divided can be protected, and all conflict and struggle between them prevented—by rendering it impossible to put or to keep it in action without the concurrent consent of all. . . .

Such an organism as this, combined with the right of suffrage, constitutes, in fact, the elements of constitutional government. The one, by rendering those who make and execute the laws responsible to those on whom they operate, prevents the rulers from oppressing the ruled; and the other, by making it impossible for any one interest or combination of interests, or class, or order, or portion of the community to obtain exclusive control . . . .

The government of the concurrent majority, where the organism is perfect, excludes the possibility of oppression by giving to each interest, or portion, or order—where there are established classes—the means of protecting itself by its negative against all measures calculated to advance the peculiar interests of others at its expense. Its effect, then, is to cause the different interests, portions, or orders, as the case may be, to desist from attempting to adopt any measure calculated to promote the prosperity of one, or more, by sacrificing that of others: and thus to force them to unite in such measures only as would promote the prosperity of all, as the only means to prevent the suspension of the action of the government, and thereby, to avoid anarchy, the greatest of all evils. It is by means of such authorized and effectual resistance that oppression is prevented and the necessity of resorting to force superseded in governments of the concurrent majority; and hence compromise, instead of force, becomes their conservative principle. . . .

Governments of concurrent majority have greatly the advantage. I allude to the difference in their respective tendency in reference to dividing or uniting the community, let its interests be ever so diversified or opposed, while that of the numerical is to divide it into two conflicting portions, let its interests be naturally ever so united and identified. It follows, from what has been stated, that it is a great and dangerous error to suppose that all people are equally entitled to liberty. It is a reward to be earned, not a blessing to be gratuitously lavished on all alike—a reward reserved for the intelligent, the patriotic, the virtuous and deserving, and not a boon to be bestowed on a people too ignorant, degraded and vicious to be capable either of appreciating or of enjoying it.

JOHN C. CALHOUN – A SIMULATED INTERVIEW

1. **What is human nature?**
   A. Human beings are social creatures. Human beings must live in a community to satisfy their physical and moral needs.
   B. Although an individual can sympathize with others, he is more likely to be concerned with what affects him directly.

2. **Is government natural to human existence?**
   A. Human beings cannot exist without government. History shows that no society has ever existed without government.
   B. Government arises naturally from a need to preserve and protect society.

3. **What are the dangers of government?**
   A. Government is composed of human beings, and since human beings naturally protect their self-interest, government has a tendency to abuse its power.
   B. Although government is natural to any society, a constitution is voluntary. However, without a constitution government is likely to abuse its power.
   C. A constitution should not only curb the abuses of government, it should also curb the abuses of an electoral majority. An unchecked majority should not be allowed to rule.
   D. Under a system of majority rule, various factions struggle to win a majority. When a majority emerges it tends to oppress the minority.
   E. The separation of powers is not enough to keep government from abusing its power. A single political party might control all three branches of government. The majority political party can oppress the minority even in a system with separation of powers.

4. **How can society control the government's abuse of power?**
   A. All societies should adopt a constitution. Constitutions impede government oppression and tyranny.
   B. Granting the people a right to vote is an essential means of control-ling government. The people's right to vote forces elected officials to become true representatives of the people's interests.
   C. A constitution should require that all power be resisted by an opposing power. Government officials are best controlled by other government officials who possess equal power.
   D. Government cannot abuse its power if minority factions possess the means to protect their interests. Minorities can be protected by requiring a concurrent majority before government takes action.

5. **What is the concurrent majority?**
    A. Society has a concurrent majority when all competing factions agree on government policy. Government is therefore powerless unless all factions allow government to take action.
    B. With a concurrent majority, the minority has the power to veto the acts of an oppressive majority.
    C. Under the restrictions of a concurrent majority, government may only act in a way that is fair to *all* factions. Concurrent majorities therefore build a stronger sense of community and a stronger Union.

6. **What is the relationship between the federal government and state governments?**
    A. The federal government possesses exclusive control over its delegated powers. State governments possess exclusive control over powers reserved to them. Neither the federal government nor state governments can interfere with each other's delegated powers.
    B. The federal government allows the states to come together and address common concerns. Outside of these common concerns all states are independent.
    C. If the federal government violates the rights of a state, the state possesses the authority to proclaim the federal law null and void. This is known as the doctrine of nullification.

7. **What is the role of slavery in the United States?**
    A. Slavery is a positive good. History shows that no wealthy and civilized society has ever existed without some form of slavery.
    B. Southerners possess a constitutional right to own slaves. The ownership of slaves is a right that should never be compromised.
    C. Congress cannot outlaw slavery in the territories. The western territories belong to the entire nation. The exclusion of slavery in the territories amounts to an exclusion of slave owners.
    D. The United States is in danger unless southerners are granted permanent protection of slavery.
    E. Whites and blacks differ to such an extent that they can never peacefully live together. Slavery is the most appropriate way to maintain safety and stability in the United States.

8. **Do all people have equal rights?**
    A. All people are not equally entitled to freedom. Freedom is a reward granted to those who are intelligent, patriotic, and virtuous. Freedom must be earned.
    B. Freedom should not be granted to those who are too ignorant and vicious to enjoy it. All people are not automatically entitled to freedom.

STUDENT ACTIVITIES

Vocabulary
Define the following terms before reading the lesson on Calhoun.

1.	aggrandize	10.	contrivance	19.	lavish
2.	anarchy	11.	diversified	20.	ordination
3.	antagonistic	12.	exclusive	21.	proximate
4.	assumption	13.	faculties	22.	sovereignty
5.	compact	14.	gratuitously	23.	suffrage
6.	concurrent	15.	incontestable	24.	sympathetic
7.	conservative	16.	indispensable	25.	unimpaired
8.	constituted	17.	injurious	26.	usurpation
9.	consummate	18.	interpose	27.	vested

Review
1. In what official capacities did Calhoun serve the U.S. government?
2. Under what presidents did Calhoun serve as vice president?
3. What president was the political enemy of Calhoun?
4. What essay did Calhoun write to advocate state nullification of federal laws?
5. What book did Calhoun write to advocate the rights of the minority?
6. Why did Calhoun believe government had a tendency to abuse its power?
7. What problems did Calhoun think should be addressed by all constitutions?
8. Why did Calhoun think separation of powers was not enough to keep government from abusing its power?
9. According to Calhoun, why is the right to vote important to society?
10. How did Calhoun think a constitution should control government misconduct?
11. What did Calhoun think was the best way to protect minority interests?
12. What is a concurrent majority?
13. What is the doctrine of nullification?
14. Why did Calhoun think slavery could not be outlawed in the territories?
15. Decide whether the following statements are **True** or **False** according to John C. Calhoun.
    A. Human beings are social creatures.
    B. Human beings are motivated by self-interest.
    C. Government is natural to human existence.
    D. A concurrent majority promotes unfair government policies.
    E. Freedom is a natural right of all human beings.
    F. Slavery is good for society.
    G. The United States is in danger unless southern slavery is granted permanent protection.

What do you think?
On a scale of one through five, rate your opinion of the following quotations by Calhoun. Write a short statement explaining your rating.

1 – You **strongly agree** with the statement *or* you feel the statement is **admirable** considering the historical circumstances surrounding it.
5 – You **strongly disagree** with the statement *or* you feel the statement is **contemptible** considering the historical circumstances surrounding it.

A. *There is often, in the affairs of government, more efficiency and wisdom in non-action than in action.*
B. *I assume as an incontestable fact that man is so constituted as to be a social being.*
C. *While man is created for the social state and is accordingly so formed as to feel what affects others as well as what affects himself, he is, at the same time, so constituted . . . that his direct or individual affections are stronger than his sympathetic or social feelings.*
D. *Man is so constituted that government is necessary to the existence of society, and society to his existence and the perfection of his faculties.*
E. *Government, although intended to protect and preserve society, has a tendency to disorder and abuse of its powers.*
F. *There is no difficulty in forming government. It is not even a matter of choice whether there shall be one or not. . . . Like breathing, it is not permitted to depend on our volition.*
G. *Constitution is the contrivance of man, while government is of divine ordination.*
H. *Power can only be resisted by power.*
I. *The dominant majority, for the time, would have the same tendency to oppression and abuse of power which, without the right of suffrage, irresponsible rulers would have.*
J. *Give to each division or interest, through its appropriate organ, either a concurrent voice in making and executing the laws or a veto on their execution.*
K. *It is a great and dangerous error to suppose that all people are equally entitled to liberty. It is a reward to be earned, not a blessing to be gratuitously lavished on all alike—a reward reserved for the intelligent, the patriotic, the virtuous and deserving, and not a boon to be bestowed on a people too ignorant, degraded and vicious to be capable either of appreciating or of enjoying it.*
L. *Many in the South once believed that it [slavery] was a moral and political evil. That folly and delusion are gone. We see it now in its true light and regard it as the most safe and stable basis for free institutions in the world.*
M. *Taking the [Declaration of Independence] literally, there is not a word of truth in it.*

CHAPTER 19

FREDERICK DOUGLASS

BACKGROUND

Frederick Douglass (1818-1895) witnessed firsthand the degradation slavery brought to millions. As a young slave he saw human beings chained, beaten, and humiliated. He saw people torn from their families and worked like animals. These experiences never left his consciousness and were a constant motivation for his desire to reform the nation. After escaping slavery at age twenty he spent over five decades promoting human rights. Throughout his life he remained true to his personal creed, "Depend upon it, men will not care much for people who care only for themselves."

In 1838 Douglass escaped to New York and began his life as a free man. At first he worked a variety of odd jobs. However, his life changed when he was drawn to the abolitionist crusade. His inspiration to attend anti-slavery meetings came from reading *The Liberator*, an abolitionist newspaper published by William Lloyd Garrison. In 1841 Douglass was asked to tell his own story. In a speech that captured the attention of five hundred listeners he began his crusade to change the United States. His dynamic speaking abilities as well as his powerful writing skills put him in the forefront of the abolitionist movement.

Douglass championed the cause of human rights in many different capacities. He spent twenty-one months in England arousing support for emancipation. At the Seneca Falls convention for women's rights he was the only male to play a leadership role. He published *The North Star*, his own anti-slavery newspaper. He helped slaves on the Underground Railroad, and he befriended the controversial John Brown. During the Civil War he met President Lincoln to offer advice. In addition, he played an indispensable role in recruiting African-American soldiers. After the war Douglass championed universal suffrage and the integration of American society. He also served as minister to Haiti.

When Douglass died of a heart attack in 1895 his pallbearers included two U.S. senators and a Supreme Court judge. Five state legislatures adopted resolutions of regret, and schools were closed in his honor. For Douglass, and the nation, the extent of change in the lifetime of a single man was tremendous.

FREDERICK DOUGLASS – IN HIS OWN WORDS

Narrative of the Life of Frederick Douglass, 1845

I have often been utterly astonished, since I came to the north, to find persons who could speak of the singing, among slaves, as evidence of their contentment and happiness. It is impossible to conceive of a greater mistake. Slaves sing most when they are most unhappy. The songs of the slave represent the sorrows of his heart; and he is relieved by them, only as an aching heart is relieved by its tears.

Message to the British, March 1847

The whole system—the whole network of American Society—is one great falsehood. Americans have become dishonest men from the very circumstances by which they are surrounded. Seventy years ago they went to the battle-field in defense of liberty. Sixty years ago they formed a Constitution, over the very gateway of which they inscribed. "To secure the blessings of liberty to ourselves and our posterity!" In their Declaration of Independence they made the loudest and clearest assertions of the rights of man; at the very same time, the men who drew up the Declaration of Independence—the very men who adopted that Constitution—were trafficking in the bodies and souls of their fellow-men. From the adoption of the Constitution of the United States downwards, everything good and great in the heart of the American people, everything patriotic, has been summoned to defend that great lie before the world; they have been driven from their very patriotism to defend this great falsehood. . . .

. . . This being the state of things in America, I cannot be very patriotic, I hope you will not expect any very eloquent outbursts of eulogy or praises of America from me on this occasion. No my friends, I am going to be honest with America; I am going to the United States soon, but I go there to do as I have done here—to unmask her pretensions to republicanism,—to unmask her hypocritical pretensions to Christianity,—to denounce her pretensions to civilization,—to proclaim in her ear the wrongs of those who cry day and night to heaven, "How long, how long, oh Lord God!" . . . This nation presents to the world an anomaly that no other nation does present. They are the boldest in their pretensions, the oldest in their profession of the love of freedom; yet no nation on the globe can present a statute book so full of all that is cruel, that is malicious, of all that is infernal, as the American statute book. Every page is red with the blood of the oppressed American slave.

Speech to the Anti-Slavery Association, June 1848

I will say . . . that we have had some advice given us lately, from very high authority, I allude to Henry Clay, who, in his last speech . . . advised the free colored people of the United States that they had better go to Africa.

He says he does not wish to coerce us, but thinks we had better go! We have as much right to stay here as he has. . . . And I want to say to our white friends that we, colored folks, have had the subject under careful consideration, and have decided to stay! I want to say to any colonization friends that they may give their minds no further uneasiness on our account, for our minds are made up. . . .

Now there is one thing about us colored folks; it is this, that under all these most adverse circumstances . . . we are almost persuaded that there is a providence in our staying here. I do not know but the United States would rot in this tyranny if there were not some Negroes in this land—some to clink their chains in the ear of listening humanity, and from whose prostrate forms the lessons of liberty can be taught to the whites.

Oration delivered in Corinthian Hall, Rochester, NY, July 1852

I say it with a sad sense of the disparity between us. I am not included within the pale of this glorious [Fourth of July] anniversary! Your high independence only reveals the immeasurable distance between us. The blessings in which you, this day, rejoice, are not enjoyed in common.—The rich inheritance of justice, liberty, prosperity and independence, bequeathed by your fathers, is shared by you, not by me. The sunlight that brought light and healing to you, has brought stripes and death to me. This Fourth of July is *yours*, not *mine*. *You* may rejoice, *I* must mourn. . . .

What, to the American slave, is your 4th of July? I answer; a day that reveals to him, more than all other days in the year, the gross injustice and cruelty to which he is the constant victim. To him, your celebration is a sham; your boasted liberty, an unholy license; your national greatness, swelling vanity; your sounds of rejoicing are empty and heartless; your denunciation of tyrants, brass fronted impudence; your shouts of liberty and equality, hollow mockery; your prayers and hymns, your sermons and thanksgivings, with all your religious parade and solemnity, are, to him, mere bombast, fraud, deception, impiety, and hypocrisy—a thin veil to cover up crimes which would disgrace a nation of savages. There is not a nation on the earth guilty of practices more shocking and bloody than are the people of the United States, at this very hour. . . .

Americans! your republican politics, not less than your republican religion, are flagrantly inconsistent. You boast of your love of liberty, your superior civilization, and your pure Christianity, while the whole political power of the nation . . . is solemnly pledged to support and perpetuate the enslavement of three millions of your countrymen.

Letter to Harriet Beecher Stowe, March 1853

I assert then, that *poverty*, *ignorance*, and *degradation* are the combined evil, or in other words, these constitute the social disease of the Free Colored people in the United States. . . .

We have now two or three colored lawyers in this country; and I rejoice in the fact; for it affords very gratifying evidence of our progress. Yet it must be confessed that, in point of success, our lawyers are . . . great failures. . . . White people will not employ them . . . and the blacks, taking their *cue* from the whites, have not sufficient confidence in their abilities to employ them.

"The Various Phases of Anti-Slavery," 1855

All men desire Liberty. They desire to possess this inalienable birthright themselves, if they are not concerned about others being the recipients of its countless blessings. They instinctively shrink from the idea of having their Intellectual, their Moral, and their Physical organism, subjugated to the entire control of Tyranny, clothed in the vesture of assumed superiority. This love of their own identity is inseparably connected with their desire and hope of immortality. And even those who attack the citadel of man's personality, and seek to reduce him to a thing, are jealous of any invasion of their own Rights, and will resist to the death any encroachment upon the sacred domain of their own personal liberty. They are Abolitionists, as they seek to abolish any system of Oppression *which has them* for its victims, even though they trample their own principles in the dust, when the Rights of others are invaded. This is neither just nor generous. No man should crave the possession of that which he assiduously endeavors to withhold from another.

Again we maintain that no man has a Right to make any concession to Tyranny, which he would refuse to make if *he* were the victim.—He has no Right to make any compromise of contract in reference to the "Institution" of slavery, as it is falsely called, which he would be unwilling to make, were he, himself the slave. He should place himself, as it were, in the position of the slave, and advocate those principles and measures, which, judging from his stand-point, he would deem just and advisable.

Speech on the *Dred Scott* Decision, May 1857

This infamous decision of the Slaveholding wing of the Supreme Court maintains that slaves are within the contemplation of the Constitution of the United States, property; that slaves are property in the same sense that horses, sheep, and swine are property; that the old doctrine that slavery is a creature of local law is false; that the right of the slaveholder to his slave does not depend upon the local law, but is secured wherever the Constitution of the United States extends; that Congress has no right to prohibit slavery anywhere; that slavery may go in safety anywhere under the star-spangled banner; that colored persons of African descent have no rights that white men are bound to respect; that colored men of African descent are not and cannot be citizens of the United States.

You will readily ask me how I am affected by this devilish decision—this judicial incarnation of wolfishness? My answer is . . . my hopes were never brighter than now.

I have no fear that the National Conscience will be put to sleep by such an open, glaring, and scandalous tissue of lies as that decision is, and has been, over and over, shown to be.

The Supreme Court of the United States is not the only power in this world. It is very great, but the Supreme Court of the Almighty is greater. . . .

Happily for the whole human family, their rights have been defined, declared, and decided in a court higher than the Supreme Court. . . .

Your fathers have said that man's right to liberty is self-evident. There is no need of argument to make it clear. The voices of nature, of conscience, of reason, and of revelation, proclaim it as the right of all rights, the foundation of all trust, and of all responsibility. Man was born with it. It was his before he comprehended it. . . . To decide against this right in the person of Dred Scott, or the humblest and most whip-scarred bondman in the land, is to decide against God. It is an open rebellion against God's government. It is an attempt to undo what God has done . . . .

Such a decision cannot stand. . . .

The American people have been called upon, in a most striking manner, to abolish and put away forever the system of slavery. The subject has been pressed upon their attention in all earnestness and sincerity. The cries of the slave have gone forth to the world, and up to the throne of God. This decision, in my view, is a means of keeping the nation awake on the subject. It is another proof that God does not mean that we shall go to sleep, and forget that we are a slaveholding nation. . . .

I know of no soil better adapted to the growth of reform than American soil. I know of no country where the conditions for effecting great changes in the settled order of things, for the development of right ideas of liberty and humanity, are more favorable than here in these United States.

. . . The Constitution, as well as the Declaration of Independence, and the sentiments of the founders of the Republic, give us a platform broad enough, and strong enough, to support the most comprehensive plans for the freedom and elevation of all the people of this country.

"The Color Line," 1881

Few evils are less accessible to the force of reason, or more tenacious of life and power, than a long-standing prejudice. It is a moral disorder, which creates the conditions necessary to its own existence, and fortifies itself by refusing all contradiction. It paints a hateful picture according to its own diseased imagination, and distorts the features of the fancied original to suit the portrait. As those who believe in the visibility of ghosts can easily see them, so it is always easy to see repulsive qualities in those we despise and hate. . . .

Of all the races and varieties of men which have suffered from this feeling, the colored people of this country have endured most. They can resort to no disguises which will enable them to escape its deadly aim. They carry in front the evidence which marks them for persecution. . . . Their African origin can be instantly recognized, though they may be several removes from the typical African race. . . . They are Negroes—and that is enough, in the eye of this unreasoning prejudice, to justify indignity and violence. In nearly every department of American life they are confronted by this insidious influence. It fills the air. It meets them at the workshop and factory, when they apply for work. It meets them at the church, at the hotel, at the ballot-box, and worst of all, it meets them in the jury-box. . . .

Everything against the person with the hated color is promptly taken for granted; while everything in his favor is received with suspicion and doubt.

Speech on "A Defense of the Negro Race," 1894

It has sometimes been thought and said that Northern benevolence has already done enough for the moral and religious improvement of the Negro, and that the time has arrived when such help is no longer needed, that the Negro should now be left to take care of himself, that the duty of the white people of the country was fully and fairly performed when they restored the Negro to his freedom.

In answer to this position, I have to say that the claims of the Negro, viewed in the light of justice and fair play, are not so easily satisfied. The simple act of emancipation was indeed a great and glorious one, but it did not remove the consequences of slavery, nor could it atone for the centuries of wrong endured by the liberated bondman. It was a great and glorious thing to put an end to his physical bondage, but there was left to him a dreadful legacy of moral and intellectual deformity, which the abolition of physical bondage could not remove. . . .

In answer to the question as to what shall be done with the Negro, I have sometimes replied, "Do nothing with him, give him fair play and let him alone." But in reporting me, it has been found convenient and agreeable to place the emphasis of my speech on one part of my sentence. They willingly accepted my idea of letting the Negro alone, but not so my idea of giving the Negro fair play. . . .

With all the discouraging circumstances that now surround what is improperly called the Negro problem, I do not despair of a better day. It is sometimes said that the condition of the colored man today is worse than it was in the time of slavery. To me this is simply an extravagance. We now have the organic law of the land on our side. We have thousands of teachers, and hundreds of thousands of pupils attending schools; we can now count our friends by the million. In many of the States we have the elective franchise; in some of them we have colored office-holders. It is no small advantage that we are citizens of this Republic by special amendment of the Constitution. . . .

My hope for the Negro is largely based upon his enduring qualities. No persecutions, no hardships are able to extinguish him. He neither dies out, nor goes out. He is here to stay, and while here he will partake of the blessings of your education, your progress, your civilization, and your Christian religion. His appeal to you today is for an equal chance in the race of life; and, dark and stormy as the present appears, his appeal will not go unanswered.

FREDERICK DOUGLASS – A SIMULATED INTERVIEW

1. **What do all human beings have in common?**
   A. Every human being desires freedom. People naturally resist domination by a tyrannical power.
   B. Even tyrants fight to preserve their liberty. Tyrants become reformers when something threatens *their* liberty.

2. **How does American slavery affect individuals?**
   A. The buying and selling of slaves destroys black families.
   B. Slavery keeps blacks ignorant and unable to learn about Christianity.
   C. Slavery denies blacks the opportunity to become responsible and productive human beings.
   D. In a system without slavery individual masters might be good and moral. However, slavery requires masters to perform evil deeds. Although slaveowners may claim to hold Christian values, they cannot remain true to Christian teachings in a system of slavery.

3. **How does slavery affect the nation?**
   A. Slavery exposes the hypocrisy of Americans who proclaim beliefs in Christianity, equality, or liberty.
   B. The United States is not a civilized nation. Crimes committed by the United States would disgrace a nation of savages. The United States leads the world in all that is cruel and malicious.
   C. Americans cannot celebrate the Fourth of July without reminding blacks that the United States is a nation of injustice and cruelty.
   D. Americans who denounce the government of any other nation are hypocrites. The United States, a slave nation, is in no position to criticize other nations.

4. **Should African-Americans try to leave the United States?**
   A. Blacks should not move to Africa and surrender their birthright. Blacks are entitled to the rights of all Americans. Blacks should remain in the United States and insist on their rights as Americans.
   B. People of African ancestry are in the United States for an important reason—they are in the country to remind whites of the nation's proclaimed beliefs in rights and liberty. Blacks should force the nation to live up to its ideals.
   C. Blacks provide the ultimate test for American civilization. Only when blacks are accepted as human beings with equal rights can the United States fulfill its special purpose in the world.

5. **What should be done to improve conditions for African-Americans?**

   A. Merely ending slavery is not enough to remove the consequences of slavery. The nation must work to eliminate the moral and intellectual deformities that result from slavery.

   B. American blacks suffer from poverty, ignorance, and degradation. Blacks must overcome these three impediments to enjoy the benefits of American society.

   C. Blacks can improve their situation through economic independence and self-reliance. Blacks must learn to take care of themselves.

   D. Blacks should pursue occupations that make whites dependent on black labor. Blacks should become skilled workers and make themselves indispensable to the community.

6. **Did the Supreme Court rule correctly in *Dred Scott v. Sandford*?**

   A. Although the *Dred Scott* decision puts slaves in the same class as horses, sheep, and swine, the decision also gives hope to anyone who opposes slavery. The *Dred Scott* decision awakens the national conscience; it highlights the need to abolish slavery.

   B. The Supreme Court is not the highest authority. The *Dred Scott* decision violates God's law and undermines natural rights to liberty.

7. **What is the nature of racial prejudice in the United States?**

   A. Prejudice is the product of a "diseased imagination." Racial prejudice is a "moral disorder" that creates the conditions necessary for its continuation.

   B. Blacks are subject to prejudice more than any other group in the United States. Blacks cannot disguise themselves to escape prejudice. The ancestry of black people is enough to justify humiliation in the eyes of unreasoning people.

   C. Blacks face prejudice in every aspect of American life. Blacks face prejudice in the workplace, in hotels, in churches, in voting, and in the legal system.

   D. The situation for women in the United States is similar to that of black Americans.

8. **Is there hope for the United States?**

   A. The United States, more than any other nation, encourages reform. Reformers stand on a strong platform when they use the ideas expressed by the founders of the nation. Those ideas are strong enough to support any plan for freedom and equality.

   B. Blacks will eventually find justice in the United States. Blacks have the ability to endure; no amount of persecution or hardship has yet taken away their ability to survive.

   C. Human beings of different races can learn to live together peacefully. There is hope for the United States

STUDENT ACTIVITIES

Vocabulary
Define the following terms before reading the lesson on Douglass.

1. assiduously	9. encroachment	17. inconsistent
2. atone	10. eulogy	18. infamous
3. benevolence	11. flagrant	19. persecution
4. bombast	12. fraud	20. pretension
5. citadel	13. hypocritical	21. subjugate
6. coerce	14. immortality	22. vesture
7. deception	15. impiety	
8. degradation	16. incarnation	

Review
1. What originally inspired Douglass, an escaped slave, to attend anti-slavery meetings?
2. Who was William Lloyd Garrison?
3. What role did Douglass play at the Seneca Falls convention?
4. What anti-slavery newspaper was published by Douglass?
5. What role did Douglass play during the Civil War?
6. What did Douglass think every human being had in common?
7. According to Douglass, how did slavery affect white masters?
8. According to Douglass, what happens when Americans celebrate the Fourth of July?
9. In what way did Douglass think blacks provided the ultimate test for the United States?
10. What three things did Douglass think blacks had to overcome to enjoy the benefits of American society?
11. How did Douglass think blacks could best improve their situation?
12. Why did Douglass think blacks should become skilled workers?
13. What did Douglass think was a positive aspect to the *Dred Scott* decision?
14. How did Douglass define prejudice?
15. According to Douglass, why are blacks subject to prejudice more than any other group?
16. What did Douglass think about the conditions for women in the United States?
17. Decide whether the following statements are **True** or **False** according to Frederick Douglass.
    A. The United States is the most civilized nation in the world.
    B. Blacks will never find justice in America and should return to Africa.
    C. The United States is naturally resistant to reforming society.
    D. There is no hope for the United States because of a deep and cruel racism.

What do you think?
On a scale of one through five, rate your opinion of the following quotations by Frederick Douglass. Write a short statement explaining your rating.

1 – You **strongly agree** with the statement *or* you feel the statement is **admirable** considering the historical circumstances surrounding it.
5 – You **strongly disagree** with the statement *or* you feel the statement is **contemptible** considering the historical circumstances surrounding it.

A. *No nation on the globe can present a statute book so full of all that is cruel, that is malicious, of all that is infernal, as the American statute book.*

B. *I do not know but the United States would rot in this tyranny if there were not some Negroes in this land—some to clink their chains in the ear of listening humanity, and from whose prostrate forms the lessons of liberty can be taught to the whites.*

C. *This Fourth of July is yours, not mine. You may rejoice, I must mourn.*

D. *There is no nation on the earth guilty of practices more shocking and bloody than are the people of the United States, at this very hour.*

E. *The Supreme Court of the United States is not the only power in this world. It is very great, but the Supreme Court of the Almighty is greater.*

F. *I know of no soil better adapted to the growth of reform than American soil. I know of no country where the conditions for effecting great changes in the settled order of things, for the development of right ideas of liberty and humanity, are more favorable than here in these United States.*

G. *The Constitution, as well as the Declaration of Independence, and the sentiments of the founders of the Republic, give us a platform broad enough, and strong enough, to support the most comprehensive plans for the freedom and elevation of all the people of this country.*

H. *Few evils are less accessible to the force of reason, or more tenacious of life and power, than a long-standing prejudice.*

I. *The simple act of emancipation was indeed a great and glorious one, but it did not remove the consequences of slavery, nor could it atone for the centuries of wrong endured by the liberated bondman.*

J. *Where justice is denied, where poverty is enforced, where ignorance prevails, and where any one class is made to feel that society is in an organized conspiracy to oppress, rob, and degrade them, neither persons nor property will be safe.*

K. *The destiny of the colored American . . . is the destiny of America.*

L. *No man can put a chain about the ankle of his fellow man without at last finding the other end fastened about his own neck.*

PART 4

A NEW BIRTH OF FREEDOM

CHAPTER 20

ABRAHAM LINCOLN

BACKGROUND

Abraham Lincoln (1809-1865) was born into a poor pioneer family and received no more than a year of formal education. As a child he experienced a typical frontier life, learning to plow the land and plant crops. Longing for a better life, he sought self-improvement through reading.

As a young adult Lincoln studied law. He began a career in politics in 1834 when he was elected to the Illinois state legislature. In 1846 he was elected to the U.S. Congress. Deciding not to run for reelection, he devoted himself to his legal career, becoming one of the most important and prosperous attorneys in Illinois.

Lincoln first gained national recognition in 1854 by denouncing the Kansas-Nebraska Act and speaking eloquently against the spread of slavery. The new Republican Party, which he played a significant role in forming, nominated him to run for the U.S. Senate in 1858. Although he lost the election, the debates with his opponent Stephen Douglas made Lincoln a national figure. He was elected president in 1860.

Before Lincoln took office seven southern states seceded from the Union. He was therefore inaugurated facing one of the worst crises in United States history. Shortly after his inauguration the Civil War began and four more states seceded. Using broad presidential powers to meet the crisis, he led the Union to victory in April 1865. Tragically, he was assassinated five days after the war ended.

In addition to his status as a folk hero Lincoln was an extremely ambitious politician. He also suffered from deep bouts of depression and feelings of hopelessness. A longtime friend once described Lincoln by saying, "I never saw so gloomy and melancholy a face in my life."

President Lincoln expressed idealistic goals during one of the nation's darkest times. He never faltered in his resolve to bring the Union to victory despite public ridicule, deep personal anguish, and several humiliating military defeats. His Gettysburg Address is considered one of the most eloquent descriptions of the higher purpose of America—a government "of the people, by the people, for the people."

ABRAHAM LINCOLN – IN HIS OWN WORDS

Speech to Young Men's Lyceum of Springfield, January 1838

I hope I am over wary; but if I am not, there is, even now, something of ill-omen amongst us. I mean the increasing disregard for law which pervades the country; the growing disposition to substitute the wild and furious passions, in lieu of the sober judgement of courts; and the worse than savage mobs, for the executive ministers of justice. . . . Accounts of outrages committed by mobs, form the everyday news of the times. . . .

It would be tedious as well as useless, to recount the horrors of all of them. Those happening in the State of Mississippi, and at St. Louis, are, perhaps, the most dangerous in example, and revolting to humanity. In the Mississippi case, they first commenced by hanging the regular gamblers: a set of men, certainly not following for a livelihood, a very useful, or very honest occupation; but one which, so far from being forbidden by the laws, was actually licensed by an act of the Legislature, passed but a single year before. Next, negroes, suspected of conspiring to raise an insurrection, were caught up and hanged in all parts of the State: then, white men, supposed to be leagued with the negroes; and finally, strangers, from neighboring States, going thither on business, were, in many instances, subjected to the same fate. Thus went on this process of hanging, from gamblers to negroes, from negroes to white citizens, and from these to strangers; till, dead men were seen literally dangling from the boughs of trees upon every road side; and in numbers almost sufficient, to rival the native Spanish moss of the country, as a drapery of the forest. . . .

But you are, perhaps, ready to ask, "What has this to do with the perpetuation of our political institutions?" I answer, it has much to do with it. Its direct consequences are, comparatively speaking, but a small evil; and much of its danger consists, in the proneness of our minds, to regard its direct, as its only consequences. . . . When men take it in their heads today, to hang gamblers, or burn murderers, they should recollect, that, in the confusion usually attending such transactions they will be as likely to hang or burn some one, who is neither a gambler nor a murderer as one who is; and that, acting upon the example they set, the mob of tomorrow, may, and probably will, hang or burn some of them, by the very same mistake. And not only so; the innocent, those who have ever set their faces against violations of law in every shape, alike with the guilty, fall victims to the ravages of mob law; and thus it goes on, step by step, till all the walls erected for the defense of the persons and property of individuals, are trodden down, and disregarded. . . .

I know the American People are *much* attached to their government;—I know they would suffer *much* for its sake;—I know they would endure evils long and patiently, before they would ever think of exchanging it for another. Yet, notwithstanding all this, if the laws be continually despised and disregarded, if their rights to be secure in their persons and property, are held by no better tenure than the caprice of a mob, the alienation of their affections from the government is the natural consequence; and to that, sooner or later, it must come. . . .

The question recurs "How shall we fortify against it?" The answer is simple. Let every American, every lover of liberty, every well wisher to his posterity, swear by the blood of the Revolution, never to violate in the least particular, the laws of the country; and never to tolerate their violation by others. As the patriots of seventy-six did to the support of the Declaration of Independence, so to the support of the Constitution and Laws, let every American pledge his life, his property, and his sacred honor;—let every man remember that to violate the law, is to trample on the blood of his father, and to tear the charter of his own, and of his children's liberty. Let reverence for the laws, be breathed by every American mother, to the lisping babe, that prattles on her lap let it be taught in schools, in seminaries, and in colleges;—let it be written in primers, spelling books, and in almanacs;—let it be preached from the pulpit, proclaimed in legislative halls, and enforced in courts of justice. And, in short, let it become the *political religion* of the nation; and let the old and the young, the rich and the poor, the grave and the gay, of all sexes and tongues, and colors and conditions, sacrifice unceasingly upon its altars.

Speech at Peoria Criticizing the Kansas-Nebraska Act, October 1854

This *declared* indifference, but as I must think, covert *real* zeal for the spread of slavery, I can not but hate. I hate it because of the monstrous injustice of slavery itself. I hate it because it deprives our republican example of its just influence in the world—enables the enemies of free institutions, with plausibility, to taunt us as hypocrites—causes the real friends of freedom to doubt our sincerity, and especially because it forces so many really good men amongst ourselves into an open war with the very fundamental principles of civil liberty—criticizing the Declaration of Independence, and insisting that there is no right principle of action but *self-interest*.

Letter to Joshua Speed, August 1855

I am not a Know-Nothing. That is certain. How could I be? How can any one who abhors the oppression of negroes, be in favor of degrading classes of white people? Our progress in degeneracy appears to me to be pretty rapid. As a nation, we began by declaring that "*all men are created equal.*" We now practically read it "all men are created equal, *except negroes.*" When the Know-Nothings get control, it will read "all men are created equal, except negroes, *and foreigners, and catholics.*" When it comes to this I should prefer emigrating to some country where they make no pretense of loving liberty—to Russia, for instance, where despotism can be taken pure, and without the base alloy of hypocrisy.

Speech at Springfield Criticizing the Dred Scott Decision, June 1857

And this is the staple argument . . . for doing this obvious violence to the plain unmistakable language of the Declaration.

I think the authors of that notable instrument intended to include *all* men, but they did not intend to declare all men equal *in all respects*. They did not mean to say all were equal in color, size, intellect, moral developments, or social capacity. They defined with tolerable distinctness in what respects they did consider all men created equal—equal in "certain inalienable rights, among which are life, liberty, and the pursuit of happiness." This they said, and this they meant. They did not mean to assert the obvious untruth, that all were then actually enjoying that equality, nor yet, that they were about to confer it immediately upon them. In fact they had no power to confer such a boon. They meant simply to declare the *right*, so that the *enforcement* of it might follow as fast as circumstances should permit.

They meant to set up a standard maxim for free society which should be familiar to all, and revered by all; constantly looked to, constantly labored for, and even though never perfectly attained, constantly approximated, and thereby constantly spreading and deepening its influence, and augmenting the happiness and value of life to all people of all colors everywhere. The assertion that "all men are created equal" was of no practical use in effecting our separation from Great Britain and it was placed in the Declaration, not for that, but for future use. Its authors meant it to be, as, thank God, it is now proving itself, a stumbling block to those who in after times might seek to turn a free people back into the hateful paths of despotism. They knew the proneness of prosperity to breed tyrants, and they meant when such should re-appear in this fair land and commence their vocation they should find left for them at least one hard nut to crack.

The House Divided Speech, June 1858

If we could first know where we are, and whither we are tending we could then better judge what to do, and how to do it. We are now far into the fifth year, since a policy was initiated, with the avowed object, and confident promise, of putting an end to slavery agitation. Under the operation of that policy, that agitation has not only, not ceased, but has constantly augmented. In my opinion, it will not cease until a crisis shall have been reached, and passed. "A house divided against itself cannot stand." I believe this government cannot endure permanently half slave and half free. I do not expect the Union to be dissolved—I do not expect the house to fall—but I do expect it will cease to be divided. It will become all one thing, or all the other. Either the opponents of slavery will arrest the further spread of it, and place it where the public mind shall rest in the belief that it is in course of ultimate extinction; or its advocates will push it forward, till it shall become alike lawful in all the States, old as well as new, North as well as South.

Letter to Henry Pierce, April 1859

This is a world of compensations; and he who would *be* no slave, must consent to *have* no slave. Those who deny freedom to others, deserve it not for themselves; and, under a just God, can not long retain it. All honor to

Jefferson—to the man who, in the concrete pressure of a struggle for national independence by a single people, had the coolness, forecast, and capacity to introduce into a merely revolutionary document, an abstract truth, applicable to all men and all times, and so to embalm it there, that today, and in all coming days, it shall be a rebuke and a stumbling-block to the very harbingers of re-appearing tyranny and oppression.

Cooper Union Speech, February 1860

Wrong as we think slavery is, we can yet afford to let it alone where it is, because that much is due to the necessity arising from its actual presence in the nation; but can we, while our votes will prevent it, allow it to spread into the National Territories, and to overrun us here in these Free States?

If our sense of duty forbids this, then let us stand by our duty, fearlessly and effectively. Let us be diverted by none of those sophistical contrivances wherewith we are so industriously plied and belabored—contrivances such as groping for some middle ground between the right and the wrong; vain as the search for a man who should be neither a living man nor a dead man; such as a policy of "don't care" on a question about which all true men do care; such as Union appeals beseeching true Union men to yield to Disunionists, reversing the Divine rule, and calling, not the sinners, but the righteous to repentance; such as invocations to Washington, imploring men to unsay what Washington said, and undo what Washington did.

. . . Let us have faith that right makes might, and in that faith, let us, to the end, dare to do our duty as we understand it.

Message to Congress, December 1862

I cannot make it better known than it already is that I strongly favor colonization. And yet I wish to say there is an objection urged against free colored persons remaining in the country, which is largely imaginary, if not sometimes malicious. . . .

But it is dreaded that the freed people will swarm forth, and cover the whole land. Are they not already in the land? Will liberation make them any more numerous? Equally distributed among the whites of the whole country, and there would be but one colored to seven whites. Could the one, in any way, greatly disturb the seven? There are many communities now, having more than one free colored person, to seven whites; and this, without any apparent consciousness of evil from it. . . .

Fellow citizens, *we* cannot escape history. We of this Congress and this administration, will be remembered in spite of ourselves. No personal significance, or insignificance, can spare one or another of us. The fiery trial through which we pass, will light us down, in honor or dishonor, to the latest generation. We *say* we are for the Union. The world will not forget that we say this. We know how to save the Union. The world knows we do know how to save it. We—even *we here*—hold the power, and bear the responsibility. In *giving* freedom to the *slave*, we assure freedom to the *free*—honorable alike in what we give, and what we preserve. We shall nobly save, or meanly lose, the last best, hope of earth. Other means may succeed; this could not fail. The way is plain, peaceful, generous, just—a way which, if followed, the world will forever applaud, and God must forever bless.

"It is for Us the Living" (The Gettysburg Address), November 1863

Four score and seven years ago our fathers brought forth on this continent, a new nation, conceived in liberty, and dedicated to the proposition that all men are created equal.

Now we are engaged in a great civil war, testing whether that nation or any nation so conceived and so dedicated, can long endure. We are met on a great battle-field of that war. We have come to dedicate a portion of that field, as a final resting place for those who here gave their lives that that nation might live. It is altogether fitting and proper that we should do this.

But, in a larger sense, we can not dedicate—we can not consecrate—we can not hallow—this ground. The brave men, living and dead, who struggled here, have consecrated it far above our poor power to add or detract. The world will little note, nor long remember what we say here, but it can never forget what they did here. It is for us the living, rather, to be dedicated here to the unfinished work which they who fought here have thus far so nobly advanced. It is rather for us to be here dedicated to the great task remaining before us—that from these honored dead we take increased devotion to that cause for which they gave the last full measure of devotion—that we here highly resolve that these dead shall not have died in vain—that this nation, under God, shall have a new birth of freedom—and that government of the people, by the people, for the people, shall not perish from the earth.

Second Inaugural Address, March 1865

Neither party expected for the war the magnitude, or the duration, which it has already attained. Neither anticipated that the *cause* of the conflict might cease with, or even before, the conflict itself should cease. Each looked for an easier triumph, and a result less fundamental and astounding. Both read the same Bible, and pray to the same God; and each invokes His aid against the other. It may seem strange that any men should dare to ask a just God's assistance in wringing their bread from the sweat of other men's faces; but let us judge not that we be not judged. The prayers of both could not be answered; that of neither has been answered fully. The Almighty has His own purposes. . . .

With malice toward none; with charity for all; with firmness in the right, as God gives us to see the right, let us strive on to finish the work we are in; to bind up the nation's wounds; to care for him who shall have borne the battle, and for his widow, and his orphan—to do all which may achieve and cherish a just, and a lasting peace, among ourselves, and with all nations.

ABRAHAM LINCOLN – A SIMULATED INTERVIEW

1. **How important to society is respect for the law?**
   A. Respect for the law should become "the political religion of the nation." When people disregard the law the nation is subject to mob rule.
   B. Everyone should obey the law. Even bad laws should be obeyed until they are repealed through the process of a free government.

2. **What is the historical significance of the Declaration of Independence?**
   A. The Declaration of Independence established a central idea to direct Americans toward a good government and a good society. It should serve as a "stumbling block" for anyone who opposes freedom.
   B. The Declaration of Independence proclaimed ideas of liberty and equality. It did not declare that all people are equal in all respects; people are equal only in their rights to life, liberty, and the pursuit of happiness.
   C. The Declaration of Independence not only gives hope to Americans, but to people of all nations. The ideas expressed in the Declaration of Independence are universal ideas.

3. **Does slavery have a place in the United States?**
   A. Slavery is unjust; slavery violates the principles of the Declaration of Independence.
   B. Slavery is contrary to the central idea of the nation. Americans cannot convince the world to embrace values of liberty and equality as long as the United States allows slavery.
   C. Americans should spend no time searching for a middle ground in the debate over slavery. Slavery is wrong; opposition to slavery is right.

4. **What are the arguments against slavery?**
   A. If slavery is such a good thing, as many southerners argue, why does no white man take advantage of the good thing and become a slave himself?
   B. If "A" can prove that he may enslave "B," why should "B" not prove that he can enslave "A"?
   C. If the issue deciding slavery is intelligence, an individual should then become a slave to the first person he meets who is an intellectual superior.
   D. If the issue deciding slavery is the color of skin, an individual should then become a slave to the first person he meets with lighter colored skin.
   E. If the issue deciding slavery is self-interest, then why should a slave not declare his self-interest by enslaving his master?

F. Unlike a system of free labor, slavery does not allow people to improve. Free labor allows the workers of today to become the business owners of tomorrow. Slavery is a threat to the ideals of a nation based on the promise of free labor.

5. **Should the United States abolish slavery?**
    A. Slavery should not be allowed to spread into the western territories where the federal government has jurisdiction. However, the United States should leave slavery alone in the states where it already exists.
    B. The Constitution does not grant Congress the power to interfere with slavery in the southern states. Leaving southern slavery free from northern interference is essential for the preservation of the Union. [Lincoln expressed this idea *before* the Civil War.]
    C. Emancipation of the slaves in all states except those remaining loyal to the Union is a military necessity. Emancipation is necessary to strike at the heart of a rebellion that is trying to destroy the Union. [Lincoln expressed this idea *during* the Civil War when he issued the Emancipation Proclamation.]

6. **Should the Supreme Court be granted the right to declare a law unconstitutional as it did in *Dred Scott v. Sandford*?**
    A. The Supreme Court ruled incorrectly in the *Dred Scott* case. The framers of the Constitution accepted citizenship for black Americans. In five of the original thirteen states—Massachusetts, New Hampshire, New York, New Jersey, and North Carolina—free blacks had the right to vote. Blacks played a role in ratifying the Constitution; blacks are certainly included in the phrase, "We the people."
    B. The *Dred Scott* case is a good example of why public policy should not be decided by judges. Policy made by judges is not democratic.
    C. A law should only be declared unconstitutional with the consent of the people. The ultimate power of government rests with the people. The Supreme Court should not act without the people's consent.

7. **Should the Union be preserved?**
    A. Southern secession is the act of a minority attempting to impose its will upon a constitutional majority. Secession is not authorized by the Constitution or the ideals of the American Revolution.
    B. The people of the Confederacy inaccurately say they are fighting for self-government. In reality, the purpose of secession is to protect slavery, an institution contrary to the principles found in the Declaration of Independence.
    C. The Civil War is a test of whether self-government is workable. The Union must be preserved to show the world that self-government is possible. The United States is the "last, best hope of earth."

STUDENT ACTIVITIES

Vocabulary
Define the following terms before reading the lesson on Lincoln.

1. agitation	10. disposition	19. plausibility
2. alienation	11. embalm	20. posterity
3. augment	12. emigrate	21. proneness
4. boon	13. hallow	22. reverence
5. boughs	14. harbinger	23. staple
6. caprice	15. hypocrite	24. taunt
7. consecrate	16. lisping	25. thither
8. covert	17. malice	26. wary
9. degeneracy	18. perpetuation	27. zeal

Review
1. When did Lincoln first gain national recognition?
2. Why were the Lincoln-Douglas debates important to Lincoln's political career?
3. What did Lincoln think should be "the political religion of the nation"?
4. What did Lincoln believe was the central idea of the United States?
5. In what way are all people created equal according to Lincoln?
6. Which five of the original thirteen states granted free blacks the right to vote?
7. Why did Lincoln think the *Dred Scott* decision was an incorrect decision?
8. What was Lincoln's position on judicial review?
9. Why did Lincoln think southern secession was wrong?
10. Although the people of the South said they were fighting for self-government, why did Lincoln think they were fighting?
11. Why did Lincoln think the Union should be preserved?
12. Decide whether the following statements are **True** or **False** according to Abraham Lincoln.
    A. The ideas expressed in the Declaration of Independence are universal ideas.
    B. Slavery keeps the United States from influencing other nations to adopt values of liberty and equality.
    C. Americans should try to compromise on the issue of slavery.
    D. Slavery is a threat to the ideals of a nation based on the promise of free labor.
    E. The Emancipation Proclamation is a military necessity.
    F. Policy made by judges is not democratic.
    G. African-Americans played a role in ratifying the United States Constitution.

What do you think?
On a scale of one through five, rate your opinion of the following quotations by Lincoln. Write a short statement explaining your rating.

1 – You **strongly agree** with the statement *or* you feel the statement is **admirable** considering the historical circumstances surrounding it.
5 – You **strongly disagree** with the statement *or* you feel the statement is **contemptible** considering the historical circumstances surrounding it.

A. *When men take it in their heads today, to hang gamblers, or burn murderers, they should recollect, that, in the confusion usually attending such transactions they will be as likely to hang or burn someone, who is neither a gambler nor a murderer as one who is.*

B. *Let every American, every lover of liberty, every well wisher to his posterity, swear by the blood of the Revolution, never to violate in the least particular, the laws of the country; and never to tolerate their violation by others.*

C. *Let [reverence for the laws] become the political religion of the nation.*

D. *I think the authors of that notable instrument [the Declaration of Independence] intended to include all men, but they did not intend to declare all men equal in all respects.*

E. *[The authors of the Declaration of Independence] defined with tolerable distinctness in what respects they did consider all men created equal—equal in "certain inalienable rights, among which are life, liberty, and the pursuit of happiness." This they said and this they meant.*

F. *[The authors of the Declaration of Independence] meant to set up a standard maxim for free society which should be familiar to all, and revered by all.*

G. *Its authors meant [the Declaration of Independence] to be . . . a stumbling block to those who . . . might seek to turn a free people back into the hateful paths of despotism.*

H. *Those who deny freedom to others, deserve it not for themselves; and under a just God, can not long retain it.*

I. *In giving freedom to the slave, we assure freedom to the free—honorable alike in what we give, and what we preserve.*

J. *[The United States is] the last best hope of earth.*

K. *These capitalists generally act harmoniously, and in concert, to fleece the people.*

L. *The ballot is stronger than the bullet.*

M. *I am a firm believer in the people. If given the truth, they can be depended upon to meet any national crisis. The great point is to bring them the real facts.*

N. *To sin by silence when they should protest makes cowards of men.*

PART 5

THE
INDUSTRIAL REVOLUTION

CHAPTER 21

ADAM SMITH

BACKGROUND

Adam Smith (1723-90) received his education at Oxford University before becoming a professor at the University of Glasgow in Scotland. As a professor he gained recognition for his book *The Theory of Moral Sentiments*, a book he used to outline his belief that empathy was the basis for moral principles. He believed human beings, who were creatures of self-interest, could still be moral because of an innate ability to grasp the feelings of others.

Smith eventually resigned his professorship at Glasgow to work as a tutor for the Duke of Buccleuch. This was a fortunate assignment since Smith had the opportunity to travel throughout Europe and meet many of the great thinkers of the time. However, the assignment lasted only two years. After the Duke's brother was murdered in Paris, the Duke's family decided to return home. Smith returned with them.

Smith returned to Scotland where he wrote *The Wealth of Nations*, a book outlining his economic ideas. The book remains one of the most important works in the history of economic thought. In *Wealth of Nations* he stated his belief that the natural inclination of individuals to pursue self-interest resulted in the well-being of society. Arguing that wealth was measured by the consumable goods a nation produced, Smith assumed that if individuals pursued their self-interest when producing goods, the welfare of the entire society would come about from the power of an "invisible hand" guiding human action. In short, self-interest would be regulated by competition.

Adam Smith was respected by the public and received many honors in his lifetime. He was even a personal friend of Benjamin Franklin. Although he was highly regarded for his intellect, he was also known as a notoriously absent-minded man. People enjoyed hearing the amusing story of how he was once kidnapped and later abandoned by gypsies. Despite his fame, his death went largely unnoticed. In 1790 the people of England were evidently too preoccupied with news of the French Revolution and its possible effect on England to take much notice that Smith had passed away.

ADAM SMITH – IN HIS OWN WORDS

Theory of Moral Sentiments, 1759

To the selfish and original passions of human nature, the loss or gain of a very small interest of our own, appears to be of vastly more importance, excites a much more passionate joy or sorrow, a much more ardent desire or aversion, than the greatest concern of another with whom we have no particular connexion. His interests, as long as they are surveyed from this station, can never be put into the balance with our own, can never restrain us from doing whatever may tend to promote our own, how ruinous soever to him. Before we can make any proper comparison of those opposite interests, we must change our position. We must view them, neither from our own place nor yet from his, neither with our own eyes nor yet with his, but from the place and with the eyes of a third person, who has no particular connexion with either, and who judges with impartiality between us. Here, too, habit and experience have taught us to do this so easily and so readily, that we are scarce sensible that to do it; and it requires, in this case too, some degree of reflection, and even of philosophy, to convince us, how little interest we should take in the greatest concerns of our neighbour, how little we should be affected by whatever relates to him, if the sense of propriety and justice did not correct the otherwise natural inequality of our sentiments.

Let us suppose that the great empire of China, with all its myriads of inhabitants, was suddenly swallowed up by an earthquake, and let us consider how a man of humanity in Europe, who had no sort of connexion with that part of the world, would be affected upon receiving intelligence of this dreadful calamity. He would, I imagine, first of all, express very strongly his sorrow for the misfortune of that unhappy people, he would make many melancholy reflections upon the precariousness of human life, and the vanity of the labours of man, which could thus be annihilated in a moment. He would too, perhaps, if he was a man of speculation, enter into many reasonings concerning the effects which this disaster might produce upon the commerce of Europe, and the trade and business of the world in general. And when all this fine philosophy was over, when all these humane sentiments had been once fairly expressed, he would pursue his business or his pleasure, take his repose or his diversion, with the same ease and tranquility, as if no such accident had happened.

The most frivolous disaster which could befall himself would occasion a more real disturbance. If he was to lose his little finger tomorrow, he would not sleep tonight; but, provided he never saw them, he will snore with the most profound security over the ruin of a hundred millions of his brethren, and the destruction of that immense multitude seems plainly an object less interesting to him, than this paltry misfortune of his own. . . . When we are always so much more deeply affected by whatever concerns ourselves, than by whatever concerns other men; what is it which prompts the generous . . . to sacrifice their own interest to the greater interest of others? It is not the soft power of humanity, it is not that feeble spark of benevolence which Nature has lighted up in the human heart, that is thus capable of counteracting the strongest impulses of self-love. It is a stronger power, a more forcible motive, which exerts itself upon such occasions. It is reason, principle, conscience, the inhabitant of the breast, the man within, the great judge and arbiter of our conduct. It is he who, whenever we are about to act so as to affect the happiness of others, calls to us, with a voice capable of astonishing the most presumptuous of our passions, that we are but one of the multitude, in no respect better than any other in it . . . It is a stronger love, a more powerful affection, which generally takes place upon such occasions; the love of what is honourable and noble, of the grandeur, and dignity, and superiority of our own character. . . .

The poor man's son, whom heaven in its anger has visited with ambition, when he begins to look around him, admires the condition of the rich. He finds the cottage of his father too small for his accommodation, and fancies he should be lodged more at his ease in a palace. He is displeased with being obliged to walk-a-foot, or to endure the fatigue of riding on horseback. He sees his superiors carried about in machines, and imagines that in one of these he could travel with less inconvenience. He feels himself naturally indolent, and willing to serve himself with his own hands as little as possible; and judges, that a numerous retinue of servants would save him from a great deal of trouble. he thinks if he had attained all these, he would sit still contentedly, and be quiet, enjoying himself in the thought of the happiness and tranquility of his situation. He is enchanted with the distant idea of this felicity. It appears in his fancy like the life of some superior rank of beings, and in order to arrive at it, he devotes himself forever to the pursuit of wealth and greatness.

Wealth of Nations, 1776

This division of labour, from which so many advantages are derived, is not originally the effect of any human wisdom, which foresees and intends that general opulence to which it gives occasion. It is the necessary, though very slow and gradual consequence of a certain propensity in human nature which has in view no such extensive utility; the propensity to truck, barter, and exchange one thing for another.

Whether this propensity be one of those original principles in human nature, of which no further account can be given; or whether, as seems more probable, it be the necessary consequence of the faculties of reason and speech, it belongs not to our present subject to enquire. It is common to all men, and to be found in no other race of animals, which seem to know neither this nor any other species of contracts. Two greyhounds, in running down the same hare, have sometimes the appearance of acting in some sort of concert. Each turns her towards his companion, or endeavours to intercept her when his companion turns her towards himself.

This, however, is not the effect of any contract, but of the accidental concurrence of their passions in the same object at that particular time. Nobody ever saw a dog make a fair and deliberate exchange of one bone for another with another dog. Nobody ever saw one animal by its gestures and natural cries signify to another, this is mine, that yours; I am willing to give this for that. When an animal wants to obtain something either of a man or of another animal, it has no other means of persuasion but to gain the favour of those whose service it requires. A puppy fawns upon its dam, and a spaniel endeavours by a thousand attractions to engage the attention of its master who is at dinner, when it wants to be fed by him. Man sometimes uses the same arts with his brethren, and when he has no other means of engaging them to act according to his inclinations, endeavours by every servile and fawning attention to obtain their good will. He has not time, however, to do this upon every occasion. In civilized society he stands at all times in need of the cooperation and assistance of great multitudes, while his whole life is scarce sufficient to gain the friendship of a few persons.

In almost every other race of animals each individual, when it is grown up to maturity, is entirely independent, and in its natural state has occasion for the assistance of no other living creature. But man has almost constant occasion for the help of his brethren, and it is in vain for him to expect it from their benevolence only. He will be more likely to prevail if he can interest their self-love in his favour, and show them that it is for their own advantage to do for him what he requires of them. Whoever offers to another a bargain of any kind, proposes to do this. Give me that which I want, and you shall have this which you want, is the meaning of every such offer; and it is in this manner that we obtain from one another the far greater part of those good offices which we stand in need of. It is not from the benevolence of the butcher, the brewer, or the baker, that we expect our dinner, but from their regard to their own interest. We address ourselves, not to their humanity but to their self-love, and never talk to them of our own necessities but of their advantages. Nobody but a beggar chooses to depend chiefly upon the benevolence of his fellow-citizens. Even a beggar does not depend upon it entirely. The charity of well-disposed people, indeed, supplies him with the whole fund of his subsistence. But though this principle ultimately provides him with all the necessaries of life which he has occasion for, it neither does nor can provide him with them as he has occasion for them. The greater part of his occasional wants are supplied in the same manner as those of other people, by treaty, by barter, and by purchase. With the money which one man gives him he purchases food. The old clothes which another bestows upon him he exchanges for other old clothes which suit him better, or for lodging, or for goods, or for money, with which he can buy either food, clothes, or lodging as he has occasion.

As it is by treaty, by barter, and by purchase, that we obtain from one another the greater part of those mutual good offices which we stand in need of, so it is this same trucking disposition which originally gives occasion to the division of labour. In a tribe of hunters or shepherds a particular person makes bows and arrows, for example, with more readiness and dexterity than any other. He frequently exchanges them for cattle or for venison with his companions; and he finds at last that he can in this manner get more cattle and venison, than if he himself went to the field to catch them. From a regard to his own interest, therefore, the making of bows and arrows grows to be his chief business, and he becomes a sort of armourer. Another excels in making the frames and covers of their little huts or moveable houses. He is accustomed to be of use in this way to his neighbours, who reward him in the same manner with cattle and with venison, till at last he finds it his interest to dedicate himself entirely to this employment, and to become a sort of house-carpenter. In the same manner a third becomes a smith or a brazier, a fourth a tanner or dresser of hides or skins, the principal part of the clothing of savages. And thus the certainty of being able to exchange all that surplus part of the produce of his own labour, which is over and above his own consumption, for such parts of the produce of other men's labour as he may have occasion for, encourages every man to apply himself to a particular occupation, and to cultivate and bring to perfection whatever talent or genius he may possess for that particular species of business. . . .

Every man is rich or poor according to the degree in which he can afford to enjoy the necessaries, conveniences, and amusements of human life. But after the division of labour has once thoroughly taken place, it is but a very small part of these with which a man's own labour can supply him. The far greater part of them he must derive from the labour of other people, and he must be rich or poor according to the quantity of that labour which he can command, or which he can afford to purchase. The value of any commodity, therefore, to the person who possesses it, and who means not to use or consume it himself, but to exchange it for other commodities, is equal to the quantity of labour which it enables him to purchase or command. Labour, therefore, is the real measure of the exchangeable value of all commodities.

The real price of everything, what every thing really costs to the man who wants to acquire it, is the toil and trouble of acquiring it, and who wants to dispose of it or exchange it for something else, is the toil and trouble which it can save to himself, and which it can impose upon other people. What is bought with money or with goods is purchased by labour as much as what we acquire by the toil of our own body. That money or those goods indeed save us this toil. They contain the value of a certain quantity of labour which we exchange for what is supposed at the time to contain the value of an equal quantity. Labour was the first price, the original purchase money that was paid for all things. It was not by gold or by silver, but by labour, that all the wealth of the world was originally purchased; and its value, to those who possess it and who want to exchange it for some new productions, is precisely equal to the quantity of labour which it can enable them to purchase or command. . . .

. . . Servants, labourers, and workmen of different kinds, make up the far greater part of every great political society. But what improves the circumstances of the greater part can never be regarded as an inconvenience to the whole. No society can surely be flourishing and happy, of which the far greater part of the members are poor and miserable. It is but equity, besides, that they who feed, clothe, and lodge the whole body of the people, should have such a share of the produce of their own labour as to be themselves tolerably well fed, clothed, and lodged. . . .

. . . As every individual, therefore, endeavours as much as he can both to employ his capital in the support of domestic industry, and so to direct that industry that its produce may be of the greatest value; every individual necessarily labours to render the annual revenue of the society as great as he can. He generally, indeed, neither intends to promote the public interest, nor knows how much he is promoting it. By preferring the support of domestic to that of foreign industry, he intends only his own security; and by directing that industry in such a manner as its produce may be of the greatest value, he intends only his own gain, and he is in this, as in many other cases, led by an invisible hand to promote an end which was no part of his intention. Nor is it always the worse for the society that it was not part of it. By pursuing his own interest he frequently promotes that of the society more effectually than when he really intends to promote it. I have never known much good done by those who affected to trade for the public good. It is an affectation, indeed, not very common among merchants, and very few words need be employed in dissuading them from it. . . .

. . . Every man, as long as he does not violate the laws of justice, is left perfectly free to pursue his own interest his own way, and to bring both his industry and capital into competition with those of any other man, or order of men. The sovereign is completely discharged from a duty, in the attempting to perform which he must always be exposed to innumerable delusions, and for the proper performance of which no human wisdom or knowledge could ever be sufficient; the duty of superintending the industry of private people, and of directing it towards the employments most suitable to the interest of the society. According to the system of natural liberty, the sovereign has only three duties to attend to; three duties of great importance, indeed, but plain and intelligible to common understandings: first, the duty of protecting the society from the violence and invasion of other independent societies; secondly, the duty of protecting as far as possible, every member of the society from the injustice or oppression of every other member of it, or the duty of establishing an exact administration of justice; and, thirdly, the duty of erecting and maintaining certain public works and certain public institutions, which it can never be for the interest of any individual, or small number of individuals to erect and maintain; because the profit could never repay the expense to any individual or small number of individuals, though it may frequently do much more than repay it to a great society.

ADAM SMITH – A SIMULATED INTERVIEW

1. **What is human nature?**
   A. Human beings are creatures of self-interest.
   B. Human activity is motivated by a desire for wealth.

2. **If human beings are creatures of self-interest, what is the source of human morality?**
   A. Individuals have a natural ability to view themselves from the position of an impartial observer. From the viewpoint of an impartial observer individuals can form ideas of morality.
   B. Human beings can overcome self-interest with moral action. Knowledge of moral action arises from rational thinking and conscience.

3. **Does self-interest play a role in society?**
   A. Self-interest serves as the dominant motivating force for human beings.
   B. Individuals work best to fulfill the demands of society when they are motivated by self-interest.

4. **What is the role of competition?**
   A. Competition is the natural result of self-interest. When human beings pursue their self-interest they naturally compete with each other.
   B. Competition allows people to get the products they want at the prices they are willing to pay.
   C. Competition creates a market system that is self-regulating. Competition keeps the prices, the quantity, and the quality of products at a level satisfactory to the marketplace.

5. **What are the characteristics of a free market system?**
   A. Each individual is free to choose the place, the amount, and the kind of work that most satisfies individual needs and desires.
   B. Due to self-interest, each individual pursues work that satisfies the demands of the marketplace. Individuals are controlled by an "invisible hand" that guides them, according to their talents, to fulfill the needs and desires of society.
   C. In a free market system the value of a commodity is determined by the labor that goes into the production of the commodity.
   D. When the market system is left alone society will continually improve. The natural result of a free market system is the creation of new products and services at a better quality and price.

6. **What is the importance of a division of labor?**
   A. A division of labor allows separate individuals to produce distinct products. The division of labor is not natural to human existence. The division of labor results from the desire to trade products and services in a market place.
   B. Once the division of labor was established each individual became dependent on others for both the necessities and the luxuries of life.

7. **What most threatens the success of the market system?**
   A. The formation of monopolies destroys competition. Without competition the market cannot operate in the best interest of society.
   B. Government intervention destroys the market's natural ability to regulate itself. The economic system is self-regulating when left free of government intervention.

8. **If government should not interfere in the economy, what is the purpose of government?**
   A. Government should provide for the defense of the nation.
   B. Government should keep society secure by administering justice.
   C. Government should maintain certain public works.

9. **How do the poor affect society?**
   A. No society can truly be happy when too many people are poor.
   B. The best society is the one that most satisfies the needs of the working poor.

10. **What are the laws of economics?**
    A. *Self-Interest*: In order to satisfy personal needs and desires individuals are motivated to perform the necessary tasks for which society is willing to pay.
    B. *Competition*: Selfish motives are controlled by competition. Businessmen will lose their business if they overcharge, if they produce unsatisfactory products, or if they pay wages that are too low.
    C. *Accumulation*: Capitalists accumulate profits that can be invested in the production of more and better products. All of society therefore benefits from the profits of the capitalists.

STUDENT ACTIVITIES

Vocabulary
Define the following terms before reading the lesson on Smith.

1. accommodation	9. domestic	17. opulence
2. affectation	10. fawning	18. passions
3. aversion	11. frivolous	19. precariousness
4. benevolence	12. grandeur	20. presumptuous
5. brethren	13. impartiality	21. retinue
6. commodity	14. indolent	22. servile
7. concurrence	15. melancholy	23. subsistence
8. dexterity	16. myriad	24. venison

Review
1. What idea did Smith promote in *The Theory of Moral Sentiments*?
2. What is the title of Smith's book outlining his economic ideas?
3. What is the "invisible hand"?
4. How did Smith believe human beings gained moral knowledge?
5. What did Smith think was the natural result of self-interest?
6. What did Smith believe was the role of competition in a market system?
7. Why did Smith believe individuals pursued work that would satisfy the demands of society?
8. According to Smith, what determines the value of a commodity in a free market system?
9. What did Smith think would happen if the free market system was left alone?
10. According to Smith, what effect does a monopoly have on the free market system?
11. According to Smith, what effect does government intervention have on the free market system?
12. What role did Smith think the government should play in society?
13. According to Smith, what are the three laws of economics?
14. What is the Law of Accumulation?
15. Decide whether the following statements are **True** or **False** according to Adam Smith.
    A. Human beings are creatures of self-interest motivated by a desire for wealth.
    B. In a free market system each individual is free to choose the place, the amount, and the kind of work that most satisfies personal needs and desires.
    C. A division of labor allows individuals to produce distinct products.
    D. The division of labor makes each individual independent of others for both the necessities and the luxuries of life.
    E. No society can truly be happy when too many people are poor.
    F. All of society benefits from the accumulation of wealth.

What do you think?
On a scale of one through five, rate your opinion of the following quotations by Smith. Write a short statement explaining your rating.

1 – You **strongly agree** with the statement *or* you feel the statement is **admirable** considering the historical circumstances surrounding it.
5 – You **strongly disagree** with the statement *or* you feel the statement is **contemptible** considering the historical circumstances surrounding it.

A. *To the selfish and original passions of human nature, the loss or gain of a very small interest of our own, appears to be of vastly more importance, excites a much more passionate joy or sorrow, a much more ardent desire or aversion, than the greatest concern of another with whom we have no particular connexion.*

B. *The poor man's son, whom heaven in its anger has visited with ambition, when he begins to look around him, admires the condition of the rich.*

C. *In almost every other race of animals each individual, when it is grown up to maturity, is entirely independent . . . . But man has almost constant occasion for the help of his brethren, and it is vain for him to expect it from their benevolence only.*

D. *The value of any commodity . . . is equal to the quantity of labour which it enables him to purchase or command.*

E. *No society can surely be flourishing and happy, of which the far greater part of the members are poor and miserable.*

F. *Every man, as long as he does not violate the laws of justice, is left perfectly free to pursue his own interest in his own way.*

G. *People of the same trade seldom meet together, even for merriment and diversion, but their conversation ends in a conspiracy against the public, or in some contrivance to raise prices.*

H. *Every individual endeavors to employ his capital so that its produce may be of greatest value. . . . He intends only his own security, only his own gain. . . . by pursuing his own interest he frequently promotes that of society more effectively than when he really intends to promote it.*

I. *Science is the great antidote to the poison of enthusiasm and superstition.*

J. *Civil government, so far as it is instituted for the security of property, is in reality instituted for the defense of the rich against the poor, or of those who have some property against those who have none at all.*

K. *[The rich] are led by an invisible hand to make nearly the same distribution of the necessaries of life, which would have been made, had the earth been divided into equal portions among all its inhabitants; and thus, without intending it, without knowing it, advance the interest of the society, and afford means to the multiplication of the species.*

CHAPTER 22

KARL MARX

BACKGROUND

Karl Marx (1818-1883) was the son of a Prussian lawyer and a Dutch woman. His parents were descendants of a long line of Jewish rabbis. However, because Jews were barred from practicing law his parents decided to convert to Lutheranism. Karl Marx, who was baptized in the Lutheran church when he was six, eventually rejected all religion and became an atheist.

Marx, a philosopher with radical political and economic ideas, spent most of his life in exile. He was first exiled from his native country of Prussia in 1849. He then went to Paris where he was again exiled. He eventually moved to London where he lived in poverty and obscurity. He was virtually unknown to the English public in his lifetime.

Marx supported himself financially as a journalist for both German and English publications. He even served as a correspondent for the *New York Daily Tribune* from 1852 to 1862. Since journalism paid low wages, Marx could only avoid starvation by appealing to his friend Friedrich Engels for financial support.

Marx knew Engels from their involvement in the communist movement in Europe. Both Marx and Engels were observers of the dramatic economic and social transformation of Europe in the nineteenth century. Hoping to abolish economic injustice, they attached themselves to the growing desire for communism developing throughout Europe.

Marx's most famous work was *Das Kapital*, a 2500 page critique of capitalism. In *Das Kapital,* as well as numerous other writings, Marx described capitalism as an unworkable system that was doomed to fail. He believed capitalism was in the last stage of historical development before the establishment of communism. He also believed that after the establishment of communism there would be no further historical changes or struggles. Throughout the twentieth century his ideas had a tremendous influence on world history.

In his later years Marx became involved in a debate raging in the radical community over the meaning of his ideas. Near the end of his life he grew disgusted with the debate and intriguingly declared, "I am not a Marxist."

KARL MARX – IN HIS OWN WORDS

Economic and Philosophic Manuscripts of 1844

The separation of capital, ground-rent and labour is thus fatal for the worker.

The lowest and the only necessary wage-rate is that providing for the subsistence of the worker for the duration of his work and as much more as is necessary for him to support a family and for the race of labourers not to die out. The ordinary wage, according to Smith, is the lowest compatible with common humanity (that is, a cattle-like existence). . . .

Capital is thus the *governing power* over labour and its products. The capitalist possesses this power, not on account of his personal or human qualities, but inasmuch as he is an *owner* of capital. His power is the *purchasing* power of his capital, which nothing can withstand. . . .

When we ask, then, what is the essential relationship of labour we are asking about the relationship of the *worker* to production.

Till now we have been considering the estrangement, the alienation of the worker only in one of its aspects, i.e., the worker's *relationship to the products of his labour*. But the estrangement is manifested not only in the result but in the *act of production*—within the *productive activity* itself. How would the worker come to face the product of his activity as a stranger, were it not that in the very act of production he was estranging himself from himself? The product is after all but the summary of the activity, of production. . . .

What, then constitutes the alienation of labour?

First, the fact that labour is *external* to the worker, i.e., it does not belong to his essential being; that in his work, therefore, he does not affirm himself but denies himself, does not feel content but unhappy, does not develop freely his physical and mental energy but mortifies his body and ruins his mind. The worker therefore only feels himself outside his work, and in his work feels outside himself. He is at home when he is not working, and when he is working he is not at home. His labour is therefore not voluntary, but coerced; it is *forced labour*. It is therefore not the satisfaction of a need; it is merely a *means* to satisfy needs external to it. Its alien character emerges clearly in the fact that as soon as no physical or other compulsion exists, labour is shunned like the plague. External labour, labour in which man alienates himself, is a labour of self-sacrifice, of mortification. Lastly, the external character of labour for the worker appears in the fact that it is not his own, but someone else's, that it does not belong to him, that in it he belongs, not to himself, but to another. . . . It is the loss of his self.

The Holy Family, **1845**

Private property as private property is wealth, is compelled to maintain *itself*, and thereby its opposite, the proletariat, in *existence*. That is the *positive* side of the contradiction, self-satisfied private property.

The proletariat, on the other hand, is compelled as proletariat to abolish itself and thereby its opposite, the condition for its existence, what makes it the proletariat, i.e., private property. That is the *negative* side of the contradiction, its restlessness with its very self, dissolved and self-dissolving private property.

The German Ideology, 1846

The way in which men produce their means of subsistence depends first of all on the nature of the actual means they find in existence and have to reproduce. This mode of production must not be considered simply as being the reproduction of the physical existence of the individuals. Rather it is a definite form of activity of these individuals, a definite form of expressing their life, a definite *mode of life* on their part. As individuals express their life, so they are. What they are, therefore, coincides with their production, both with *what* they produce and with *how* they produce. The nature of individuals thus depends on the material conditions determining their production.

The Poverty of Philosophy, 1847

Economic conditions had first transformed the mass of the people of the country into workers. The combination of capital has created for this mass a common situation, common interests. This mass is thus already a class as against capital, but not yet for itself. In the struggle, of which we have noted only a few phases, this mass becomes united, and constitutes itself as a class for itself. The interests it defends become class interests. But the struggle of class against class is a political struggle. . . .

The working class, in the course of its development, will substitute for the old civil society an association which will exclude classes and their antagonism, and there will be no more political power properly so-called, since political power is precisely the official expression of antagonism in civil society.

The Communist Manifesto, 1848
[Written with Friedrich Engels]

A spectre is haunting Europe—the spectre of Communism. All the Powers of old Europe have entered into a holy alliance to exorcise this spectre . . . .

. . . It is enough to mention the commercial crises that by their periodical return put on its trial, each time more threateningly, the existence of the entire bourgeois society. In these crises a great part not only of the existing products, but also of the previously created productive forces, are periodically destroyed. In these crises there breaks out an epidemic that, in all earlier epochs, would have seemed an absurdity—the epidemic of over production. Society suddenly finds itself put back into a state of momentary barbarism; it appears as if a famine, a universal war of devastation had cut off the supply of every means of subsistence; industry and commerce seem to be destroyed; and why? Because there is too much civilisation, too much means of subsistence, too much industry, too much commerce.

In this sense, the theory of the Communists may be summed up in the single sentence: Abolition of private property. . . .

Does it require deep intuition to comprehend that man's ideas, views and conceptions, in one word, man's consciousness, changes with every change in the conditions of his material existence, in his social relations and in his social life?

What else does the history of ideas prove, than that intellectual production changes its character in proportion as material production is changed? The ruling ideas of each age have ever been the ideas of its ruling class. . . .

Nevertheless, in the most advanced countries, the following will be pretty generally applicable.

1. Abolition of property in land and application of all rents on land to public purposes.

2. A heavy progressive or graduated income tax.

3. Abolition of all right of inheritance.

4. Confiscation of the property of all emigrants and rebels.

5. Centralization of credit in the hands of the State, by means of a national bank with State capital and an exclusive monopoly.

6. Centralization of the means of communication and transport in the hands of the State.

7. Extension of factories and instruments of production owned by the State; the bringing into cultivation of wastelands, and the improvement of the soil generally in accordance with a common plan.

8. Equal liability of all to labour. Establishment of industrial armies, especially for agriculture.

9. Combination of agriculture with manufacturing industries; gradual abolition of the distinction between town and country, by a more equable distribution of the population over the country.

10. Free education for all children in public schools. Abolition of children's factory labour in its present form. combination of education with industrial production, etc., etc.

Letter to Joseph Wedemeyer, March 1852

What was new on my part was to prove the following:

1. that the existence of classes is connected only with certain historical struggles which arise out of the development of production;

2. that the class struggle necessarily leads to the dictatorship of the proletariat;

3. that this dictatorship itself is only a transition to the *abolition of all classes* and to a *classless society*.

Preface to *A Contribution to the Critique of Political Economy*, 1859
In the social production of their life, men enter definite relations that are indispensable and independent of their will, relations of production which correspond to a definite stage of development of their material productive forces. The sum total of these relations of production constitutes the economic structure of society, the real foundation, on which rises a legal and political superstructure and to which correspond definite forms of social consciousness. The mode of production of material life conditions the social, political and intellectual life process in general. It is not the consciousness of men that determines their being, but, on the contrary their social being that determines their consciousness. At a certain stage of their development, the material productive forces of society come in conflict with the existing relations of production, or—what is but a legal expression for the same thing—with the property relations within which they have been at work hitherto. From forms of development of the productive forces these relations turn into their fetters. Then begins an epoch of social revolution. With the change of the economic foundation the entire immense superstructure is more or less rapidly transformed. In considering such transformations a distinction should always be made between the material transformation of the economic conditions of production, which can be determined with the precision of natural science, and the legal, political, religious, aesthetic or philosophic—in short, ideological forms in which men become conscious of this conflict and fight it out. Just as our opinion of an individual is not based on what he thinks of himself, so can we not judge of such a period of transformation by its own consciousness; on the contrary, this consciousness must be explained rather from the contradictions of material life, from the existing conflict between the social productive forces and the relations of production. No social order ever perishes before all the productive forces for which there is room in it have developed; and new, higher relations of production never appear before the material conditions of their existence have matured in the womb of the old society itself. Therefore mankind always sets itself only such tasks as it can solve; since, looking at the matter more closely, it will always be found that the task itself arises only when the material conditions for its solution already exist or are at least in the process of formation.

"Wages, Prices and Profit," 1865
What, then, is the general law which determines the rise and fall of wages and profit in their reciprocal relation?

They stand in inverse ratio to each other. Capital's share, profit, rises in the same proportion as labour's share, wages, falls, and vice versa. Profit rises to the extent that wages fall; it falls to the extent that wages rise.

To explain, therefore, the *general nature of profits*, you must start from the theorem that, on an average, commodities are *sold at their real value*, and *that profits are derived from selling them at their values*, that is, in proportion to the quantity of labour realised in them. If you cannot explain profit upon this supposition, you cannot explain it at all. This seems paradox and contrary to everyday observation. It is also paradox that the earth moves round the sun, and that water consists of two highly flammable gases. Scientific truth is always paradox, if judged by everyday experience, which catches only the delusive appearance of things. . . .

. . . The capitalist will daily advance three shillings and daily pocket six shillings, . . . half of which will form *surplus value* . . . .

The rate of surplus value, all other circumstances remaining the same, will depend on the proportion between that part of the working day necessary to reproduce the value of the labouring power and the *surplus time* or *surplus* labour performed for the capitalist. It will, therefore, depend on the *ratio in which the working day is prolonged over and above that extent*, by working which the working man would only reproduce the value of his labouring power, or replace his wages.

Das Kapital, 1867

'What is a working-day? What is the length of time during which capital may consume the labour-power whose daily value it buys? How far may the working-day be extended beyond the working-time necessary for the reproduction of labour-power itself?' It has been seen that to these questions capital replies: the working-day contains the full 24 hours, with the deduction of the few hours of repose without which labour-power absolutely refuses its services again. Hence it is self-evident that the labourer is nothing else, his whole life through, than labour-power, that therefore all his disposable time is by nature and law labour-time, to be devoted to the self-expansion of capital. Time for education, for intellectual development, for the fulfilling of his bodily and mental activity, even the rest time of Sunday (and that in a country of Sabbatarians!)—moonshine! But in its blind unrestrainable passion, its werewolf hunger for surplus labour, capital oversteps not only the moral, but even the merely physical maximum bounds of the working day. It usurps the time for growth, development, and healthy maintenance of the body. It steals the time required for the consumption of fresh air and sunlight. It higgles over a meal-time, incorporating it where possible with the process of production itself, so that food is given to the labourer as to a mere means of production, as coal is supplied to the boiler, grease and oil to the machinery. It reduces the sound sleep needed for the restoration, reputation, refreshment of the bodily powers to just so many hours of torpor as the revival of an organism, absolutely exhausted, renders essential. It is not the normal maintenance of the labour-power, no matter how diseased, compulsory, and painful it may be, which is to determine the limits of the labourers' period of repose. Capital cares nothing for the length of life of labour-power. All that concerns it is simply and solely the maximum of labour-power, that can be rendered fluent in a working-day. It attains this end by shortening the extent of the labourer's life, as a greedy farmer snatches increased produce from the soil by robbing it of its fertility.

KARL MARX – A SIMULATED INTERVIEW

1. **What determines the character of human existence?**
    A. The character of individuals, groups, or institutions is determined by the economic conditions under which they exist.
    B. The character of ideas is determined by the economic circumstances of those who express the ideas. The ideas that rule society are the ideas of the ruling classes.

2. **What is the character of the working class in a capitalist society?**
    A. Capitalists pay workers no more than subsistence wages. Workers are doomed to a life of "cattle-like" existence.
    B. Workers gain no benefit from their labor; they are alienated from the product of their labor.
    C. Workers live under conditions that do not allow them to refuse work; they are in a situation of forced labor.

3. **How do capitalists operate in a capitalist society?**
    A. Capitalists control the means of production. However, they do not have control because of superior personal qualities; they have control simply because they possess capital.
    B. Capitalists profit from the destruction of competition. With the destruction of competition capitalists can more easily increase their profits.
    C. Capitalists profit from paying workers subsistence wages. Capitalists will never threaten their own profits by allowing workers a way out of an unhappy existence.

4. **What is the relationship between workers and capitalists?**
    A. Work does not belong to the worker. Capitalists control employment; the worker is at the mercy of the capitalist.
    B. Capitalists work to protect capitalism while workers struggle to destroy capitalism. Class conflict is inevitable in a capitalist system.

5. **What will be the final outcome of the struggle between workers and capitalists?**
    A. Capitalism is destined for a revolution in which the workers abolish private property. Economic classes will disappear.
    B. Class struggle will lead to a dictatorship of the working classes. The dictatorship will serve as a transitional stage in the development of a classless society.
    C. After workers destroy private property and class division, political authority will eventually be unnecessary.

6. **What is the cyclical process that causes a continuing economic crisis in the capitalist system?**
   A. A desire to sell more products motivates capitalists to hire more workers.
   B. The desire for more workers drives up wages.
   C. More workers at higher wages leads to a crisis of overproduction during which capitalists witness a decline in profits.
   D. A decline in profits causes capitalists to reduce the cost of labor.
   E. When labor costs are reduced society faces a crisis of underconsumption. During this crisis smaller businesses are taken over by larger businesses. The circle of capitalists narrows; huge business organizations begin to dominate the economy.
   F. The crisis of underconsumption gives capitalists a desire to sell more products. The cycle starts over.
   G. The cycle of overproduction and underconsumption will continue until society experiences a final economic crisis in which the workers will overthrow the capitalists.

7. **What are the characteristics of a society moving beyond capitalism and toward communism?**
   A. After capitalism is destroyed inheritance will be abolished, child labor will be abolished and free public schools will be established for all children. In addition, government will own all banking and credit as well as the means of production.
   B. Capitalism eventually will be replaced by communism. Communism is defined as the abolition of private property.
   C. The destruction of private property will bring about a change in human nature. Selfishness will disappear with the absence of private property.

8. **What are the laws of history?**
   A. *Economic Determinism*: Economic conditions determine the character of all institutions. The character of government, religion, art, and ideas is determined by the economic environment.
   B. *Dialectical Materialism (Class Struggle)*: Economic classes naturally struggle against each other. This struggle produces constant change in history.
   C. *Inevitability of Communism*: The working classes will eventually overthrow the capitalists. This final historical change will result in a dictatorship of the working class that will bring about the abolition of private property and the creation of a classless society.

STUDENT ACTIVITIES

Vocabulary
Define the following terms before reading the lesson on Marx.

1. aesthetic	10. compulsory	19. manifested
2. alienation	11. confiscation	20. mortify
3. antagonism	12. contradiction	21. paradox
4. bourgeois	13. diabolical	22. progressive
5. centralization	14. epoch	23. proletariat
6. coerced	15. estrangement	24. reciprocal
7. commodity	16. exorcize	25. spectre
8. compatible	17. graduated	26. subsistence
9. compulsion	18. ideological	27. superstructure

Review
1. How did Marx support himself financially?
2. What friend of Karl Marx joined him in the European communist movement?
3. What was the title of Marx's most famous book?
4. What did Marx believe determined the character of individuals, groups, and institutions?
5. What did Marx believe determined the character of ideas?
6. According to Marx, why do capitalists control the means of production?
7. According to Marx, why do capitalists refuse to pay more than subsistence wages to workers?
8. Why did Marx think class conflict was inevitable in a capitalist system?
9. What did Marx believe would happen when workers destroyed private property?
10. According to Marx, what is the role of a proletariat dictatorship?
11. What was the cycle of overproduction and underconsumption described by Marx?
12. What did Marx believe society would witness after the destruction of capitalism?
13. What is communism?
14. How did Marx believe communism would change human nature?
15. According to Marx, what are the three laws of history?
16. Decide whether the following statements are **True** or **False** according to Karl Marx.
    A. Workers are doomed to a life of "cattle-like" existence.
    B. Workers are not in a position to refuse work.
    C. Capitalists depend on competition to increase their profits.
    D. Workers are at the mercy of the capitalists.
    E. The abolition of private property is inevitable.
    F. Class struggle produces constant change in history.
    G. Communism is inevitable.

What do you think?
On a scale of one through five, rate your opinion of the following quotations by Marx. Write a short statement explaining your rating.

1 – You **strongly agree** with the statement *or* you feel the statement is **admirable** considering the historical circumstances surrounding it.
5 – You **strongly disagree** with the statement *or* you feel the statement is **contemptible** considering the historical circumstances surrounding it.

A. *Capital is the governing power over labour and its products. The capitalist possesses this power, not on account of his personal or human qualities, but inasmuch as he is an owner of capital.*
B. *[A worker's] labour is . . . not voluntary, but coerced; it is forced labour.*
C. *Private property as private property is wealth, is compelled to maintain itself, and thereby its opposite, the proletariat, in existence. . . . The proletariat, on the other hand, is compelled as proletariat to abolish itself and thereby its opposite, the condition for its existence, what makes it the proletariat, i.e., private property.*
D. *Does it require deep intuition to comprehend that man's ideas, views and conceptions, in one word, man's consciousness, changes with every change in the conditions of his material existence?*
E. *The ruling ideas of each age have ever been the ideas of its ruling class.*
F. *In its blind unrestrainable passion, its werewolf hunger for surplus labour, capital oversteps not only the moral, but even the merely physical maximum bounds of the working day..*
G. *When labor has become not only a means of living, but itself the first necessity of life . . . it will be possible . . . for society to inscribe on its banners: From each according to his abilities to each according to his needs.*
H. *Capital is dead labor that, vampire-like, lives only by sucking living labor, and lives more, the more labor it sucks.*
I. *Let the ruling classes tremble at a communist revolution. The proletarians have nothing to lose but their chains. They have a world to win. Working men of all countries, unite!*
J. *The philosophers have only interpreted the world differently, the point is to change it.*
K. *Political power, properly so called, is merely the organized power of one class for oppressing another.*
L. *Modern society . . . greets gold as its Holy Grail, as the glittering incarnation of the very principle of its own life.*
M. *Force is the midwife of every old society pregnant with a new one.*
N. *The rich will do everything for the poor except get off their backs.*

CHAPTER 23

WILLIAM GRAHAM SUMNER

BACKGROUND

In the 1870s the English philosopher Herbert Spencer gained popularity in the United States as an advocate of social Darwinism. Applying Charles Darwin's theory of evolution to society, Spencer believed society operated like a jungle in which only the fittest survived. He admitted that survival of the fittest was a cruel process. However, he also believed the process promised long-term benefits. He thought human beings, if left alone, would slowly evolve into citizens of a more perfect society. His ideas gave corporate leaders of the late 1800s a philosophy that justified the acquisition of tremendous wealth without interference from the government.

Spencer's ideas had a tremendous influence on William Graham Sumner (1840-1910). The child of an immigrant working-class family, Sumner studied theology and, for a time, served as an ordained Episcopal minister. In Spencer's writings Sumner found a philosophy that conformed with his view of the world. He decided to quit the ministry and become a teacher of social Darwinism. In 1872 he became a professor at Yale.

A tough-minded man with a sharp tongue, Sumner was a popular professor. In his lectures he denounced government aid to the poor *and* to the industrialists. His expression, "It's root, hog, or die," became a characteristic description of social Darwinism. A student once asked Sumner, "Suppose some professor of political science came along and took your job away from you. Wouldn't you be sore?" Sumner responded, "Any other professor is welcome to try. If he gets my job, it is my fault. My business is to teach the subject so well that no one can take the job away from me." In this short statement Sumner summed up the essence of social Darwinism and the law of the jungle—only the fittest survive.

Sumner described his personal philosophy through lectures, magazine articles, and his most famous book *Folkways*. He opposed all government intervention in economic affairs. He felt that any attempt to reform society would fail. In short, he did not think society needed any care, supervision, or social engineering.

WILLIAM GRAHAM SUMNER – IN HIS OWN WORDS

"The Forgotten Man," 1883

Now who is the Forgotten Man? He is the simple, honest laborer, ready to earn his living by productive work. We pass him by because he is independent, self-supporting, and asks no favors. He does not appeal to the emotions or excite the sentiments. He only wants to make a contract and fulfill it, with respect on both sides and favor on neither side. He must get his living out of the capital of the country. The larger the capital is, the better living he can get. Every particle of capital which is wasted on the vicious, the idle, and the shiftless is so much taken from the capital available to reward the independent and productive laborer.

What Social Classes Owe to Each Other, 1883

It is commonly asserted that there are in the United States no classes, and any allusion to classes is resented. On the other hand, we constantly read and hear discussion of social topics in which the existence of social classes is assumed as a simple fact. "The poor," "the weak," "the laborers," are expressions which are used as if they had exact and well-understood definition. Discussions are made to bear upon the assumed rights, wrongs, and misfortunes of certain social classes; and all public speaking and writing consists, in a large measure, of the discussion of general plans for meeting the wishes of classes of people who have not been able to satisfy their own desires. These classes are sometimes discontented, and sometimes not. Sometimes they do not know that anything is amiss with them until the "friends of humanity" come to them with offers of aid. . . . Sometimes they claim that they have a right to everything of which they feel the need for their happiness on earth. . . . They formulate their claims as rights against society—that is, against some other men. In their view they have a right, not only to *pursue* happiness, but to *get* it; and if they fail to get it, they think they have a claim to the aid of other men—that is, to the labor and self-denial of other men—to get it for them. They find orators and poets who tell them that they have grievances, so long as they have unsatisfied desires. . . .

A free man in a free democracy has no duty whatever toward other men of the same rank and standing, except respect, courtesy, and good-will. . . . In a free state every man is held and expected to take care of himself and his family, to make no trouble for his neighbor, and to contribute his full share to public interests and common necessities. If he fails in this he throws burdens on others. He does not thereby acquire rights against the others. On the contrary, he only accumulates obligations toward them; and if he is allowed to make his deficiencies a ground of new claims, he passes over into the position of a privileged or petted person—emancipated from duties, endowed with claims. This is the inevitable result of combining democratic political theories with humanitarian social theories. . . . One result of such inconsistency must surely be to undermine democracy, to increase the power of wealth in the democracy, and to hasten the subjection of democracy to plutocracy; for a man who accepts any share which he has not earned in another man's capital cannot be an independent citizen. . . .

. . . I never have known a man of ordinary common-sense who did not urge upon his sons, from earliest childhood, doctrines of economy and the practice of accumulation. A good father believes that he does wisely to encourage enterprise, productive skill, prudent self-denial, and the judicious expenditure on the part of his son. The object is to teach the boy to accumulate capital. If, however, the boy should read many of the diatribes against "the rich" which are afloat in our literature; if he should read or hear some of the current discussion about "capital"; and if, with the ingenuousness of youth, he should take these productions at their literal sense, instead of discounting them, as his father does, he would be forced to believe that he was on the path of infamy when he was earning and saving capital. It is worthwhile to consider which we mean or what we mean. Is it wicked to be rich? Is it mean to be a capitalist? If the question is one of degree only, and it is right to be rich up to a certain point and wrong to be richer, how shall we find the point? . . .

The aggregation of large fortunes is not at all a thing to be regretted. On the contrary, it is a necessary condition of many forms of social advance. If we should set a limit to the accumulation of wealth, we should say to our most valuable producers, "We do not want you to do us the services which you best understand how to perform, beyond a certain point." It would be like killing off our generals in war. . . .

. . . I have never seen a defense of the employer. Who dares say that he is not the friend of the poor man? Who dares say that he is the friend of the employer? I will try to say what I think is true. There are bad, harsh, cross employers; there are slovenly, negligent workmen; there are just about as many proportionately of one of these classes as of the other. The employers of the United States—as a class, proper exceptions being understood—have no advantage over their workmen. They could not oppress them if they wanted to do so. The advantage, taking good and bad times together, is with the workmen. The employers wish the welfare of the workmen in all respects, and would give redress for any grievance which was brought to their attention. They are considerate of the circumstances and interests of the laborers. They remember the interests of the workmen when driven to consider the necessity of closing or reducing hours. They go on, and take risk and trouble on themselves in working through bad times, rather than close their works. The whole class of those-who-have are quick in their sympathy for any form of distress or suffering. They are too quick. Their sympathies need regulating, not stimulating. They are more likely to give away capital recklessly than to withhold it stingily when any alleged case of misfortune is before them. . . .

Every man and woman in society has one big duty. That is, to take care of his or her own self. This is a social duty. For, fortunately, the matter stands so that the duty of making the best of one's self individually is not a separate thing from the duty of filling one's place in society, but the two are one, and the latter is accomplished when the former is done. The common notion, however, seems to be that one has a duty to society, as a special and separate thing, and that this duty consists in considering and deciding what other people ought to do. Now, the man who can do anything for or about anybody else than himself is fit to be head of a family; and when he becomes head of a family he has duties to his wife and his children, in addition to the former big duty. Then, again, any man who can take care of himself and his family is in a very exceptional position, if he does not find in his immediate surroundings people who need his care and have some sort of a personal claim upon him. If, now, he is able to fulfill all this, and to take care of anybody outside his family and his dependents, he must have a surplus of energy, wisdom, and moral virtue beyond what he needs for his own business. No man has this; for a family is a charge which is capable of infinite development, and no man could suffice to the full measure of duty for which a family may draw upon him. Neither can a man give to society so advantageous an employment of his services, whatever they are, in any other way as by spending them on his family. . . .

The danger of minding other people's business is twofold. First, there is the danger that a man may leave his own business unattended to; and second, there is the danger of an impertinent interference with another's affairs. The "friends of humanity" almost always run into both dangers. . . .

The social doctors enjoy the satisfaction of feeling themselves to be more moral or more enlightened than their fellow-men. They are able to see what other men ought to do when the other men do not see it. An examination of the work of the social doctors, however shows that they are only more ignorant and more presumptuous than other people. . . .

Society does not need any care or supervision. If we can acquire a science of society, based on observation of phenomena and study of forces, we may hope to gain some ground slowly toward the elimination of a sound and natural social order. Whatever we gain that way will be by growth, never in the world by any reconstruction of society on the plan of some enthusiastic social architect. The latter is only repeating the old error over again, and postponing all our chances of real improvement. Society needs first of all to be freed from these meddlers—that is, to be let alone. Here we are, then, once more back at the old doctrine—*laissez faire*. Let us translate it into blunt English, and it will read, "Mind your own business." It is nothing but the doctrine of liberty. Let every man be happy in his own way. . . .

The type and formula of most schemes of philanthropy and humanitarianism is this: A and B put their heads together to decide what C shall be made to do for D. The radical vice of all these schemes, from a sociological point of view, is that C is not allowed a voice in the matter, and his position, character, and interests, as well as the ultimate effects on society through C's interests, are entirely overlooked. I call C the Forgotten Man. . . .

. . . Capital is the force by which civilization is maintained and carried on. The same piece of capital cannot be used in two ways. Every bit of capital, therefore, which is given to a shiftless and inefficient member of society, who makes no return for it, is diverted from a reproductive use; but if it was put to reproductive use, it would have to be granted in wages to an efficient and productive laborer. Hence the real sufferer by that kind of benevolence which consists in an expenditure of capital to protect the good-for-nothing is the industrious laborer. . . . There is an almost invincible prejudice that a man who gives a dollar to a beggar is generous and kind-hearted, but that a man who refuses the beggar and puts the dollar in a savings-bank is stingy and mean. The former is putting capital where it is very sure to be wasted, and where it will be a kind of seed for a long succession of future dollars, which must be wasted to ward off a greater strain on the sympathies than would have been occasioned by a refusal in the first place. . . .

There is a beautiful notion afloat in our literature and in the minds of our people that men are born to certain "natural rights." If that were true, there would be something on earth which was got for nothing, and this world would not be the place it is at all. The fact is, that there is no right whatever inherited by man which has not an equivalent and corresponding duty by the side of it, as the price of it. . . . Something for nothing is not to be found on earth.

If there were such things as natural rights, the question would arise, Against whom are they good? Who has the corresponding obligation to satisfy these rights? There can be no rights against Nature, except to get out of her whatever we can, which is only the fact of the struggle for existence stated over again. The common assertion is, that the rights are good against society; that is; that society is bound to obtain and secure them for the person interested. Society, however, is only the persons interested plus some other person; and as the persons interested have by the hypothesis failed to win the rights, we come to this, that natural rights are the claims which certain persons have by prerogative against some other person. Such is the actual interpretation in practice of natural rights—claims which some people have by prerogative on other people.

This theory is a very far-reaching one, and of course it is adequate to furnish a foundation for a whole social philosophy. In its widest extension it comes to mean that if any man finds himself uncomfortable in this world, it must be somebody else's fault, and that somebody is bound to come and make him comfortable. Now, the people who are most uncomfortable in this world . . . are those who have neglected their duties, and consequently have failed to get their rights. The people who can be called upon to serve the uncomfortable must be those who have done their duty, as the world goes, tolerably well. Consequently the doctrine which we are discussing turns out to be in practice only a scheme for making injustice prevail in human society by reversing the distribution of rewards and punishments between those who have done their duty and those who have not.

The "Challenge of Facts," 1880s

Private property, which we have seen to be a feature of society organized in accordance with the natural conditions of the struggle for existence, produces inequalities between men. The struggle for existence is aimed against nature. It is from her niggardly hand that we have to wrest the satisfactions for our needs, but our fellow-men are our competitors for the meager supply. Competition, therefore, is a law of nature. Nature is entirely neutral; she submits to him who most energetically and resolutely assails her. She grants her rewards to the fittest, therefore, without regard to other considerations of any kind. If, then, there be liberty, men get from her just in proportion to their works, and their having and enjoying are just in proportion to their being and their doing. Such is the system of nature. If we do not like it, and if we try to amend it, there is only one way in which we can do it. We can take from the better and give to the worse. We can deflect the penalties of those who have done ill and throw them on those who have done better. We can take the rewards from those who have done better and give them to those who have done worse. We shall thus lessen the inequalities. We shall favor the survival of the unfittest, and we shall accomplish this by destroying liberty. Let it be understood that we cannot go outside of this alternative: liberty, inequality, survival of the fittest; not-liberty, equality, survival of the unfittest. The former carries society forward and favors all its best members; the latter carries society downwards and favors all its worst members. . . .

. . . The socialist regards misery as the fault of society. He thinks that we can organize society as we like and that an organization can be devised in which poverty and misery shall disappear. He goes even further than this. He assumes that men have artificially organized society as it now exists. Hence, if anything is disagreeable or hard in the present state of society it follows, on that view, that the task of organizing society has been imperfectly and badly performed, and that it needs to be done over again. . . .

The truth is that the social order is fixed by laws of nature precisely analogous to those of the physical order. The most that man can do is by ignorance and self-conceit to mar the operation of social laws. The evils of society are to a great extent the result of the dogmatism and self-interest of statesmen, philosophers, and ecclesiastics who in past time have done just what the socialists now want to do. Instead of studying the natural laws of the social order, they assumed that they could organize society as they chose, they made up their minds what kind of a society they wanted to make, and they planned their little measures for the ends they had resolved upon. It will take centuries of scientific study of the facts of nature to eliminate from human society the mischievous institutions and traditions which the said statesmen, philosophers, and ecclesiastics have introduced into it.

WILLIAM GRAHAM SUMNER – A SIMULATED INTERVIEW

1. **Do human beings possess natural rights?**
    A. If human beings possessed natural rights, nature would be granting something for nothing. Something for nothing is not found on earth. No person possesses rights unaccompanied by responsibilities.
    B. Nature does not grant rights; nature requires human beings to struggle for survival in a brutal world. The best that human beings can hope for is to soften the brutality of life through knowledge, discipline, and technology.
    C. Some people inaccurately claim they not only have a natural right to *pursue* happiness, they also have a right to *receive* happiness. If they do not achieve happiness they blame other people.

2. **Should people with money take care of the disadvantaged?**
    A. Each individual has one primary responsibility—to take care of himself. All that an individual owes other people is respect, courtesy, and goodwill.
    B. An individual who is fit to take care of himself *and* to take care of others should restrict himself to caring for a family. No individual has enough energy, wisdom, and moral virtue to provide for more than himself and his family.
    C. A person who tries to take care of someone else's business risks leaving his own business unattended.
    D. Although a person who gives a dollar to a beggar is seen as generous and kind, that person has in fact put his money where it is sure to be wasted. All money given to people who do not take care of themselves is money that could instead reward independent and productive workers.
    E. People who fail to take care of themselves become a burden for others. People who accept money they do not earn are released from the responsibility of having to care for themselves—they are undeservedly placed in a privileged class.
    F. Society should give more credit to the average person who is hard-working, self- supporting, honest, and contributes to society. This person is the Forgotten Man.

3. **Are capitalists the enemies of society?**
    A. Wealthy capitalists are unjustly portrayed as disgraceful human beings. The accumulation of a large fortune is not disgraceful. The accumulation of wealth is necessary for the improvement of society.
    B. Capitalists are unjustly portrayed as enemies of the workers. Capitalists desire the best for their workers and are concerned for their workers. In fact, a capitalist's sympathy for workers should be regulated rather than encouraged.

C. Capitalists have no advantages over their workers. Capitalists could not oppress their workers if they wanted. Workers have the advantage over capitalists.

4. Should society be reformed?
    A. Society does not need care or supervision. All attempts at reform and social engineering should be resisted.
    B. Private property, inequality, and competition are natural to human existence. Human beings are engaged in a never-ending struggle against nature for their very existence. Nature does not provide enough for all human beings. Society cannot be reformed.
    C. Human beings are molded by circumstances beyond their control. Human beings do not possess the power to reform their environment. Reformers should leave society alone and mind their own business. *Laissez faire* is the best policy.
    D. Any attempt to improve society by limiting wealth requires asking wealthy people to stop providing the service they know best. Limiting wealth is similar to killing off generals during wartime.
    E. Reformers who try to fix society's problems feel they are more enlightened than others. In fact, reformers are simply more ignorant and more arrogant.
    F. The only proper role of government is to provide peace, order, and security. Reformers mistakenly believe the role of government should be expanded.

5. What most threatens progress in society?
    A. The biggest threat to American society is the tendency of a government chosen by the masses to intervene in economic affairs. Society improves naturally if those who are most fit are allowed to work and invest without restrictions.
    B. Industry and state should be separate in the same manner as church and state. A relationship between government and business would be disastrous. If capitalists used their power for political rather than industrial purposes, society would be in danger.
    C. When democratic reformers successfully use the state to regulate economic conditions they force capitalists to protect themselves with the power of government. Corruption in politics is inevitable when reformers try to regulate capitalists.

6. What determines the character of society?
    A. Industrial groups determine the character of society through the use of technology.
    B. Tradition and habit provide society with gradual progress.

STUDENT ACTIVITIES

Vocabulary
Define the following terms before reading the lesson on Sumner.

1. accumulation	8. dogmatism	15. petted
2. aggregation	9. ecclesiastics	16. plutocracy
3. analogous	10. grievance	17. prerogative
4. assertion	11. inefficient	18. presumptuous
5. benevolence	12. judicious	19. redress
6. diatribe	13. negligent	20. shiftless
7. discontented	14. niggardly	21. slovenly

Review
1. What is social Darwinism?
2. In what way did Herbert Spencer believe social Darwinism provided long-term benefits?
3. What did corporate leaders justify with social Darwinism in the late 1800s?
4. What was Sumner's most famous book?
5. Why did Sumner believe people did not possess natural rights?
6. What situation did Sumner believe is thrust upon people by nature?
7. How did Sumner think human beings could soften the world's brutality?
8. According to Sumner, what is each individual's primary responsibility?
9. Why did Sumner think money should not be given to the poor?
10. What did Sumner think happened to people who accepted money they did not earn?
11. Who did Sumner think was the Forgotten Man?
12. In what way did Sumner think capitalists were unjustly portrayed as enemies of the workers?
13. What did Sumner think was the proper role of government?
14. What did Sumner think was the biggest threat to American society?
15. What happens when democratic reformers use the state to regulate economic conditions?
16. Decide whether the following statements are **True** or **False** according to William Graham Sumner.
    A. Some people inaccurately claim they have a right to happiness.
    B. All that an individual owes other people is respect, courtesy, and goodwill.
    C. Wealthy capitalists are disgraceful human beings.
    D. Workers hold an advantage over capitalists.
    E. All attempts at social reform should be resisted.
    F. Nature does not provide enough for all human beings.
    G. Reformers should quit trying to improve society; *laissez faire* is the best policy.
    H. Industry and state, like church and state, should be separate.

What do you think?
On a scale of one through five, rate your opinion of the following quotations by Sumner. Write a short statement explaining your rating.

1 – You **strongly agree** with the statement *or* you feel the statement is **admirable** considering the historical circumstances surrounding it.
5 – You **strongly disagree** with the statement *or* you feel the statement is **contemptible** considering the historical circumstances surrounding it.

A. *Every particle of capital which is wasted on the vicious, the idle, and the shiftless is so much taken from the capital available to reward the independent and productive laborer.*
B. *A free man in a free democracy has no duty whatever toward other men of the same rank and standing, except respect, courtesy, and good-will.*
C. *In a free society every man is held and expected to take care of himself and his family, to make no trouble for his neighbor, and to contribute his full share to public interests and common necessities.*
D. *The aggregation of large fortunes is not at all a thing to be regretted. On the contrary, it is a necessary condition of many forms of social advance.*
E. *The employers wish the welfare of the workmen in all respects, and would give redress for any grievance which was brought to their attention. They are considerate of the circumstances and interests of the workmen.*
F. *An examination of the social doctors . . . shows that they are . . . more ignorant and more presumptuous than other people.*
G. *Mind your own business. It is nothing but the doctrine of liberty. Let every man be happy in his own way.*
H. *There is no right whatever inherited by man which has not an equivalent and corresponding duty by the side of it, as the price of it.*
I. *The people who are most uncomfortable in this world . . . are those who have neglected their duties, and consequently have failed to get their rights.*
J. *Competition . . . is a law of nature. Nature is entirely neutral; she submits to him who most energetically and resolutely assails her.*
K. *The yearning after equality is the offspring of covetousness, and there is no possible plan for satisfying that yearning which can do aught else than rob A to give to B; consequently all such plans nourish some of the meanest vices of human nature, waste capital, and overthrow of civilization.*
L. *The state, it cannot be too often repeated, does nothing and can give nothing which it does not take from somebody.*

CHAPTER 24

HENRY GEORGE

BACKGROUND

Few American reformers have ever gained as devoted a following as Henry George (1839-1897). George began a reform movement that won the admiration of such well-known men as Sun Yat Sen, Leo Tolstoy, George Bernard Shaw, and Woodrow Wilson. Some people were so committed to George's message that fifty years after his death his daughter witnessed old men crying when her father's name was mentioned.

Throughout his life George worked a variety of jobs. He left home at age thirteen and spent time as a gold prospector, sailor, and typesetter. In his early twenties he endured several years of wretched poverty. Having to beg for money to stay alive gave him a profound understanding of the dark side of the Industrial Revolution.

After gaining employment as a journalist George began writing about people who suffered under the American capitalist system. He brought attention to the abusive power of monopolies, the discrimination against immigrants, and the desperate poverty for many Americans. He was outraged that a nation of great wealth would allow such injustice. A deeply religious man, he shaped his criticisms in moral terms. Writing with great passion, he never came across as an impersonal economist viewing the world in technical terms.

After publishing his masterpiece *Progress and Poverty* he saw his ideas championed by people around the world. The book was a huge bestseller and made his name a household word in both the United States and England. He was even asked to run for mayor of New York in 1886. Although he did not win the three-way mayoral race, he did beat Teddy Roosevelt. He was asked to run again for mayor in 1897, but died before the election. Over 100,000 people attended his funeral.

In spite of the fact his proposals met almost universal rejection by academic economists, he was a powerful symbol of a desire for justice. During the industrial takeoff of the late 1800s he reminded Americans that traditional ideas of equality and republicanism should not be discarded. His importance to the growing desire for the reforms finally instituted in the early 1900s cannot be underestimated.

HENRY GEORGE – IN HIS OWN WORDS

Progress and Poverty, 1879

The present century has been marked by a prodigious increase in wealth-producing power. The utilization of steam and electricity, the introduction of improved processes and labor-saving machinery, the greater subdivision and grander scale of production, the wonderful facilitation of exchanges, have multiplied enormously the effectiveness of labor.

At the beginning of this marvelous era it was natural to expect, and it was expected, that labor-saving inventions would lighten the toil and improve the condition of the laborer; that the enormous increase in the power of producing wealth would make real poverty a thing of the past. . . .

Out of these bounteous material conditions [we] would have seen arising . . . moral conditions realizing the golden age of which mankind have always dreamed. Youth no longer stunted and starved; age no longer harried by avarice; the child at play with the tiger; the man with the muck-rake drinking in the glory of the stars! Foul things fled, fierce things tame; discord turned to harmony! For how could there be greed where all had enough? How could the vice, the crime, the ignorance, the brutality, that spring from poverty and the fear of poverty, exist where poverty had vanished? Who should crouch where all were freemen; who oppress where all were peers? . . .

Now, however, we are coming into collision with facts which there can be no mistaking. From all parts of the civilized world come complaints of industrial depression; of labor condemned to involuntary idleness; of capital massed and wasting; of pecuniary distress among business men; of want and suffering and anxiety among the working classes. All the dull, deadening pain, all the keen, maddening anguish, that to great masses of men are involved in the words "hard times," afflict the world today. . . .

And, unpleasant as it may be to admit it, it is at last becoming evident that the enormous increase in productive power which has marked the present century and is still going on with accelerating ratio, has no tendency to extirpate poverty or to lighten the burdens of those compelled to toil. . . . The march of invention has clothed mankind with powers of which a century ago the boldest imagination could not have dreamed. But in factories where labor-saving machinery has reached its most wonderful development, little children are at work; wherever the new forces are anything like fully utilized, large classes are maintained by charity or live on the verge of recourse to it; amid the greatest accumulations of wealth, men die of starvation, and puny infants suckle dry breasts; while everywhere the greed of gain, the worship of wealth, shows the force of the fear of want. The promised land flies before us like the mirage. The fruits of the tree of knowledge turn as we grasp them to apples of Sodom that crumble at the touch.

It is true that wealth has been greatly increased, and that the average of comfort, leisure, and refinement has been raised; but these gains are not general. In them the lowest class do not share. . . .

This association of poverty with progress is the great enigma of our times. It is the central fact from which spring industrial, social, and political difficulties that perplex the world, and with which statesmanship and philanthropy and education grapple in vain. From it come the clouds that overhang the future of the most progressive and self-reliant nations. It is the riddle which the Sphinx of Fate puts to our civilization, and which not to answer is to be destroyed. So long as all the increased wealth which modern progress brings goes but to build up great fortunes, to increase luxury and make sharper the contrast between the House of Have and the House of Want, progress is not real and cannot be permanent. The reaction must come. The tower leans from its foundations, and every new story but hastens the final catastrophe. To educate men who must be condemned to poverty, is but to make them restive; to base on a state of most glaring social inequality political institutions under which men are theoretically equal, is to stand a pyramid on its apex. . . .

Land, labor, and capital are the three factors of production. If we remember that capital is thus a term used in contradistinction to land and labor, we at once see that nothing properly included under either one of these terms can be properly classed as capital. The term land necessarily includes, not merely the surface of the earth as distinguished from the water and the air, but the whole material universe outside of man himself, for it is only by having access to land, from which his very body is drawn, that man can come in contact with or use nature. The term land embraces, in short all natural materials, forces, and opportunities, and, therefore, nothing that is freely supplied by nature can be properly classed as capital. . . . The term labor, in like manner, includes all human exertion, and hence human powers whether natural or acquired can never properly be classed as capital. . . .

We must exclude from the category of capital everything that may be included either as land or labor. Doing so, there remain only things which are neither land nor labor, but which have resulted from the union of these two original factors of production. Nothing can be properly capital that does not consist of these—that is to say, nothing can be capital that is not wealth. . . .

. . . That as land is necessary to the exertion of labor in the production of wealth, to command the land which is necessary to labor, is to command all the fruits of labor save enough to enable labor to exist. . . . This simple truth, in its application to social and political problems, is hid from the great masses of men partly by its very simplicity, and in greater part by widespread fallacies and erroneous habits of thought which lead them to look in every direction but the right one for an explanation of the evils which oppress and threaten the civilized world. . . .

There is but one way to remove an evil—and that is, to remove its cause. Poverty deepens as wealth increases, and wages are forced down while productive power grows, because land, which is the source of all wealth and the field of all labor is monopolized. To extirpate poverty, to make wages what justice commands they should be, the full earnings of the laborer, we must therefore substitute for the individual ownership of land a common ownership. Nothing else will go to the cause of the evil—in nothing else is there the slightest hope.

This, then, is the remedy for the unjust and unequal distribution of wealth apparent in modern civilization, and for all the evils which flow from it:

We must make land common property. . . .

Whatever may be said for the institution of private property in land, it is therefore plain that it cannot be defended on the score of justice.

The equal right of all men to the use of land is as clear as their equal right to breathe the air—it is a right proclaimed by the fact of their existence. For we cannot suppose that some men have a right to be in this world and others no right. . . .

Our boasted freedom necessarily involves slavery, so long as we recognize property in land. Until that is abolished, Declarations of Independence and Acts of Emancipation are in vain. So long as one man can claim the exclusive ownership of the land from which other men must live, slavery will exist, and as material progress goes on, must grow and deepen! . . .

Now, insomuch as the taxation of rent, or land values, must necessarily be increased just as we abolish other taxes, we may put the proposition into practical form by proposing—

To abolish all taxation save that upon land values.

As we have seen, the value of land is at the beginning of society nothing, but as society develops by the increase of population and the advance of the arts, it becomes greater and greater. In every civilized country, even the newest, the value of the land taken as a whole is sufficient to bear the entire expenses of government. . . .

The tax upon land values is . . . the most just and equal of all taxes. It falls only upon those who receive from society a peculiar and valuable benefit, and upon them in proportion to the benefit they receive. It is the taking by the community, for the use of the community, of that value which is the creation of the community. It is the application of the common property to common uses. When all rent is taken by taxation for the needs of the community, then will the equality ordained by nature be attained. No citizen will have an advantage over any other citizen save as is given by his industry, skill, and intelligence; and each will obtain what he fairly earns. Then, but not till then, will labor get its full reward, and capital its natural return. . . .

To abolish [all] taxes [except on land value] would be to lift the whole enormous weight of taxation from productive industry. The needle of the seamstress and the great manufactory; the cart-horse and the locomotive; the fishing boat and the steamship; the farmer's plow and the merchant's stock, would be alike untaxed. All would be free to make or to save, to buy or to sell, unfined by taxes, unannoyed by the tax-gatherer. Instead of saying to the producer, as it does now, "The more you add to the general wealth the more shall you be taxed!" the state would say to the producer, "Be as industrious, as thrifty, as enterprising as you choose, you shall have your full reward! You shall not be fined for making two blades of grass grow where one grew before; you shall not be taxed for adding to the aggregate wealth." . . .

The evils arising from the unjust and unequal distribution of wealth, which are becoming more and more apparent as modern civilization goes on, are not incidents of progress, but tendencies which must bring progress to a halt; that they will not cure themselves, but, on the contrary, must, unless their cause is removed, grow greater and greater, until they sweep us back into barbarism by the road every previous civilization has trod. But it also shows that these evils are not imposed by natural laws; that they spring solely from social maladjustments which ignore natural laws, and that in removing their cause we shall be giving an enormous impetus to progress.

The poverty which in the midst of abundance pinches and embrutes men, and all the manifold evils which flow from it, spring from a denial of justice. In permitting the monopolization of the opportunities which nature freely offers to all, we have ignored the fundamental law of justice—for, so far as we can see, when we view things upon a large scale, justice seems to be the supreme law of the universe. But by sweeping away this injustice and asserting the rights of all men to natural opportunities, we shall conform ourselves to the law—we shall remove the great cause of unnatural inequality in the distribution of wealth and power; we shall abolish poverty; tame the ruthless passions of greed; dry up the springs of vice and misery; light in dark places the lamp of knowledge; give new vigor to invention and a fresh impulse to discovery; substitute political strength for political weakness; and make tyranny and anarchy impossible.

The reform I have proposed accords with all that is politically, socially, or morally desirable. . . . What is it but the carrying out in letter and spirit of the truth enunciated in the Declaration of Independence—the "self-evident" truth that is the heart and soul of the Declaration— *"That all men are created equal; that they are endowed by their Creator with certain unalienable rights; that among these are life, liberty, and the pursuit of happiness!"*

These rights are denied when the equal right to land—on which and by which men alone can live—is denied. Equality of political rights will not compensate for the denial of the equal right to the bounty of nature. Political liberty, when the equal right to land is denied, becomes, as population increases and invention goes on, merely the liberty to compete for employment at starvation wages. This is the truth that we have ignored. And so there come beggars in our streets and tramps on our roads; and poverty enslaves men whom we boast are political sovereigns; and want breeds ignorance that our schools cannot enlighten; and citizens vote as their masters dictate; and the demagogue usurps the part of the statesman; and gold weighs in the scales of justice; and in high places sit those who do not pay to civic virtue even the compliment of hypocrisy; and the pillars of the republic that we thought so strong already bend under an increasing strain.

Social Problems, 1883

The terms rich and poor are of course frequently used in a relative sense. . . . Now, we cannot, of course, all be rich in the sense of having more than others; but when people say, as they so often do, that we cannot all be rich, or when they say that we must always have the poor with us, they do not use the words in this comparative sense. They mean by the rich those who have enough, or more than enough wealth to gratify all reasonable wants, and by the poor, those who have not.

Now, using the words in this sense, I join issue with those who say that we cannot all be rich; with those who declare that in human society the poor must always exist. . . . What I mean is, that we all might have leisure, comfort, and abundance, not merely of the necessaries but even of what are now esteemed the elegancies and luxuries of life. . . . I do mean to say that we might all have enough wealth to satisfy reasonable desires; that we might all have so much of the material things we now struggle for that no one would want to rob or swindle his neighbor; that no one would worry all day or lie awake at nights fearing he might be brought to poverty or thinking how he might acquire wealth.

Does this seem a utopian dream? What would people of fifty years ago have thought of one who would have told them that it was possible to sow by steam power; to cross the Atlantic in six days or the continent in three; to have a message sent from London at noon delivered in Boston three hours before noon; to hear in New York the voice of a man talking in Chicago. . . .

Who can look about him without seeing that to whatever cause poverty may be due, it is not due to the niggardliness of nature; without seeing that it is blindness or blasphemy to assume that the Creator has condemned the masses of men to hard toil for a bare living? . . .

"The poor ye have always with you." If ever a scripture has been wrested to the devil's service, this is the scripture. How often have these words been distorted from their obvious meaning to soothe conscience into acquiescence in human misery and degradation—to bolster that blasphemy, the very negation and denial of Christ's teaching, that the All-Wise and Most Merciful, the Infinite Father, has decreed that so many of His creatures but be poor in order that others of His creatures to whom He wills the good things of life should enjoy the pleasure and virtue of doling out alms! . . .

It is not necessary that anyone should be condemned to monotonous toil; it is not necessary that anyone should lack the wealth and the leisure which permit the development of the faculties that raise man above the animal. . . . In turning men into machines we are wasting the highest powers.

HENRY GEORGE – A SIMULATED INTERVIEW

1. **How did the Industrial Revolution affect American society?**
    A. The Industrial Revolution brought about great progress in productive capabilities. The productive power of labor was tremendously multiplied.
    B. The economic progress of the Industrial Revolution was not accompanied by progress for the lower classes. Too many people are stuck in a life of desperate poverty.

2. **Why must society try to solve the problem of poverty?**
    A. In a time of enormous economic progress poverty is more visible and less acceptable.
    B. All human beings have a right to the necessities and comforts of life.
    C. All people have an equal right to apply their labor to the earth's natural resources.
    D. The Industrial Revolution allowed people to become wealthy without working; this is morally wrong. Wealth goes primarily to those who own land. Land should belong to all people, and wealth should not come from the mere ownership of land.
    E. If the problem of poverty is not solved, civilization faces a return to barbarism. An unequal distribution of wealth is dangerous to society. The problems of an unequal distribution of wealth threaten the progress of society.

3. **Is there a solution to the problem of poverty?**
    A. Nature provides enough resources that no person should have to live a life of poverty.
    B. The root cause of poverty is the private ownership of land. Land should be made common property.

4. **What are the three factors of production?**
    A. *Land*: Land includes all material not made by human beings.
    B. *Labor*: Labor includes all human work.
    C. *Capital*: Capital includes everything that is not classified as land or labor.

5. **Does the ownership of land involve a financial risk?**
    A. The value of land increases as society increases in population. Landlords do not have to develop their land or invest capital to increase the value of their land. Owning land involves no financial risk.
    B. Landlords merely own land. They gain great wealth at no risk and they provide no service to society. This situation is morally wrong and should be corrected.

6. How does the monopolization of land affect the capitalist system?
  A. Land is necessary to both workers and capitalists for the production of wealth. Those who own land control the production of wealth.
  B. Landlords gain great wealth at the expense of the capitalists and the workers. Private ownership of land leads to slavery for those who do not own land.
  C. Rent charged by landlords for the use of land robs capitalists and workers of honest profit. Capitalists risk their wealth. Workers give their time and their labor. Landlords offer no services and gain wealth through mere ownership.
  D. An increase in population creates a higher demand for land. In turn, a higher demand for land creates higher rents demanded by landlords. An increase in rent causes wages and profits to fall.
  E. Landlords monopolize resources that are granted equally to all human beings by nature. All people should have an equal right to land.

7. How can the monopolization of land be abolished?
  A. Land should be made common property. All human beings have an equal and natural right to use land.
  B. Landlords should be taxed for the value of their land.
  C. A single massive tax on the value of land would absorb all rents and end the monopolization of land. The market value of land (known as rent) should be confiscated through taxation.

8. How will a single tax on the value of land affect society?
  A. A tax on the value of land will be the only tax necessary to fund government. All other taxes can be abolished.
  B. When all taxes are abolished except the land tax, an enormous weight will be lifted from productive industry. People will be free to buy or sell in a market uninhibited by taxes.
  C. A single tax on the value of land will lead to the abolition of all rent. The abolition of rent will raise wages and profits, abolish poverty, and create full employment.
  D. The land tax or "single tax" will stimulate economic production and progress.
  E. Revenue from the land tax can be used to improve society.

STUDENT ACTIVITIES

Vocabulary
Define the following terms before reading the lesson on George.

1. acquiescence	8. contradistinction	15. fallacy
2. aggregate	9. degradation	16. maladjustment
3. apex	10. enigma	17. niggardly
4. avarice	11. enunciated	18. pecuniary
5. barbarism	12. erroneous	19. philanthropy
6. blasphemy	13. extirpate	20. prodigious
7. bounteous	14. facilitation	

Review

1. What well-known men admired George's reform movement?
2. What is George's most important book?
3. What did George think was the positive aspect of the industrial revolution?
4. What did George think was the negative aspect of the industrial revolution?
5. What did George think would happen to society if the problem of poverty was not solved?
6. What did George think was morally wrong with the changes brought about by the industrial revolution?
7. What did George think was the root cause of poverty?
8. What are the three factors of production according to George?
9. According to George, what is land?
10. Why did George think ownership of land involved no financial risk?
11. What did George think was the status of people who did not own land?
12. According to George, what situation creates a higher demand for land?
13. What did George think was the solution to the landlords' monopolization of land?
14. What did George think would happen if all taxes were abolished except the land tax?
15. Decide whether the following statements are **True** or **False** according to Henry George.
    A. Landlords gain great wealth without providing a service to society.
    B. People who control capital control the production of wealth.
    C. Society needs a single massive tax on the value of land.
    D. All taxes should be abolished except the land tax and an income tax.
    E. A single tax on the value of land would slow down economic production.
    F. All people should have an equal right to land.

What do you think?
On a scale of one through five, rate your opinion of the following quotations by George. Write a short statement explaining your rating.

1 – You **strongly agree** with the statement *or* you feel the statement is **admirable** considering the historical circumstances surrounding it.
5 – You **strongly disagree** with the statement *or* you feel the statement is **contemptible** considering the historical circumstances surrounding it.

A. *It is becoming evident that the enormous increase in productive power which has marked the present century and is still going on with accelerating ratio, has no tendency to extirpate poverty or to lighten the burdens of those compelled to toil.*
B. *This association of poverty with progress is the great enigma of our times. It is the central fact from which spring industrial, social, and political difficulties that perplex the world, and with which statesmanship and philanthropy and education grapple in vain.*
C. *So long as all the increased wealth which modern progress brings goes but to build up great fortunes, to increase luxury and make sharper the contrast between the House of Have and the House of Want, progress is not real and cannot be permanent.*
D. *We must make land common property.*
E. *The equal right of all men to the use of land is as clear as their equal right to breathe the air—it is a right proclaimed by the fact of their existence.*
F. *The evils arising from the unjust and unequal distribution of wealth, which are becoming more and more apparent as modern civilization goes on, are not incidents of progress, but tendencies which must bring progress to a halt.*
G. *I join issue with those who say that we cannot all be rich; with those who declare that in human society the poor must always exist. . . . We might all have enough wealth to satisfy reasonable desires.*
H. *It is not necessary that anyone should be condemned to monotonous toil; it is not necessary that anyone should lack the wealth and the leisure which permit the development of the faculties that raise man above the animal.*
I. *There is danger in reckless change; but greater danger in blind conservatism.*
J. *There are three ways by which an individual can get wealthy—by work, by gift, and by theft. And, clearly, the reason why the workers get so little is that the beggars and thieves get so much.*
K. *How can a man be said to have a country when he has not right to a square inch of it?*
L. *Property in land is as indefensible as property in man.*

CHAPTER 25

THORSTEIN VEBLEN

BACKGROUND

Thorstein Veblen (1857-1929), the son of Norwegian immigrants, grew up in an environment that seemed unlikely to produce one of the world's great intellectuals. As a boy on his father's Minnesota farm he learned English as a second language. When he entered college at age nineteen he still spoke primarily Norwegian. He would, however, eventually learn twenty-six languages. He would also become an expert in philosophy, history, economics, sociology, psychology, anthropology, and engineering. Many people referred to Veblen as "the last man to know everything."

After earning a doctorate in philosophy from Yale, Veblen returned to his father's farm. For seven years he tinkered with farm machinery while privately continuing his academic studies. At age thirty-five he secured his first job when he was hired to work as a professor at the University of Chicago.

As a scholar Veblen came across as an uninvolved spectator of human behavior. He wrote as a scientist who merely observed, described, and analyzed human society. In his personal life he seemed alienated from society. A nonconformist, he remained aloof from his colleagues and had no close friends. He was seen as an eccentric who refused to use a telephone, make his bed, or wash his dishes. As a teacher he mumbled through lectures. He gave every student a "C" unless a student needed a higher grade to retain a scholarship. He posted his office hours as 10:00 to 10:05 on Mondays. He had trouble maintaining employment and was asked to leave several universities. He died in poverty.

His best known works are *The Theory of the Leisure Class* and *The Theory of Business Enterprise*. In these books, and many others, he developed his general thesis that classical economic theories were no longer compatible with modern industry. He brought attention to how small-scale capitalism was giving way to large-scale monopolies. Veblen, like Karl Marx, predicted social upheaval. After his death his stature as an outstanding social scientist grew steadily. He influenced many economists and political scientists. During the New Deal of the 1930s several public policy makers claimed Veblen as their primary influence.

THORSTEIN VEBLEN – IN HIS OWN WORDS

The Theory of the Leisure Class, 1899

It is as elements of social structure—conventional facts—that leisure and ownership are matters of interest for the purpose in hand. An habitual neglect of work does not constitute a leisure class; neither does the mechanical fact of use and consumption constitute ownership. . . .

If its working were not disturbed by other economic forces or other features of the emulative process, the immediate effect of such a pecuniary struggle . . . would be to make men industrious and frugal. This result actually follows, in some measure, so far as regards the lower classes, whose ordinary means of acquiring goods is productive labor. . . . These lower classes can in any case not avoid labor, and the imputation of labor is therefore not greatly derogatory to them, at least not within their class. Rather, since labor is their recognized and accepted mode of life, they take some emulative pride in a reputation for efficiency in their work, this being often the only line of emulation that is open to them. . . .

But it is otherwise with the superior pecuniary class, with which we are here immediately concerned. For this class also the incentive to diligence and thrift is not absent; but its action is so greatly qualified by the secondary demands of pecuniary emulation, that any inclination in this direction is practically overborne and any incentive to diligence tends to be of no effect. The most imperative of these secondary demands of emulation, as well as the one of widest scope, is the requirement of abstention from productive work. . . . During the predatory culture labor comes to be associated in men's habits of thought with weakness and subjection to a master. It is therefore a mark of inferiority, and therefore comes to be accounted unworthy of man in his best estate. By virtue of this tradition labor is felt to be debasing, and this tradition has never died out. . . .

In order to gain and to hold the esteem of men it is not sufficient merely to possess wealth or power. The wealth or power must be put in evidence, for esteem is awarded only on evidence. And not only does the evidence of wealth serve to impress one's importance on others and to keep their sense of his importance alive and alert, but it is of scarcely less use in building up and preserving one's self-complacency. In all but the lowest stages of culture the normally constituted man is comforted and upheld in his self-respect by "decent surroundings" and by exemption from "menial offices." . . .

Abstention from labor is not only an honorific or meritorious act, but it presently comes to be a requisite of decency. The insistence on property as the basis of reputability is very naïve and very imperious during the early stages of the accumulation of wealth. Abstention from labor is the conventional evidence of wealth and is therefore the conventional mark of social standing; and this insistence on the meritoriousness of wealth leads to a more strenuous insistence on leisure. . . . According to well-established laws of human nature, prescription presently seizes upon this conventional evidence of wealth and fixes it in men's habits of thought as something that is in itself substantially meritorious and ennobling; while productive labor at the same time and by a like process becomes in a double sense intrinsically unworthy. Prescription ends by making labor not only disreputable in the eyes of the community, but morally impossible to the noble, freeborn man, and incompatible with a worthy life. . . .

For the great body of the people in any modern community, the proximate ground of expenditure in excess of what is required for physical comfort is not a conscious effort to excel in the expensiveness of their visible consumption, so much as it is a desire to live up to the conventional standard of decency in the amount and grade of goods consumed. This desire is not guided by a rigidly invariable standard, which must be lived up to, and beyond which there is no incentive to go. The standard is flexible; and especially it is indefinitely extensible, if only time is allowed for habituation to any increase in pecuniary ability and for acquiring facility in the new and larger scale of expenditure that follows such an increase. It is much more difficult to recede from a scale of expenditure once adopted than it is to extend the accustomed scale in response to an accession of wealth. Many items of customary expenditure prove on analysis to be almost purely wasteful, and they are therefore honorific only, but after they have once been incorporated into the scale of decent consumption, and so have become an integral part of one's scheme of life, it is quite as hard to give up these as it is to give up many items that conduce directly to one's physical comfort, or even that may be necessary to life and health. That is to say, the conspicuously wasteful honorific expenditure that confers spiritual well-being may become more indispensable than much of that expenditure which ministers to the "lower" wants of physical well-being or sustenance only. It is notoriously just as difficult to recede from a "high" standard of living as it is to lower a standard which is already relatively low; although in the former case the difficulty is a moral one, while in the latter it may involve a material deduction from the physical comforts of life. . . .

It is for this [leisure] class to determine, in general outline, what scheme of life the community shall accept as decent or honorific; and it is their office by precept and example to set forth this scheme of social salvation in its highest, ideal form. . . .

This conservatism of the wealthy class is so obvious a feature that it has even come to be recognized as a mark of respectability. Since conservatism is a characteristic of the wealthier and therefore more reputable portion of the community, it has acquired a certain honorific or decorative value. It has become prescriptive to such an extent that an adherence to conservative views is comprised as a matter of course in our notions of respectability; and it is imperatively incumbent on all who would lead a blameless life in point of social repute. Conservatism, being an upper-class characteristic, is decorous; and conversely, innovation, being a lower-class phenomenon, is vulgar. . . .

The revulsion felt by good people at any proposed departure from the accepted methods of life is a familiar fact of everyday experience. . . .

The institution of a leisure class acts to make the lower classes conservative by withdrawing from them as much as it may of the means of sustenance and so reducing their consumption, and consequently their available energy, to such a point as to make them incapable of the effort required for the learning and adoption of new habits of thought. The accumulation of wealth at the upper end of the pecuniary scale implies privation at the lower end of the scale. It is a commonplace that, wherever it occurs, a considerable degree of privation among the body of the people is a serious obstacle to any innovation.

The Theory of Business Enterprise, 1904

The scope and method of modern industry are given by the machine. This may not seem to hold true for all industries, perhaps, not for the greater part of industry as rated by the bulk of the output or by the aggregate volume of labor expended. But it holds true to such an extent and in such a pervasive manner that a modern industrial community cannot go on except by the help of the accepted mechanical appliances and processes. The machine industries—those portions of the industrial system in which the machine process is paramount—are in a dominant position; they set the pace for the rest of the industrial system. In this sense the present is the age of the machine process. This dominance of the machine process in industry marks off the present industrial situation from all else of its kind.

In a like sense the present is the age of business enterprise. Not that all industrial activity is carried on by the rule of investment for profits, but an effective majority of the industrial forces are organized on that basis. There are many items of great volume and consequence that do not fall within the immediate scope of these principles. . . . But those elements in the industrial world that take the initiative and exert a far-reaching coercive guidance in matters of industry go to their work with a view to profits on investment, and are guided by the principles and exigencies of business. The business man, especially the business man of wide and authoritative discretion, has become a controlling force in industry, because through the mechanism of investments and markets, he controls the plants and processes, and these set the pace and determine the direction of movement for the rest. His control in those portions of the field that are not immediately under his hand is, no doubt, somewhat loose and uncertain; but in the long run his discretion is in great measure decisive even for these outlying portions of the field, for he is the only large self-directing economic factor. His control of the motions of other men is not strict, for they are not under coercion from him except through the coercion exercised by the exigencies of the situation in which their lives are cast; but as near as it may be said of any human power in modern times, the large business man controls the exigencies of life under which the community lives. Hence, upon him and his fortunes centers the abiding interest of civilized mankind. . . .

Under modern circumstances, where industry is carried on on a large scale, the discretionary head of an industrial enterprise is commonly removed from all personal contact with the body of customers for whom the industrial process under his control purveys goods or services. The mitigating effect which personal contact may have in dealings between man and man is therefore in great measure eliminated. The whole takes on something of an impersonal character. One can with an easier conscience and with less of a sense of meanness take advantage of the necessities of people whom one knows of only as an indiscriminate aggregate of consumers. . . .

. . . Under the old order, industry, and even such trade as there was, was a quest of livelihood; under the new order industry is directed by the quest of profits. Formerly, therefore, times were good or bad according as the industrial processes yielded a sufficient or an insufficient output of the means of life. Latterly times are good or bad according as the process of business yields an adequate or inadequate rate of profits. The controlling end is different in the present, and the question of welfare turns on the degree of success with which this different ulterior end is achieved. Prosperity now means, primarily, business prosperity; whereas it used to mean industrial sufficiency. . . .

Popular welfare is bound up with the conduct of business, because industry is managed for business ends; and also because there prevails throughout modern communities a settled habit of rating the means of livelihood and the amenities of life in pecuniary terms. But apart from their effect in controlling the terms of livelihood from day to day, these principles are also in great measure decisive in the larger affairs of life, both for the individual in his civil relations and for the community at large in its political concerns. Modern (civilized) institutions rest, in great part, on business principles. . . .

Because of this settled habit of seeing all the conjunctures of life from the business point of view, in terms of profit and loss, the management of the affairs of the community at large falls by common consent into the hands of businessmen, and is guided by business considerations. Hence, modern politics is business politics, even apart from the sinister application of the phrase to what is invidiously called corrupt politics. This is true both of foreign and domestic policy. Legislation, police surveillance, the administration of justice, the military and diplomatic service, all are chiefly concerned with business relations, pecuniary interest, and they have little more than an incidental bearing on other human interests. All this apparatus is also charged with the protection of life and personal liberty, but its work in this bearing has much of a pecuniary color. . . .

Representative government means, chiefly, representation of business interests. The government commonly works in the interest of the businessmen with a fairly consistent singleness of purpose. And in its solicitude for the businessmen's interests, it is borne out by current public sentiment, for there is a naïve, unquestioning persuasion abroad among the body of the people to the effect that, in some occult way, the material interests of the populace coincide with the pecuniary interests of those businessmen who live within the scope of the same set of governmental contrivances. . . .

The ground of sentiment on which rests the popular approval of a government for business ends may be summed up under two heads: patriotism and property. Both of these terms stand for institutional facts that have come down out of a past which differed substantially from the present situation. The substance of both is of the nature of unreasoning sentiment, in the sense that both are insisted on as a matter of course, as self-legitimating grounds of action which, it is felt, not only give expedient rules of conduct but admit of no question as to their ulterior consequences or their value for the life purposes of the community. . . .

. . . The common man is enabled to feel that he has some sort of metaphysical share in the gains which accrue to the businessmen who are citizens of the same "commonwealth"; so that whatever policy furthers the commercial gains of those businessmen, whose domicile is within the national boundaries, is felt to be beneficial to all the rest of the population. . . .

. . . Under this current business regime, business gains are the basis of individual wealth, and the (pseudo) notion of joint acquisition has taken the place of the manorial notion of joint work. The institutional animus of ownership, as it took shape under the discipline of early modern handicraft awards the ownership of property to the workman who has produced. By a dialectical conversion of the terms, this metaphysical dictum is made to fit the circumstances of later competitive business by construing acquisition of property to mean production of wealth; so that a businessman is looked upon as the putative producer of whatever wealth he acquires. By force of this sophistication the acquisition of property by any person is held to be, not only expedient for the owner, but meritorious as an action serving the common good. Failure to bargain shrewdly or to accumulate more goods than one has produced by the work of one's own hands is looked upon with a feeling of annoyance, as a neglect, not only of opportunity, but of duty. The pecuniary conscience commonly does not, of course, go to quixotic lengths in a public-spirited insistence on everybody's acquiring more than an aliquot part of the aggregate wealth on hand, but it is felt that he best serves the common good who, other things equal, diverts the larger share of the aggregate wealth to his own possession. His acquiring a defensible title to it makes him the putative producer of it. . . .

The quest of profits leads to a predatory national policy. The resulting large fortunes call for a massive government apparatus to secure the accumulations, on the one hand, and for large and conspicuous opportunities to spend the resulting income, on the other hand; which means a militant, coercive home administration and something in the way of an imperial court life—a dynastic fountain of honor and a courtly bureau of ceremonial amenities.

THORSTEIN VEBLEN – A SIMULATED INTERVIEW

1. **What is conspicuous consumption?**
   A. Conspicuous consumption occurs when people spend money in excess of what is necessary to fulfill their needs. People openly consume products they don't need in order to gain social status.
   B. People in the leisure class advertise their perceived superiority through conspicuous consumption. The leisure class flaunts its wealth and power by purchasing status items. More expensive products are considered better products.

2. **Besides conspicuous consumption, what are other characteristics of the leisure class?**
   A. Although people in the leisure class possess enough wealth to avoid work, they are not idle. Indeed, they are the busiest members of society.
   B. The work of the leisure class is predatory. They seize wealth through force. They do nothing to contribute to true productivity.
   C. The leisure class is composed of people who consume without producing.
   D. The leisure class is by nature conservative. Wealthy people oppose changing a society in which they profit.

3. **How does society view the leisure class?**
   A. Society views the leisure class as superior because of their public exhibition of wealth and power.
   B. The leisure class pursues its predatory activities with the full approval of society. The leisure class is seen as strong and able. The predatory behavior of the leisure class is honored by society.
   C. Society most honors people who are not involved in productive labor. The ability to avoid productive labor is seen as a mark of superiority. Gaining wealth by force is admired by society, while pure productive labor is considered undignified.`
   D. The leisure class determines the values of society. People aspire to the same beliefs and values as those held by the leisure class. For example, since conservatism is a characteristic of the leisure class, conservatism is honored and respected by the lower class.

4. **What are the characteristics of the lower class?**
   A. People in the lower class work hard out of necessity. Work is an accepted fact of life for people in the lower class.
   B. The productive labor of the lower class is seen as a sign of weakness and inferiority. Productive labor is seen as unworthy of respect.
   C. People in the lower class try to imitate the leisure class. Predatory force is admired.

5. How do individuals gain status in modern society?
  A. Since the leisure class is considered superior, individuals gain status by imitating people in the leisure class. Individuals gain self-respect by purchasing status items.
  B. Since individuals care how they are perceived by others, personal pleasure and self-respect depend on conspicuous consumption.

6. What are the characteristics of modern society?
  A. Society rates success in monetary terms. People with more money are considered more successful.
  B. Since modern life is viewed in monetary terms of profit and loss, the affairs of society are in the hands of businessmen.
  C. By trying to imitate the leisure class people do not consume simply to satisfy their needs. People consume in a way that they might gain status in society.

7. What is the role of government in modern society?
  A. Government operates for the good of businessmen. Representative government does not represent the people; it represents business.
  B. Wealthy businessmen use government to protect and advance their wealth. Their desire for profit leads to a predatory national policy.
  C. Modern politics is based upon the needs of businessmen. Both foreign and domestic policies are determined by business concerns.

8. What are the characteristics of the modern economy?
  A. At one time business production was based upon the needs of society. In modern times, however, business is operated solely to produce profit, and prosperity is based upon what is prosperous for business rather than what is prosperous for society.
  B. Modern business is impersonal. Business is run on such a large scale that businessmen are removed from personal contact with their workers and their customers.
  C. In the modern economy businessmen are predators who conspire against the economic machine. They cause values to fluctuate and create confusion. Businessmen are preoccupied with credit and loans; they are preoccupied with a make-believe capitalism.
  D. In the modern economy there is no place for the businessman whose only aim is profit. The economic machine wants to produce goods to fulfill the needs of society and therefore requires technicians and engineers to make the economic machine work efficiently.
  E. The modern economy no longer needs businessmen; it needs technicians to run the economy like a well-oiled productive machine. The days of the businessman are numbered. A corps of engineers will eventually take over the chaos of the business system. If not, the system will degenerate into a system based upon naked force.

STUDENT ACTIVITIES

Vocabulary
Define the following terms before reading the lesson on Veblen.

1.	aggregate	10.	ennobling	19.	manorial
2.	aliquot	11.	exigencies	20.	mitigating
3.	conjunctures	12.	expedient	21.	pecuniary
4.	conspicuous	13.	extensible	22.	predatory
5.	contrivance	14.	frugal	23.	privation
6.	dialectical	15.	indiscriminate	24.	proximate
7.	dictum	16.	intrinsically	25.	quixotic
8.	discretion	17.	invidiously	26.	solicitude
9.	emulative	18.	latterly	27.	sustenance

Review
1. In what way did Veblen write as a scientist?
2. What were Veblen's best known books?
3. According to Veblen, when does conspicuous consumption occur?
4. How did Veblen think people in the leisure class used conspicuous consumption?
5. According to Veblen, the leisure class works hard at what type of work?
6. Why did Veblen believe the leisure class was naturally conservative?
7. Why did Veblen think society viewed the leisure class as superior to other classes?
8. According to Veblen, who is most honored by society?
9. Who did Veblen believe determined the values of society?
10. How did Veblen think society viewed productive labor?
11. How did Veblen think people in society gained status?
12. Why did Veblen think people consumed more than necessary to satisfy their needs?
13. What did Veblen think was needed by the modern economic machine?
14. Who did Veblen believe should take control of the modern business system?
15. Decide whether the following statements are **True** or **False** according to Thorstein Veblen.
    A. People in the lower classes are naturally at war with people in the leisure class.
    B. Society views products that are more expensive as better products.
    C. The affairs of society are in the hands of businessmen.
    D. Government operates for the good of businessmen.
    E. Although domestic policies are determined by the needs of businessmen, foreign policies are determined by the desire to promote democracy.
    F. Modern business is predatory and impersonal.

What do you think?
On a scale of one through five, rate your opinion of the following quotations by Veblen. Write a short statement explaining your rating.

1 – You **strongly agree** with the statement *or* you feel the statement is **admirable** considering the historical circumstances surrounding it.
5 – You **strongly disagree** with the statement *or* you feel the statement is **contemptible** considering the historical circumstances surrounding it.

A. *These lower classes can in any case not avoid labor, and the imputation of labor is therefore not greatly derogatory to them, at least not within their class.*
B. *During the predatory culture labor comes to be associated in men's habits of thought with weakness and subjection to a master.*
C. *In order to gain and to hold the esteem of men it is not sufficient merely to possess wealth or power. The wealth or power must be put in evidence, for esteem is awarded only on evidence.*
D. *Prescription ends by making labor not only disreputable in the eyes of the community, but morally impossible to the noble, freeborn man, and incompatible with a worthy life.*
E. *It is notoriously just as difficult to recede from a "high" standard of living as it is to lower a standard which is relatively low; although in the former case the difficulty is a moral one, while in the latter it may involve a material deduction from the physical comforts of life.*
F. *It is for this [leisure] class to determine, in general outline, what scheme of life the community shall accept as decent or honorific.*
G. *This conservatism of the wealthy class is so obvious a feature that it has even come to be recognized as a mark of respectability.*
H. *Popular welfare is bound up with the conduct of business, because industry is managed for business ends; and also because there prevails throughout modern communities a settled habit of rating the means of livelihood and the amenities of life in pecuniary terms.*
I. *Modern politics is business politics.*
J. *Representative government means, chiefly, representation of business interests.*
K. *The quest of profits leads to a predatory national policy.*
L. *The institution of a leisure class hinders cultural development immediately (1) by the inertia proper of the class itself, (2) through its prescriptive example of conspicuous waste and conservatism, and (3) indirectly through that system of unequal distribution of wealth and sustenance on which the institution itself rests.*
M. *The addiction to sports, therefore, in a peculiar degree marks an arrested development of man's moral nature.*

CHAPTER 26

EUGENE DEBS

BACKGROUND

As a young man Eugene V. Debs (1855-1926) appeared destined for a career as a labor leader and Democratic politician. However, after losing faith in American capitalism he turned to socialism. His commitment to humanitarian reform led him to believe the capitalist control of society should be terminated.

At the age of fifteen Debs went to work for the railroad in his home town of Terre Haute, Indiana. After rising through the ranks of his local union he gained recognition as a promising young politician. He was twice elected city clerk before his election to the Indiana State Assembly.

In 1894, when Debs was president of the American Railway Union, he led a strike against industrialist George Pullman. During an economic depression Pullman instituted harsh pay cuts while refusing to cut prices in his company town. Pullman believed workers should suffer more than anyone during a depression since he believed workers contributed little to the success of a business. The strike against Pullman was declared illegal. Debs, however, refused to end the strike and spent six months in prison for contempt of court.

In prison Debs had time to read and reflect. Believing that unions would fail against capitalist power, he concluded that European ideas of socialism were the answer to labor's problems. After his release from prison he helped organize the Socialist party. As a popular and legendary personality Debs was nominated five times by the Socialist party to run for president of the United States. In the elections of 1912 and 1920 he received over one million votes.

In the 1920 election Debs had to campaign from a prison cell. During World War I the government passed the Sedition Act effectively making criticism of the government a criminal offense. Debs, who opposed World War I, was not swayed by the Sedition Act and made a speech questioning the traditional idea of wartime patriotism. Although he defended himself on the grounds that the First Amendment guaranteed freedom of speech, he was sentenced to ten years in prison. After serving five years he was pardoned by President Harding. Debs died in his home town of Terre Haute in 1926.

EUGENE DEBS – IN HIS OWN WORDS

"Outlook for Socialism in the United States," 1900

As a rule, large capitalists are Republicans and small capitalists are Democrats, but workingmen must remember that they are all capitalists, and that the many small ones, like the fewer large ones, are all politically supporting their class interests, and this is always and everywhere the capitalist class.

Whether the means of production—that is to say, the land, mines, factories, machinery, etc.—are owned by a few large Republican capitalists, who organize a trust, or whether they be owned by a lot of small Democratic capitalists, who are opposed to the trust, is all the same to the working class. Let the capitalists, large and small, fight this out among themselves.

The working class must get rid of the whole brood of masters and exploiters, and put themselves in possession and control of the means of production, that they may have steady employment without consulting a capitalist employer, large or small, and that they may get the wealth their labor produces, all of it, and enjoy with their families the fruits of their industry in comfortable and happy homes, abundant and wholesome food, proper clothing, and all other things necessary to "life, liberty and the pursuit of happiness." It is therefore a question not of "reform," the mask of fraud, but of revolution. The capitalist system must be overthrown, class-rule abolished, and wage-slavery supplanted by cooperative industry.

"The Negro in the Class Struggle," 1903

The history of the Negro in the United States is a history of crime without parallel.

Why should the white man hate him? Because he stole him from his native land and for two centuries and a half robbed him of the fruit of his labor, kept him in beastly ignorance, and subjected him to the brutal domination of the lash? Because he tore the black child from the breasts of its mother and ravished the black man's daughter before her father's eyes? . . .

I have said and say again that, properly speaking, there is no Negro question outside of the labor question—the working-class struggle. Our position as Socialists and as a party is perfectly plain. We have simply to say: "The class struggle is colorless." The capitalists, white, black, and other shades, are on one side and the workers, white, black, and all other colors, on the other side. . . .

We have nothing special to offer the Negro, and we cannot make separate appeals to all the races.

The Socialist party is the party of the working class, regardless of color—the whole working class of the whole world.

"Woman–Comrade and Equal," undated

I am glad to align myself with a party that declares for absolute equality between the sexes. Anything less than this is too narrow for twentieth-century civilization, and too small for a man who has a right conception of manhood. . . .

Under our brutal forms of existence, beating womanhood to dust, we have raged in passion for the individual woman, for use only. Some day we shall develop the social passion for womanhood, and then the gross will disappear in service and justice and companionship. Then we shall lift woman from the mire where our fists have struck her, and set her by our side as our comrade and equal and that will be love indeed.

"Revolutionary Unionism," 1905

We are engaged today in a class war; and why? For the simple reason that in the evolution of the capitalist system in which we live, society has been mainly divided into two economic classes—a small class of capitalists who own the tools with which work is done and wealth is produced, and a great mass of workers who are compelled to use those tools. Between these two classes there is an irrepressible economic conflict. . . .

By virtue of his private ownership of the social tool—made and used by the cooperative labor of the working class—the employer has the economic power to appropriate to himself, as a capitalist, what is produced by the social labor of the working class. This accounts for the fact that the capitalist becomes fabulously rich, lives in a palace where there is music and singing and dancing, and where there is the luxury of all climes, while the working-men who do the work and produce the wealth and endure the privations and make the sacrifices of health and limb and life, remain in a wretched state of poverty and dependence. . . .

We insist that all the workers in the whole of any given plant shall belong to one and the same union.

This is the very thing the workers need and the capitalist who owns the establishment does not want. . . .

The capitalists are perfectly willing that you shall organize, as long as you don't do a thing against them; as long as you don't do a thing for yourselves. You cannot do a thing for yourselves without antagonizing them; and you don't antagonize them through your craft unions nearly as much as you buttress their interests and prolong their mastery. . . .

Since you have looked yourself over thoroughly, you realize by this time that, as a workingman, you have been supporting, through your craft unions and through your ballots, a social system that is the negation of your manhood. . . .

[The capitalist] doesn't own you under the law, but he does under the fact.

Why? Because he owns the tool with which you work, and you have got to have access to that tool if you work; and if you want to live you have got to work. If you don't work you don't eat; and so, scourged by hunger pangs, you look about for that tool and you locate it, and you soon discover that between yourself, a workingman, and that tool that is an essential part of yourself in industry, there stands the capitalist who owns it. He is your boss; he owns your job, takes your product, and controls your destiny. Before you can touch that tool to earn a dime you must petition the owner of it to allow you to use it, in consideration of your giving to him all you produce with it, except just enough to keep you alive and in working order.

Speech at Girard, Kansas, 1908
We were taught under the old ethic that man's business upon this earth was to look out for himself. That was the ethic of the jungle; the ethic of the wild beast. Take care of yourself, no matter what may become of your fellowman. Thousands of years ago the question was asked: "Am I my brother's keeper?" That question has never yet been answered in a way that is satisfactory to civilized society.

Yes, I am my brother's keeper. I am under a moral obligation to him that is inspired, not by any maudlin sentimentality, but by the higher duty I owe to myself. What would you think of me if I were capable of seating myself at a table and gorging myself with food and saw about me the children of my fellow beings starving to death?

Speech accepting the Socialist nomination for President, 1912
The Socialist party's mission is not only to destroy capitalist despotism but to establish industrial and social democracy. To this end the workers are steadily organizing and fitting themselves for the day when they shall take control of the people's industries and when the right to work shall be as inviolate as the right to breathe the breath of life.

Standing as it does for the emancipation of the working class from wage-slavery, for the equal rights and opportunities of all men and all women, for the abolition of child labor and the conservation of all childhood, for social self-rule and the equal freedom of all, the Socialist party is the party of progress, the party of the future, and its triumph will signalize the birth of a new civilization and the dawn of a happier day for all humanity.

"Jesus the Supreme Leader," 1914
Jesus was the grandest and loftiest of human souls—sun-crowned and God-inspired; a full-statured man, red-blooded and lion-hearted, yet sweet and gentle as the noble mother who gave him birth.

He had the majesty and poise of a god, the prophetic vision of a seer, the great, loving heart of a woman, and the unaffected innocence and simplicity of a child.

This was and is the martyred Christ of the working class, the inspired evangel of the downtrodden masses, the world's supreme revolutionary leader, whose love for the poor and the children of the poor hallowed all the days of his consecrated life, of his death, and gave to the ages his divine inspiration and his deathless name.

Speech to the Jury, 1918

I have read some history. I know that it is ruling classes that make war upon one another, and not the people. In all the history of this world the people have never yet declared a war. Not one. I do not believe that really civilized nations would murder one another. I would refuse to kill a human being on my own account. Why should I at the command of any one else, or at the command of any power on earth?

Twenty centuries ago there was one appeared upon earth we know as the Prince of Peace. He issued a command in which I believe. He said, "Love one another." He did not say, "Kill one another," but "Love one another." He espoused the cause of the suffering poor . . . and the poor heard him gladly. It was not long before he aroused the ill will and hatred of the usurers, the money changers, the profiteers, the high priests, the lawyers—in a word, the ruling class. They said of him just what the ruling class says of the Socialist today, "He is preaching dangerous doctrine. He is inciting the common rabble. He is a menace to peace and order." And they had him arraigned, tried, convicted, condemned, and they had his quivering body spiked to the gates of Jerusalem. . . .

War does not come by chance. War is not the result of accident. There is a definite cause for war, especially a modern war. The war that began in Europe can readily be accounted for. For the last forty years, under this international capitalist system, this exploiting system, these various nations of Europe have been preparing for the inevitable. And why? In all these nations the great industries are owned by a relatively small class. They are operated for the profit of that class. And great abundance is produced by the workers; but their wages will only buy back a small part of their product. What is the result? They have a vast surplus on hand; they have got to export it; they have got to find a foreign market for it. As a result of this these nations are pitted against each other. They are industrial rivals—competitors. They begin to arm themselves to open, to maintain the market and quickly dispose of their surplus. There is but the one market. All these nations are competitors for it, and sooner or later every war of trade becomes a war of blood.

Now where there is exploitation there must be some form of militarism to support it. Wherever you find exploitation you find some form of military force.

Walls and Bars, 1926

I marvel at the incredible stupidity that blinds the men in control of prisons to the redeeming power of kindness as a substitute for the destructive power of brutality. Every instinct of our nature protests against cruelty to the helpless and defenseless, yet of all places where it is most needed mercy is least practiced in the treatment of convicts. I have seen men of mild temper and gentle disposition made sullen and vicious by harshness and I have also seen the toughest specimens of "bad men" softened and made gentle by a kind word and the touch of a friendly hand. . . .

Crime in all of its varied forms and manifestations is of such a common nature under the capitalist system that capitalism and crime have become almost synonymous terms.

Private appropriation of the earth's surface, the natural resources, and the means of life is nothing less than a crime against humanity, but the comparative few who are the beneficiaries of this iniquitous social arrangement, far from being viewed as criminals meriting punishment, are the exalted rulers of society and the people they exploit gladly render them homage and obeisance. . . .

Multiplied thousands of men, women and children are killed and maimed in American industry by absolutely preventable accidents every year, yet no one ever dreams of indicting the capitalist masters who are guilty of the crime. The capitalist owners of fire traps and of fetid sweating dens, where the lives of the workers are ruthlessly sacrificed and their health wantonly undermined, are not indicted and sent to prison for the reason that they own and control the indicting machinery just as they own and control the industrial machinery in their system. . . .

Capitalism needs and must have the prison to protect itself from the criminals it has created. It not only impoverishes the masses when they are at work, but it still further reduces them by not allowing millions to work at all. The capitalist's profit has supreme consideration; the life of the workers is of little consequence.

If a hundred men are blown up in a mine a hundred others rush there eagerly to take the places of the dead even before the remnants of their bodies have been laid away. Protracted periods of enforced idleness under capitalism have resulted in thousands of industrious working men becoming tramps and vagabonds, and in thousands of tramps and vagabonds becoming outcasts and criminals.

It is in this process that crime is generated and proceeds in its logical stages from petty larceny to highway robbery and homicide. Getting a living under capitalism—the system in which the few who toil not are millionaires and billionaires, while the mass of the people who toil and sweat and produce all the wealth are victims of poverty and pauperism—getting a living under this inexpressibly cruel and inhuman system is so precarious, so uncertain, fraught with such pain and struggle that the wonder is not that so many people become vicious and criminal, but that so many remain in docile submission to such a tyrannous and debasing condition. . . .

. . . The most casual examination of the inmates of jails and prisons shows the great majority of them at a glance to be of the poorer classes.

When, perchance, some rich man goes to prison the instance is so remarkable that it excites great curiosity and amazement. A rich man does not fit in prison. The prison was not made for him; he does not belong there and he does not stay there. The rich man goes to prison only as the exception to prove the rule.

EUGENE DEBS – A SIMULATED INTERVIEW

1. **What is wrong with capitalism?**
   A. Capitalism divides society into two classes—a small class of capitalists who own the tools of production and the great mass of workers who use the tools of production.
   B. Capitalists use their ownership of the tools of production to accumulate wealth and support an extravagant lifestyle. Workers, who do all the work and produce all the wealth, are condemned to a state of poverty and dependence.
   C. Capitalism enriches a few while the mass of people struggle for a minimal existence. Capitalists care only about profit; the life of a worker is of little consequence.
   D. Workers are slaves to the capitalists. Workers are denied a livelihood unless the capitalist provides a job. Workers do not control their own destiny.
   E. The capitalist wage system breeds oppression, exploitation, and war.

2. **What causes crime?**
   A. Crime is synonymous with capitalism. Capitalist society needs prisons to protect itself from the criminals it creates.
   B. Millions of people are unemployed in a capitalist system. Extended periods of joblessness turn workers into tramps and criminals. The capitalist system generates crime.
   C. In a capitalist system workers do not control their own destiny; the ability to make a living is doubtful. In such an inhumane system many people become vicious criminals.
   D. Capitalists are guilty of vast crimes against humanity. They destroy natural resources. They kill and maim workers in factories. These are great crimes that should be punished. Rather than receiving punishment, however, capitalists are glorified as the leaders of society.
   E. The great majority of people in prison are from the poorer classes. When a rich man happens to go to jail great curiosity and excitement are aroused. In a capitalist system a rich person in prison is a rarity.

3. **Should American workers support Democrats or Republicans?**
   A. Both Republicans and Democrats represent capitalist interests. Republicans are big business capitalists who organize trusts. Democrats are small business capitalists who oppose trusts. Whether Republicans or Democrats control political power makes no difference to the working class.
   B. When Democrats or Republicans promise reform, they are guilty of fraud. Workers will never achieve life, liberty, and the pursuit of happiness until the capitalist system is overthrown.

4. How can society be improved?
    A. The Socialist Party proposes several fundamental changes:
        1. Capitalism should be abolished.
        2. Workers should be freed from the slavery of the wage system.
        3. Workers should own and control the tools of production.
        4. The right to work should be as important as the right to breathe.
        5. All men and women should have equal rights and opportunities.
        6. Child labor should be abolished.
    B. Each individual should recognize a moral obligation to help others. The idea of living according to the law of the jungle violates the moral truth that we are our brother's keeper.
    C. People should recognize the benefits of treating others with kindness. Harsh treatment makes all people, even criminals, more vicious. The toughest people are softened by gentle and kind treatment.

5. How will the Socialist party help African-Americans and women?
    A. Crimes committed against blacks are without parallel in history. Africans were stolen from their native land, robbed of the product of their labor, kept in ignorance, and subjected to severe punishment. The Socialist party, however, offers no program just for blacks. The Socialist party is for the entire working class regardless of color. All races are equal.
    B. The Socialist party believes in the absolute equality of the sexes.

6. How does socialism correspond to the teachings of Jesus?
    A. The socialist desire to help the poor stems from the teachings of Jesus. Jesus was a revolutionary leader who loved the poor and valued all life.
    B. Jesus fought for peace and brotherhood; socialists believe in peace and brotherhood.
    C. Jesus, like those who are socialist, was denounced for preaching what was considered a dangerous doctrine.
    D. Socialists are opposed to war. Jesus, the Prince of Peace, said "Love one another." Jesus did not say "Kill one another."

7. Why do nations go to war?
    A. War is made by the ruling classes. The people never make war.
    B. War is inevitable between competitive capitalist nations. The causes of war are grounded in the capitalist system:
        1. Workers produce a surplus of products, but are not paid enough to buy the products.
        2. Capitalists who cannot sell their products domestically are forced to find foreign markets.
        3. Capitalist nations must arm themselves and go to war to protect their foreign markets.

STUDENT ACTIVITIES

Vocabulary
Define the following terms before reading the lesson on Debs.

1. buttress	7. iniquitous	13. sullen
2. docile	8. maudlin	14. supplant
3. evangel	9. obeisance	15. synonymous
4. exploiter	10. privation	16. usurer
5. fetid	11. rabble	17. vagabond
6. homage	12. scourged	18. wantonly

Review
1. Whom did Debs lead a strike against in 1894 when he was head of the American Railway Union?
2. Why did Debs go to jail during the Pullman strike?
3. How many times did the Socialist party nominate Debs for president of the United States?
4. Why did Debs go to jail during World War I?
5. According to Debs, what two social classes does capitalism produce?
6. In what way did Debs think workers were slaves to capitalists?
7. In what way did Debs think capitalism generated crime?
8. In what way did Debs think capitalists were guilty of great crimes against humanity?
9. What did Debs believe was the chief difference between Democrats and Republicans?
10. What did Debs believe was necessary for American workers to achieve "life, liberty, and the pursuit of happiness"?
11. What did Debs feel was a moral obligation of each individual?
12. How did Debs think society would benefit from people treating others with kindness?
13. What program did Debs offer to help African-Americans?
14. What did Debs believe was the basis of the socialist desire to help the poor?
15. In what way did Debs think Jesus was like a socialist?
16. Who did Debs think was responsible for war?
17. Why did Debs think war was inevitable between capitalist nations?
18. Decide whether the following statements are **True** or **False** according to Eugene Debs.
    A. Although workers produce all wealth, they are condemned to a state of poverty.
    B. Oppression, exploitation, and war are natural consequences of the capitalist system.
    C. A rich person is as likely to go to prison as a poor person.
    D. Capitalism should be abolished.
    E. Child labor should be abolished.

What do you think?
On a scale of one through five, rate your opinion of the following quotations by Debs. Write a short statement explaining your rating.

1 – You **strongly agree** with the statement *or* you feel the statement is **admirable** considering the historical circumstances surrounding it.
5 – You **strongly disagree** with the statement *or* you feel the statement is **contemptible** considering the historical circumstances surrounding it.

A. *As a rule, large capitalists are Republicans and small capitalists are Democrats, but workingmen must remember that they are all capitalists, and that the many small ones, like the fewer large ones, are all politically supporting their class interests, and this is always and everywhere the capitalist class.*
B. *The working class must get rid of the whole brood of masters and exploiters, and put themselves in possession and control of the means of production.*
C. *It is therefore a question not of "reform," the mask of fraud, but of revolution.*
D. *Yes, I am my brother's keeper. I am under a moral obligation to him that is inspired, not by any maudlin sentimentality, but by the higher duty I owe myself.*
E. *[Jesus was] the inspired evangel of the downtrodden masses, the world's supreme revolutionary leader, whose love for the poor and the children of the poor hallowed all the days of his consecrated life, of his death, and gave to the ages his divine inspiration and his deathless name.*
F. *It is the ruling classes that make war upon one another, and not the people.*
G. *I marvel at the incredible stupidity that blinds the men in control of prisons to the redeeming power of kindness as a substitute for the destructive power of brutality.*
H. *Crime in all of its varied forms and manifestations is of such a common nature under the capitalist system that capitalism and crime have become almost synonymous terms.*
I. *The most casual examination of the inmates of jails and prisons shows the great majority of them at a glance to be of the poorer classes.*
J. *A rich man does not fit in prison. The prison was not made for him; he does not belong there and he does not stay there.*
K. *I have no country to fight for; my country is the earth, and I am a citizen of the world.*
L. *When great changes occur in history, when great principles are involved, as a rule the majority are wrong.*

PART 6

THE END OF THE FRONTIER

CHAPTER 27

FREDERICK JACKSON TURNER

BACKGROUND

Historians work to keep alive the stories of people who made history and shaped our lives. Sometimes, however, a historian will make history by describing the past in a way that transforms how we view ourselves. One such historian was Frederick Jackson Turner (1861-1932).

A professor at the University of Wisconsin and at Harvard, Turner pioneered new methodologies of historical research. He urged historians to look into all aspects of history in order to gain a more accurate interpretation of the past. He thought American historians should study immigration, urbanization, diplomacy, economics, politics, and culture. He believed research in a variety of disciplines allowed historians to assemble a more complete description of the past.

In 1893 Turner delivered "The Significance of the Frontier in American History," a speech that forever changed how Americans described their nation. In the speech Turner referred to the announcement based on 1890 census findings that the government could no longer designate frontier boundaries in the United States. He used his speech to argue that the frontier was the most important force in determining the American character. The speech was largely ignored until Turner's friend Woodrow Wilson, a professor at Princeton, used the frontier thesis in his own academic research. Turner's ideas eventually became a topic of considerable discussion and debate.

Turner's frontier thesis made Americans rethink their past. Before 1900 the importance of the West was generally overlooked in U.S. history textbooks. Historians had traditionally argued that American institutions originated with early Germanic tribes, an approach known as the germ theory. Turner, however, emphasized the importance of the frontier in forming the American character rather than the influence of early Germanic tribes. His thesis became the dominant interpretation of United States history until the 1930s. Even today, historians feel compelled to address Turner's writings whether they agree or disagree with his thesis. Turner has influenced the writing of American history as much as any other historian. His ideas have even penetrated the social consciousness.

FREDERICK JACKSON TURNER – IN HIS OWN WORDS

"The Significance of the Frontier in American History," 1893
In a recent bulletin of the superintendent of the census for 1890 appear these significant words: "Up to and including 1880 the country had a frontier of settlement, but at present the unsettled area has been so broken into by isolated bodies of settlement that there can hardly be said to be a frontier line. In the discussion of its extent, its westward movement, etc., it cannot, therefore, any longer have a place in the census reports." This brief official statement marks the closing of a great historic movement. Up to our own day American history has been in a large degree the history of the colonization of the Great West. The existence of an area of free land, its continuous recession, and the advance of American settlement westward, explain American development.

Behind institutions, behind constitutional forms and modifications, lie the vital forces that call these organs into life, and shape them to meet changing conditions. Now, the peculiarity of American institutions is the fact that they have been compelled to adapt themselves to the changes of an expanding people—to the changes involved in crossing a continent, in winning a wilderness, and in developing at each area of this progress out of the primitive economic and political conditions of the frontier into the complexity of city life. . . . American development has exhibited not merely advance along a single line, but a return to primitive conditions on a continually advancing frontier line, and a new development for that area. American social development has been continually beginning over again on the frontier. This perennial rebirth, this fluidity of American life, this expansion westward with its new opportunities, its continuous touch with the simplicity of primitive society, furnish the forces dominating American character. The true point of view in the history of this nation is not the Atlantic coast, it is the Great West. . . .

In the settlement of America we have to observe how European life entered the continent, and how America modified and developed that life, and reacted on Europe. Our early history is the study of European germs developing in an American environment. Too exclusive attention has been paid by institutional students to the Germanic origins, too little to the American factors. Now, the frontier is the line of most rapid and effective Americanization. The wilderness masters the colonist. It finds him a European in dress, industries, tools, modes of travel, and thought. It takes him from the railroad car and puts him in the birch canoe. It strips off the garments of civilization, and arrays him in the hunting shirt and the moccasin. It puts him in the log cabin of the Cherokee and the Iroquois, and runs an Indian palisade around him. . . . In short, at the frontier the environment is at first too strong for the man. He must accept the conditions which it furnishes, or perish, and so he fits himself into the Indian clearings and follows the Indian trails. Little by little he transforms the wilderness, but the outcome is not the old Europe, not simply the development of Germanic germs, any more than the first phenomenon was a case of reversion to the Germanic mark. The fact is, that here is a new product that is American. At first, the frontier was the Atlantic coast. It was the frontier of Europe in a very real sense. Moving westward, the frontier became more and more American. As successive terminal moraines result from successive glaciations, so each frontier leaves its traces behind it, and when it becomes a settled area the region still partakes of the frontier characteristics. Thus the advance of the frontier has meant a steady movement away from the influence of Europe, a steady growth of independence on American lines. And to study this advance, the men who grew up under these conditions, and the political, economic and social results of it, is to study the really American part of our history. . . .

The most important effect of the frontier has been in the promotion of democracy here and in Europe. As has been pointed out, the frontier is productive of individualism. Complex society is precipitated by the wilderness into a kind of primitive organization based on the family. The tendency is anti-social. It produces antipathy to control, and particularly to any direct control. The tax-gatherer is viewed as a representative of oppression. . . . The frontier individualism has from the beginning promoted democracy. . . .

. . . The democracy born of free land, strong in selfishness and individualism, intolerant of administrative experience and education, and pressing individual liberty beyond its proper bounds, has its dangers as well as its benefits. Individualism in America has allowed a laxity in regard to governmental affairs which has rendered possible the spoils system, and all the manifest evils that follow from the lack of a highly developed civic spirit. . . .

From the conditions of frontier life came intellectual traits of profound importance. The works of travelers along each frontier from colonial days onward describe for each certain common traits, and these traits have, while softening down, still persisted as survivals in the place of their origin, even when a higher social organization succeeded. The result is that to the frontier the American intellect owes its striking characteristics. That coarseness and strength combined with acuteness and inquisitiveness, that practical, inventive turn of mind, quick to find expedients, that masterful grasp of material things, lacking in the artistic but powerful to effect great ends, that restless nervous energy, that dominant individualism, working for good and for evil, and withal that buoyancy and exuberance which comes with freedom—these are traits of the frontier, or traits called out elsewhere because of the existence of the frontier. Since the days when the fleet of Columbus sailed into the waters of the New World, America has been another name for opportunity, and the people of the United States have taken their tone from the incessant expansion which has not only been open but has even been forced upon them. He would be a rash prophet who should assert that the expansive character of American life has now entirely ceased. Movement has been its dominant fact, and, unless this training has no effect upon a people, the American energy will continually demand a wider field for its exercise. But never again will such gifts of free land offer themselves. For a moment at the frontier the bonds of custom are broken, and unrestraint is triumphant. There is not *tabula rasa*. The stubborn American environment is there with its imperious summons to accept its conditions; the inherited ways of doing things are also there; and yet, in spite of environment, and in spite of custom, each frontier did indeed furnish a new field of opportunity, a gate of escape from the bondage of the past; and freshness, and confidence, and scorn of older society, impatience of its restraints and its ideas, and indifference to its lessons, have accompanied the frontier. What the Mediterranean Sea was to the Greeks, breaking the bond of custom, offering new experiences, calling out new institutions and activities, that, and more, the ever retreating frontier has been to the United States directly, and to the nations of Europe more remotely. And now, four centuries from the discovery of America, at the end of a hundred years of life under the Constitution, the frontier has gone, and with its going has closed the first period of American history.

"Contributions of the West to American Democracy," 1903

The careful student of history must seek the explanation of the forms and changes of political institutions in the social and economic forces that determine them. To know that at any one time a nation may be called a democracy, an aristocracy, or a monarchy, is not so important as to know what are the social and economic tendencies of the state. These are the vital forces that work beneath the surface and dominate external form. It is to changes in the economic and social life of a people that we must look for the forces that ultimately create and modify organs of political action. . . .

. . . We find ourselves at the present time in an era of such profound economic and social transformation as to raise the question of the effect of these changes upon the democratic institutions of the United States. Within a decade four marked changes have occurred in our national development; taken together they constitute a revolution.

First, there is the exhaustion of the supply of free land and the closing of the movement of Western advance as an effective factor in American development. The first rough conquest of the wilderness is accomplished, and that great supply of free lands which year after year has served to reinforce the democratic influences in the United States is exhausted. . . . The free lands that made the American pioneer have gone.

In the second place, contemporaneously with this there has been such a concentration of capital in the control of fundamental industries as to make a new epoch in the economic development of the United States. . . .

A third phenomenon connected with the two just mentioned is the expansion of the United States politically and commercially into lands beyond the seas. . . . Having completed the conquest of the wilderness, and having consolidated our interests, we are beginning to consider the relations of democracy and empire.

And fourth, the political parties of the United States now tend to divide on issues that involve the question of Socialism. The rise of the Populist party in the last decade, and the acceptance of so many of its principles by the Democratic party under the leadership of Mr. Bryan, show in striking manner the birth of new political ideas, the reformation of the lines of political conflict.

It is doubtful if in any ten years of American history more significant factors in our growth have revealed themselves. . . . As a contribution to this inquiry, let us now turn to an examination of the part that the West has played in shaping our democracy.

From the beginning of the settlement of America, the frontier regions have exercised a steady influence toward democracy. . . .

. . . If now in the way of recapitulation we try to pick out from the influences that have gone to the making of Western democracy the factors which constitute the net result of the movement, we shall have to mention at least the following:—

Most important of all has been the fact that an area of free land has continually lain on the western border of the settled area of the United States. Whenever social conditions tended to crystallize in the East, whenever capital tended to press upon labor or political restraints to impede the freedom of the mass, there was this gate of escape to the free conditions of the frontier. These free lands promoted individualism, economic equality, freedom to rise, democracy. Men would not accept inferior wages and a permanent position of social subordination when this promised land of freedom and equality was theirs for the taking. Who would rest content under oppressive legislative conditions when with a slight effort he might reach a land wherein to become a co-worker in the building of free cities and free States on the lines of his own ideal? In a word, then, free lands meant free opportunities. Their existence has differentiated the American democracy from the democracies which have preceded it, because ever, as democracy in the East took the form of highly specialized and complicated industrial society, in the West it kept in touch with primitive conditions, and by action and reaction these two forces have shaped our history.

In the next place, these free lands and this treasury of industrial resources have existed over such vast spaces that they have demanded of democracy increasing spaciousness of design and power of execution. Western democracy is contrasted with the democracy of all other times in the largeness of the tasks to which it set its hand, and in the vast achievements which it has wrought out in the control of nature and of politics. It would be difficult to over-emphasize the importance of this training upon democracy. Never before in the history of the world has a democracy existed on so vast an area and handled things in the gross with such success, with such largeness of design, and such grasp upon the means of execution. In short, democracy has learned in the West of the United States how to deal with the problem of magnitude. The old historic democracies were but little states with primitive economic conditions. . . .

The question is imperative, then, What ideals persist from this democratic experience of the West; and have they acquired sufficient momentum to sustain themselves under conditions so radically unlike those in the days of their origin? . . . The free lands are gone. The material forces that gave vitality to Western democracy are passing away. It is to the realm of the spirit, to the domain of ideals and legislation, that we must look for Western influence upon democracy in our own days.

Western democracy has been from the time of its birth idealistic. The very fact of the wilderness appealed to men as a fair, blank page on which to write a new chapter in the story of man's struggle for a higher type of society. . . . The existence of this land of opportunity has made America the goal of idealists from the days of the Pilgrim Fathers. . . .

. . . But the idealistic influence is not limited to the dreamers' conception of a new State. It gave to the pioneer farmer and city builder a restless energy, a quick capacity for judgement and action, a belief in liberty, freedom of opportunity, and a resistance to the domination of class which infused a vitality and power into the individual atoms of this democratic mass. . . .

It must also be remembered that these democratic ideals have existed at each stage of the advance of the frontier, and have left behind them deep and enduring effects on the thinking of the whole country. Long after the frontier period of a particular region of the Untied States has passed away, the conception of society, the ideals and aspirations which it produced, persist in the minds of the people. . . .

This, at least, is clear: American democracy is fundamentally the outcome of the experiences of the American people in dealing with the West. Western democracy through the whole of its earlier period tended to the production of a society of which the most distinctive fact was the freedom of the individual to rise under conditions of social mobility, and whose ambition was the liberty and well-being of the masses. This conception has vitalized all American democracy, and has brought it into sharp contrasts with the democracies of history, and with those modern efforts of Europe to create an artificial democratic order by legislation. . . .

. . . Best of all, the West gave, not only to the American, but to the unhappy and oppressed of all lands, a vision of hope, and assurance that the world held a place where were to be found high faith in man and the will and power to furnish him the opportunity to grow to the full measure of his own capacity. Great and powerful as are the new sons of her loins, the Republic is greater than they. The paths of the pioneer have widened into broad highways. The forest clearing has expanded into affluent commonwealths. Let us see to it that the ideals of the pioneer in his log cabin shall enlarge into the spiritual life of a democracy where civic power shall dominate and utilize individual achievement for the common good.

FREDERICK JACKSON TURNER – A SIMULATED INTERVIEW

1. **How important was Europe to the development of the United States?**
    A. Historians have paid too much attention to the European roots of the United States. More attention should be given to the *American* factors that developed the character of the United States.
    B. Although Europeans migrated to America, the wilderness transformed the fundamental character of Europeans to create a uniquely American character. The ideas and traditions that Europeans brought to America were changed by the frontier experience.
    C. The continuous movement of Americans onto new frontiers marked a steady movement away from European influences. European traditions became gradually less important to the development of the American character.

2. **What force most shaped the development of the United States?**
    A. The United States was shaped primarily by the frontier conditions that existed in America for 300 years. The American character is the product of people who have been in continuous contact with primitive frontier conditions.
    B. The continuing nature of the frontier led to the constant restructuring of society. The United States is the product of new societies created as people continuously moved west.

3. **What American characteristics are a product of the frontier?**
    A. The frontier fostered a spirit of individualism. People on the frontier faced primitive conditions forcing them to rely on themselves and their family for survival.
    B. The frontier gave Americans an enthusiasm for freedom.
    C. The frontier made Americans inquisitive, inventive, materialistic, energetic, and independent.
    D. The frontier nourished a sense of social equality. Birthright did not matter on the frontier; all that mattered was what an individual could do for himself.
    E. Americans lack a sense of tradition because of the frontier. A continuous frontier meant that society was constantly reborn.

4. **How did the frontier affect American democracy?**
    A. The most important aspect of America's frontier experience was the development of democracy. American democracy is fundamentally a product of the western frontier experience.
    B. Americans built something unique in human history—they constructed a democracy that functions over a vast territory. More than any other people, Americans understand how to deal with problems on a vast scale.

5. How did the frontier affect American society?

   A. Although people moving onto the frontier carried their social traditions with them, life on the frontier thrust them into a state of near savagery. The frontier therefore transformed social traditions into something new.

   B. The frontier allowed social mobility. On the frontier an individual could improve himself through his own abilities.

   C. The continuous existence of free land gave people a safety valve to escape hardship. Whenever conditions became intolerable the West served as an escape to freedom and opportunity.

6. How did the American frontier affect other nations?

   A. The American frontier gave a vision of hope not only to Americans, but also to people of other nations. The American frontier provided people of many nations an opportunity to better their lives according to their own abilities.

   B. Since the time of Columbus, America has been a land of opportunity.

   C. Free land on the American frontier served as a magnet to bring people west, including people from Europe.

7. Should Americans be concerned about the closing of the frontier?

   A. The frontier promoted qualities of individualism, equality, freedom and democracy. At the beginning of the twentieth century Americans faced the question of whether these qualities would continue when there was no frontier to nurture their growth.

   B. At the beginning of the twentieth century Americans faced challenges resulting from four dramatic changes:

       1. The end of the westward movement due to the absence of free land.

       2. The concentration of wealth among a few fundamental industries.

       3. The expansion of the United States overseas.

       4. The division of political parties over the issue of socialism.

Only time would tell if the frontier qualities of individualism, equality, freedom, and democracy would survive these dramatic changes. One could only wonder what would happen to the American character without the presence of a frontier to conquer.

STUDENT ACTIVITIES

Vocabulary
Define the following terms before reading the lesson on Turner.

1. antipathy
2. buoyancy
3. epoch
4. exuberance
5. glaciation
6. indifference
7. moraine
8. precipitate
9. subordination
10. *tabula rasa*

Review
1. Turner was a professor of history at what two universities?
2. Why did Turner think historians should research in a variety of disciplines?
3. What speech given by Turner in 1893 changed how Americans described their nation?
4. What was significant about the 1890 census?
5. What was the germ theory of American history?
6. What did Turner believe should be given more attention when historians described the character of the United States?
7. What did Turner believe changed the fundamental character of Europeans when they came to America?
8. What effect did Turner think the continuing nature of the frontier had on American society?
9. In what way did Turner think the frontier fostered individualism?
10. In what way did Turner think the frontier nourished social equality?
11. Why did Turner think Americans lacked a sense of tradition?
12. What did Turner think was the most important aspect of America's frontier experience?
13. According to Turner, what did Americans build that was unique in human history?
14. In what way did Turner think the frontier was a safety valve?
15. How did Turner think the American frontier influenced people of other nations?
16. What question did Turner think Americans faced at the beginning of the twentieth century?
17. What four challenges did Turner think Americans faced at the beginning of the twentieth century?
18. Decide whether the following statements are **True** or **False** according to Frederick Jackson Turner.
   A. The frontier made Americans inventive, energetic, and independent.
   B. On the frontier people could improve themselves through their own individual abilities.
   C. The frontier served as a magnet to bring people west.
   D. A person could only guess what would happen to the United States without the frontier to nurture the American character.

What do you think?
On a scale of one through five, rate your opinion of the following quotations by Turner. Write a short statement explaining your rating.

1 – You **strongly agree** with the statement *or* you feel the statement is **admirable** considering the historical circumstances surrounding it.
5 – You **strongly disagree** with the statement *or* you feel the statement is **contemptible** considering the historical circumstances surrounding it.

A. *Up to our own day [1893] American history has been in a large degree the history of the colonization of the Great West.*
B. *This perennial rebirth [on the frontier], this fluidity of American life, this expansion westward with its new opportunities, its continuous touch with the simplicity of primitive society, furnish the forces dominating American character.*
C. *The advance of the frontier has meant a steady movement away from the influence of Europe, a steady growth of independence on American lines.*
D. *The frontier individualism has from the beginning promoted democracy.*
E. *And now, four centuries from the discovery of America, at the end of a hundred years of life under the Constitution, the frontier has gone, and with its going has closed the first period of American history.*
F. *In a word, then, free lands meant free opportunities.*
G. *Never before in the history of the world has a democracy existed on so vast an area and handled things in the gross with such success, with such largeness of design, and such grasp upon the means of execution.*
H. *Western democracy has been from the time of its birth idealistic.*
I. *Best of all, the West gave, not only to the American, but to the unhappy and oppressed of all lands, a vision of hope, and assurance that the world held a place where were to be found high faith in man and the will and power to furnish him the opportunity to grow to the full measure of his own capacity.*
J. *The result is that to the frontier the American intellect owes its striking characteristics. The coarseness and strength combined with acuteness and inquisitiveness; that practical inventive turn of mind, quick to find expedients; that masterful grasp of material things, lacking in the artistic but powerful to effect great ends; that restless, nervous energy; that dominant individualism, working for good and for evil, and with all that buoyancy and exuberance which comes from freedom—these are traits of the frontier.*

PART 7

ECONOMIC AND POLITICAL DEVELOPMENTS OF THE TWENTIETH CENTURY

CHAPTER 28

WOODROW WILSON

BACKGROUND

Woodrow Wilson (1856-1924) spent most of his adult life as a professor and did not enter politics until he was in his fifties. As a young man he practiced law for a short time. However, he came to believe the legal profession was full of money-grubbing, intellectually-narrow men. He therefore decided to quit his work as a lawyer and pursue a career in academics. In 1886 he received his Ph.D. from Johns Hopkins University and began his career as a professor.

His scholarly work received much attention in the academic community. Writing primarily about the administration of government, he was considered one of the founders of political science. *Congressional Government*, his doctoral thesis, remains a classic work of political science.

In 1902 he was appointed president of Princeton University. In that position he initiated several reforms. Contemporaries gave him credit for turning what was already a respected university into a world-class institution. However, conflicts over his reform efforts as well as his growing interest in running for political office led to his resignation in 1910. That same year he was elected governor of New Jersey.

As governor he promoted many progressive reforms. His work caught the attention of Democrats, and in 1912 he earned the nomination of the Democratic Party for president. In a tough three-way race against William Howard Taft and Theodore Roosevelt, Wilson was elected 28th president of the United States.

Wilson is considered one of the more important presidents in United States history. His domestic reforms, known as the New Freedom, were significant and far-reaching. His reforms defined twentieth century liberalism by combining the Jeffersonian idea of a popular-based government with the Hamiltonian desire for a strong federal government. During World War I he played an important role in establishing the United States as a world power. Although he failed in his struggle with Republican senators to gain American entry into the League of Nations, he was awarded the Nobel Prize for Peace as a result of his efforts.

WOODROW WILSON – IN HIS OWN WORDS

Inaugural Address as Governor of New Jersey, 1911
The whole world has changed within the lifetime of men not yet in their thirties; the world of business, and therefore the world of society and the world of politics. The organization and movement of business are new and upon a novel scale. Business has changed so rapidly that for a long time we were confused, alarmed, bewildered, in a sort of terror of the things we had ourselves raised up. We talked about them either in sensational articles in the magazines which distorted every line of the picture, or in conservative editorials in our newspapers, which stoutly denied that anything at all had happened, or in grave discourses which tried to treat them as perfectly normal phenomena, or in legislative debates which sought to govern them with statutes which matched them neither in size nor in shape.

But, if only by sheer dint of talking about them, either to frighten or to reassure one another, or to make ourselves out wiser or more knowing than our fellows, we have at last turned them about and looked at them from almost every angle and begun to see them whole, as they are. Corporations are no longer hobgoblins which have sprung at us out of some mysterious ambush, nor yet unholy inventions of rascally rich men, nor yet the puzzling devices by which ingenious lawyers build up huge rights of a multitude of small wrongs; but merely organizations of a perfectly intelligible sort which the law has licensed for the convenience of extensive business; organizations which have proved very useful but which have for the time being slipped out of the control of the very law that gave them leave to be and that can make or unmake them at pleasure. We have now to set ourselves to control them, soberly but effectively, and to bring them thoroughly within the regulation of the law.

The New Freedom Speeches, 1912
I admit the popularity of the theory that the trusts have come about through the natural development of business conditions in the United States, and that it is a mistake to try to oppose the processes by which they have been built up, because those processes belong to the very nature of business in our time, and that therefore the only thing we can do, and the only thing we ought to attempt to do, is to accept them as inevitable arrangements and make the best out of it that we can by regulation.

I answer, nevertheless, that this attitude rests upon a confusion of thought. Big business is no doubt to a large extent necessary and natural. The development of business upon a great scale, upon a great scale of co-operation, is inevitable, and, let me add, is probably desirable. But that is a very different matter from the development of trusts, because the trusts have not grown. They have been artificially created; they have been put together, not by natural processes, but by the will, the deliberate planning will, of men who were more powerful than their neighbors in the business world, and who wished to make their power secure against competition. . . . I take my stand absolutely, where every progressive ought to take his stand, on the proposition that private monopoly is indefensible and intolerable. And there I will fight my battle. And I know how to fight it. Everybody who has even read the newspapers knows the means by which these men built up their power and created these monopolies. Any decently equipped lawyer can suggest to you statutes by which the whole business can be stopped. What these gentlemen do not want is this: they do not want to be compelled to meet all comers on equal terms. I am perfectly willing that they should beat any competitor by fair means; but I know the foul means they have adopted, and I know that they can be stopped by law. If they think that coming into the market upon the basis of mere efficiency, upon the mere basis of knowing how to manufacture goods better than anybody else, they can carry the immense amount of water that they have put into their enterprises in order to buy up rivals, they are perfectly welcome to try it. But there must be no squeezing out of the beginner, no crippling his credit; no discrimination against retailers who buy from a rival; no threats against concerns who sell supplies to a rival; no holding back of raw material from him; no secret arrangements against him. All the fair competition you choose, but no unfair competition of any kind. . . .

I have been told by a great many men that the idea I have, that by restoring competition you can restore industrial freedom, is based upon a failure to observe the actual happenings of the last decades in this country; because, they say, it is just free competition that has made it possible for the big to crush the little.

I reply, it is not free competition that has done that; it is illicit competition. It is competition of the kind that the law ought to stop, and can stop—this crushing of the little man. . . .

. . . There has come about an extraordinary and very sinister concentration in the control of business in the country. . . . It is more important still that the control of credit also has become dangerously centralized. . . . The growth of the nation, therefore, and all our activities are in the hands of a few men who, even if their action be honest and intended for the public interest, are necessarily concentrated upon the great undertakings in which their own money is involved and who necessarily, by very reason of their own limitations, chill and check and destroy genuine economic freedom. This is the greatest question of all, and to this statesmen must address themselves with an earnest determination to serve the long future and the true liberties of men. . . .

When we undertake the strategy which is going to be necessary to overcome and destroy this far-reaching system of monopoly, we are rescuing the business of this country, we are not injuring it. . . . Limit opportunity, restrict the field of originative achievement, and you have cut out the heart and root of all prosperity.

The only thing that can ever make a free country is to keep a free and hopeful heart under every jacket in it. Honest American industry has always thriven, when it has thriven at all, on freedom; it has never thriven on monopoly. It is a great deal better to shift for yourselves than to be taken care of by a great combination of capital. I, for my part, do not want to be taken care of. I would rather starve a free man than be fed a mere thing at the caprice of those who are organizing American industry as they please to organize it. I know, and every man in his heart knows, that the only way to enrich America is to make it possible for any man who has the brains to get into the game. I am not jealous of the size of any business that has grown to that size. I am not jealous of any process of growth, no matter how huge the result, provided the result was indeed obtained by the processes of wholesome development, which are the process of efficiency, of economy, of intelligence, and of invention.

Speech on "The Meaning of Democracy," 1912

I know that the government of the United States is not a free instrument, and that it is our duty to set it free. . . .

Of course, this was intended to be a government of free citizens and of equal opportunity, but how are we going to make it such? That is the question. Because I realize that while we are followers of Jefferson, there is one principle of Jefferson's which no longer can obtain in the practical politics of America. You know that it was Jefferson who said that the best government is that which does as little governing as possible, which exercises its power as little as possible. That was said in a day when the opportunities of America were so obvious to every man, when every individual was so free to use his powers without let or hindrance, that all that was necessary was the government should withhold its hand and see to it that every man got an opportunity to act if he would. But that time is past. America is not now, and cannot be, a place for unrestricted individual enterprise. . . .

When you offer the securities of a great corporation to anybody who wishes to purchase them, you must open that corporation to the inspection of everybody who wants to purchase. There must, to follow out the figure of the tenement house, be lights along the corridor, there must be police patrolling the openings, there must be inspection wherever it is known that men may be deceived with regard to the contents of the premises. . . . Similarly, treatment of labor by the great corporations is not now what it was in Jefferson's time. Who in this great audience knows his employer? . . . You probably don't know the directors of the corporation by sight. The only thing you know is that by the score, by the hundred, by the thousand, you are employed with your fellow workmen by some agent of an invisible employer. Therefore, whenever bodies of men employ bodies of men, it ceases to be a private relationship. . . . This dealing of great bodies of men with other bodies of men is a matter of public regulation.

Similarly, it was no business of the law in the time of Jefferson to come into my house and see how I kept house. But when my house, when my property, when my so-called private property, became a great mine, and men went along dark corridors amidst every kind of danger to dig out of the bowels of the earth things necessary for the industries of a whole nation, and when it was known that no individual owned these mines, that they were owned by great stock companies, that their partnership was as wide as great communities, that all the old analogies absolutely collapsed and it became the right of the government to go down into those mines and see whether human beings were properly treated in them or not; to see whether accidents were properly safeguarded against; to see whether the modern methods of using these inestimable riches of the world were followed or were not followed. . . .

I say then, the proposition is this: that there shall be two masters, the great corporation and over it the government of the United States; and I ask: Who is going to be the master of the government of the Untied States? It has a master now—those who in combination control these monopolies. And if the government controlled by the monopolies in its turn controls the monopolies, the partnership is finally consummated.

I don't care how benevolent the master is going to be. I will not live under a master. That is not what America was created for. America was created in order that every man should have the same chance with every other man to exercise mastery over his own fortunes. . . .

The vision of America will never change. America once, when she was a little people, sat upon a hill of privilege and had a vision of the future. She saw men happy because they were free. She saw them free because they were equal. She saw them banded together because they had the spirit of brothers. She saw them safe because they did not wish to impose upon one another. And the vision is not changed. The multitude has grown, that welcome multitude that comes from all parts of the world to seek a safe place of life and of hope in America. And so America will move forward, if she moves forward at all, only with her face to that same sun of promise. Just so soon as she forgets the sun in the heavens, just so soon as she looks so intently upon the road before her and around her that she does not know where it leads, then will she forget what America was created for; her light will go out; the nations will grope again in darkness and they will say: "Where are those who prophesied a day of freedom for us? Where are the lights that we followed? Where is the torch that the runners bore? Where are those who bade us hope? Where came in these whispers of dull despair? Has America turned back? Has America forgotten her mission? Has America forgotten that her politics are part of her life, and that only as the red blood of her people flows in the veins of her polity shall she occupy that point of vantage which has made her the beacon and the leader of mankind?"

War Message to Congress, 1917

The present German submarine warfare against commerce is a warfare against mankind.

It is a war against all nations. American ships have been sunk, American lives taken, in ways which it has stirred us very deeply to learn of, but the ships and people of other neutral and friendly nations have been sunk and overwhelmed in the waters in the same way. There has been no discrimination. The challenge is to all mankind. Each nation must decide for itself how it will meet it. The choice we make for ourselves must be made with a moderation of counsel and a temperateness of judgement befitting our character and our motives as a nation. We must put excited feeling away. Our motive will not be revenge or the victorious assertion of the physical might of the nation, but only the vindication of right, of human right, of which we are only a single champion. . . .

Let us be very clear, and make very clear to all the world what our motives and our objects are. . . . Our object . . . is to vindicate the principles of peace and justice in the life of the world as against selfish and autocratic power and to set up amongst the really free and self-governed peoples of the world such a concert of purpose and of action as will henceforth insure the observance of those principles. Neutrality is no longer feasible or desirable where the peace of the world is involved and the freedom of its peoples, and the menace to that peace and freedom lies in the existence of autocratic governments backed by organized force which is controlled wholly by their will, not by the will of their people. We have seen the last of neutrality in such circumstances. We are at the beginning of an age in which it will be insisted that the same standards of conduct and of responsibility for wrong done shall be observed among nations and their governments that are observed among the individual citizens of civilized states. . . .

. . . The world must be made safe for democracy. Its peace must be planted upon the tested foundations of political liberty. We have no selfish ends to serve. We desire no conquest, no dominion. We seek no indemnities for ourselves, no material compensation for the sacrifices we shall freely make. We are but one of the champions of the rights of mankind. We shall be satisfied when those rights have been made as secure as the faith and the freedom of nations can make them.

Speech on the Versailles Treaty, 1919

At the front of this great treaty is put the Covenant of the League of Nations. . . . Unless you get the united, concerted purpose and power of the great Governments of the world behind this settlement, it will fall down like a house of cards. There is only one power to put behind the liberation of mankind, and that is the power of mankind. It is the power of the united moral forces of the world, and in the Covenant of the League of Nations the moral forces of the world are mobilized. . . .

Speech Defending the League of Nations, 1919

Sometimes people call me an idealist. Well, that is the way I know I am an American. America is the only idealistic nation in the world.

WOODROW WILSON – A SIMULATED INTERVIEW

1. **How has the Industrial Revolution changed the United States?**
    A. With the development of giant corporations the United States no longer grants every person an opportunity to profit from his talent. Talented individuals can no longer enter the business world because monopolies have taken control of the economy.
    B. In the early days of the United States, Thomas Jefferson desired minimal government in order that individuals could freely develop their talents. However, giant corporations now dominate the nation. Individuals no longer possess economic freedom. The United States is witnessing a concentration of wealth and credit that has destroyed economic freedom.
    C. The relationship between workers and employers has changed. Workers employed by big business no longer have a personal relationship with their employers.

2. **Are big corporations always a problem?**
    A. To a large extent big business was necessary and desirable. The development of big business was inevitable.
    B. A business that defeats its competitors by producing better products in a more efficient manner deserves to win the economic competition. However, the development of a monopoly through the illegitimate destruction of competition is harmful to the nation.

3. **How do monopolies threaten the United States?**
    A. Monopolies are the result of a deliberate elimination of competition. The men who form monopolies do not allow newcomers into the business world. Individual Americans do not enjoy *economic* freedom in a nation of monopolies.
    B. Monopolies are so powerful they have taken control of the United States government. Individual Americans do not enjoy *political* freedom in a nation of monopolies.
    C. Monopolies create misery on a large scale. Monopolies are not accountable for their actions, and they are harmful to the public.
    D. Monopolies exploit the public and control the government. The formation of monopolies leads to a concentration of wealth and power that denies freedom to the American people.

4. **What should be done about the power of monopolies?**
    A. Thomas Jefferson's support for minimal government should be replaced by support for federal action that restores economic liberty.
    B. Federal power should be used to restore economic competition. The American people should be given a "new freedom" in which they are free from the power of monopolies.

5. **Why should the government regulate business activity?**
   A. If a corporation serves the public it should be open to public inspection.
   B. The government is justified in regulating a corporation if the actions of the corporation affect large numbers of people.
   C. Monopolies control the United States to such an extent that their actions cannot be ignored by a government based on the consent of the people. Public interest must be protected by the government.
   D. Even monopolies operating in a humane manner control the nation illegitimately. The United States was established in order that every individual could be his own master. No person should serve a master that has gained power without the consent of the people.

6. **Will government regulation of business threaten the capitalist system?**
   A. Regulating monopolies will not harm capitalism. Instead, regulation will revive economic competition and bring about a new prosperity that better serves the public interest.
   B. Capitalism thrives on freedom; monopolies destroy freedom. Regulation of monopolies is necessary in order that talented individuals can again enter a competitive capitalist market place.
   C. Free market capitalism should remain the basis of American liberty. However, private ambition should be balanced with a public regulation that stimulates the competitive energy of *all* Americans.

7. **Why is the United States justified in declaring war on Germany?**
   A. The German submarine warfare is warfare against humanity. The United States cannot be neutral when humanity is threatened.
   B. The United States should go to war with Germany to fight for peace and justice. The United States should make the world safe for democracy.
   C. The United States is on a mission of peace and sacrifice that promotes the welfare of all human beings. The United States must be the "beacon and the leader of mankind."

8. **Why should the United States join the League of Nations?**
   A. If the United States joined the League of Nations, it would join an organization that could energize the moral forces of the world.
   B. Through the League of Nations the United States can lead the world into a new international community based upon peace and freedom.

9. **What is the function of the presidency in American society?**
   A. The president has a duty to unify the nation as well as to give direction to the nation.
   B. The president should establish moral principles that guide the nation.

STUDENT ACTIVITIES

Vocabulary
Define the following terms before reading the lesson on Wilson.

1. analogies	10. consummated	19. originative
2. autocratic	11. dint	20. score
3. beacon	12. hobgoblin	21. temperateness
4. benevolent	13. idealistic	22. tenement
5. bowels	14. illicit	23. thriven
6. caprice	15. indemnity	24. trust
7. centralized	16. inestimable	25. vantage
8. compensation	17. monopoly	26. vindicate
9. concentration	18. multitude	

Review
1. What was Wilson's profession before he entered politics?
2. Wilson served as president of what university?
3. What two candidates did Wilson defeat in the presidential election of 1912?
4. What name was given to President Wilson's domestic reforms?
5. In what way did Wilson's reforms define twentieth century liberalism?
6. How did Wilson think the development of giant corporations had changed the United States?
7. How did Wilson think the relationship between workers and employers had changed?
8. According to Wilson, what type of monopolies are legitimate?
9. According to Wilson, how did monopolies affect American freedom?
10. What did Wilson think should replace Jefferson's support for minimal government?
11. According to Wilson, what is the "new freedom"?
12. In what situation did Wilson believe the government should be allowed to inspect corporations?
13. Why did Wilson think monopolies should be regulated even if they acted in a humane manner?
14. What did Wilson believe should balance the private ambition of free market capitalism?
15. Why did Wilson think the United States should join a League of Nations?
16. What did Wilson believe was the role of the president of the United States?
17. Decide whether the following statements are **True** or **False** according to Woodrow Wilson.
    A. The United States is witnessing a concentration of wealth and credit that is expanding economic opportunities for all Americans.
    B. Monopolies have taken control of the United States.

    C. Capitalism does not allow freedom.

    D. The United States should remain neutral on the issue of German submarine warfare.

    E. The United States should be the "beacon and the leader of mankind."

What do you think?

On a scale of one through five, rate your opinion of the following quotations by Wilson. Write a short statement explaining your rating.

1 – You **strongly agree** with the statement *or* you feel the statement is **admirable** considering the historical circumstances surrounding it.

5 – You **strongly disagree** with the statement *or* you feel the statement is **contemptible** considering the historical circumstances surrounding it.

A. *Big business is no doubt to a large extent necessary and natural. The development of business upon a great scale, upon a great scale of co-operation, is inevitable, and, let me add, is probably desirable.*

B. *[Trusts] have been artificially created; they have been put together, not by natural processes, but by the will, the deliberate planning will, of men who were more powerful than their neighbors in the business world, and who wished to make their power secure against competition.*

C. *I know, and every man in his heart knows that the only way to enrich America is to make it possible for any man who has the brains to get into the game.*

D. *America was created in order that every man should have the same chance with every other man to exercise mastery over his own fortunes.*

E. *Neutrality is no longer feasible or desirable where the peace of the world is involved and the freedom of its peoples, and the menace to that peace and freedom lies in the existence of autocratic governments backed by organized force which is controlled wholly by their will, not by the will of their people.*

F. *The world must be made safe for democracy. Its peace must be planted upon the tested foundations of political liberty.*

G. *America was established not to create wealth but to realize a vision, to realize an ideal—to discover and maintain liberty among men.*

H. *Big business is not dangerous because it is big, but because its bigness is an unwholesome inflation created by privileges and exemptions which it ought not to enjoy.*

I. *To conquer with arms is to make only a temporary conquest; to conquer the world by earning its esteem is to make a permanent conquest.*

J. *Energy in a nation is like sap in a tree; it rises from bottom up.*

K. *A Presidential campaign may easily degenerate into a mere personal contest, and so lose its real dignity.*

CHAPTER 29

FRANKLIN ROOSEVELT

BACKGROUND

Franklin Roosevelt (1882-1945) grew up in the midst of great wealth and privilege. The only child of overindulgent parents, he graduated from such bulwarks of the privileged class as Groton, Harvard, and Columbia. Although he seemed ill-prepared to understand the problems of common Americans, his political philosophy was shaped during the Progressive Era when government worked to bring monopolistic abuse under control. He was persuaded by the actions of his cousin Theodore Roosevelt and by Woodrow Wilson to believe in federal regulation of business and the enforcement of antitrust legislation.

In 1921 Franklin Roosevelt contracted polio, an experience that gave him a deep appreciation for people who struggled against life's adversities. Although he never recovered the use of his legs, he survived severe pain and years of rehabilitation. He was able to make a political comeback in 1928 when he was elected governor of New York.

In 1932 Roosevelt was elected president of the United States. Confronted with the worst depression in United States history, he restored the nation's confidence with the New Deal, a program that provided direct government relief to the unemployed. In almost every area of national concern his leadership produced substantial change. He permanently reshaped the presidency as well as the federal government's domestic responsibilities. In addition, World War II established Roosevelt as a leader of international significance. He played an integral role in organizing a new international order for the post-war world.

Roosevelt, the only person elected to the presidency four times, was one of the most admired and, at the same time, one of the most hated presidents of the twentieth century. His supporters viewed him as a man whose bold leadership transformed the nation's domestic policies to serve common Americans. His critics thought he destroyed the values of rugged individualism that many people believed made America great. Few people, however, doubted FDR's status as one of the most important presidents of the twentieth century.

FRANKLIN ROOSEVELT – IN HIS OWN WORDS

First Gubernatorial Inaugural Address, January 1929

I object to having this spirit of personal civil responsibility to the state and to the individual . . . described as "humanitarian." It is far more than that. It is the recognition that our civilization cannot endure unless we, as individuals, realize our personal responsibility to and dependence on the rest of the world. For it is literally true that the "self-supporting" man or woman has become as extinct as the man of the stone age. Without the help of thousands of others, any one of us would die, naked and starved. Consider the bread upon our table, the clothes upon our backs, the luxuries that make life pleasant; how many men worked in sunlit fields, in dark mines, in the fierce heat of molten metal, and among the looms and wheels of countless factories, in order to create them for our use and enjoyment.

Second Annual Message to Congress, January 1935

The lessons of history . . . show conclusively that continued dependence upon relief induces a spiritual and moral disintegration fundamentally destructive to the national fiber. To dole out relief in this way is to administer a narcotic, a subtle destroyer of the human spirit. . . .

Work must be found for able-bodied but destitute workers.

Speech before the 1936 Democratic National Convention, June 1936

That very word *freedom*, in itself and of necessity, suggests freedom from some restraining power. In 1776 we sought freedom from the tyranny of a political autocracy—from the eighteenth-century royalists who held special privileges from the crown. It was to perpetuate their privilege that they governed without the consent of the governed . . . .

And so it was to win freedom from the tyranny of political autocracy that the American Revolution was fought. That victory gave the business of governing into the hands of the average man, who won the right with his neighbors to make and order his own destiny through his own government. Political tyranny was wiped out at Philadelphia on July 4, 1776.

Since that struggle, however, man's inventive genius released new forces in our land which reordered the lives of our people. The age of machinery, of railroads; of steam and electricity; the telegraph and the radio; mass production, mass distribution—all of these combined to bring forward a new civilization and with it a new problem for those who sought to remain free.

For out of this modern civilization economic royalists carved new dynasties. New kingdoms were built upon concentration of control over material things. Through new uses of corporations, banks and securities, new machinery of industry and agriculture, of labor and capital—all undreamed of by the Fathers—the whole structure of modern life was impressed into this royal service.

There was no place among this royalty for our many thousands of small-businessmen and merchants who sought to make a worthy use of the American system of initiative and profit. They were no more free than the worker or the farmer. Even honest and progressive-minded men of wealth, aware of their obligation to their generation, could never know just where they fitted into this dynastic scheme of things.

It was natural and perhaps human that the privileged princes of these new economic dynasties, thirsting for power, reached out for control over government itself. They created a new despotism and wrapped it in the robes of legal sanction. In its service new mercenaries sought to regiment the people, their labor, and their property. And as a result the average man once more confronts the problem that faced the Minute Man.

The hours men and women worked, the wages they received, the conditions of their labor—these had passed beyond the control of the people, and were imposed by this new industrial dictatorship. The savings of the average family, the capital of the small-businessman, the investments set aside for old age—other people's money—these were tools which the new economic royalty used to dig itself in.

Those who tilled the soil no longer reaped the rewards which were their right. The small measure of their gain was decreed by men in distant cities.

Throughout the nation, opportunity was limited by monopoly. Individual initiative was crushed in the cogs of a great machine. The field open for free business was more and more restricted. Private enterprise, indeed, became too private. It became privileged enterprise, not free enterprise.

An old English judge once said: "Necessitous men are not free men." Liberty requires opportunity to make a living—a living decent according to the standard of the time, a living which gives man not only enough to live by, but something to live for.

For too many of us the political equality we once had won was meaningless in the face of economic inequality. A small group had concentrated into their own hands an almost complete control over other people's property, other people's money, other people's labor—other people's lives. For too many of us life was no longer free; liberty no longer real; men could no longer follow the pursuit of happiness.

Against economic tyranny such as this, the American citizen could appeal only to the organized power of government. . . .

The royalists of the economic order have conceded that political freedom was the business of the government, but they have maintained that economic slavery was nobody's business. They granted that the government could protect the citizen in his right to vote, but they denied that the government could do anything to protect the citizen in his right to work and right to live.

Today we stand committed to the proposition that freedom is no half-and-half affair. If the average citizen is guaranteed equal opportunity in the polling place, he must have equal opportunity in the market place.

These economic royalists complain that we seek to overthrow the institutions of America. What they really complain of is that we seek to take away their power. Our allegiance to American institutions requires the overthrow of this kind of power. In vain they seek to hide behind the flag and the Constitution. In their blindness they forget what the flag and the Constitution stand for. Now, as always, they stand for democracy, not tyranny; for freedom, not subjection; and against a dictatorship by mob rule and the overprivileged alike.

The brave and clear platform adopted by this convention, to which I heartily subscribe, sets forth that government in a modern civilization has certain inescapable obligations to its citizens, among which are protection of the family and the home, the establishment of a democracy of opportunity, and aid to those overtaken by disaster. . . .

Better the occasional faults of a government that lives in a spirit of charity than the consistent omissions of a government frozen in the ice of its own indifference. . . .

. . . Here in America we are waging a great and successful war. It is not alone a war against want and destitution and economic demoralization. It is more than that; it is a war for the survival of democracy. We are fighting to save a great and precious form of government for ourselves and for the world.

Second Inaugural Address, January 1937

This year marks the 150th anniversary of the Constitutional Convention which made us a nation. At that Convention our forefathers found the way out of the chaos which followed the Revolutionary War; they created a strong government with powers of united action sufficient then and now to solve problems utterly beyond individual or local solution. A century and a half ago they established the federal government in order to promote the general welfare and secure the blessings of liberty to the American people.

Today we invoke those same powers of government to achieve the same objectives. . . .

. . . The essential democracy of our nation, and the safety of our people depend not upon the absence of power, but upon lodging it with those whom the people can change or continue at stated intervals through an honest and free system of elections. The Constitution of 1787 did not make our democracy impotent.

In fact, . . . we have made the exercise of all power more democratic; for we have begun to bring private autocratic powers into their proper subordination to the public's government. The legend that they were invincible—above and beyond the processes of a democracy—has been shattered. They have been challenged and beaten. . . .

But here is the challenge to our democracy: in this nation I see tens of millions of its citizens—a substantial part of its whole population—who at this very moment are denied the greater part of what the very lowest standards of today call the necessities of life. . . .

I see one-third of a nation ill-housed, ill-clad, ill-nourished.

. . . We are determined to make every American citizen the subject of his country's interest and concern; and we will never regard any faithful, law-abiding group within our borders as superfluous. The test of our progress is not whether we add more to the abundance of those who have much; it is whether we provide enough for those who have too little.

Speech at the University of Virginia, June 1940

Some, indeed, still hold to the now somewhat obvious delusion that we of the United States can safely permit the United States to become a lone island in a world dominated by the philosophy of force.

Such an island may be the dream of those who still talk and vote as isolationists. Such an island represents to me and to the overwhelming majority of Americans today a helpless nightmare, the helpless nightmare of a people lodged in prison, handcuffed, hungry, and fed through the bars from day to day by the contemptuous, unpitying masters of other continents.

Press Conference on the Lend-Lease Act, December 1940

What I am trying to do is to eliminate the dollar sign. That is something brand new in the thoughts of practically everybody in this room, I think—get rid of the silly, foolish, old dollar sign.

Well, let me give you an illustration: Suppose my neighbor's home catches fire, and I have a length of garden hose 400 or 500 feet away. If he can take my garden hose and connect it up with his hydrant, I may help him to put out his fire. Now, what do I do? I don't say to him before that operation, "Neighbor, my garden hose cost me $15; you have to pay me $15 for it." What is the transaction that goes on? I don't want $15—I want my garden hose back after the fire is over. All right. If it goes through the fire all right, intact, without any damage to it, he gives it back to me and thanks me very much for the use of it. But suppose it gets smashed up—holes in it—during the fire; we don't have to have too much formality about it, but I say to him, "I was glad to lend you that hose; I see I can't use it any more, it's all smashed up." He says "How many feet of it were there?" I tell him, "There were 150 feet of it." He says, "All right, I will replace it." Now, if I get a nice garden hose back, I am in pretty good shape.

In other words, if you lend certain munitions and get munitions back at the end of the war, if they are intact—haven't been hurt—you are all right; if they have been damaged or have deteriorated or have been lost completely, it seems to me you come out pretty well if you have them replaced by the fellow to whom you have lent them.

Eighth Annual Message to Congress, January 1941

We look forward to a world founded upon four essential human freedoms.

The first is freedom of speech and expression—everywhere in the world.

The second is freedom of every person to worship God in his own way—everywhere in the world.

The third is freedom from want—which, translated into world terms, means economic understandings which will secure to every nation a healthy peacetime life for its inhabitants—everywhere in the world.

The fourth is freedom from fear—which, translated into world terms, means a worldwide reduction of armaments to such a point and in such a thorough fashion that no nation will be in a position to commit an act of physical aggression against any neighbor—anywhere in the world. . . .

Since the beginning of our American history, we have been engaged in change—in perpetual peaceful revolution, a revolution which goes on steadily, quietly adjusting itself to changing conditions . . . . The world order which we seek is the cooperation of free countries, working together in a friendly, civilized society.

Eleventh Annual Message to Congress, January 1944

This Republic had its beginning, and grew to its present strength, under the protection of certain inalienable political rights—among them the right of free speech, free press, free worship, trial by jury, freedom from unreasonable searches and seizures. They were our rights to life and liberty.

As our nation has grown in size and stature, however—as our industrial economy expanded—these political rights proved inadequate to assure us equality in the pursuit of happiness.

We have come to a clear realization of the fact that true individual freedom cannot exist without economic security and independence. "Necessitous men are not free men." People who are hungry and out of a job are the stuff of which dictatorships are made.

In our day these economic truths have become accepted as self-evident. We have accepted, so to speak, a second Bill of Rights under which a new basis of security and prosperity can be established for all—regardless of station, race, or creed.

Among these are:

The right to a useful and remunerative job in the industries or shops or farms or mines of the nation;

The right to earn enough to provide adequate food and clothing and recreation;

The right of every farmer to raise and sell his products at a return which will give him and his family a decent living;

The right of every businessman, large and small, to trade in an atmosphere of freedom from unfair competition and domination by monopolies at home or abroad;

The right of every family to a decent home.

The right of adequate medical care and the opportunity to achieve and enjoy good health;

The right to adequate protection from the economic fears of old age, sickness, accident, and unemployment;

The right to a good education.

I ask the Congress to explore the means for implementing this economic Bill of Rights.

FRANKLIN ROOSEVELT – A SIMULATED INTERVIEW

1. **How did the Industrial Revolution change the United States?**
   A. America flourished in its early years because of democracy and an abundance of natural resources. During the Industrial Revolution, however, ruthless and wasteful men took control of the economy. These economic royalists took control of property, capital, and labor. Average Americans no longer controlled their own destiny.
   B. The Industrial Revolution created a new class of privileged Americans who not only controlled the economy, but also controlled the government. Average Americans no longer controlled their own government. Workers, farmers, and small businessmen were no longer free and independent.
   C. In the modern industrial society average Americans face the same problems they confronted during the American Revolution—they do not control their own destiny.
   D. In the modern industrial society economic opportunity for the average American has been limited by monopolies. Individual initiative has been destroyed. Private enterprise has become privileged enterprise.
   E. America has reached its last frontier by establishing an industrial economy. There is no longer an abundance of land, and Americans no longer possess a safety valve on the western frontier.

2. **Should government extend its powers to bring order to the industrial economy?**
   A. Big business and monopoly are a threat to democracy. The federal government has a responsibility to use its powers to protect economic rights and create economic order.
   B. Although government should be controlled through free elections, the framers of the Constitution did not intend to make government powerless. Government should exercise the power necessary to protect democracy and freedom.
   C. The American Revolution was fought to win freedom from oppression. Average people wanted the right to control their own destiny and pursue happiness in their own way. Government should guarantee freedom by using its constitutional power to promote the general welfare and secure the blessings of liberty.
   D. Government should use its power to fight underconsumption. Antitrust laws should not only be used to break up big corporations, they also should be used to control pricing. Purchasing power should be stimulated throughout the nation.
   E. Government should provide relief to the unemployed. People who depend on the dole, however, face spiritual and moral disintegration. Life on the dole destroys the human spirit. Work is better than the dole, and government should create jobs for the unemployed.

3. **Will government's control of the economy threaten individual freedom?**
   A. The United States stands for democracy, not tyranny. To protect individual freedom the power of the economic royalists must be overthrown. Government should guarantee each citizen the right to work and the right to make a decent living.
   B. Citizens guaranteed political freedom must also be guaranteed economic freedom. Freedom is not only an opportunity to speak and worship freely, it is also the opportunity to make a decent living.
   C. Government control of the economy does not limit freedom. Government control of the economy *protects* freedom. Economic royalists who complain about a loss of freedom are really complaining that their privileges have been limited.

4. **What are the responsibilities of government?**
   A. Government has a responsibility to protect the rights of every citizen. Government should measure its success by how it provides for those who have too little, not how it enriches those who already have much.
   B. Government's responsibility to the welfare of society does not stem from simple humanitarian concerns. Civilization cannot survive unless all individuals are responsible to each other. In the modern industrial society self-supporting individuals are extinct; every individual is dependent on others for survival.
   C. Government has a responsibility to protect individual rights. In addition to political rights the United States should also guarantee several economic rights:
      1. The right to a useful and profitable job.
      2. The right to earn enough for an adequate standard of living.
      3. The right to operate a business free of unfair competition.
      4. The right to live in a decent home.
      5. The right to adequate medical care.
      6. The right to economic security.
      7. The right to a good education.

5. **What should be the basis of United States foreign policy?**
   A. The United States cannot isolate itself from a world dominated by those who believe in ruling through the use of force.
   B. The United States should support nations fighting against dictatorships. Support should be offered through the lending of weapons.
   C. The United States should work toward a world based on international cooperation. Free countries should work together in a civilized manner.
   D. The United States should fight to establish four essential freedoms throughout the world: freedom of expression, freedom of religion, freedom from want, and freedom from fear.

STUDENT ACTIVITIES

Vocabulary
Define the following terms before reading the lesson on Roosevelt.

1. autocracy	5. dole	9. munition
2. contemptuous	6. dynastic	10. remunerative
3. demoralization	7. inalienable	11. sanction
4. destitute	8. mercenaries	12. subordination

Review
1. From what schools did Roosevelt graduate?
2. What two men shaped Roosevelt's political philosophy?
3. What gave Roosevelt an appreciation for people who face adversity?
4. What name was given to Roosevelt's program to help the unemployed?
5. What did Roosevelt think happened to the United States during the Industrial Revolution?
6. Why did Roosevelt think average Americans no longer controlled their own destiny?
7. What did Roosevelt think was responsible for limiting opportunities for average Americans?
8. What did Roosevelt think was a threat to democracy in an industrial society?
9. How did Roosevelt think government should fight underconsumption?
10. According to Roosevelt, what effect does the dole have on the unemployed?
11. What did Roosevelt think government should guarantee each citizen?
12. How did Roosevelt define freedom?
13. Why did Roosevelt think economic royalists complained about government control of the economy?
14. What did Roosevelt believe was necessary for the survival of civilization?
15. What economic rights did Roosevelt believe should be guaranteed to each citizen?
16. What four freedoms did Roosevelt think the United States should protect?
17. Decide whether the following statements are **True** or **False** according to Franklin Roosevelt.
    A. The Industrial Revolution created a new class of privileged Americans who controlled the economy and the government.
    B. Although the United States changed dramatically in the Industrial Revolution, Americans still possessed a safety valve on the western frontier.
    C. The United States should adopt an isolationist foreign policy.
    D. The United States should work toward a world based on international cooperation.

What do you think?
On a scale of one through five, rate your opinion of the following quotations by Roosevelt. Write a short statement explaining your rating.

1 – You **strongly agree** with the statement *or* you feel the statement is **admirable** considering the historical circumstances surrounding it.
5 – You **strongly disagree** with the statement *or* you feel the statement is **contemptible** considering the historical circumstances surrounding it.

A. *Our civilization cannot endure unless we, as individuals, realize our personal responsibility to and dependence on the rest of the world. For it is literally true that the "self-supporting" man or woman has become as extinct as the man of the stone age.*

B. *The lessons of history . . . show conclusively that continued dependence upon relief induces a spiritual and moral disintegration fundamentally destructive to the national fiber.*

C. *We stand committed to the proposition that freedom is no half-and-half affair. If the average citizen is guaranteed equal opportunity in the polling place, he must have equal opportunity in the market place.*

D. *These economic royalists complain that we seek to overthrow the institutions of America. What they really complain of is that we seek to take away their power.*

E. *The test of our progress is not whether we add more to the abundance of those who have much; it is whether we provide enough for those who have too little.*

F. *We have come to a clear realization of the fact that true individual freedom cannot exist without economic security and independence. . . . People who are hungry and out of a job are the stuff of which dictatorships are made.*

G. *I sometimes think that the saving grace of America lies in the fact that the overwhelming majority of Americans are possessed of two great qualities—a sense of humor and a sense of proportion.*

H. *Taxes, after all, are the dues that we pay for the privileges of membership in an organized society.*

I. *No man can tame a tiger into a kitten by stroking it. There can be no appeasement with ruthlessness. There can be no reasoning with an incendiary bomb.*

J. *No business which depends for existence by paying less than living wages to its workers has any right to continue in this country.*

K. *[Business and finance are] unanimous in their hate for me—and I welcome their hatred. . . . I should like to have it said of my first Administration that in it the forces of selfishness and of lust for power met their match; I would like to have it said of my second administration that in it these forces met their match.*

CHAPTER 30

JOHN MAYNARD KEYNES

BACKGROUND

John Maynard Keynes (1883-1946) was born into an upper-class British family and never knew economic hardship. He married a famous Russian ballerina, collected rare books and fine art, ran a theater, and was the director of the Bank of England. He lived such a charmed life that he once mentioned his only regret in life was not drinking enough champagne.

Educated in England's finest schools, Keynes spent time in the civil service before becoming the editor of the *Economic Journal*. During World War I he worked for the British Treasury as an unofficial and unpaid assistant. By the end of the war he held a high position in the government and was asked to attend the Versailles Conference. After witnessing the drafting of what he felt was an unworkable treaty Keynes wrote *The Economic Consequences of the Peace*. With this book he gained international recognition as a critic of the Treaty of Versailles.

After the war Keynes wrote several books describing his ideas on economics. In 1936 he published his most important work, *The General Theory of Employment, Interest and Money*. In the *General Theory* Keynes revolutionized economics. Several nations instituted Keynesian economics, and, consequently, his ideas directly influenced a large portion of the world's population. Franklin Roosevelt's New Deal was a good example of Keynesian economics.

Although he was often criticized by advocates of *laissez faire*, Keynes saw himself as providing a way to save capitalism. He believed free market nations needed to adopt a system of managed capitalism. Specifically, he felt that nations needed to link employment and income to public as well as private investment. Only then could a nation work toward full employment. As Keynes pointed out, the problem of unemployment was a serious threat to the survival of capitalism. Ironically, Keynes, a man who wanted to save capitalism, was born the same year that Karl Marx, capitalism's most severe critic, died.

JOHN MAYNARD KEYNES – IN HIS OWN WORDS

The General Theory of Employment, Interest and Money, 1936

I have called this book the *General Theory of Employment, Interest and Money*, placing the emphasis on the prefix *general*. The object of such a title is to contrast the character of my arguments and conclusions with those of the *classical* theory of the subject, upon which I was brought up and which dominates the economic thought, both practical and theoretical, of the governing and academic classes of this generation, as it has for a hundred years past. I shall argue that the postulates of the classical theory are applicable to a special case only and not to the general case, the situation which it assumes being a limiting point of the possible positions of equilibrium. Moreover, the characteristics of the special case assumed by the classical theory happen not to be those of the economic society in which we actually live, with the result that its teaching is misleading and disastrous if we attempt to apply it to the facts of experience. . . . The outstanding faults of the economic society in which we live are its failure to provide for full employment and its arbitrary and inequitable distribution of wealth and incomes. . . .

Thus our argument leads towards the conclusion that in contemporary conditions the growth of wealth, so far from being dependent on the abstinence of the rich, as is commonly supposed, is more likely to be impeded by it. One of the chief social justifications of great inequality of wealth is, therefore, removed. I am not saying that there are no other reasons, unaffected by our theory, capable of justifying some measure of inequality in some circumstances. But it does dispose of the most important of the reasons why hitherto we have thought it prudent to move carefully. . . .

For my own part, I believe that there is social and psychological justification for significant inequalities of incomes and wealth, but not for such large disparities as exist today. There are valuable human activities which require the motive of money-making and the environment of private wealth-ownership for their full fruition. Moreover, dangerous human proclivities can be canalised into comparatively harmless channels by the existence of opportunities for money-making and private wealth, which, if they cannot be satisfied in this way, may find their outlet in cruelty, the reckless pursuit of personal power and authority, and other forms of self-aggrandizement. It is better that a man should tyrannize over his bank balance than over his fellow-citizens; and whilst the former is sometimes denounced as being but a means to the latter, sometimes at least it is an alternative. But it is not necessary for the stimulation of these activities and the satisfaction of these proclivities that the game should be played for such high stakes as at present. Much lower stakes will serve the purpose equally well, as soon as the players are accustomed to them. The task of transmuting human nature must not be confused with the task of managing it. Though in the ideal commonwealth men may have been taught or inspired or bred to take no interest in the stakes, it may still be wise and prudent statesmanship to allow the game to be played, subject to rules and limitations, so long as the average man, or even a significant section of the community is in fact strongly addicted to the money-making passion. . . .

We must recognize that only experience can show how far the common will, embodied in the policy of the State, ought to be directed to invest; and how far it is safe to stimulate the average propensity to consume, without foregoing our aim of depriving capital of its scarcity-value within one or two generations. It may turn out the propensity to consume will be so easily strengthened by the effects of a falling rate of interest, that full employment can be reached with a rate of accumulation little greater than at present. In this event a scheme for the higher taxation of large incomes and inheritances might be open to the objection that it would lead to full employment with a rate of accumulation which was reduced considerably below the current level. I must not be supposed to deny the possibility, or even the probability, of this outcome. For in such matter it is rash to predict how the average man will react to a changed environment. If, however, it should prove easy to secure an approximation to full employment with a rate of accumulation not much greater than at present, an outstanding problem will at least have been solved. And it would remain for separate decision on what scale and by what means it is right and reasonable to call on the living generation to restrict their consumption, so as to establish, in course of time, a state of full investment for their successors.

In some other respects the foregoing theory is moderately conservative in its implications. For whilst it indicates the vital importance of establishing certain central controls in matters which are now left in the main to individual initiative, there are wide fields of activity which are unaffected. The state will have to exercise a guiding influence on the propensity to consume partly through its scheme of taxation, partly by fixing the rate of interest, and partly, perhaps in other ways. Furthermore, it seems unlikely that the influence of banking policy on the rate of interest will be sufficient by itself to determine an optimum rate of investment. I conceive, therefore, that a somewhat comprehensive socialisation of investment will prove the only means of securing an approximation to full employment; though this need not exclude all manner of compromises and of devices by which public authority will co-operate with private initiative. But beyond this no obvious case is made out for a system of State Socialism which would embrace most of the economic life of the community. It is not the ownership of the instruments of production which it is important for the State to assume. If the State is able to determine the aggregate amount of resources devoted to augmenting the instruments and the basic rate of reward to those who own them, it will have accomplished all that is necessary. Moreover, the necessary measures of socialisation can be introduced gradually and without a break in the general traditions of society.

Our criticism of the accepted classical theory of economics has consisted not so much in finding logical flaws in its analysis as in pointing out that its tacit assumptions are seldom or never satisfied, with the result that it cannot solve the economic problems of the actual world. But if our central controls succeed in establishing an aggregate volume of output corresponding to full employment as nearly as is practicable, the classical theory comes into its own again from this point onwards. If we suppose the volume of output to be given, i.e. to be determined by forces outside the classical scheme of thought, then there is no objection to be raised against the classical analysis of the manner in which private self-interest will determine what in particular is produced, in what proportions the factors of production will be combined to produce it, and how the value of the final product will be distributed between them. Again, if we have dealt otherwise with the problem of thrift, there is no objection to be raised against the modern classical theory as to the degree of consilience between private and public advantage in conditions of perfect and imperfect competition respectively. Thus, apart from the necessity of central controls to bring about an adjustment between the propensity to consume and the inducement to invest, there is no more reason to socialise economic life than there was before.

To put the point concretely, I see no reason to suppose that the existing system seriously misemploys the factors of production which are in use. There are, of course, errors of foresight; but these would not be avoided by centralising decisions. When 9,000,000 men are employed out of 10,000,000 willing and able to work, there is no evidence that the labour of these 9,000,000 men is misdirected. The complaint against the present system is not that these 9,000,000 men ought to be employed on different tasks, but that tasks should be available for the remaining 1,000,000 men. It is in determining the volume, not the direction, of actual employment that the existing system has broken down.

. . . The central controls necessary to ensure full employment will, of course, involve a large extension of the traditional functions of government. Furthermore, the modern classical theory has itself called attention to various conditions in which the free play of economic forces may need to be curbed or guided. But there will still remain a wide field for the exercise of private initiative and responsibility. Within this field the traditional advantages of individualism will still hold good.

Let us stop for a moment to remind ourselves what these advantages are. They are partly advantages of efficiency—the advantages of decentralisation and of the play of self-interest. The advantage to efficiency of the decentralisation of decisions and of individual responsibility is even greater, perhaps, than the nineteenth century supposed; and the reaction against the appeal to self-interest may have gone too far. But, above all, individualism, if it can be purged of its defects and its abuses, is the best safeguard of personal liberty in the sense that, compared with any other system, it greatly widens the field for the exercise of personal choice. It is also the best safeguard of the variety of life, which emerges precisely from this extended field of personal choice, and the loss of which is the greatest of all the losses of the homogeneous or totalitarian state. For this variety preserves the traditions which embody the most secure and successful choices of former generations; it colours the present with the diversification of its fancy; and, being the handmaid of experiment as well as of tradition and fancy, it is the most powerful instrument to better the future.

Whilst, therefore, the enlargement of the functions of government, involved in the task of adjusting to one another the propensity to consume and the inducement to invest, would seem to a nineteenth-century publicist or to a contemporary American financier to be a terrific encroachment on individualism, I defend it, on the contrary, both as the only practicable means of avoiding the destruction of existing economic forms in their entirety and as the condition of the successful functioning of individual initiative.

For if effective demand is deficient, not only is the public scandal of wasted resources intolerable, but the individual enterpriser who seeks to bring these resources into action is operating with the odds loaded against him. The game of hazard which he plays is furnished with many zeros, so that the players *as a whole* will lose if they have the energy and hope to deal all the cards. Hitherto the increment of the world's wealth has fallen short of the aggregate of positive individual savings; and the difference has been made up by the losses of those whose courage and initiative have not been supplemented by exceptional skill or unusual good fortune. But if effective demand is adequate average skill and average fortune will be enough.

The authoritarian state systems of today seem to solve the problem of unemployment at the expense of efficiency and of freedom. It is certain that the world will not much longer tolerate the unemployment which apart from brief intervals of excitement, is associated—and, in my opinion, inevitably associated—with present-day capitalistic individualism. But it may be possible by a right analysis of the problem to cure the disease whilst preserving efficiency and freedom. . . .

I have mentioned in passing that the new system might be more favourable to peace than the old has been. It is worth while to repeat and emphasize that aspect.

War has several causes. Dictators and others such, to whom war offers, in expectation at least, a pleasurable excitement, find it easy to work on the natural bellicosity of their peoples. But, over and above this, facilitating their task of fanning the popular flame, are the economic causes of war, namely, the pressure of population and the competitive struggle for markets. It is the second factor, which probably played a predominant part in the nineteenth century, and might again, that is germane to this discussion.

I have pointed out . . . that, under the system of domestic *laissez-faire* and an international gold standard such as was orthodox in the latter half of the nineteenth century, there was no means open to a government whereby to mitigate economic distress at home except through the competitive struggle for markets. For all measures helpful to a state of chronic or intermittent under-employment were ruled out, except measures to improve the balance of trade on income account.

. . . But if nations can learn to provide themselves with full employment by their domestic policy (and, we must add, if they can also attain equilibrium in the trend of their population), there need be no important economic forces calculated to set the interest of one country against that of its neighbours. There would still be room for the international division of labour and for international lending in appropriate conditions. But there would no longer be a pressing motive why one country need force its wares on another or repulse the offerings of its neighbour, not because this was necessary to enable it to pay for what it wished to purchase, but with the express object of upsetting the equilibrium of payments so as to develop a balance of trade in its own favour. International trade would cease to be what it is, namely, a desperate expedient to maintain employment at home by forcing sales on foreign markets and restricting purchases, which, if successful, will merely shift the problem of unemployment to the neighbour which is worsted in the struggle, but a willing and unimpeded exchange of goods and services in conditions of mutual advantage. . . .

Is the fulfilment of these ideas a visionary hope? Have they insufficient roots in the motives which govern the evolution of political society? Are the interests which they will thwart stronger and more obvious than those which they will serve?

I do not attempt an answer in this place. It would need a volume of a different character from this one to indicate even in outline the practical measures in which they might be gradually clothed. But if the ideas are correct—an hypothesis on which the author himself must necessarily base what he writes—it would be a mistake, I predict, to dispute their potency over a period of time. At the present moment people are unusually expectant of a more fundamental diagnosis; more particularly ready to receive it; eager to try it out, if it should be even plausible. But apart from this contemporary mood, the ideas of economists and political philosophers, both when they are right and when they are wrong, are more powerful than is commonly understood. Indeed the world is ruled by little else. Practical men, who believe themselves to be quite exempt from any intellectual influences, are usually the slaves of some defunct economist. Madmen in authority, who hear voices in the air, are distilling their frenzy from some academic scribblers of a few years back. I am sure that the power of vested interests is vastly exaggerated compared with the gradual encroachment of ideas. Not indeed, immediately, but after a certain interval; for in the field of economic and political philosophy there are not many who are influenced by new theories after they are twenty-five or thirty years of age, so that the ideas which civil servants and politicians and even agitators apply to current events are not likely to be the newest. But, soon or late, it is ideas, not vested interests, which are dangerous for good or evil.

JOHN MAYNARD KEYNES – A SIMULATED INTERVIEW

1. **How do classical economists explain a depression?**
   A. Classical economists contend that an excess of savings not only causes a depression, but also ends a depression. Classical economists argue that an excess of savings causes banks to bring down interest rates. Lower interest rates then serve as an incentive for the investment needed to end a depression.
   B. Classical economists contend that all depressions are temporary. In reality, an economy might remain in a depression; there is no automatic end to a depression.

2. **If classical economists are wrong, how can depressions be explained?**
   A. Depressions are not necessarily caused by an excess of savings. Depressions are caused by savings that remain idle. An economy enters a depression when savings are not invested in business expansion.
   B. An excess of savings does not necessarily bring about lower interest rates. During a depression savings might dry up as banks fail. When banks fail on a wide scale capital simply might not be available for investment.
   C. Investment is the key to economic prosperity. When an economy moves into a depression there is no incentive to invest.
   D. Businessmen and bankers should not be blamed for a reluctance to invest. There is no incentive to invest when there is no market for products. The capitalist system has no villain; the capitalist system simply suffers from a technical defect.

3. **What is the technical defect in the capitalist system?**
   A. A depression might be permanent; there is no automatic solution to a depression.
   B. Economic prosperity depends on investment. When businesses do not expand an economy falls into a depression.
   C. Businesses do not always have an incentive to expand. In fact, businesses are least likely to invest during a depression, a time when business investment is most needed.

4. **Other than the technical defect, what is wrong with the capitalist system?**
   A. No system is safe when it permits a wide gap between the rich and the poor. Although wealth should not be divided equally, capitalism in the 1930s allows too wide a division between economic classes.
   B. No system is safe when it permits widespread unemployment. All capitalist societies should commit themselves to full employment.

5. **What is the best way to achieve full employment?**
    A. Full employment can best be achieved through government control of investment.
    B. When private businesses have no incentive to expand, government should "prime the pump." Pump priming means that government spends heavily to stimulate economic activity.
    C. Government should regulate consumer demand through taxation and interest rates. Lower taxes and lower interest rates stimulate demand. In turn, increased demand inspires business expansion and a subsequent increase in employment.
    D. Full employment should be achieved in a way that preserves freedom. Dictatorships achieve full employment at the expense of freedom. Government control of investment does not mean that government should inhibit private initiative.

6. **Does allowing government to control investment threaten private initiative?**
    A. Government does not threaten private initiative by providing full employment. Instead, government serves as a practical means of saving capitalism and therefore preserves private initiative.
    B. Government should not control the means of production and exchange. The government should only take control of economic investment. Government spending is simply a means to stimulate economic activity.

7. **How will full employment affect the problem of war?**
    A. War is caused by economic factors. Government cannot ignore the social pressure to provide employment for its people. Government too often tries to provide employment by fighting for control of foreign markets. War would be unnecessary if a nation had full employment
    B. Nations that achieve full employment through government spending eliminate the pressing need for foreign markets. A new system of economics based on full employment through government investment will bring peace to the world.

8. **In what way is Keynesian economics a conservative idea?**
    A. Although Keynesian economics increases the role of government, widespread areas of the economy should be left to private initiative.
    B. Keynesian reforms should be introduced gradually without interfering with the traditions of society.
    C. Government should be granted the power to stimulate economic activity in order that capitalism can be saved from its greatest threat—unemployment. The fundamental point of Keynesian economics is to *conserve* the capitalist system.

STUDENT ACTIVITIES

Vocabulary
Define the following terms before reading the lesson on Keynes.

1. accumulation	10. equilibrium	19. propensity
2. aggregate	11. homogeneous	20. prudent
3. augmenting	12. impede	21. self-aggrandizement
4. canalized	13. inequitable	22. socialization
5. consilience	14. intermittent	23. totalitarian
6. disparity	15. mitigate	24. transmute
7. distilling	16. postulate	25. vested
8. diversification	17. predominant	
9. encroachment	18. proclivity	

Review
1. Where was Keynes employed during World War I?
2. What important book on economics did Keynes publish in 1936?
3. What program of the United States government was a good example of Keynesian economics?
4. According to classical economists, what causes a depression?
5. According to classical economists, what brings an end to a depression?
6. According to Keynes, what causes a depression?
7. Why did Keynes believe an excess of savings might not bring about lower interest rates?
8. What did Keynes think was the key to economic prosperity?
9. When did Keynes think business was least likely to expand?
10. What did Keynes believe should be the goal of every capitalist society?
11. What did Keynes think was the best way to achieve full employment?
12. What is pump priming?
13. How did Keynes think government should regulate consumer demand?
14. According to Keynes, what is the cause of war?
15. What did Keynes believe would bring peace to the world?
16. What was the fundamental point of Keynesian economics?
17. Decide whether the following statements are **True** or **False** according to John Maynard Keynes.
    A. Classical economists contend there is no automatic end to a depression.
    B. Businessmen and bankers are often to blame for depressions.
    C. A depression might be permanent; there is no automatic solution to a depression.
    D. Society should not allow too wide a gap between rich and poor.
    E. Government should not inhibit private enterprise.
    F. Government should control the means of production and exchange.

What do you think?
On a scale of one through five, rate your opinion of the following quotations by Keynes. Write a short statement explaining your rating.

1 – You **strongly agree** with the statement *or* you feel the statement is **admirable** considering the historical circumstances surrounding it.
5 – You **strongly disagree** with the statement *or* you feel the statement is **contemptible** considering the historical circumstances surrounding it.

A. *The outstanding faults of the economic society in which we live are its failure to provide for full employment and its arbitrary and inequitable distribution of wealth and incomes.*
B. *I believe that there is social and psychological justification for significant inequalities of incomes and wealth, but not for such large disparities as exist today.*
C. *It is not the ownership of the instruments of production which it is important for the State to assume. If the State is able to determine the aggregate amount of resources devoted to augmenting the instruments and the basic rate of reward to those who own them, it will have accomplished all that is necessary.*
D. *The central controls necessary to ensure full employment will, of course, involve a large extension of the traditional functions of government.*
E. *If nations can learn to provide themselves with full employment by their domestic policy . . . there need be no important economic forces calculated to set the interest of one country against that of its neighbour.*
F. *The ideas of economists and political philosophers, both when they are right and when they are wrong, are more powerful than is commonly understood. Indeed the world is ruled by little else.*
G. *It is ideas, not vested interest, which are dangerous for good or evil.*
H. *Marxian Socialism must always remain a portent to the historians of opinion—how a doctrine so illogical and so dull can have exercised so powerful and enduring an influence on the minds of men, and, through them, the events of history.*
I. *When the accumulation of wealth is no longer of high social importance, there will be great changes in the code of morals. We shall be able to rid ourselves of many of the pseudo-moral principles which have hagridden us for two hundred years, by which we have exalted some of the most distasteful of human qualities into the position of highest virtues.*
J. *Capitalism . . . is not intelligent, it is not beautiful, it is not just, it is not virtuous—and it doesn't deliver the goods.*

CHAPTER 31

RONALD REAGAN

BACKGROUND

Ronald Reagan (1911-2004) acquired an appreciation for conventional middle class values as a child in Illinois. Despite the fact his father was often unemployed and drank heavily, Reagan learned to admire hard work and individual initiative. After graduating from college with an economics degree he worked as a radio sports announcer until 1937 when he traveled to California.

A Hollywood screen test led to the offer of an acting job and Reagan began a career in which he would act in fifty-two motion pictures. In 1947 he was chosen president of the Screen Actors Guild, a position he used to prevent communist influence in Hollywood. In fact, he served as an FBI informant passing on names of actors he believed were communists.

In 1954 Reagan signed a contract with General Electric and became a spokesman for the political concerns of large corporations. He made his first national political speech in 1964 when he went on television to endorse conservative Barry Goldwater for president. Reagan's speech was such a success with conservatives that he was encouraged to run for political office. In 1966 he was elected to the first of two terms as governor of California.

In 1980 Reagan was elected president in an election that marked a great triumph for conservative ideas. As president he attacked anti-poverty programs and called for a sharp reduction in taxes. Although he professed a firm belief in balanced budgets, the national debt tripled during his presidency. He also presided over the largest military buildup in United States history. During his presidency tensions with the Soviet Union eased as the cold war came to an end.

For over twenty years Reagan was the leading spokesman for a new conservative movement that began in the 1950s with the political commentary of William F. Buckley, the founder of *National Review* magazine. Reagan played an integral role in creating a conservative coalition of intellectuals, business leaders, middle-class voters, and fundamentalist Christians. His leadership was essential to the success of a movement that would transform American politics and public policy in the late twentieth century.

RONALD REAGAN – IN HIS OWN WORDS

Televised Nationwide Address on Behalf of Senator Barry Goldwater, October 1964

We have so many people who can't see a fat man standing beside a thin one without coming to the conclusion that the fat man got that way by taking advantage of the thin one! So they are going to solve all the problems of human misery through government and government planning. Well, now if government planning and welfare had the answer, and they've had almost thirty years of it, shouldn't we expect government to read the score to us once in a while? Shouldn't they be telling us about the decline each year in the number of people needing help? . . . the reduction in the need for public housing?

But the reverse is true. Each year the need grows greater, the program grows greater.

The Creative Society, 1968

The theory of Communism holds that government eventually will wither away. The theory of Socialism says that government is the answer to all the people's problems. The theory of the Creative Society says that government is best when kept closest to and most responsive to the people. That is the direction in which we are attempting to move. . . .

. . . I do not hold with the theory that says society is to blame when a man commits a robbery or a murder and therefore we must be understanding and as sympathetic for the criminal as we are for the victim. Nor do I hold with the spirit of permissiveness abroad in the land that has undoubtedly added to the juvenile delinquency problem.

This is an era, not only of permissiveness, but also of affluence. As a result many young people often have time on their hands. Many who might otherwise find jobs have no need to work. . . .

I cannot help but believe that goods and privileges carelessly given or lightly earned are lightly regarded. A boy who works for the money to buy a car and keep it in gasoline is much more likely to appreciate it and care for it than the youth whose car has been given to him and whose gas is purchased on his father's credit card. Likewise the boy or girl who can go out at night only if he or she behaves is more apt to behave than those who have no set rules to follow, and no responsibilities to accept.

This brings me down to two points. First, are we doing enough for our children by doing too much for them? Aren't they really better off if they are taught to accept responsibility and to learn that in the long run we all must earn what we get and that we usually get what we earn?

The second point is, haven't we made it almost impossible for many of our young people to earn legitimately the things they need and want?

In some cases we have taught them by example that they don't have to earn, that instead they have a right to expect to be given. I challenge that this is wrong, I challenge that nobody does any young person any favor by this approach. . . .

My administration makes no bones about being business-oriented. A healthy business climate means a healthy economy and a healthy economy benefits all our people in jobs, in added tax revenues for added government services, in many other ways.

In addition, we believed and we are finding out it is true, that a government operated on business-like principles is a more efficient, more economical government.

Speech to the American Textile Manufacturers Institute, March 1973

When government sets out to solve a problem, the cure may not be worse than the disease. But it is bigger and it costs more. Government does not really solve problems; it subsidizes them. And it does not produce a dime of revenue. It can spend only what it first takes from the pockets of the working men and women of this country.

In the past few years, there has been an increasing assault on the very economic system that built America from a small backward country into the world's strongest. You as businessmen are blamed for many things you have not done, and given little credit for a number of things you have done very well. . . .

To some people, profit is a six-letter dirty word. Business is viewed with suspicion while government, big government, is hailed as a panacea. There is an appalling lack of understanding of the simple workings of the marketplace and the competitive economic system. . . .

No government agency can match the genius of the private sector in solving problems, in meeting new conditions, in providing services for the people. . . .

Why shouldn't business silence the political demagogue once and for all by explaining that business does not pay taxes. Business *collects* taxes for government—the kind of hidden taxes that are so favored by the demagogues.

Yet we are told that if business is just taxed a little more, this would produce more than enough money to finance whatever spending scheme anyone could dream up. Of course the inference is that we can have more goodies from government at no cost to the people.

Speech to the California Federation of Women's Clubs, May 1973

Our economic experts pointed out to us that in 1930 governments—federal, state and local combined—only took 15 percent of the people's earnings. By 1950, this had become 32 percent, and today government at all levels is taking 44.7 cents out of every income dollar. . . .

Government is an umpire—a policeman if you will. It is not a producer of goods or wealth. When government takes this much of the people's money, it creates a drag on the economy, causing economic slump and unemployment. History reveals that no society has long survived a tax burden that reached one-third of the people's earnings. Looking back on the fallen empires of the past, one sees the first warning signs appear. As the burden grows heavier, there is growing a lack of respect for government and the law. Fraud becomes widespread and crime increases. Are we to say none of those things are taking place here? . . .

Most of the opposition to this idea has come from within government. One legislator has told us such a plan would make it impossible for government to "continue re-distributing the earnings of the people." I submit that that is not a proper function of government. You and I do not have the right to take the earnings of one to give to another, and therefore we cannot give such power to government.

Speech at the American Conservative Union Banquet, February 1977
If there is any political viewpoint in this world which is free of slavish adherence to abstraction, it is American conservatism.

When a conservative states that the free market is the best mechanism ever devised by the mind of man to meet material needs, he is merely stating what a careful examination of the real world has told him is the truth.

When a conservative says it is bad for the government to spend more than it takes in, he is simply showing the same common sense that tells him to come in out of the rain. . . .

When a conservative quotes Jefferson that government closest to the people is best, it is because he knows that Jefferson risked his life, his fortune, and his sacred honor to make certain that what he and his fellow patriots learned from experience was not crushed by an ideology of empire.

. . . Conservative wisdom and principles are derived from willingness to learn—not just from what is going on *now*, but from what has happened before.

The principles of conservatism are sound because they are based on what men and women have discovered through experience in not just one generation or a dozen, but in all the combined experience of mankind. When we conservatives say that we know something about political affairs, and that what we know can be stated as principles, we are saying that the principles we hold dear are those that have been found, through experience, to be ultimately beneficial for individuals, for families, for communities and for nations—found through the often bitter testing of pain, or sacrifice and sorrow.

First Inaugural Address, January 1981
In this present crisis, government is not the solution to our problem; government is the problem. From time to time we've been tempted to believe that society has become too complex to be managed by self-rule, that government by an elite group is superior to government for, by, and of the people. Well, if no one among us is capable of governing himself, then who among us has the capacity to govern someone else? All of us together, in and out of government, must bear the burden. The solutions we seek must be

equitable, with no one group singled out to pay a higher price.

. . . We are a nation that has a government—not the other way around. And this makes us special among the nations of the earth. Our government has no power except that granted it by the people. It is time to check and reverse the growth of government, which shows signs of having grown beyond the consent of the governed.

It is my intention to curb the size and the influence of the federal establishment and to demand recognition of the distinction between the powers granted to the federal government and those reserved to the states or to the people. All of us need to be reminded that the federal government did not create the states; the states created the federal government.

Now, so there will be no misunderstanding, it's not my intention to do away with government. It is rather to make it work—work with us, not over us; to stand by our side, not ride on our back. Government can and must provide opportunity, not smother it; foster productivity, not stifle it.

If we look to the answer as to why for so many years we achieved so much, prospered as no other people on earth, it was because here in this land we unleashed the energy and individual genius of man to a greater extent than has ever been done before. Freedom and the dignity of the individual have been more available and assured here than in any other place on earth. The price for this freedom at times has been high, but we have never been unwilling to pay that price.

Remarks at the White House Meeting of State Legislators and County Executives, February 1981

I've long believed that State and local governments have a better chance to be efficient and responsive than does the Federal bureaucracy, which tries to fit solutions to problems that vary from one locale to another, and all too often they end up with their own bureaucracy the beneficiary of whatever program they administer.

Remarks at the Conservative Political Action Conference, March 1981

This is the real task before us: to reassert our commitment as a nation to a law higher than our own, to renew our spiritual strength. Only by building a wall of such spiritual resolve can we, as a free people, hope to protect our own heritage and make it someday the birthright of all men.

Remarks to the International Association of the Chiefs of Police, September 1981

Controlling crime in American society is not simply a question of more money, more police, more courts, more prosecutors; it's ultimately a moral dilemma, one that calls for a moral, or, if you will, a spiritual solution . . . in the end, the war on crime will only be won when an attitude of mind and a change of heart takes place in America, when certain truths take hold again and plant their roots deep in our national consciousness, truths like: right and wrong matters; individuals are responsible for their actions; retribution should be swift and sure for those who prey on the innocent.

Many of the social thinkers of the 1950s and 60s who discussed crime only in the context of disadvantaged childhoods and poverty-stricken neighborhoods were the same people who thought that massive government spending could wipe away our social ills. The underlying premise in both cases was a belief that there was nothing permanent or absolute about any man's nature, that he was a product of his material environment—with government as the chief vehicle of change through educational, health, housing, and other programs—we could permanently change man and usher in a great new era . . . . It's time, too, that we acknowledge the solution to the crime problem will not be found in the social worker's files, the psychiatrist's notes, or the bureaucrat's budgets. It's a problem of the human heart, and it's there we must look for the answer.

Remarks at the Recommissioning of the USS *New Jersey*, December 1982

Since the founding of our armed forces during the Revolutionary War, our country has always done without large standing armies and navies. Our great success story—unique in history—has been based on peaceful achievements in every sphere of human experience. In our two centuries of continuous democracy, we've been the envy of the world in technology, commerce, agriculture, and economic potential.

Our status as a free society and world power is not based on brute strength. When we've taken up arms, it has been for the defense of freedom for ourselves and for other peaceful nations who needed our help. But now, faced with the development of weapons with immense destructive power, we've no choice but to maintain ready defense forces that are second to none. Yes, the cost is high, but the price of neglect would be infinitely higher. . . .

America's strength is the bedrock of the free world's security, for the freedom we guard is not just our own. . . .

The United States is a naval power by necessity, critically dependent on the transoceanic import of vital strategic materials. . . . Freedom to use the seas is our nation's lifeblood. For that reason, our Navy is designed to keep the sea-lanes open worldwide, a far greater task than closing those sea-lanes at strategic choke points.

Remarks at the Conservative Political Action Conference, March 1985

The new conservatives made anew the connection between economic justice and economic growth. Growth in the economy would not only create jobs and paychecks, they said; it would enhance familial stability and encourage a healthy optimism about the future. Lower those tax rates, they said, and let the economy become the engine of our dreams. Pull back regulations, and encourage free and open competition. Let the men and women of the marketplace decide what they want.

RONALD REAGAN – A SIMULATED INTERVIEW

1. **Why is the United States a great nation?**
   A. The United States is a great nation because it allows for the freedom of the individual.
   B. The United States is a great nation because the government is based upon the will of the people.
   C. The United States is a great nation because of its free market system. The free market is the best system ever devised to fulfill the material needs of the people. Businessmen are not given enough credit for all the good they have done for the nation.
   D. For two hundred years the U.S. has been the envy of the world in regard to technology, commerce, agriculture, and economic potential. American power has not been based simply on military strength.

2. **How could the government of the United States be improved?**
   A. More power should be given to state and local governments. The best government is one that is close to the people and responsive to the needs of the people. State and local governments have a better chance to serve the people than the federal government.
   B. Government should be business oriented. A healthy business climate creates a healthy economy. In turn, a healthy economy benefits all people by providing jobs and higher tax revenues for increased government services.
   C. Government should operate according to the principles of business. Government would be more efficient and economical if it were run like a business.
   D. Government should not spend more than it takes in. Federal spending should be cut by eliminating useless and wasteful programs.
   E. The size of government should be reduced.

3. **Why should the role of the United States government be reduced?**
   A. Government cannot solve the problems of human misery. Although several decades of welfare have tried to end poverty, the number of people needing government help keeps increasing. The private sector can solve problems more successfully than government.
   B. The U.S. government has grown beyond the consent of the governed.
   C. Excessive taxation prevents people from investing in factories, equipment, and research. Excessive taxation causes unemployment and a slump in economic activity.
   D. Excessive regulation of business stifles creativity. Government should not present a barrier to creativity and prosperity.

E. Government cannot and should not try to do everything for its citizens. When government tries to satisfy every desire of its citizens, the result is tyranny.

F. Big government suppresses individual excellence and personal freedom. Government should not rob the people of their ability to think and act for themselves.

4. Should government try to redistribute wealth?

A. Government should not try to redistribute wealth. No one has the right to take the earnings of one person to give to another.

B. Government should not involve itself in producing goods or creating wealth. Government should serve only as an umpire in the economy.

C. Government cannot provide solutions to economic problems—government is the problem.

5. Should government stimulate economic growth?

A. Government should cut taxes particularly for corporations and wealthy individuals. Taxes should be cut for those who are most likely to invest in productive enterprises.

B. Government should promote economic growth because economic growth provides economic justice. Economic growth not only creates jobs, it enhances the stability of the family and encourages a healthy optimism about the future.

6. How should American society change?

A. The nation should commit itself to a higher law than human-made law. Americans can only protect their heritage by building a society based on spiritual strength.

B. The problems that Americans confront do not call for complex solutions. The answers to all the problems that Americans face are found in one book—the *Bible*.

C. Too many people have adopted an attitude of permissiveness toward children. This is particularly dangerous in an affluent society. Children with much time on their hands and the permission to do what they want do not learn good values. They do not learn responsibility; they do not learn they must earn what they receive.

D. Too many people inaccurately blame society for the actions of criminals. Crime in the United States is ultimately a moral problem. Crime cannot be stopped with simply more money, more policemen, and more courts. The problem of crime demands a spiritual solution.

7. Why should the United States maintain a strong military?

A. Although the United States has survived in the past without a large standing army, the modern world presents the threat of weapons with immense destructive power. The United States must defend itself with a strong military.

B. The United States needs a strong military to protect freedom throughout the world.

C. The United States navy should be strong enough to keep the sea-lanes of the world open to free trade.

D. The United States needs a strong military to resist Soviet aggression. The Soviet Union is an evil empire that threatens individual freedom and human dignity.

STUDENT ACTIVITIES

Vocabulary
Define the following terms before reading the lesson on Reagan.
1. abstraction
2. adherence
3. beneficiary
4. delinquency
5. demagogue
6. juvenile
7. panacea
8. permissiveness
9. slavish
10. sympathetic

Review
1. What career did Reagan begin after traveling to California in 1937?
2. What did Reagan work to prevent as president of the Screen Actors Guild?
3. When did Reagan make his first national political speech?
4. What elected office did Reagan win in 1966?
5. What were some of Reagan's achievements as president?
6. Who is William F. Buckley?
7. Why did Reagan believe the United States was a great nation?
8. Why did Reagan think the United States was the envy of the world?
9. Why did Reagan want to give more power to state and local governments?
10. Why did Reagan think government should be business oriented?
11. How did Reagan think government should reduce spending?
12. What did Reagan think was more successful than government at solving problems of human misery?
13. How did Reagan think excessive taxation affected the economy?
14. Why did Reagan think government should cut taxes for corporations and wealthy individuals?
15. Why did Reagan think government should promote economic growth?
16. What did Reagan believe happened to children raised with an attitude of permissiveness?
17. What did Reagan believe was the cause of crime?
18. Decide whether the following statements are **True** or **False** according to Ronald Reagan.
    A. Businessmen receive too much credit for their actions in helping the nation.
    B. The size of government should be reduced.

C. Big government is necessary to regulate big business.
D. Government should work to redistribute wealth.
E. Americans should commit themselves to a higher law than human-made law.
F. The answers to all the problems in America are found in the *Bible*.
G. The United States must defend itself with a strong military.
H. The Soviet Union threatens individual freedom and human dignity.

What do you think?
On a scale of one through five, rate your opinion of the following quotations by Reagan. Write a short statement explaining your rating.

1 – You **strongly agree** with the statement *or* you feel the statement is **admirable** considering the historical circumstances surrounding it.
5 – You **strongly disagree** with the statement *or* you feel the statement is **contemptible** considering the historical circumstances surrounding it.

A. *I do not hold with the theory that says society is to blame when a man commits a robbery or a murder and therefore we must be understanding and as sympathetic for the criminal as we are for the victim.*
B. *My administration makes no bones about being business-oriented. A healthy business climate means a healthy economy and a healthy economy benefits all our people in jobs, in added tax revenues for added government services, in many other ways.*
C. *In this present crisis, government is not the solution to our problem; government is the problem.*
D. *We are a nation that has a government—not the other way around. And this makes us special among the nations of the earth.*
E. *I've long believed that State and local governments have a better chance to be efficient and responsive than does the Federal bureaucracy, which tries to fit solutions to problems that vary from one locale to another.*
F. *In the end, the war on crime will only be won when an attitude of mind and a change of heart takes place in America, when certain truths take hold again and plant their roots deep in our national consciousness, truths like: right and wrong matters; individuals are responsible for their actions; retribution should be swift and sure for those who prey on the innocent.*
G. *Let us be aware that while [the Soviets] preach the supremacy of the state and predict its eventual domination of all peoples on earth, they are the focus of evil in the modern world. Let us pray for the salvation of all those who live in that totalitarian darkness—pray they will discover the joy of knowing God. But until they do, let us be aware they are the focus of evil in the world.*
H. *Government exists to protect us from each other. Where Government has gone beyond its limits is in deciding to protect us from ourselves.*

PART 8

A NEW SENSE OF JUSTICE

CHAPTER 32

WILLIAM O. DOUGLAS

BACKGROUND

Under Chief Justice John Marshall, who served from 1801 to 1835, the Supreme Court laid the foundation of the American legal system, and not until the 1950s and 1960s was constitutional law significantly redefined. Under Chief Justice Earl Warren, who served from 1954 to 1969, the Supreme Court provided the nation with fundamental changes in constitutional law. Warren's impact as chief justice is comparable only to that of John Marshall.

In several landmark cases the Warren Court changed American society. *Brown v. The Board of Education* declared that segregated schools were unconstitutional and set off the civil rights movement of the 1950s and 1960s. *Baker v. Carr* began the process of establishing a principle of "one man-one vote," shifting political power from rural to urban and suburban areas. Cases such as *Gideon v. Wainwright, Mapp v. Ohio*, and *Miranda v. Arizona,* protected the rights of individuals accused of a crime. Overall, the Warren Court shifted the emphasis of constitutional law from property rights to personal rights. In short, the Warren Court led a profound, but peaceful revolution in the United States.

Several justices on the Warren Court rank among the most important in United States history. The legal writings of Hugo Black, William Brennan, Felix Frankfurter, and Thurgood Marshall will be studied for generations. Their rulings expanded civil and individual rights as well as provided legal protection for the poor and the powerless. No member of the Warren Court argued for the protection of rights more than William O. Douglas (1898-1975).

Douglas joined the Supreme Court in 1939 when he was appointed by President Roosevelt. As a youth he developed his social conscience by witnessing firsthand the mistreatment of poor migrant workers and the violence against union members. He never lost his concern for the downtrodden, and in his thirty-six years on the Supreme Court he demonstrated a determination to use the judiciary to improve society. Few public figures have challenged established legal principles more than William O. Douglas.

WILLIAM O. DOUGLAS – IN HIS OWN WORDS

"The Black Silence of Fear," 1952

The democratic way of life rejects standardized thought. It rejects orthodoxy. It wants the fullest and freest discussion, within peaceful limits, of all public issues. It encourages constant search for truth at the periphery of knowledge.

We as a people have probably never lived up to that standard in any of our communities. But it has been an ideal toward which most of our communities have strived. We have over the years swung from tolerance to intolerance and back again. There have been eras of intolerance when the views of minorities have been suppressed. But there probably has not been a period of greater intolerance than we witness today. . . .

This pattern of orthodoxy that is shaping our thinking has dangerous implications. No one man, no one group can have the answer to the many perplexing problems that today confront the management of world affairs. The scene is a troubled and complicated one. The problems require the pooling of many ideas, the exposure of different points of view, the hammering out in public discussions of the pros and cons of this policy or of that. . . .

The great danger of this period is not inflation, nor the national debt, nor atomic warfare. The great, the critical danger is that we will so limit or narrow the range of permissible discussion and permissible thought that we will become victims of the orthodox school. If we do, we will lose flexibility. We will lose the capacity for expert management. We will then become wedded to a few techniques, to a few devices. They will define our policy and at the same time limit our ability to alter or modify it. Once we narrow the range of thought and discussion, we will surrender a great deal of our power. We will become like the man on the toboggan who can ride it but who can neither steer it nor stop it.

The mind of man must always be free. The strong society is one that sanctions and encourages freedom of thought and expression. When there is that freedom, a nation has resiliency and adaptability. When freedom of expression is supreme, a nation will keep its balance and stability. Our real power is our spiritual strength, and that spiritual strength stems from our civil liberties. If we are true to our traditions, if we are tolerant of a whole market place of ideas, we will always be strong. Our weakness grows when we become intolerant of opposing ideas [and] depart from our standards of civil liberties.

An Almanac of Liberty, 1954

Our freedom and liberty will be easy to redeem if we remember the fundamentals. First, our way of life is greatly concerned with *method* and *means*. The history of man's struggle to be free is in large degree a struggle to be free of oppressive procedures—the right to be free from torture and the hated oaths; the right to trial by jury; the right to confront the accuser face to face; the right to know the charge and to have a fair opportunity to defend. Second, we have principles or articles of faith to which we are committed. Of these, none is more important than the right to speak and to write freely; the right to worship God as one chooses; the sanctity of the conscience; the right to be let alone; the dependency of government on "the consent of the governed." . . .

In the field of constitutional law, judges do not feel bound by rulings of their predecessors. It is the *Constitution* they swore to support and defend, not the gloss which an earlier Court has put on it. And so it is that decisions on the construction of the *Constitution* have been constantly re-examined. . . .

Age does not necessarily give sanctity to a decision. In 1837, the Supreme Court overruled a ninety-five-year-old decision and in 1938 a sixty-eight-year old one. These involved constructions of the *Constitution*. From 1937 to 1949, the Supreme Court overruled 30 decisions, 21 involving constitutional questions. The great majority of the 30 had been decided within the previous twenty years.

In general each generation has taken unto itself the construction of the *Constitution* that best fits its needs. . . .

The first Ten Amendments to our *Constitution*—commonly referred to as the *Bill of Rights*—were held to be restrictions on the power of the federal government, not the States. Madison had endeavored to include provisions that no State should infringe "the equal rights of conscience, nor the freedom of speech or of the press, nor of the right of trial by jury in criminal cases." But that proposal was rejected.

Though the Fourteenth Amendment, adopted after the Civil War, says that no State shall deprive any person of "life, liberty, or property, without due process of law," it was assumed, up to 1925, that "liberty," as so used, did not include freedom of speech. In that year the Supreme Court, in passing on the constitutionality of a New York law which made it a crime to advocate the overthrow of the government by force or violence, assumed that freedom of speech and of the press, protected by the First Amendment, were also included within "liberty," as that word is used in the Fourteenth Amendment. In 1927, the first state law abridging free speech was struck down on that ground. Since then, that rule has been repeatedly applied to cases where the States have restrained free speech and freedom of the press. Soon it was applied to situations involving freedom of religion and to rights of assembly.

That is the reason why First Amendment rights are often said to have a preferred position in our constitutional scheme. They are preferred because the *Constitution*, as construed, protects them against abridgement by either the States or the federal government. . . .

"We the People of the United States" established the *Constitution*. "We the People" are the source of all governing power. The executive, the legislative, and the judicial branches are our agents, commissioned to express our will. "We the People" no longer have to beg for rights. We are the source of political power, and we may not be deprived of any of that power by any branch of the government.

This is the philosophy behind the command of the First Amendment that Congress shall make "no" law abridging freedom of speech and of the press. "We the People" are the governing body, who are not dependent on the legislature for what we may say or print. Our philosophy is premised on the belief that national security will be better assured through political freedom, than through repression. Once we start restraining that political freedom, we evince a lack of faith in the boldest political principle the world has known. . . .

The Fifth Amendment is an old friend, and a good friend. It is one of the great landmarks in man's struggle to be free of tyranny, to be decent and civilized. It is our way of escape from the use of torture. It protects man against any form of the Inquisition. It is part of our respect for the dignity of man. It reflects our ideas of the worth of rugged individualism.

A person who refuses to answer a question on the ground that it might incriminate him may ruin his reputation, though he saves his neck. The protection of the Fifth Amendment does not extend to condemnations which his neighbors or his employer may make because of his refusal to testify. The immunity does not afford a witness a certificate of good character. . . .

The Fifth Amendment, it should be remembered, was written for the protection of the innocent and guilty alike . . . . An act that in fact is wholly innocent may fit logically into a pattern of evidence, indicating guilt. Hence, if the innocent witness testifies, he may be furnishing the prosecution with a case against himself and be forced to depend on a jury to clear him. . . .

"A man's house is his castle" is a principle deep in our traditions. The home is a place of privacy, a sanctuary from the world. The police may not come night or day to search the premises as they desire. This was not always so. In colonial days, writs of assistance were issued authorizing officers to search places of business and homes from top to bottom, and to seize property and papers of every nature. They were used principally by custom inspectors seeking to find violations of the revenue laws. No showing was required that there were reasons to believe the person whose place was searched had violated any law. They were fishing expeditions, whereby officers ransacked houses looking for violations of the law. . . .

Experience with the writs of assistance produced the Fourth Amendment . . . .

Thus was the right of the *Constitution* placed behind the right of privacy—the right which Justice Brandeis once described as "the right to be let alone." . . .

The United States is a constant, eternal threat to any political oligarchy, to any totalitarian regime in the world. It is a threat because it is founded on the "consent of the governed" and because it grants civil rights to all people, regardless of race or creed. Our very existence is therefore a more potent threat than any stock pile of bombs.

Ideas are indeed the most dangerous weapons in the world. Our ideas of freedom are the most powerful political weapons man has ever forged. If we remember that, we will never have much to fear from communism. The force we generate with our ideas of liberty can give powerful impetus to freedom on other continents, as well as at home; in another century, as well as today.

Roth v. The United States, 1957
If the First Amendment means anything . . . it must allow protests even against the moral code that the standard of the day sets for the community. In other words, literature should not be suppressed merely because it offends the moral code of the censor.

Points of Rebellion, 1969
All branches of the government are bound by the Bill of Rights. It is of no concern to government what a person believes, what he thinks, what philosophy he embraces.

— "What church do you belong to?"

— "Are you an atheist?"

— "What are your views on the United Nations?"

These and like inquiries are irrelevant.

A man's belief is his own; he is the keeper of his conscience; Big Brother has no rightful concern in these areas.

The Court Years, 1980
The great work of the Warren Court was in making the standards of the Bill of Rights applicable to state action. . . .

Indeed, all of the important protective safeguards afforded to the accused by the Bill of Rights have been made applicable to the states. As this was happening a great howl went up in some quarters that the states' rights were being abridged and the lives of criminals made easier.

Making the Bill of Rights applicable to the states raised the level of law enforcement practices that states may permissibly use. . . . Those knowledgeable in the field know that crime springs from poverty, insufferable living conditions and from involvement in drugs. The presumption of innocence is proclaimed not only for the rich and prestigious members of the community but also for the lowliest members. . . .

If the judiciary bows to expediency and puts questions in the "political" rather than in the justiciable category merely because they are troublesome or embarrassing or pregnant with great emotion, the judiciary has become a political instrument itself. Courts sit to determine questions on stormy as well as on calm days. The Constitution is the measure of their duty. And it is the Constitution, not the judges' individual preferences, that marks the line between what is justiciable on the one hand and, on the other, what is political and therefore beyond the reach or competence of courts. A question is "political" only if the Constitution has assigned it to one of the other two departments for solution. . . .

The First Amendment tolerates a wide range of utterances. Whether in the field of obscenity or subversion, an utterance which incites to unlawful acts is irrelevant to the protection afforded by the first Amendment. Of course a legislature can deal with sexual conduct; unfortunately, the easy way is to strike at the speaker and suppress him. Our constitutional philosophy is that mature people will pick and choose among speakers, writers and publishers, turning their backs on those ideas that are repulsive but suppressing none. But in politics there are the untouchables, just as in religion there are heretics. Until Americans grow up and become sophisticated, they will continue to produce legislators and judges who will find applause somewhere in the mob. . . .

. . . Some critics have said that the Court should apply only "neutral" principles. But on most issues, the Constitution is not "neutral." It vigorously champions freedom of expression, not censorship; it declares against self-incrimination, not for inquisition; it proclaims against the establishment of a religion by the state; and in numerous like ways, picks and chooses one set of values as against others. The Constitution is not neutral when it comes to race; and a Court, therefore, that undertook to pose as neutral would not be faithful to the constitutional scheme. . . .

In time I wrote many opinions sustaining and defending the press. I . . . thought the First Amendment meant what it said when it commanded that Congress shall make "no law . . . abridging" freedom of the press. . . . I also felt that the same restrictions were imposed on the states when it was held that the First Amendment was applicable to them, as I have discussed, by reason of the Fourteenth Amendment—in a decision rendered by the Hughes Court, and in an opinion written by him in 1930.

My defense of the press did not stem from my personal opinion of its quality. It was, I thought, as depraved as it had been in Jefferson's time. My feelings, however, were like Jefferson's—that craven and abusive and self-seeking as the press is, a much worse press would result from government surveillance. . . .

The First Amendment always seemed to . . . me to be a "preferred" guarantee of the Bill of Rights. That idea was often ridiculed. But it is "preferred" because when it says "no law," that is in terms absolute and quite unlike the word "unreasonable" search or seizure in the Fourth Amendment or "speedy" trial in the Sixth or "excessive" bail in the Eighth. The values the First Amendment protects are necessary in a multiracial, multireligious, multi-ideological society of the kind we profess to be. The First Amendment sets us apart from most other nations. It marks the end of all censorship. It allows the ability of the mind to roam at will over the entire spectrum of ideas, and the sanctity of one's beliefs. It—not our bombs or air force or missiles or manufacturing skills or merchandising methods of GNP—sets us apart. A symbol of our health is the respect we show to First Amendment values.

WILLIAM O. DOUGLAS – A SIMULATED INTERVIEW

1. **Should judges follow judicial precedent when deciding constitutional issues?**
    A. Judges should rule according to the Constitution rather than previous legal decisions. Judges should overturn a previous decision if the decision was wrong according to the Constitution.
    B. Judges should rule according to the Constitution regardless of personal preference.
    C. Each generation should interpret the Constitution according to the needs of the time. If previous decisions are wrong for modern times, they should be overturned.

2. **Should freedom of expression be protected in every situation?**
    A. Democracy rejects standardized thinking. Democracy demands full and free debate of all public issues. Democracy works best when citizens are free to speak.
    B. No single person or group can have the answer to the many problems facing the nation. Modern problems require a combination of various ideas filtered through public debate.
    C. The United States should not limit itself to established ideas while being intolerant of new or different ideas. The nation will be weakened if Americans limit themselves to a narrow range of thought and discussion.
    D. Freedom of thought and expression will strengthen society by making the nation resilient and adaptable.
    E. Freedom of thought and expression are essential in a society as diverse as the United States.
    F. The people can be trusted to deal with speech that is considered dangerous, obscene, or offensive. Judges are wrong when they deny freedom of speech on the grounds that the people are too uninformed and unreliable for absolute freedom of speech.
    G. Government exists to serve the people. Government serves the people best if the people are left free to experiment with new ideas.

3. **Does the federal Bill of Rights restrict the actions of state governments?**
    A. The Bill of Rights was originally considered a means of restricting the actions of the federal government, not the states. However, the Fourteenth Amendment allows judges to use the Bill of Rights to restrict the actions of state governments.
    B. The Fourteenth Amendment protects life, liberty, and property. These rights are also protected by the Bill of Rights. The Fourteenth Amendment requires that state governments as well as the federal government refrain from denying these rights.

    C. All branches of government must obey the Bill of Rights. No part of government at the federal or state level should be concerned with what someone thinks.

    D. The Warren Court's greatest contribution was its requirement that the Bill of Rights apply to the actions of state governments.

4. What is the importance of the First Amendment in constitutional law?

    A. First Amendment rights have a *preferred position* in constitutional law. First Amendment rights are preferred because they are protected at both the federal and state level.

    B. First Amendment rights are absolute; they cannot be denied under any condition. The Constitution clearly states that Congress shall make *no* law denying First Amendment rights.

    C. The First Amendment marks the end of all censorship and sets the United States apart from other nations. The health of the nation is determined by the respect shown for First Amendment values.

    D. The First Amendment protects *all* speech. It even protects speech considered offensive to the moral standards of the community.

    E. Even symbolic speech, such as picketing, sit-ins, and demonstrations, is protected by the First Amendment.

    F. Freedom of the press cannot be denied under any condition. Questions about the quality of the press are insignificant when considering First Amendment rights.

5. Besides the rights stated in the First Amendment, what other rights are essential to American freedom?

    A. The Fifth Amendment protects an individual from testifying against himself. This amendment is one of the landmarks of human freedom. It protects individuals from any form of Inquisition; it allows Americans to live in a decent and civilized society.

    B. Although the Constitution does not expressly protect privacy, the right to privacy is implied. The Fourth Amendment, which protects people from unwarranted search and seizure, implies a protection of the right to privacy.

6. Should controversial issues be restricted to the elected legislative and executive branches of government?

    A. The judicial branch of government should not avoid controversial issues. The fact that judges are not elected does not mean they should avoid controversial issues.

    B. The Constitution is not neutral on controversial issues. The Constitution has something to say about issues such as religion and racial discrimination. When judges rule according to the Constitution they will find themselves facing controversial issues.

7. **What role should the United States play in the world?**
   A. The United States is a constant threat to governments that deny freedom. Governments that deny freedom are threatened by a successful government based on the consent of the people and a government guaranteeing the protection of civil rights.
   B. American ideas of freedom are the most powerful political weapons ever created. Ideas are the most dangerous weapons in the world.

STUDENT ACTIVITIES

Vocabulary
Define the following terms before reading the lesson on Douglas.

1. abridge	9. incite	17. perplexing
2. abusive	10. incriminate	18. predecessor
3. condemnation	11. infringe	19. ransack
4. craven	12. inquisition	20. repression
5. evince	13. intolerance	21. sanctuary
6. heretic	14. ominous	22. self-incrimination
7. immunity	15. oppressive	23. subversion
8. impetus	16. periphery	24. writ of assistance

Review
1. What chief justice laid the foundation of the American legal system?
2. What chief justice of the 1950s and 1960s provided the nation with fundamental changes in constitutional law?
3. Who were some of the important members of the Warren Court?
4. In what decision did the Supreme Court declare segregated schools unconstitutional?
5. In what decision did the Supreme Court begin the process of establishing "one man-one vote"?
6. What were three Warren Court decisions that protected the rights of people accused of a crime?
7. What did Douglas think was more important than judicial precedent?
8. Why did Douglas desire free public debate over a variety of ideas?
9. Why did Douglas think free thought and expression would strengthen society?
10. Why did Douglas think the federal Bill of Rights could restrict the actions of state governments?
11. What did Douglas think was the Warren Court's greatest contribution?
12. Why did Douglas think First Amendment rights held a preferred position in constitutional law?
13. Why did Douglas think First Amendment rights were absolute?
14. Why did Douglas think the Fifth Amendment was a landmark of human freedom?

15. On what grounds did Douglas think the right to privacy was implied in the Constitution?
16. Why did Douglas feel the United States was an important nation?
17. Decide whether the following statements are **True** or **False** according to William O. Douglas.
    A. The Warren Court emphasized property rights over personal rights.
    B. Each generation should interpret the Constitution in its own way.
    C. In some cases the people are too uninformed to allow absolute freedom of speech.
    D. Controversial issues should be limited to the elected legislative and executive branches of government.

What do you think?
On a scale of one through five, rate your opinion of the following quotations by Douglas. Write a short statement explaining your rating.

1 – You **strongly agree** with the statement *or* you feel the statement is **admirable** considering the historical circumstances surrounding it.
5 – You **strongly disagree** with the statement *or* you feel the statement is **contemptible** considering the historical circumstances surrounding it.

A. *The democratic way of life rejects standardized thought.*
B. *[The Fifth Amendment] is one of the great landmarks in man's struggle to be free of tyranny, to be decent and civilized. It is our way of escape from the use of torture.*
C. *The home is a place of privacy, a sanctuary from the world. The police may not come night or day to search the premises as they desire.*
D. *The United States is a constant, eternal threat to any political oligarchy, to any totalitarian regime in the world.*
E. *A symbol of our health is the respect we show to First Amendment values.*
F. *Men may believe what they cannot prove. . . . Religious experiences which are as real as life to some may be incomprehensible to others.*
G. *Government should be concerned with anti-social conduct, not with utterances.*
H. *The great and invigorating influences in American life have been the unorthodox; the people who challenge an existing institution or way of life, or say and do things that make people think.*
I. *Free speech is not to be regulated like diseased cattle and impure butter. The audience . . . that hissed yesterday may applaud today, even for the same performance.*
J. *The right to be let alone is indeed the beginning of all freedoms.*
K. *The American Government is premised on the theory that if the mind of man is to be free, his ideas, his beliefs, his ideology, his philosophy must be placed beyond the reach of government.*

CHAPTER 33

MARTIN LUTHER KING, JR.

BACKGROUND

Dr. Martin Luther King, Jr. (1929-1968) committed his life to the ideas of social justice and nonviolence he derived from the teachings of Jesus and Gandhi. King first gained international recognition as a minister in Montgomery, Alabama, when he helped organize a year-long boycott of the city's segregated bus system. During the boycott his philosophy of nonviolence, his outstanding speaking skills, and his personal courage inspired a generation to fight for social change.

After the boycott he continued his fight for racial justice by helping to create the Southern Christian Leadership Conference. At first, SCLC focused on a campaign to register black voters; however, when black college students began staging protests and sit-ins King joined their cause. Demonstrations, often led by King, spread throughout the nation and the movement for civil rights gained momentum. In 1963 over 250,000 people marched on Washington, D.C., where King delivered his famous "I Have a Dream" speech. The following year he was awarded the Nobel Prize for Peace.

By the mid-1960s King's leadership in the civil rights movement diminished. Many black leaders disagreed with his message of nonviolence and integration. In addition, he faced resistance from the United States Government. The FBI worked to prove he was a communist. The FBI even eavesdropped on his personal life and sent him a message suggesting he commit suicide. J. Edgar Hoover, the head of the FBI, referred to King as the most "notorious liar" in America. After King denounced the Vietnam War he also faced the wrath of President Lyndon Johnson.

In 1968 King was assassinated in Memphis, Tennessee. During his short life he sacrificed much for social change. His home was bombed in Montgomery; he was stabbed in Harlem; he was physically assaulted in Chicago; he was jailed in several communities. Nevertheless, he did not abandon his beliefs. Working to improve our world, he combined the universal ideals of love and brotherhood with the traditional American ideals of freedom and equality. In 1986 his birthday, January 15, became a national holiday.

MARTIN LUTHER KING, JR. – IN HIS OWN WORDS

Stride Toward Freedom, **1958**
Ever since the signing of the Declaration of Independence, America has manifested a schizophrenic personality on the question of race. She has been torn between selves—a self in which she has proudly professed democracy and a self in which she has sadly practiced the antithesis of democracy. The reality of segregation, like slavery, has always had to confront the ideals of democracy and Christianity. Indeed, segregation and discrimination are strange paradoxes in a nation founded on the principle that all men are created equal. . . .

. . . The shape of the world today does not permit us the luxury of a faltering democracy. The United States cannot hope to attain the respect of the vital and growing colored nations of the world unless it remedies its racial problems at home. If America is to remain a first-class nation, it cannot have a second-class citizenship.

Speech at Lincoln University ("The American Dream"), June 1961
America is essentially a dream, a dream as yet unfulfilled. It is a dream of a land where men of all races, of all nationalities and of all creeds can live together as brothers. The substance of the dream is expressed in these sublime words, words lifted to cosmic proportions: "We hold these truths to be self-evident, that all men are created equal, that they are endowed by their Creator with certain unalienable rights, that among these are life, liberty, and the pursuit of happiness." This is the dream. . . .

And there is another thing we see in this dream that ultimately distinguishes . . . our form of government from all of the totalitarian regimes that emerge in history. It says that each individual has certain basic rights that are neither conferred by nor derived from the state. To discover where they came from it is necessary to move back behind the dim mist of eternity, for they are God-given. Very seldom if ever in the history of the world has a sociopolitical document expressed in such profoundly eloquent and unequivocal language the dignity and the worth of human personality. The American dream reminds us that every man is heir to the legacy of worthiness. . . .

. . . I think all of us must develop a world perspective if we are to survive. The American dream will not become a reality devoid of the larger dream of a world of brotherhood and peace and good will. The world in which we live is a world of geographical oneness and we are challenged now to make it spiritually one. . . .

Through our scientific genius we have made of this world a neighborhood; now through our moral and spiritual development we must make of it a brotherhood. In a real sense, we must all learn to live together as brothers, or we will all perish together as fools. We must come to see that no individual can live alone; no nation can live alone. We must all live together; we must all be concerned about each other.

Letter from Birmingham City Jail, April 1963

I think I should give the reason for my being in Birmingham, since you have been influenced by the argument of "outsiders coming in." . . .

I am in Birmingham because injustice is here. . . .

Moreover, I am cognizant of the interrelatedness of all communities and states. I cannot sit idly by in Atlanta and not be concerned about what happens in Birmingham. Injustice anywhere is a threat to justice everywhere. We are caught in an inescapable network of mutuality, tied in a single garment of destiny. Whatever affects one directly affects all indirectly. . . .

You may well ask, "Why direct action? Why sit-ins, marches, etc.? Isn't negotiation a better path?" You are exactly right in your call for negotiation. Indeed, this is the purpose of direct action. Nonviolent direct action seeks to create such a crisis and establish such creative tension that a community that has constantly refused to negotiate is forced to confront the issue. It seeks so to dramatize the issue that it can no longer be ignored. . . . I must confess that I am not afraid of the word tension. I have earnestly worked and preached against violent tension, but there is a type of constructive nonviolent tension that is necessary for growth. . . . So the purpose of the direct action is to create a situation so crisis-packed that it will inevitably open the door to negotiation. . . .

You express a great deal of anxiety over our willingness to break laws. . . . One may well ask, "How can you advocate breaking some laws and obeying others?" The answer is found in the fact that there are two types of laws: there are *just* and there are *unjust* laws. . . .

Now what is the difference between the two? How does one determine when a law is just or unjust? A just law is a man-made code that squares with the moral law or the law of God. An unjust law is a code that is out of harmony with the moral law. . . . Any law that uplifts human personality is just. Any law that degrades human personality is unjust. All segregation statutes are unjust because segregation distorts the soul and damages the personality. It gives the segregator a false sense of superiority, and the segregated a false sense of inferiority. . . .

An unjust law is a code that a majority inflicts on a minority that is not binding on itself. This is difference made legal. . . .

. . . An unjust law is a code inflicted upon a minority which that minority had no part in enacting or creating because they did not have the unhampered right to vote. . . .

I hope you see the distinction I am trying to point out. In no sense do I advocate evading or defying the law as the rabid segregationist would do. This would lead to anarchy. One who breaks an unjust law must do it *openly, lovingly,* . . . and with a willingness to accept the penalty. I submit that an individual who breaks a law that conscience tells him is unjust, and willingly accepts the penalty by staying in jail to arouse the conscience of the community over its injustice, is in reality expressing the very highest respect for law.

We can never forget that everything Hitler did in Germany was "legal" and everything Hungarian freedom fighters did in Hungary was "illegal." It was "illegal" to aid and comfort a Jew in Hitler's Germany. But I am sure that if I had lived in Germany during that time I would have aided and comforted my Jewish brothers even though it was illegal. If I lived in a Communist country today where certain principles dear to the Christian faith are suppressed, I believe I would openly advocate disobeying these anti-religious laws. . . .

. . . We who engage in nonviolent direct action are not the creators of tension. We merely bring to the surface the hidden tension that is already alive. We bring it out in the open where it can be seen and dealt with. Like a boil that can never be cured as long as it is covered up but must be opened with all its pus-flowing ugliness to the natural medicines of air and light, injustice must likewise be exposed, with all of the tension its exposing creates, to the light of human conscience and the air of national opinion before it can be cured. . . .

Oppressed people cannot remain oppressed forever. The urge for freedom will eventually come. . . . The Negro has many pent-up resentments and latent frustrations. He has to get them out. So let him march sometime; let him have his prayer pilgrimages to the city hall; understand why he must have sit-ins and freedom rides. If his repressed emotions do not come out in these nonviolent ways, they will come out in ominous expressions of violence. This is not a threat; it is a fact of history. . . .

. . . I have no fear about the outcome of our struggle in Birmingham, even if our motives are presently misunderstood. We will reach the goal of freedom in Birmingham and all over the nation, because the goal of America is freedom. Abused and scorned though we may be, our destiny is tied up with the destiny of America. . . . We will win our freedom because the sacred heritage of our nation and the eternal will of God are embodied in our echoing demands.

Speech at the Lincoln Memorial ("I Have a Dream"), August 1963

So I say to you, my friends, that even though we must face the difficulties of today and tomorrow, I still have a dream. It is a dream deeply rooted in the American dream that one day this nation will rise up and live out the true meaning of its creed—we hold these truths to be self-evident, that all men are created equal.

I have a dream that one day on the red hills of Georgia, sons of former slaves and sons of former slave-owners will be able to sit down together at the table of brotherhood.

I have a dream that one day, even the state of Mississippi, a state sweltering with the heat of injustice, sweltering with the heat of oppression, will be transformed into an oasis of freedom and justice.

I have a dream my four little children will one day live in a nation where they will be judged not by the color of their skin but by the content of their character. I have a dream today!

I have a dream that one day, down in Alabama, with its vicious racists, with its governor having his lips dripping with the words of interposition and nullification, that one day, right there in Alabama, little black boys and black girls will be able to join hands with little white boys and white girls as sisters and brothers. I have a dream today!

I have a dream that one day every valley shall be exalted, every hill and mountain shall be made low, the rough places shall be made plain, and the crooked places shall be made straight and the glory of the Lord will be revealed and all flesh shall see it together.

This is our hope. This is the faith that I go back to the South with.

With this faith we will be able to hew out of the mountain of despair a stone of hope. With this faith we will be able to transform the jangling discords of our nation into a beautiful symphony of brotherhood.

With this faith we will be able to work together, to pray together, to struggle together, to go to jail together, to stand up for freedom together, knowing that we will be free one day. This will be the day when all of God's children will be able to sing with new meaning—"my country 'tis of thee; sweet land of liberty; of thee I sing; land where my fathers died, land of the pilgrim's pride; from every mountain side, let freedom ring"—and if America is to be a great nation, this must become true. . . .

And when we allow freedom to ring, when we let it ring from every village and hamlet, from every state and city, we will be able to speed up that day when all of God's children—black men and white men, Jews and Gentiles, Catholics and Protestants—will be able to join hands and to sing in the words of the old Negro spiritual, "Free at last, free at last; thank God Almighty, we are free at last."

The Strength to Love, 1963

Softmindedness is one of the basic causes of race prejudice. The toughminded person always examines the facts before he reaches conclusions; in short, he postjudges. The tenderminded person reaches a conclusion before he has examined the first fact; in short, he prejudges and is prejudiced. Race prejudice is based on groundless fears, suspicions, and misunderstandings. There are those who are sufficiently softminded to believe in the superiority of the white race and the inferiority of the Negro race in spite of the toughminded research of anthropologists who reveal the falsity of such a notion. There are softminded persons who argue that racial segregation should be perpetuated because Negroes lag behind in academic, health, and moral standards. They are not toughminded enough to realize that lagging standards are the result of segregation and discrimination. They do not recognize that it is rationally unsound and sociologically untenable to use the tragic effects of segregation as an argument for its continuation. . . .

There is little hope for us until we become toughminded enough to break loose from the shackles of prejudice, half-truths, and downright ignorance. The shape of the world today does not permit us the luxury of softmindedness. A nation or a civilization that continues to produce softminded men purchases its own spiritual death on an installment plan.

But we must not stop with the cultivation of a tough mind. The gospel also demands a tender heart. Toughmindedness without tenderheartedness is cold and detached, leaving one's life in a perpetual winter devoid of the warmth of spring and the gentle heat of summer. What is more tragic than to see a person who has risen to the disciplined heights of toughmindedness but has at the same time sunk to the passionless depths of hardheartedness?

The hardhearted person never truly loves. He engages in a crass utilitarianism which values other people mainly according to their usefulness to him. He never experiences the beauty of friendship, because he is too cold to feel affection for another and is too self-centered to share another's joy and sorrow. He is an isolated island. No outpouring of love links him with the mainland of humanity.

Sermon on "The Drum Major Instinct," February 1968

If any of you are around when I have to meet my day, I don't want a long funeral. And if you get somebody to deliver the eulogy, tell them not to talk too long. . . . Tell them not to mention that I have a Nobel Peace Prize, that isn't important. Tell them not to mention that I have three or four hundred other awards, that's not important. Tell him not to mention where I went to school.

I'd like somebody to mention that day, that Martin Luther King, Jr., tried to give his life serving others. I'd like for somebody to say that day, that Martin Luther King, Jr., tried to love somebody. I want you to say that day, that I tried to be right on the war question. I want you to be able to say that day, that I did try to feed the hungry. And I want you to be able to say that day, that I did try, in my life, to clothe those who were naked. I want you to say, on that day, that I did try, in my life, to visit those who were in prison. I want you to say that I tried to love and serve humanity.

. . . Say that I was a drum major for justice; say that I was a drum major for peace; I was a drum major for righteousness. And all of the other shallow things will not matter. I won't have any money to leave behind. I won't have the fine and luxurious things of life to leave behind. But I just want to leave a committed life behind.

And that's all I want to say . . . if I can help somebody as I pass along, if I can cheer somebody with a word or song, if I can show somebody he's traveling wrong, then my living will not be in vain. If I can do my duty as a Christian ought, if I can bring salvation to a world once wrought, if I can spread the message as the master taught, then my living will not be in vain.

Yes, Jesus, I want to be on your right side or your left side, not for any selfish reason. I want to be on your right or your best side, not in terms of some political kingdom or ambition, but I just want to be there in love and in justice and in truth and in commitment to others, so that we can make of this old world a new world.

MARTIN LUTHER KING, JR. – A SIMULATED INTERVIEW

1. **What is the defining purpose of the United States?**
    A. The American dream is found in the words of the Declaration of Independence. All people are created equal with natural rights to life, liberty, and the pursuit of happiness.
    B. The philosophy of the United States maintains that each individual possesses fundamental rights that cannot be denied. The goal of the United States is freedom.
    C. The United States is based upon a dream that people of all races, nationalities, and beliefs can live together in peace.
    D. The United States has a split personality. On the one hand, the nation claims to believe in the principles of the Declaration of Independence. On the other hand, the nation allows segregation of the races and discrimination against minorities.

2. **What is the nature of racial prejudice?**
    A. Racial prejudice is found in people who are "softminded" and reach conclusions before studying the facts. Racial prejudice is based upon fears, suspicions, and misunderstandings that have no basis in fact.
    B. Racial prejudice is a denial of the unity of all people in God's eyes. We are all God's children.

3. **What can be done to achieve social change in the United States?**
    A. People must learn to develop tender hearts. People must learn to love others and to care about all human beings.
    B. People should feel a responsibility to fight injustice everywhere it is found. Whatever affects one individual affects all individuals.
    C. Oppressed people must fight for their freedom. Freedom is never freely given to anybody. Privileged people will not give up their privileges voluntarily.
    D. People should take direct action to fight injustice. Direct action should create a tense situation that dramatizes injustice and sets off a crisis that will open the door to change.
    E. People should be willing to break the law to protest injustice. A just law should be obeyed; an unjust law should be disobeyed. The difference between a just law and an unjust law is simple. A just law conforms to moral law and the law of God. An unjust law does not conform to moral law; an unjust law degrades human beings.
    F. People should not arbitrarily break the law—this leads to anarchy. However, unjust laws should be broken openly with a willingness to accept the penalty.
    G. People must possess the courage to bring about social change. The key to happiness is freedom; the key to freedom is courage. A person who fears death is not free.

4. Why is nonviolence the best method to achieve social change?
A. Nonviolence does not mean people refuse to fight; nonviolence means people choose to fight in a productive manner. The aftermath of violence is bitterness and hatred. The aftermath of nonviolence is peace and brotherhood.
B. Nonviolence allows people to achieve a permanent victory instead of a temporary advantage. Nonviolence is a way of overcoming evil without acting in an evil manner. Nonviolence does not try to defeat an enemy; nonviolence tries to win an enemy's friendship and understanding.

5. What role should the United States play in the world?
A. The United States must show the world that people of different races and beliefs can live together in peace.
B. Americans are fighting more than racial injustice when they fight for civil rights—they are developing a concept of brotherhood that can be an example to the world. The greatest contribution of the civil rights revolution may be its enhancement of world peace.
C. Unless Americans deal with their racial problems they cannot gain respect in the international community.

6. What should be the ultimate goal for humanity?
A. Moral progress lags behind scientific progress. Human beings have used scientific genius to transform the world into a neighborhood. However, human beings have not used moral genius to allow people to live together in peace.
B. Humanity's ultimate goal should be the creation of a Beloved Community. A Beloved Community is an integrated community where men and women of all races and beliefs live together in peace.
C. After civil rights are achieved the problem of economic rights should be addressed. Freedom involves more than civil rights. People must be free from poverty to experience true freedom.

7. Is there hope for humanity?
A. The world has little hope unless it rejects prejudice and ignorance. The modern world demands that people learn to live with those who are different.
B. Oppressed people will not remain oppressed forever. Human beings naturally desire freedom, and freedom will eventually win. Those who deny freedom should be aware that if a desire for freedom is not allowed to be expressed in nonviolent ways, people will demand their freedom through acts of violence.
C. People who fight for freedom and social justice will eventually succeed. The American heritage, as well as the will of God, is linked to the principles of freedom and justice.

STUDENT ACTIVITIES

Vocabulary
Define the following terms before reading the lesson on King.
1. advocate
2. anarchy
3. cognizant
4. crass
5. discrimination
6. interposition
7. latent
8. manifested
9. mutuality
10. nullification
11. ominous
12. paradox
13. perpetuate
14. pilgrimage
15. resentment
16. schizophrenic
17. segregation
18. totalitarian
19. unequivocal
20. utilitarianism

Review
1. From what two persons did King derive his ideas on social justice?
2. In what city did King help organize a boycott of the segregated bus system?
3. What organization for social justice did King help create?
4. What speech did King deliver at the March on Washington in 1963?
5. Why did the FBI investigate King?
6. Where did King think people could find the American dream?
7. In what way did King think the United States had a split personality?
8. What did King believe was the basis of racial prejudice?
9. What did King believe was the purpose of direct action in fighting injustice?
10. What did King think was the difference between a just law and an unjust law?
11. Why did King believe people should not break the law arbitrarily?
12. How did King believe people should react to unjust laws?
13. What did King think was the key to freedom?
14. According to King, what is the goal of nonviolence?
15. What did King believe the United States should show the world?
16. What did King believe might have been the greatest contribution of the civil rights movement?
17. What is the Beloved Community?
18. What did King think should be addressed after civil rights are achieved?
19. Why did King think people who fought for freedom and social justice would eventually succeed?
20. Decide whether the following statements are **True** or **False** according to Martin Luther King, Jr.
    A. People must develop tender hearts by learning to love others and to care about others.
    B. People should obey the law in all situations.
    C. Nonviolence means that people must refuse to fight.
    D. Moral progress lags behind scientific progress.
    E. Human beings naturally desire freedom.

What do you think?
On a scale of one through five, rate your opinion of the following quotations by King. Write a short statement explaining your rating.

1 – You **strongly agree** with the statement *or* you feel the statement is **admirable** considering the historical circumstances surrounding it.
5 – You **strongly disagree** with the statement *or* you feel the statement is **contemptible** considering the historical circumstances surrounding it.

A. *America is essentially a dream, a dream as yet unfulfilled. It is a dream of a land where men of all races, of all nationalities and of all creeds can live together as brothers.*
B. *Through our scientific genius we have made of this world a neighborhood; now through our moral and spiritual development we must make of it a brotherhood.*
C. *I submit that an individual who breaks a law that conscience tells him is unjust, and willingly accepts the penalty by staying in jail to arouse the conscience of the community over its injustice, is in reality expressing the very highest respect for law.*
D. *Oppressed people cannot remain oppressed forever. The urge for freedom will eventually come.*
E. *Race prejudice is based on groundless fears, suspicions, and misunderstandings.*
F. *The church must be reminded that it is not the master or the servant of the state, but rather the conscience of the state.*
G. *Success, recognition, and conformity are the bywords of the modern world where everyone seems to crave the anesthetizing security of being identified with the majority.*
H. *Morality cannot be legislated, but behavior can be regulated. Judicial decrees may not change the heart, but they can restrain the heartless.*
I. *In the guilt and confusion confronting our society, violence only adds to the chaos. It deepens the brutality of the oppressor and increases the bitterness of the oppressed. Violence is the antithesis of creativity and wholeness. It destroys community and makes brotherhood impossible.*
J. *If a man hasn't discovered something that he will die for, he isn't fit to live.*
K. *The question is not whether we will be extremists, but what kind of extremists we will be. . . . The nation and the world are in dire need of creative extremists.*
L. *The choice today is not between violence and non-violence. It is either non-violence or non-existence.*
M. *We will have to repent in this generation not merely for the vitriolic words and actions of the bad people, but for the appalling silence of the good people.*
N. *War is a poor chisel to carve out tomorrow.*

CHAPTER 34

MALCOLM X

BACKGROUND

Malcolm X (1925-1965) was the son of Earl Little, a Baptist preacher. In 1931 Earl was found with one side of his head crushed and almost detached from his body. The murderers, who were most likely a white lynch mob, were never found. Earl's death was ruled a suicide, and because the death was a "suicide," Malcolm's mother was denied death benefits. She therefore had to accept welfare to care for her seven children. The welfare agency, however, decided to take six-year-old Malcolm away from his mother and put him in a foster home. Malcolm's mother eventually suffered a nervous breakdown and was placed in a mental institution.

After the eighth grade Malcolm dropped out of school and turned to a life of crime. Known as "Detroit Red," he spent time as a drug dealer and a pimp. In 1946 he was arrested for burglary. In prison he became a Muslim after studying the teachings of Elijah Muhammad, the leader of the Nation of Islam. Following the Nation's custom of dropping slave names, Malcolm replaced his surname Little with the letter X.

After Malcolm was paroled in 1962 he served as a Muslim minister in Harlem. An articulate spokesperson for the Nation of Islam, he referred to white people as the devil and argued for racial separation. However, he soon became disappointed with the Nation's refusal to challenge white authority. In turn, Elijah Muhammad seemed threatened by Malcolm's growing popularity. In 1963 Malcolm was censored by Elijah Muhammad. Elijah used Malcolm's description of John Kennedy's assassination as "the chickens coming home to roost" to justify the period of censorship.

In 1964 Malcolm's life changed dramatically. After leaving the Nation of Islam he made two trips to Africa and the Middle East. On a pilgrimage to Mecca he discovered that traditional Muslims accepted racial equality. Although he continued to criticize American racism, he abandoned the idea that all white people were evil. Just as he was gaining international stature as a spokesperson for human rights he was assassinated by Black Muslims in February 1965.

MALCOLM X – IN HIS OWN WORDS

The Autobiography of Malcolm X, 1964 [As told to Alex Haley]
"The devil white man," down through history, out of his devilish nature, had pillaged, murdered, raped, and exploited every race of man not white.

Human history's greatest crime was the traffic in black flesh when the devil white man went into Africa and murdered and kidnapped to bring to the West in chains, in slave ships, millions of black men, women, and children, who were worked and beaten and tortured as slaves.

The devil white man cut these black people off from all knowledge of their own kind, and cut them off from any knowledge of their own language, religion, and past culture, until the black man in America was the earth's only race of people who had absolutely no knowledge of his true identity. . . .

This "Negro" was taught of his native Africa that it was peopled by heathen black savages, swinging like monkeys from trees. This "Negro" accepted this along with every other teaching of the slavemaster that was designed to make him accept and obey and worship the white man. . . .

. . . The white man *wants* black men to stay immoral, unclean and ignorant. As long as we stay in these conditions we will keep on begging him and he will control us. We never can win freedom and justice and equality until we are doing something for ourselves! . . .

Since slavery, the American white man has always kept some hand-picked Negroes who fared much better than the black masses suffering and slaving out in the hot fields. The white man had these "house" and "yard" Negroes for his special servants. He threw them more crumbs from his rich table, he even let them eat in his kitchen. He knew that he could always count on them to keep "good massa" happy in his self-image of being so "good" and "righteous." "Good massa" always heard just what he wanted to hear from these "house" and "yard" blacks. "You're such a good, *fine* massa!" Or, "Oh, massa, those old black fieldhands out there, they're happy just like they are; why, massa, they're not intelligent enough for you to try and do any better for them, massa—"

Well, slavery time's "house" and "yard" Negroes had become more sophisticated, that was all. When now the white man picked up his telephone and dialed his "house" and "yard" Negroes—why, he didn't even need to instruct the trained black puppets. They had seen the television program; had read the newspapers. They were already composing their lines. They knew what to do.

I'm not going to call any names, but if you make a list of the biggest Negro "leaders," so-called, in 1960, then you've named the ones who began to attack us "field" Negroes who were sounding *insane*, talking that way about good massa.

"By no means do these Muslims represent the Negro masses—" That was the first worry, to reassure "good massa" that he had no reason to be concerned about his fieldhands in the ghettoes. "An irresponsible hate cult" . . . "an unfortunate Negro image, just when the racial picture is improving—" . . .

For the white man to ask the black man if he hates him is just like the rapist asking the *raped*, or the wolf asking the *sheep*, "Do you hate me?" The white man is in no moral *position* to accuse anyone else of hate!

Why, when all of my ancestors are snake-bitten, and I'm snake-bitten, and I warn my children to avoid snakes, what does that *snake* sound like accusing *me* of hate-teaching? . . .

No *sane* black man really wants integration! No *sane* white man really wants integration! No sane black man really believes that the white man ever will give the black man anything more than token integration. No! The Honorable Elijah Muhammad teaches that for the black man in America the only solution is complete *separation* from the white man! . . .

The Honorable Elijah Muhammad teaches us that since Western society is deteriorating, it has become overrun with immorality, and God is going to judge it, and destroy it. And the only way the black people caught up in the society can be saved is not to *integrate* into this corrupt society, but to *separate* from it, to a land of our *own*, where we can reform ourselves, lift up our moral standards, and try to be godly. The Western world's most learned diplomats have failed to solve this grave race problem. Her learned legal experts have failed. Her sociologists have failed. Her civil leaders have failed. Her fraternal leaders have failed. Since all of these have *failed* to solve this race problem, it is time for us to sit down and *reason*! I am certain that we will be forced to agree that it takes *God Himself* to solve this grave racial dilemma.

Every time I mentioned "separation," some of them would cry that we Muslims were standing for the same thing that white racists and demagogues stood for. I would explain the difference. "No! We reject *segregation* even more militantly than you say you do! We want *separation*, which is not the same! The Honorable Elijah Muhammad teaches us that *segregation* is when your life and liberty are controlled, regulated, by *someone else*. To *segregate* means to control. Segregation is that which is forced upon inferiors by superiors. But *separation* is that which is done voluntarily, by two equals—for the good of both! The Honorable Elijah Muhammad teaches us that as long as our people here in America are dependent upon the white man, we will always be begging him for jobs, food, clothing, and housing. And he will always control our lives, regulate our lives, and have the power to segregate us. The Negro here in America has been treated like a child. A child stays within the mother until the time of birth! When the time of birth arrives, the child must be separated, or it will *destroy* its mother and itself. The mother can't carry that child after its time. The child cries for and needs its own world!" . . .

So let us, the black people, *separate* ourselves from this white man slavemaster, who despises us so much! You are out here begging him for some so-called "integration!" But what is this slavemaster white, *rapist*, going about saying! He is saying *he* won't integrate because black blood will *mongrelize* his race. . . .

Unless we call one white man, by name, a "devil," we are not speaking of any *individual* white man. We are speaking of the *collective* white man's *historical* record. We are speaking of the collective white man's cruelties, and evils, and greeds, that have seen him *act* like a devil toward the non-white man. Any intelligent, honest, objective person cannot fail to realize that this white man's slave trade, and his subsequent devilish actions are directly *responsible* for not only the *condition* in which we find this black man here. You cannot find *one* black man, I do not care who he is, who has not been personally damaged in some way by the devilish acts of the collective white man! . . .

Human rights! Respect as *human beings*! That's what America's black masses want. That's the true problem. The black masses want not to be shrunk from as though they are plague-ridden. They want not to be walled up in slums, in the ghettoes, like animals. They want to live in an open, free society where they can walk with their heads up, like men, and women!

Few white people realize that many black people today dislike and avoid spending any more time than they must around white people. This "integration" image, as it is popularly interpreted, has millions of vain, self-exalted white people convinced that black people want to sleep in bed with them—and that's a lie! . . . Like a black brother recently observed to me, "Look, you ever smell one of them *wet*?" . . .

The American black man should be focusing his every effort toward building his *own* businesses, and decent homes for himself. As other ethnic groups have done let the black people, wherever possible, however possible, patronize their own kind, hire their own kind, and start in those ways to build up the black race's ability to do for itself. That's the only way the American black man is ever going to get respect. One thing the white man never can give the black man is self-respect! The black man never can become independent and recognized as a human being who is truly equal with other human beings until he has what they have and until he is doing for himself what others are doing for themselves.

The black man in the ghettoes, for instance, has to start self-correcting his own material, moral, and spiritual defects and evils. The black man needs to start his own program to get rid of drunkenness, drug addiction, prostitution. The black man in America has to lift up his own sense of values. . . .

. . . I was convinced that our Nation of Islam could be an even greater force in the American black man's overall struggle—if we engaged in more *action*. By that, I mean I thought privately that we should have amended, or relaxed, our general non-engagement policy. I felt that, wherever black people committed themselves, in the Little Rocks and the Birminghams and other places, militantly disciplined Muslims should also be there—for all the world to see, and respect, and discuss.

It could be heard increasingly in the Negro communities: "Those Muslims *talk* tough but they never *do* anything, unless somebody bothers Muslims." . . .I moved around among outsiders more than most other

Muslim officials. I felt the very real potentiality that, considering the mercurial moods of the black masses, this labeling of Muslims as "talk only" could see us, powerful as we were, one day suddenly separated from the Negroes' front-line struggle. . . .

The black man in North America was sickest of all politically. He let the white man divide him into such foolishness as considering himself a black "Democrat," a black "Republican," a black "Conservative," or a black "Liberal" . . . when a ten-million black vote bloc could be the deciding balance of power in American politics, because the white man's vote is almost always evenly divided. The polls are one place where every black man could fight the black man's cause with dignity, and with the power and the tools that the white man understands, and respects, and fears, and cooperates with. . . .

. . . I said that the American black man needed to recognize that he had a strong, airtight case to take the United States before the United Nations on a formal accusation of "denial of human rights"—and that if Angola and South Africa were precedent cases, then there would be no easy way that the U.S. could escape being censured, right on its own home ground. . . .

My pilgrimage broadened my scope. It blessed me with a new insight. In two weeks in the Holy Land, I saw what I never had seen in thirty-nine years here in America. I saw all *races*, all *colors*,—blue-eyed blonds to black-skinned Africans—in *true* brotherhood! In unity! Living as one! Worshiping as one! No segregationists—no liberals; they would not have known how to interpret the meaning of those words.

In the past, yes, I have made sweeping indictments of *all* white people. I never will be guilty of that again—as I know now that some white people *are* truly sincere, that some truly are capable of being brotherly toward a black man. The true Islam has shown me that a blanket indictment of all white people is as wrong as when whites make blanket indictments against blacks.

Yes, I have been convinced that *some* American whites do want to help cure the rampant racism which is on the path to *destroying* this country! . . .

I tried in every speech I made to clarify my new position regarding white people—"I don't speak against the sincere, well-meaning, good white people. I have learned that there *are* some. I have learned that not all white people are racists. I am speaking against and my fight is against the white *racists*. I firmly believe that Negroes have the right to fight against these racists, by any means that are necessary." . . .

I said that on the American racial level, we had to approach the black man's struggle against the white man's racism as a human problem, that we had to forget hypocritical politics and propaganda. I said that both races, as human beings, had the obligation, the responsibility, of helping to correct America's human problem. The well-meaning white people, I said, had to combat, actively and directly, the racism in other white people. And the black people had to build within themselves much greater awareness that along with equal rights there had to be the bearing of equal responsibilities.

I knew, better than most Negroes, how many white people truly wanted to see American racial problems solved. I knew that many whites were as frustrated as Negroes. I'll bet I got fifty letters some days from white people. The white people in meeting audiences would throng around me, asking me, after I had addressed them somewhere, "What *can* a sincere white person do?"

When I say that here now, it makes me think about that little co-ed I told you about, the one who flew from her New England college down to New York and came up to me in the Nation of Islam's restaurant in Harlem, and I told her that there was "nothing" she could do. I regret that I told her that. I wish that now I knew her name, or where I could telephone her, or write to her, and tell her what I tell white people now when they present themselves as being sincere, and ask me, one way or another, the same thing that she asked.

The first thing I tell them is that at least where my own particular Black Nationalist organization, the Organization of Afro-American Unity, is concerned, they can't *join* us. I have these very deep feelings that white people who want to join black organizations are really just taking the escapist way to salve their consciences. By visibly hovering near us, they are "proving" that they are "with us." But the hard truth is this *isn't* helping to solve America's racist problem. The Negroes aren't the racists. Where the really sincere white people have got to do their "proving" of themselves is not among the black *victims*, but out on the battle lines of where America's racism really *is*—and that's in their own home communities; America's racism is among their own fellow whites. That's where the sincere whites who really mean to accomplish something have got to work.

Aside from that, I mean nothing against any sincere whites when I say that as members of black organizations, generally whites' very presence subtly renders the black organization automatically less effective. Even the best white members will slow down the Negroes' discovery of what they need to do, and particularly of what they can do—for themselves, working by themselves, among their own kind, in their own communities. . . .

I tell sincere white people, "Work in conjunction with us—each of us working among our own kind." Let sincere white individuals find all other white people they can who feel as they do—and let them form their own all-white groups, to work trying to convert other white people who are thinking and acting so racist. Let sincere whites go and teach non-violence to white people! . . .

Sometimes, I have dared to dream to myself that one day, history may even say that my voice—which disturbed the white man's smugness, and his arrogance, and his complacency—that my voice helped to save America from a grave, possibly even a fatal catastrophe.

MALCOLM X – A SIMULATED INTERVIEW

1. **Do Black Muslims hate white people?**
   A. Black Muslims who refer to whites as the devil are responding to continuing white racism and injustice. No black person should be blamed for how he responds to the actions of whites. Black hatred for whites is the result of white racism.
   B. The African slave trade was history's greatest crime. White society teaches blacks that Africans are savages. Blacks in America are denied knowledge of their ancestry; blacks are taught to hate themselves.
   C. A sweeping indictment of *all* white people is wrong. Some whites are capable of brotherhood with blacks. Not all whites are racists; some whites hate racism.

2. **Should African-Americans support racial integration?**
   A. America does not need racial integration. America simply needs to allow all human beings to live with freedom and dignity.
   B. Whites and blacks have already been separated in the United States. Since blacks will never be allowed out of the ghettos, they should run the ghettos.
   C. When blacks demand integrated schools they wrongly concede the inferiority of their own children. Black communities should build black-run schools for black children.

3. **Should African-Americans support the civil rights movement?**
   A. The struggle to gain *human* rights is more important than the struggle to gain *civil* rights.
   B. Federal civil rights legislation is a fraud on black people. Civil rights legislation gives blacks a paycheck that whites will never cash.
   C. Blacks who fight for civil rights confine themselves to the boundaries of the United States; they spend time trying to prove they are Americans. Blacks should never demean themselves by begging for justice; blacks should never compromise to gain rights.

4. **Should African-Americans vote?**
   A. Blacks should control the politics and the politicians of their own community.
   B. Blacks should vote, but they should not compromise with their votes. If blacks have no person or policy that deserves their vote, they should save their votes.
   C. Blacks should register to vote in large numbers. However, they should not align themselves with either the Republican Party or the Democratic Party. Blacks should form an independent third political force that can determine the balance of power in close elections.

5. Is nonviolence the best method for African-Americans to achieve justice?

    A. Blacks should be nonviolent only when treated nonviolently. Blacks should not be nonviolent when groups like the Ku Klux Klan act violently. Nonviolence does not work unless everyone is nonviolent.

    B. A bloodless revolution in the United States is possible, but not likely. Even Patrick Henry and George Washington understood that bloodless, nonviolent revolutions were not possible.

6. What can African-Americans do to improve their situation?

    A. The Nation of Islam is wrong when it refuses to challenge white authority. Black Muslims should actively commit themselves to helping others fight American racism.

    B. People of all colors and philosophies should work together to abolish injustice in the United States.

    C. The best way for blacks to improve their situation is to control their own communities and their own lives. Blacks should get rid of their dependence on whites.

    D. Blacks should own and operate the businesses in black communities.

    E. Blacks should be in a position to create job opportunities for their own people. Blacks should not have to beg whites for a job.

    F. Blacks should abolish the vices that destroy the moral fiber of black communities. Blacks should work to remove alcoholism, drugs, and other social evils from their communities.

    G. Blacks should work on improving themselves. Blacks cannot change the attitude or the behavior of whites; blacks should change their own attitude and behavior.

    H. American blacks should adopt an international view. Blacks in the United States are a minority. Internationally, blacks are the majority.

    I. The plight of black Americans should be brought before the United Nations. The United Nations should condemn American injustice and bring charges against the United States.

7. Is there hope for the United States?

    A. American democracy and capitalism are cruel, hypocritical institutions.

    B. Appealing to America's conscience is a waste of time. The United States has no conscience; Americans know nothing about morals. If the United States had a conscience, changes would be made without having to put pressure on the system.

    C. The American political, economic, and social system will never produce freedom for black people. The system should be abolished, and those who desire human rights should not compromise.

    D. The United States might be at the point where things can no longer be changed through voting.

STUDENT ACTIVITIES

Vocabulary
Define the following terms before reading the lesson on Malcolm X.
1. arrogance
2. complacency
3. demagogue
4. exploited
5. fraternal
6. hypocritical
7. militantly
8. mongrelize
9. pilgrimage
10. propaganda
11. rampant
12. segregationist
13. self-exalted
14. smugness

Review
1. Why was six-year-old Malcolm taken away from his mother?
2. Why did Malcolm spend time in prison?
3. Who was Elijah Muhammad?
4. Why did Malcolm Little replace his surname with X?
5. In what city did Malcolm X serve as a Muslim minister?
6. What did Malcolm X discover on his pilgrimage to Mecca?
7. Who assassinated Malcolm X?
8. What did Malcolm X believe white society taught blacks?
9. What did Malcolm X believe was the basis of black hatred for whites?
10. Why did Malcolm X believe a sweeping indictment of all white people was wrong?
11. Why did Malcolm X believe blacks should build their own schools?
12. Why did Malcolm X believe federal civil rights legislation was fraudulent?
13. What political party did Malcolm X believe blacks should support?
14. Why did Malcolm X believe blacks should adopt an international view?
15. Why did Malcolm X believe an appeal to America's conscience was a waste of time?
16. Decide whether the following statements are **True** or **False** according to Malcolm X.
    A. The United States should allow all human beings to live with freedom and dignity.
    B. Blacks should control the politics and the politicians of their own community.
    C. Nonviolence does not work unless everyone is nonviolent.
    D. Patrick Henry and George Washington were wrong to advocate bloodless revolution.
    E. People of all colors and philosophies should work to abolish injustice in the United States.
    F. Blacks should own and operate businesses in black communities.
    G. Blacks should work to change the attitude and behavior of whites.
    H. The United Nations should bring charges against the United States.
    I. The United States might be at the point where things can no longer be changed with voting.

What do you think?
On a scale of one through five, rate your opinion of the following quotations by Malcolm X. Write a short statement explaining your rating.

1 – You **strongly agree** with the statement *or* you feel the statement is **admirable** considering the historical circumstances surrounding it.
5 – You **strongly disagree** with the statement *or* you feel the statement is **contemptible** considering the historical circumstances surrounding it.

A. *History's greatest crime was the traffic in black flesh.*
B. *The white man wants black men to stay immoral, unclean and ignorant. As long as we stay in these conditions we will keep on begging him and he will control us. We never can win freedom and justice and equality until we are doing something for ourselves!*
C. *For the white man to ask the black man if he hates him is just like the rapist asking the raped, or the wolf asking the sheep, "Do you hate me?" The white man is in no moral position to accuse anyone else of hate.*
D. *Unless we call one white man, by name, a "devil," we are not speaking of any individual white man. We are speaking of the collective white man's historical record.*
E. *The American black man should be focusing his every effort toward building his own businesses, and decent homes for himself.*
F. *Be peaceful, be courteous, obey the law, respect everyone; but if someone puts his hand on you, send him to the cemetery.*
G. *A segregated school system produces children who, when they graduate, graduate with crippled minds.*
H. *Nobody can give you freedom. Nobody can give you equality or justice or anything. If you're a man, you take it.*
I. *You show me a capitalist, I'll show you a bloodsucker.*
J. *You can't separate peace from freedom because no one can be at peace unless he has his freedom.*
K. *Power never takes a back step—only in the face of more power.*
L. *This country can seduce God. Yes, it has that seductive power—the power of dollarism.*
M. *You're not supposed to be so blind with patriotism that you can't face reality. Wrong is wrong, no matter who does it or who says it.*
N. *The political philosophy of black nationalism means that the black man should control the politics and the politicians in his own community; no more.*
O. *Speaking like this doesn't mean that we're anti-white, but it does mean we're anti-exploitation, we're anti-degradation, we're anti-oppression.*

CHAPTER 35

BETTY FRIEDAN

BACKGROUND

When Betty Friedan (1921-) graduated summa cum laude from Smith College in 1942 she felt prepared for a life of intellectual excitement. However, after several years as a housewife she questioned the usefulness of her excellent education. At her fifteen year college reunion she sent questionnaires to her female classmates asking them to describe their lives since college. The response showed that many women were utterly bored with their lives as housewives. To report on her findings Friedan wrote *The Feminine Mystique*, a best-selling book that brought about profound social change. Quite simply, *The Feminine Mystique* was the catalytic work of the modern women's movement.

In a mockery of the women's movement, U.S. Representative Howard Smith proposed a law in 1964 prohibiting discrimination on the basis of sex. Smith was against women's rights and thought his proposal would be taken as a joke. He only introduced the legislation to help defeat civil rights reform. To his surprise, the law, known as Title VII to the Civil Rights Act of 1964, was passed by Congress.

Friedan and many other women distrusted the government's desire to enforce Title VII. Friedan therefore helped organize the National Organization for Women (NOW) in 1966. As president of NOW, Friedan fought for legalized abortion and for an Equal Rights Amendment (ERA) to the Constitution. Although the Supreme Court protected abortion rights, the Equal Rights Amendment was not ratified.

In 1981 Friedan published *The Second Stage*, describing new goals for the women's movement. In the book she expressed her opinion that during the 1970s feminism had been too confrontational. She hoped that women and men would begin working together on family issues.

When *The Feminine Mystique* became a best-seller in 1963 it ignited a movement that changed American society. Today, women pursue careers that were formerly restricted to men. To be sure, the United States has changed profoundly because of the ideas and the activism of Betty Friedan.

BETTY FRIEDAN – IN HER OWN WORDS

The Feminine Mystique, 1963

The problem lay buried, unspoken, for many years in the minds of American women. It was a strange stirring, a sense of dissatisfaction, a yearning that women suffered in the middle of the twentieth century in the United States. Each suburban wife struggled with it alone. As she made the beds, shopped for groceries, matched slipcover material, ate peanut butter sandwiches with her children, chauffeured Cub Scouts and Brownies, lay beside her husband at night—she was afraid to ask even of herself the silent question— "Is this all?"

For over fifteen years there was no word of this yearning in the millions of words written about women, for women, in all the columns, books and articles by experts telling women their role was to seek fulfillment as wives and mothers. Over and over women heard . . . that they could desire no greater destiny than to glory in their own femininity. Experts told them how to catch a man and keep him, how to breastfeed children and handle their toilet training, how to cope with sibling rivalry and adolescent rebellion; how to buy a dishwasher, bake bread, cook gourmet snails, and build a swimming pool with their own hands; how to dress, look, and act more feminine and make marriage more exciting; how to keep their husbands from dying young and their sons from growing into delinquents. They were taught to pity the neurotic, unfeminine, unhappy women who wanted to be poets or physicists or presidents. They learned that truly feminine women do not want careers, higher education, political rights—the independence and the opportunities that the old-fashioned feminists fought for. Some women, in their forties and fifties, still remembered painfully giving up those dreams, but most of the younger women no longer even thought about them. . . . All they had to do was devote their lives from earliest girlhood to finding a husband and bearing children. . . . (pps. 15-16)

If I am right, the problem that has no name stirring in the minds of so many American women today is not a matter of loss of femininity or too much education, or the demands of domesticity. It is far more important than anyone recognizes. . . . It may well be the key to our future as a nation and a culture. We can no longer ignore that voice within women that says: "I want something more than my husband and my children and my home." . . . (p. 32)

The feminine mystique says that the highest value and the only commitment for women is the fulfillment of their own femininity. . . . The mistake, says the mystique, the root of women's troubles in the past is that women envied men, women tried to be like men, instead of accepting their own nature, which can find fulfillment only in sexual passivity, male domination, and nurturing maternal love.

But the new image this mystique gives to American women is the old image: "Occupation: housewife." The new mystique makes the housewife-mothers, who never had a chance to be anything else, the model for all women; it presupposes that history has reached a final and glorious end in the here and now, as far as women are concerned. Beneath the sophisticated trappings, it simply makes certain concrete, finite, domestic aspects of feminine existence—as it was lived by women whose lives were confined, by necessity, to cooking, cleaning, washing, bearing children—into a religion, a pattern by which all women must now live or deny their femininity. . . . (p. 43)

. . . Ideas are not like instincts of the blood that spring into the mind intact. They are communicated by education, by the printed word. The new young housewives; who leave high school or college to marry, do not read books, the psychological surveys say. They only read magazines. Magazines today assume women are not interested in ideas. But going back to the bound volumes in the library, I found in the thirties and forties that the mass circulation magazines like *Ladies' Home Journal* carried hundreds of articles about the world outside the home. "The first inside story of American diplomatic relations preceding declared war"; "Can the U.S. Have Peace After This War?" by Walter Lippman; "Stalin at Midnight," by Harold Stassen; "General Stilwell Reports on China"; articles about the last days of Czechoslovakia by Vincent Sheean; the persecution of Jews in Germany; the New Deal; Carl Sandburg's account of Lincoln's assassination; Faulkner's stories of Mississippi, and Margaret Sanger's battle for birth control.

In the 1950's they printed virtually no articles except those that serviced women as housewives, or described women as housewives, or permitted a purely feminine identification like the Duchess of Windsor or Princess Margaret. "If we get an article about a woman who does anything adventurous, out of the way, something by herself, you know, we figure she must be terribly aggressive, neurotic," a *Ladies' Home Journal* editor told me. . . . (pps. 51-52)

A baked potato is not as big as the world, and vacuuming the living room floor—with or without makeup—is not work that takes enough thought or energy to challenge any woman's full capacity. Women are human beings, not stuffed dolls, not animals. . . . (p. 67)

The feminine mystique is so powerful that women grow up no longer knowing that they have the desires and capacities the mystique forbids. . . . (p. 68)

The feminine mystique permits, even encourages, women to ignore the question of their identity. The mystique says they can answer the question "Who am I?" by saying "Tom's wife . . . Mary's mother." But I don't think the mystique would have such power over American women if they did not fear to face this terrifying blank which makes them unable to see themselves after twenty-one. The truth is—and how long it has been true, I'm not sure, but it was true in my generation and it is true of girls growing up today—an American woman no longer has a private image to tell her who she is, or can be, or wants to be.

The public image, in the magazines and television commercials, is designed to sell washing machines, cake mixes, deodorants, detergents, rejuvenating face creams, hair tints. But the power of that image, on which companies spend millions of dollars for television time and ad space, comes from this: American women no longer know who they are. They are sorely in need of a new image to help them find their identity. As the motivational researchers keep telling the advertisers, American women are so unsure of who they should be that they look to this glossy public image to decide every detail of their lives. . . . (pps. 71-72)

It is my thesis that the core of the problem for women today is . . . a problem of identity—a stunting or evasion of growth that is perpetuated by the feminine mystique. It is my thesis that . . . our culture does not permit women to accept or gratify their basic need to grow and fulfill their potentialities as human beings . . . . (p. 77)

There are certain facts of life so obvious and mundane that one never talks about them. Only the child blurts out: "Why do people in books never go to the toilet?" Why is it never said that the really crucial function, the really important role that women serve as housewives is *to buy more things for the house*. In all the talk of femininity and woman's role, one forgets that the real business of America is business. But the perpetuation of housewifery, the growth of the feminine mystique, makes sense (and dollars) when one realizes that women are the chief customers of American business. Somehow, somewhere, someone must have figured out that women will buy more things if they are kept in the underused, nameless-yearning, energy-to-get-rid-of state of being housewives. . . . (pps. 206-07)

. . . I noticed something else about these women who were leading their lives in the protective shade of the feminine mystique. They were so *busy*—busy shopping, chauffeuring, using their dishwashers and dryers and electric mixers, busy gardening, waxing, polishing, helping with the children's homework, collecting for mental health, and doing thousands of little chores. In the course of my interviews with these women, I began to see that there was something peculiar about the *time* housework takes today. . . . (pps. 236-37)

The mystique would have women renounce ambition for themselves. Marriage and motherhood is the end; after that, women are supposed to be ambitious only for their husbands and their children. . . . (pps. 355-56)

The key to the trap is, of course, education. The feminine mystique has made higher education for women seem suspect, unnecessary and even dangerous. But I think that education, and only education, has saved, and can continue to save, American women from the greater dangers of the feminine mystique. . . . (p. 357)

It is essential, above all, for educators themselves to say "no" to the feminine mystique and face the fact that the only point in educating women is to educate them to the limit of their ability. Women do not need courses in "marriage and the family" to marry and raise families; they do not need courses in homemaking to make homes. But they must study science—to discover in science; study the thought of the past—to create new thought; study society—to pioneer in society. (p. 368)

The Second Stage, 1981

There is no going back. The women's movement was necessary. But the liberation that began with the women's movement isn't finished. The equality we fought for isn't livable, isn't workable, isn't comfortable in the terms that structured our battle. The first stage, the women's movement, was fought within, and against, and defined by that old structure of unequal, polarized male and female sex roles. But to continue reacting against that structure is still to be defined and limited by its terms. What's needed now is to transcend those terms, transform the structure itself. Maybe the women's movement, as such, can't do that. The experts of psychology, sociology, economics, biology, even the feminist experts are still engaged in the old battles, of women versus men. . . . We have to break out of feminist rhetoric, go beyond the assumptions of the first stage of the women's movement and test life again—with personal truth—to turn this new corner, just as we had to break through the feminine mystique twenty years ago to begin our modern movement toward equality.

Saying no to the feminine mystique and organizing to confront sex discrimination was only the first stage. We have somehow to transcend the polarities of the first stage, and even the rage of our own "no," to get on to the second stage: the restructuring of our institutions on a basis of real equality for women and men, so we can live a new "yes" to life and love, and can *choose* to have children. . . .

Around 1969, when that anti-man, anti-family, bra-burning image of "women's lib" was built up in *Newsweek* and *Time* cover stories exaggerating the antics of the most extremist voices in the movement, I remember the helpless feeling shared by the founding mothers of NOW: "But that's not what we meant, not at all." For us, with our roots in the middle American mainstream and our own fifties' families, equality and the personhood of women never meant destruction of the family, repudiation of marriage, and motherhood, or implacable sexual war against men. That "bra-burning" note shocked and outraged us, and we knew it was wrong—personally and politically—though we never said so, then, as loudly as we should have. We were intimidated by the conformities of the women's movement and the reality of "sisterhood is powerful," as we never would have been by "the enemy." . . .

The new frontier where the issues of the second stage will be joined is, I believe, the family . . . .

On the economic bottom line, after nearly twenty years of the women's movement, it becomes clear that most women are still saddled with the work they used to do in the family . . . in addition to their hard new "male" jobs, at a price of fatigue and stress only superwomen can endure. Or they are facing economic misery in divorce and the loss of whatever power they had through that "female" family role—devalued and sometimes even replaced by other women who got into the men's world and sometimes took away their husbands. . . .

Was it all an illusion, women's movement toward equality—since no matter what we have done or are doing, it's still a men's world, and they call the shots? Not quite, not any longer. But the bridge we have to cross to live that equality we fought for is *the family*.

It is hardly new for women to be concerned with the family, I realize. But weren't feminists supposed to be liberating themselves *from* the family? . . .

I believe that feminism must, in fact, confront the family, albeit in new terms, if the movement is to fulfill its own revolutionary function in modern society. Otherwise it will abort or be put on history's shelf—its real promise and significance obscured, distorted, by its denial of life's realities for too many millions of women. . . .

In the second stage of this struggle that is changing everyone's life, men's and women's needs converge. There are conscious choices now, for men as well as women—to set up their lives in such a way as to achieve a more equitable balance between success in work and gratification in personal life. And here is the missing link, the power that was lacking when women tried to solve these problems by taking it all on themselves as superwomen, the power women did not and will not have, to change the structure of jobs by and for themselves alone. But if young men now need and want self-fulfillment beyond their jobs and the life-grounding women have always had in the family—as much as women now need and want some voice and active power in the world—there will be a new, and sufficient, *combined* force for the second stage.

So this is the other half of Stage Two of the struggle that began with women's movement for equality—men's liberation. . . .

In the second stage, perhaps, the daughters will stop looking for supermen. They've begun to understand that their own superwoman drive and assertion of absolute independence is a mask for that residue of soft need to remain dependent. They have begun to realize that a little dependence is nothing to be afraid of, and that they won't drown in it—they wouldn't have to drive themselves so hard if they let themselves have those feelings once in a while. And they have also begun to see that those young men are just as afraid as they are—maybe more afraid, if they're still expected to be supermen. The sons are just beginning to be able to express those feelings the daughters now know are their life's blood.

I expect my daughter will be a better mother than I was. She won't have my guilts and driven-ness, and the self-doubts that kept me from enjoying those years even more than I did. She will simply have the practical problems. I expect the daughters will work those out. Not even the most rigidly traditional institutions can resist evolutionary change, if the daughters don't give up the dream, if they let the men join them in the parenting and the work of restructuring. They may not be able to have it all, either their way or even my way, all at the same time. But maybe they won't even want to.

BETTY FRIEDAN – A SIMULATED INTERVIEW

1. **What is the feminine mystique?**
   A. The feminine mystique is a concept of femininity that women feel compelled to fulfill.
   B. According to the feminine mystique, a woman's identity derives from the success of her husband and her children.
   C. The feminine mystique requires women to accept their role as housewives and mothers rather than desire opportunities open to men. Women are taught to pity any woman who wants a career, an education, or a role in politics.
   D. The feminine mystique requires women to ignore an internal voice that says, "I want something more than my husband, my children and my home." The feminine mystique does not allow women to dream of a life outside the home.

2. **What role does advertising play in promoting the feminine mystique?**
   A. Women are America's chief consumers. Corporate leaders believe women buy more if they are kept in their position as housewives.
   B. When women remain in their role as housewives they conform to the needs of businessmen who need to sell products. Advertisers create a public image of women necessary to selling household products.
   C. Advertisers exploit a woman's feeling of emptiness by encouraging her to fill her home with the latest products.

3. **Why would a woman limit herself to the life of a housewife?**
   A. American culture does not permit women to satisfy their basic need to grow as human beings. The core problem for women is therefore a problem of identity. Women have no image of themselves in a career outside the home.
   B. The feminine mystique encourages women to ignore the question of their identity. Women grow up denying personal desires and capabilities forbidden by the feminine mystique.
   C. The feminine mystique requires women to renounce personal ambition. Women are only allowed to be ambitious about marriage and motherhood. After marriage and motherhood, women are only permitted to be ambitious for their husbands and their children.
   D. Women are not necessarily fulfilled as housewives and mothers. Many women become restless when the measure of their personal fulfillment is limited to the achievements of their husband and children.

4. How should women change their lives?

   A. Women should pursue fulfillment in careers outside the home. The feminine mystique will be destroyed when women find stimulating and rewarding work outside the home. Women need either a career that can be interrupted for childbearing or an interesting part-time job.

   B. The feminine mystique makes higher education for women unnecessary. Education, however, can save women from the dangers of the feminine mystique.

5. What problems confront women who pursue careers outside the home?

   A. When women enter the workplace they are too often burdened with the same duties they performed as housewives. Housework takes much time.

   B. The double duty of career and family can only be completed at the high price of fatigue and stress.

   C. Women must not carry the sole burden of taking care of the home and raising children. Men must learn to share in household duties.

6. What was wrong with the women's movement in the 1970s?

   A. News stories in the 1970s exaggerated the actions of the most extreme elements of the women's movement. The media portrayed feminists as anti-man and anti-family.

   B. Feminism was too women-centered in the 1970s. Men and women should not be in a state of confrontation; men and women should join together to solve family problems.

7.   How should the women's movement change?

   A. The second stage of the women's movement should focus on achieving real equality for men and women.

   B. The new frontier for the women's movement is the family. Women should not work to liberate themselves from the family. Women must confront the problems of family.

   C. Both women and men should be allowed to gain fulfillment through marriage, children, and career.

   D. Women and men must work together to achieve an equal balance between success in their work and gratification in their personal lives.

STUDENT ACTIVITIES

Vocabulary
Define the following terms before reading the lesson on Friedan.

1. adolescent
2. chauffeur
3. converge
4. domesticity
5. feminine
6. implacable
7. maternal
8. mundane
9. mystique
10. perpetuation
11. polarize
12. sibling

Review

1. Friedan graduated summa cum laude from what college?
2. What did Friedan learn from a survey she sent to her classmates at their fifteen year reunion?
3. What best-selling book written by Friedan brought about profound social change?
4. Why did U.S. Representative Howard Smith propose a law prohibiting discrimination on the basis of sex?
5. What was protected in Title VII of the Civil Rights Act of 1964?
6. What organization did Friedan help create to fight for women's rights?
7. What was the ERA?
8. In what book did Friedan point out that the women's movement was too confrontational?
9. What was a woman's identity based upon according to the feminine mystique?
10. What does the feminine mystique teach a woman to think about other women who want a career or a role in politics?
11. Why did Friedan think the business community preferred women as housewives?
12. How did Friedan think that advertisers took advantage of women?
13. How did Friedan think the feminine mystique would be destroyed?
14. What did Friedan think was the new frontier for the women's movement?
15. Decide whether the following statements are **True** or **False** according to Betty Friedan.
    A. The feminine mystique demands that women dream about a life outside the home.
    B. The feminine mystique allows women to pursue personal ambition outside the home.
    C. Women who work outside the home face a double duty of career and family.
    D. Men must learn to share household duties.
    E. Feminists are anti-man and anti-family.
    F. Feminists should adopt a confrontational attitude toward the male-dominated society.

What do you think?

On a scale of one through five, rate your opinion of the following quotations by Friedan. Write a short statement explaining your rating.

1 – You **strongly agree** with the statement *or* you feel the statement is **admirable** considering the historical circumstances surrounding it.

5 – You **strongly disagree** with the statement *or* you feel the statement is **contemptible** considering the historical circumstances surrounding it.

A. *[Women] were taught to pity the neurotic, unfeminine, unhappy women who wanted to be poets or physicists or presidents.*

B. *We can no longer ignore that voice within women that says: "I want something more than my husband and my children and my home."*

C. *Ideas are not like instincts of the blood that spring into the mind intact. They are communicated by education, by the printed word.*

D. *Magazines today assume women are not interested in ideas.*

E. *A baked potato is not as big as the world, and vacuuming the living room floor—with or without makeup— is not work that takes enough thought or energy to challenge any woman's full capacity.*

F. *Our culture does not permit women to accept or gratify their basic need to grow and fulfill their potentialities as human beings.*

G. *Why is it never said that the really crucial function, the really important role that women serve as housewives is to buy more things for the house? In all the talk of femininity and woman's role, one forgets that the real business of America is business.*

H. *The new frontier where the issues of the second stage will be joined is, I believe, the family.*

I. *After nearly twenty years of the women's movement, it becomes clear that most women are still saddled with the work they used to do in the family . . . in addition to their hard new "male" jobs, at a price of fatigue and stress only superwomen can endure.*

J. *There are conscious choices now, for men as well as women—to set up their lives in such a way as to achieve a more equitable balance between success in work and gratification in personal life.*

K. *Our society forces boys, insofar as it can, to grow up, to endure the pains of growth, to educate themselves to work, to move on. Why aren't girls forced to grow up—to achieve somewhere the core of self that will end the unnecessary dilemma, the mistaken choice between femaleness and humanness that is implied in the feminine mystique?*

CHAPTER 36

THE AMERICAN INDIAN

BACKGROUND

Before Europeans colonized America hundreds of Indian tribes lived within what is today the United States. Indian history is therefore the story of many different groups and individuals exhibiting wide differences in language, religion, custom, and lifestyle. Although Indian history is characterized by diversity, Indians are united in their traditional love of the land, their love of freedom, and their common mistreatment at the hands of the United States government.

All Indian tribes shared the loss of life, land, and human rights at the hands of whites. Before Europeans arrived the estimated Indian population was 10-13 million. Contact with whites led to the near destruction of Indians. By 1890 the Indian population of the United States was only 228,000. Indians had been decimated by disease, the destruction of the buffalo, a growing number of hostile white settlers, and brute military force.

Indians have endured the wholesale denial of human rights in the United States. After first deciding in the 1830s that Indian tribes constituted "dependent" nations, the Supreme Court ruled in the 1880s that the federal government had ultimate control of tribal nations. Indians were therefore not allowed to determine their own destiny. Congress could legislate Indian affairs any way it saw fit. What might be unconstitutional treatment for white Americans was legal when applied to Indians.

Numerous Indian groups joined the civil rights protests of the 1960s, and the struggle for the rights of Indians led to many subsequent legal victories. In 1968 Congress extended the protection of the Constitution and the Bill of Rights to Indians. In the 1970s courts allowed Indian tribes greater self-determination. In the 1980s Congress allowed tribes to generate revenue through gambling. In 1990 a law was passed to protect Indian burial sites.

Indians today are a rapidly growing minority group with improved prosperity. Although many tribes suffer from high levels of unemployment and cultural stereotyping, they have achieved a unique legal status that would have been unimaginable in the nineteenth century.

AMERICAN INDIANS – IN THEIR OWN WORDS

Chief Logan's Lament, 1774

I appeal to any white man to say, if ever he entered Logan's cabin hungry, and he gave him not meat: if ever he came cold and naked, and he cloathed him not. During the course of the last long and bloody war Logan remained idle in his cabin, an advocate for peace. Such was my love for the whites, that my countrymen pointed as they passed, and said, "Logan is the friend of white man." I had even thought to have lived with you, but for the injuries of one man. Colonel Cresap, the last spring, in cold blood, and unprovoked, murdered all the relations of Logan, not even sparing my women and children. There runs not a drop of my blood in the veins of any living creature. This called on me for revenge. I have sought it: I have killed many: I have fully glutted my vengeance: for my country I rejoice at the beams of peace. But do not harbour a thought that mine is the joy of fear. Logan never felt fear. He will not turn on his heel to save his life. Who is there to mourn for Logan?—Not one.

Black Hawk (Sac-Potawatomi), Farewell Speech at the End of the Black Hawk War, 1835

An Indian, who is as bad as the white men, could not live in our nation; he would be put to death, and eat up by the wolves. The white men are bad schoolmasters; they carry false looks, and deal in false actions; they smile in the face of the poor Indian to cheat him; they shake them by the hand to gain their confidence, to make them drunk, to deceive them, and ruin our wives. We told them to let us alone, and keep away from us; but they followed on, and beset our paths, and they coiled themselves among us, like the snake. They poisoned us by their touch. We were not safe. We lived in danger. We were becoming like them, hypocrites and liars, adulterers, lazy drones, all talkers, and no workers.

John Quinney (Mahican), Fourth of July Speech at New York, 1854

The Indian is said to be the ward of the white man, and the negro his slave. Has it ever occurred to you, my friend, that while the negro is increasing and increased by every appliance, the Indian is left to rot and die before the inhumanities of this model republic?

You have your tears and groans and mobs and riots for the individuals of the former, while your indifference of purpose and vacillation of policy is hurrying to extinction whole communities of the latter.

Chief Joseph (Nez Percés), "The Fate of the Nez Percés Tribe, 1879

When I think of our condition my heart is heavy. I see men of my race treated as outlaws and driven from country to country, or shot down like animals.

I know that my race must change. We can not hold our own with the white men as we are. We only ask an even chance to live as other men live.

We ask to be recognized as men. We ask that the same law shall work alike on all men. If the Indian breaks the law, punish him by the law. If the white man breaks the laws, punish him also.

Let me be a free man—free to travel, free to stop, free to work, free to trade where I choose, free to choose my own teachers, free to follow the religion of my fathers, free to think and talk and act for myself—and I will obey every law, or submit to the penalty.

Whenever the white man treats the Indian as they treat each other, then, we will have no more wars. We shall all be alike—brothers of one father and one mother, with one sky above us and one country around us, and one government for all. Then the Great Spirit Chief who rules above will smile upon this land, and send rain to wash out the bloody spots made by brothers' hands from the face of the earth. For this time the Indian race are waiting and praying. I hope that no more groans of wounded men and women will ever go to the ear of the Great Spirit Chief above, and that all people may be one people.

Masse Hadjo (Sioux), "A Defense of the Ghost Dance Religion," 1890

The Indians have never taken kindly to the Christian religion as preached and practiced by whites. Do you know why this is the case? Because the Good Father of all has given us a better religion—a religion that is all good and no bad, a religion that is adapted to our wants. You say if we are good, obey the Ten Commandments and never sin any more, we may be permitted eventually to sit upon a white rock and sing praises to God forevermore, and look down upon our heathen fathers, mothers, brothers and sisters who are howling in hell.

It won't do. The code of morals as practiced by the white race will not compare with the morals of the Indians. We pay no lawyers or preachers, but we have not one-tenth part of the crime that you do. If our Messiah does come we shall not try to force you into our belief. We will never burn innocent women at the stake or pull men to pieces with horses because they refuse to join in our ghost dances. . . . The white man's heaven is repulsive to the Indian nature, and if the white man's hell suits you, why, you keep it. I think there will be white rogues enough to fill it.

Carlos Montezuma (Apache), "Let My People Go," 1915

It is appalling and inexplicable that the palefaces have taken all of the Indian's property—the continent of America—which was all he had in the world. The Indian asks for public school, college, and university education for his children. To refuse such a noble request would be as cruel as to give a stone when he asks for bread. Will the department defray the expenses of any college or university Indian students? The Indian Bureau's motto seems to be, "Eighth grade and no more." And therefore we may assume that the Indian Department does not want the Indian educated. It may be wise, and is afraid that they will make too many lawyers who will fight to a finish. It may be that the Indian Bureau fears something may happen from the

Indian's knowledge of doing something.

To dominate a race you do not want to educate them. All one needs to do is to make them believe black is white and get them to believe everything you do is all right. . . .

The reservation Indians are prisoners; they cannot do anything for themselves. . . . There is no fear of the general public; they are our friends. When they find out that we are not free they will free us. We have a running chance with the public, but no chance with the Indian Bureau.

The abolishment of the Indian Bureau will not only benefit the Indians, but the country will derive more money annually from the Indians than the Government has appropriated to them. Why? Because by doing away with the Indian Bureau you stop making paupers and useless beings and start making of producers and workers.

Luther Standing Bear (Sioux), "What the Indian Means to America," 1933

The white man does not understand the Indian for the reason that he does not understand America. He is too far removed from its formative processes. The roots of the tree of his life have not yet grasped the rock and soil. The white man is still troubled with primitive fears; he still has in his consciousness the perils of this frontier continent, some of its fastnesses not yet having yielded to his questing footsteps and inquiring eyes. He shudders still with the memory of the loss of his forefathers upon its scorching deserts and forbidding mountain-tops. The man from Europe is still a foreigner and an alien. And he still hates the man who questioned his path across the continent.

But in the Indian the spirit of the land is still vested; it will be until other men are able to divine and meet its rhythm. . . .

The attempted transformation of the Indian by the white man and the chaos that has resulted are but the fruits of the white man's disobedience of a fundamental and spiritual law. The pressure that has been brought to bear upon the native people, since the cessation of armed conflict, in the attempt to force conformity of custom and habit has caused a reaction more destructive than war, and the injury has not only affected the Indian, but has extended to the white population as well. Tyranny, stupidity, and lack of vision have brought about the situation now alluded to as the "Indian Problem."

There is, I insist, no Indian problem as created by the Indian himself. Every problem that exists today in regard to the native population is due to the white man's cast of mind, which is unable, at least reluctant, to seek understanding and achieve adjustment in a new and a significant environment into which it has so recently come.

The white man excused his presence here by saying that he had been guided by the will of his God; and in so saying absolved himself of all responsibility for his appearance in a land occupied by other men.

American Indian Chicago Conference, *Declaration of Indian Purpose,* **1961**

We believe in the inherent right of all people to retain spiritual and cultural values, and that the free exercise of these values is necessary to the normal development of any people. Indians exercised this inherent right to live their own lives for thousands of years before the white man came and took their lands. It is a more complex world in which Indians live today, but the Indian people who first settled in the New World and built the great civilizations which only now are being dug out of the past, long ago demonstrated that they could master complexity.

We believe that the history and development of America show that the Indian has been subjected to duress, stifling influence, unwarranted pressures, and self-destroying policies which have produced uncertainty, frustration, and despair. Only when the public understands these conditions and is moved to take action toward the formulation and adoption of sound and consistent policies and programs will these destroying factors be removed and the Indian resume his normal growth and make his maximum contribution to modern society.

We believe in the future of a greater America, an America which we were the first to love, where life, liberty, and the pursuit of happiness will be a reality. In such a future, with Indians and all other Americans cooperating, a cultural climate will be created in which the Indian people will grow and develop as members of a free society. . . .

The time came when the Indian people were no longer the masters of their situation. Their life ways survived subject to the will of a dominant sovereign power. This is said, not in a spirit of complaint; we understand that in the lives of all nations of people, there are times of plenty and times of famine. But we do speak out in a plea for understanding.

When we go before the American people . . . and ask for material assistance in developing our resources and developing our opportunities, we pose a moral problem which cannot be left unanswered. For the problem we raise affects the standing which our nation sustains before world opinion.

Our situation cannot be relieved by appropriated funds alone, though it is equally obvious that without capital investment and funded services, solutions will be delayed. Nor will the passage of time lessen the complexities which beset a people moving toward new meaning and purpose.

The answers we seek are not commodities to be purchased; neither are they evolved automatically through the passing of time.

The effort to place social adjustment on a money-time interval scale which has characterized Indian administration, has resulted in unwanted pressure and frustration.

When Indians speak of the continent they yielded, they are not referring only to the loss of some millions of acres in real estate. They have in mind that the land supported a universe of things they knew, valued, and loved.

With that continent gone, except for the few poor parcels they still retain, the basis of life is precariously held, but they mean to hold the scraps and parcels as earnestly as any small nation or ethnic group was ever determined to hold to identity and survival.

What we ask of America is not charity, not paternalism, even when benevolent. We ask only that the nature of our situation be recognized and made the basis of policy and action.

In short, the Indians ask for assistance, technical and financial, for the time needed, however long that may be, to regain in the America of the space age some measure of the adjustment they enjoyed as the original possessors of their native land.

Clyde Warrior (Ponca), "The War on Poverty," 1967

In recent days . . . some of us have been thinking that perhaps the damage done to our community by forced assimilation and directed acculturation programs was minor compared to the situation in which our children find themselves. There is a whole generation of Indian children who are growing up in the American school system. They still look to their relatives, my generation and my fathers, to see if they are worthy people. Their judgment and definition of what is worthy is now the judgment which most Americans make. They judge worthiness as competence and competence as worthiness. And I am afraid my fathers and I do not fare well in the light of this situation and judgment. Our children are learning that their people are not worthy and thus that they individually are not worthy. But even if by some stroke of good fortune prosperity was handed to us on a platter, that still would not soften the negative judgment our youngsters have of their people and themselves. As you know, people who feel themselves to be unworthy and feel they cannot escape this unworthiness turn to drink and crime and self-destructive acts. Unless there is some way that we as Indian individuals and communities can prove ourselves competent and worthy in the eyes of our youngsters there will be a generation of Indians grown to adulthood whose reactions to their situation will make previous social ills seem like a Sunday school picnic.

For the sake of our children, for the sake of the spiritual and material well-being of our total community, we must be able to demonstrate competence to ourselves. For the sake of our psychic stability as well as our physical well-being, we must be free men and exercise free choices. We must make decisions about our own destinies. We must be able to learn and profit by our own mistakes. Only then can we become competent and prosperous communities. We must be free in the most literal sense of the word, not sold or coerced into accepting programs for our own good, not of our own making or choice. Too much of what passes for grassroots democracy on the American scene is really a slick job of salesmanship. It is not hard for sophisticated administrators to sell tinsel and glitter programs to simple people, programs which are not theirs, which they do not understand, and which cannot but ultimately fail to contribute to already strong feelings of inadequacy.

THE AMERICAN INDIAN – A SIMULATED INTERVIEW

1. **What was the importance of land in Indian history?**
   A. Indian land was sacred. Indian land has witnessed a long history of events, both happy and sad. Whites who took control of the land are haunted by the ghosts of Indian history.
   B. The land was all that Indians had in this world. When whites took away the land they took away the Indian way of life.
   C. The concept of "yours" and "mine" was foreign to most Indians. Indians had no concept of marking areas of land for individual or group ownership.

2. **What role did freedom play in Indian history?**
   A. Indians were the original Americans. Indians believed in a community based on the idea of life, liberty, and the pursuit of happiness.
   B. Indians lived a life of pure freedom until white settlers arrived and took away their land.
   C. Although Indians lost their freedom when they were defeated by whites, they still fought for a life of freedom and equality under American law.
   D. Indians have always fought for the inherent right to protect their spiritual and cultural values. Indians exercised this right for thousands of years until whites took away their land.

3. **How did government policies during the first two hundred years of United States history change the Indian way of life?**
   A. The Indian population was decimated.
   B. Indians lost their freedom and independence.
   C. Indians were denied their rights.

4. **Should Indians have trusted the United States government?**
   A. Historically, whites could not be trusted. Whites treated Indians like outlaws and shot them down like animals. Whites violated every treaty signed with Indians.
   B. Indians could not trust the government because government policies destroyed the Indian way of life. The government caused Indians to live with uncertainty, frustration, and despair.

5. **What major problems confronted Indians in the twentieth century?**
   A. Indians were handicapped by crippling stereotypes.
   B. Indians suffered from a lack of understanding by non-Indians.
   C. Indian society suffered from a high level of alcoholism.
   D. Indians were divided into factions.
   E. Indians lost their self-esteem.

6. **Why did Indians have a difficult time joining white society?**
   A. Indians were prisoners on the reservation; they could not do anything for themselves. The Bureau of Indian Affairs did not allow Indians to control their own destiny.
   B. The code of morality practiced by whites never compared to the morality practiced by Indians. The religion of whites was repulsive to Indians.
   C. Whites were unwilling to educate Indians. The motto of the Bureau of Indian Affairs seemed to be "eighth grade and no more." Whites did not want Indians educated because Indian lawyers would then be available to fight the policies of the Indian Bureau. In addition, whites could not dominate Indians if Indians were educated.
   D. The attempt to destroy Indian culture led to a reaction against whites in the Indian world. White tyranny, stupidity, and lack of vision created what whites called the "Indian problem."
   E. History books filled young minds with false ideas about Indians. Indians were portrayed as uncivilized underachievers who were inferior to whites. Indians not only lost their land, they lost their culture and their history. American society saw Indians as curiosities.
   F. Indian children growing up in public schools learned that Indians were not worthy of respect. People who felt they were unworthy turned to alcohol and crime.

7. **Since the 1960s what demands have Indians made to improve their lives?**
   A. Demands have been made for children to be taught that Indians are competent and worthy of respect. Indians have tried to develop a pride in their cultural traditions.
   B. In 1972 a march on Washington known as the Trail of Broken Treaties led to the presentation of specific Indian demands. These demands, known as the *Twenty Points*, presented a new framework for considering the status of Indian tribes. A few significant items in the *Twenty Points* are listed below:
      1. Indians should be allowed to govern themselves. The Bureau of Indian Affairs should be abolished. The 1871 ban on treaty-making with Indians should be repealed, and Indian relations with the federal government should be decided by treaty. The jurisdiction that state courts have over Indians should be ended.
      2. United States treaty violations of the past should be reviewed. All past violations should be corrected.
      3. Congress should protect the religious freedom and the cultural integrity of Indians.
      4. The Indian land base should be doubled.
      5. Indian tribes should be given criminal jurisdiction over non-Indians on the reservations.

STUDENT ACTIVITIES

Vocabulary

Define the following terms before reading the lesson on the American Indian.

1. acculturation	6. hypocrite	11. repulsive
2. assimilation	7. inexplicable	12. rogue
3. competence	8. molestation	13. solitude
4. defray	9. pauper	14. vacillation
5. drone	10. precarious	

Review

1. In what three ways are diverse Indian groups united?
2. What factors led to the decline of the American Indian population?
3. What ruling did the Supreme Court make in the 1830s about the status of Indian tribes?
4. What ruling did the Supreme Court make in the 1880s about the status of Indian tribes?
5. What legal victories have Indians made from 1968 to the present?
6. What status does Indian land hold in Indian culture?
7. What happened to Indians when their land was taken away?
8. In what three ways did U.S. government policies change the Indian way of life?
9. What problems have confronted Indians in the twentieth century?
10. Why did Indians feel that whites did not want Indians to receive an education?
11. What did Indians think was the cause of the "Indian problem"?
12. How do Indians feel they have been portrayed in history books?
13. What do Indians believe is the cause of alcoholism, crime, and self-destructive acts?
14. Why have Indians called for the abolishment of the Bureau of Indian Affairs?
15. What are the *Twenty Points*?
16. What demands did the *Twenty Points* make about the (1) Bureau of Indian Affairs, (2) past treaty violations, (3) religious freedom, (4) tribal jurisdiction over crime, and (5) Indian land?
17. Decide whether the following statements are **True** or **False** according to American Indians.
    A. The concept of "yours" and "mine" was foreign to Indians at one time.
    B. Indians lived a life of pure freedom until white settlers arrived.
    C. U.S. government policies have caused Indians to live with uncertainty, frustration, and despair.
    D. The Bureau of Indian Affairs has historically helped Indians maintain their way of life.
    E. Indians should develop pride in their cultural traditions.

What do you think?
On a scale of one through five, rate your opinion of the following quotations by American Indians. Write a short statement explaining your rating.

1 – You **strongly agree** with the statement *or* you feel the statement is **admirable** considering the historical circumstances surrounding it.
5 – You **strongly disagree** with the statement *or* you feel the statement is **contemptible** considering the historical circumstances surrounding it.

A. *An Indian, who is as bad as the white men, could not live in our nation; he would be put to death, and eat up by the wolves.* (Black Hawk)
B. *Every part of the soil is sacred, in the estimation of my people. Every hillside, every valley, every plain and grove, has been hallowed by some sad or happy event in days long vanished.* (John Quinney)
C. *I know that my race must change. We can not hold our own with the white men as we are. We only ask an even chance to live as other men live.* (Chief Joseph)
D. *Let me be a free man—free to travel, free to stop, free to work, free to trade where I choose, free to choose my own teachers, free to follow the religion of my fathers, free to think and talk and act for myself—and I will obey every law, or submit to the penalty.* (Chief Joseph)
E. *Tyranny, stupidity, and lack of vision have brought about the situation now alluded to as the "Indian Problem."* (Luther Standing Bear)
F. *We believe in the inherent right of all people to retain spiritual and cultural values, and that the free exercise of these values is necessary to the normal development of any people.* (Declaration of Indian Purpose)
G. *We believe in the future of a greater America, an America which we were the first to love, where life, liberty, and the pursuit of happiness will be a reality.* (Declaration of Indian Purpose)
H. *Our children are learning that their people are not worthy and thus that they individually are not worthy.* (Clyde Warrior)
I. *For the sake of our children, for the sake of the spiritual and material well-being of our total community, we must be able to demonstrate competence to ourselves.* (Clyde Warrior)
J. *Sell the country? Why not sell the air, the clouds, the great sea?* (Tecumseh, 1810)
K. *This we know: The earth does not belong to man, man belongs to the Earth. All things are connected like the blood that unites us all: Man did not weave the web of life, he is but a strand in it. Whatever he does to the web he does to himself.* (attributed to Chief Seattle, 1852)
L. *The white man knows how to make everything, but he does not know how to distribute it.* (Sitting Bull on seeing the slums of American cities, 1885)

CHAPTER 37

CÉSAR CHÁVEZ

BACKGROUND

Born to immigrant parents in Yuma, Arizona, César Chávez (1927-1993) grew up as a migrant farm worker picking carrots, cotton, and grapes. He attended almost forty elementary schools while his family moved around looking for work. After he dropped out of the seventh grade he worked full-time in the fields, an experience that gave him first-hand knowledge of the shameful conditions farm workers encountered. As an adult, Chávez dedicated himself to changing conditions for farm workers. Today he is recognized as one of the most important labor leaders in United States history.

After serving in the U.S. Navy during World War II, Chávez moved to California where he joined the Community Service Organization (CSO). His work in the CSO included helping Mexican-Americans register to vote and serving as their advocate before government agencies. Although Chávez eventually became national director of the CSO, he resigned in 1962 to devote himself full-time to organizing a union for farm workers.

By 1965 Chávez had organized almost 1,700 families and had convinced two large California growers to raise the wages of migrant workers. He next led a strike, known as La Huelga, against California grape growers. La Huelga lasted five years and included a successful national boycott of grapes. Peaceful demonstrations accompanied by the seventeen million people who joined the boycott forced grape growers to sign a contract in 1970 granting rights and higher wages to farm workers. La Huelga's success was only the first of many successful boycotts led by Chávez.

Chávez was an extremely religious man who believed in self-sacrifice. He lived most of his life penniless and without property, giving everything to help his union, the United Farm Workers. He often fasted, which he viewed as a form of individual sacrifice, to bring attention to his cause.

In addition to fighting for farm workers, Chávez also helped inspire the Chicano movement, creating a new consciousness among Mexican-Americans of all classes. After he died in his sleep of natural causes California state flags were lowered to half-mast and messages poured in from heads of church and state, including Pope John Paul II and President Bill Clinton. Today his legacy is not only marked by the numerous schools, public buildings, parks, and streets named after him, but also by the many lives he improved.

CÉSAR CHÁVEZ – IN HIS OWN WORDS

César Chávez: Autobiography of La Causa, **1975** [As told to Jacques Levy]
I like the whole idea of sacrifice to do things. If they are done that way, they are more lasting. If they cost more, then we will value them more.

If you're outraged at conditions, then you can't possibly be free or happy until you devote all your time to changing them and do nothing but that. The affluence in this country is our biggest trap, because we can't change anything if we want to hold on to a good job, a good way of life, and avoid sacrifice. . . .

Only my financial security had me tied up and kept me from moving. There was my wife, Helen, and I knew it would be asking a lot of her to give up what we had. Here I was already thirty-five, with my first steady job in one location, after years of constantly drifting from one place to another, first as a migrant hunting for work and then as a CSO organizer. We had about twelve hundred dollars in the bank that wouldn't last six months if I left my job. And more importantly there were our eight children, the oldest thirteen and the two youngest only four and two and a half.

Finally one day I said, "We can't organize farm workers like this. I can talk about how bad conditions are for them, how much I've done for them, and how much I'd like to do, and I can stay here and keep my job. Or we give up the paycheck, nobody tells us what to do, and we organize the way we want to do it."

So I resigned my job and set out to found a union. At first I was frightened, very frightened. But by the time I had missed the fourth paycheck and found things were still going, that the moon was still there and the sky and the flowers, I began to laugh. I really began to feel free. It was one of my biggest triumphs in terms of finding myself and of being able to discipline myself.

The need for radical change is great and urgent, in the cities as well as in the fields, and if we don't succeed, violence will spread. Other movements will try to do it with violence.

But in seeking social change, I am positive nonviolence is the way, morally and tactically, especially in our society where those in power resort to clubs, tear gas, and guns. I have seen nonviolence work many times in many ways. When we organized California's vineyards, for example, it was the grower's violence, their manipulation of the police and the courts, that helped win support for our cause.

We can remain nonviolent because people outside the Movement by and large don't want violence. By remaining nonviolent in the face of violence, we win them to our side, and that's what makes the strength. And we organize that strength to fight for change. . . .

[When I was young my mother] gave us a lot of consejos—advice. She didn't wait until something went wrong, nor was she scolding when she was doing it. It was part of the training. At first I didn't understand, but she would make it easy for us. She would say, "He who never listens to consejos will never grow to be old." . . .

When I look back, I see her sermons had tremendous impact on me. I didn't know it was nonviolence then, but after reading Gandhi, St. Francis, and other exponents of nonviolence, I began to clarify that in my mind. Now that I'm older I see she is nonviolent, if anybody is, both by word and deed. She would always talk about not fighting. Despite a culture where you're not a man if you don't fight back, she would say, "No, it's best to turn the other cheek. God gave you senses like eyes and mind and tongue, and you can get out of anything." She would say, "It takes two to fight." That was her favorite. "It takes two to fight, and one can't do it alone." She had all kinds of proverbs for that. "It's better to say that he ran from here than to say he died here." When I was young I didn't realize the wisdom in her words, but it has been proved to me so many times since. Today I appreciate the advice, and I use quite a few of the dichos, especially in Spanish. . . .

I remember her story of the stone freezing in the boy's hand. It was a very disobedient son who came home drunk and got real mad at his mother. He picked up a rock and was about to throw it at her when it froze to his hand. Her stories were about obedience and honesty and some of the virtues. There were others that dealt with miracles. The range was very wide. . . .

When we apply Gandhi's philosophy of nonviolence, it really forces us to think, really forces us to work hard. But it has power. It attracts the support of the people. I've learned that, if any movement is on the move, violence is the last thing wanted. Violence only seems necessary when people are desperate; frustration often leads to violence.

For example, a supermarket boycott is an effective nonviolent weapon. Fire is not. When a fire destroys a supermarket, the company collects the insurance and rebuilds the store bigger and better, and also marks off the loss on its income tax. But picket lines take away customers and reduce business, and there is no way for the store to compensate for that. It is driven by sheer economics to want to avoid picket lines.

Gandhi described his tactics as moral jujitsu—always hitting the opposition off balance, but keeping his principles. His tactics of civil disobedience haven't hit this country on a massive scale, but they will. Anybody who comes out with the right way of doing it is going to throw the government into a real uproar. If they have a good issue, and they find a good vehicle for civil disobedience, they're going to be devastating. . . .

Although my mother opposed violence, I think the thing she really cracked down on the most was being selfish. She made us share everything we had. If we had an apple or a tiny piece of candy, we had to cut it into five pieces. . . .

She also taught us never to lend money to our brothers or sisters. "If you were really brothers, you wouldn't let money come between you. You'd trust them." So instead of lending, we'd give them the money. Even today, none of us really cares much about money. We never make loans. If we have it, we give it. . . .

Since those days [of going to church with my family], my need for religion has deepened. Today I don't think that I could base my will to struggle on cold economics or on some political doctrine. I don't think there would be enough to sustain me. For me the base must be faith.

It's not necessary to have a religion to act selflessly. I know many agnostics who are more religious in their own way than most people who claim to be believers. While most people drawn toward liberalism or radicalism leave the church, I went the other way. I drew closer to the church the more I learned and understood.

To me, religion is a most beautiful thing. And over the years, I have come to realize that all religions are beautiful. Your religion just happens to depend a lot on your upbringing and your culture.

For me, Christianity happens to be a natural source of faith. . . .

Because my mother was illiterate, she made us go to school She would say, "I didn't learn, but you can learn, so you have to go." Even if we were in a place only one or two or three days, we'd go. Once Richard, Rita, and I counted the schools we each attended. The total was about thirty-seven, and I went to most of them. From the accumulation of all the things we had to go through, I can see now that we were really pushed back, beaten back, that education had nothing to do with our way of life.

School was just a nightmare. Probably the one I hated the most was in Fresno where Richard and I were the only two Mexicans in the whole school. When we went to the principal's office to register, we had to stand there almost all morning while he worked.

Later we listened to him on the phone saying, "Well, we've got these kids. I don't know what to do with them." Then he said, "Oh, yea, they're in the fourth grade, but they couldn't do that work." I thought to myself, how does he know I can't do that work?

And I heard him say things like, "What will we do with them? You wouldn't want them in your class."—right in front of us! I don't think he really gave a damn. He didn't even realize what he was doing, which probably hurt more than if he did it calculatingly.

This happened many times. They would say, "the Mexicans," or "Yea, they're farm workers," or "these farm workers." Always their tone dripped with contempt.

Then when I came to class, I was frightened. I didn't know the lesson. I was given a seat, and the next morning I wasn't sure if that was really my seat. I was so frightened I was afraid to even ask the teacher for permission to go to the restroom. I didn't dare ask very often, as the kids laughed at my accent, the way I talked. . . .

We had a very strong commitment to civil rights. But if we wanted civil rights for us, then we certainly had to respect the rights of blacks, Jews, and other minorities. . . .

That's why today we oppose some of this La Raza business so much. We know what it does. When La Raza means or implies racism, we don't support it. But if it means our struggle, our dignity, or our cultural roots, then we're for it. I guess many times people don't know what they mean by La Raza, but we can't be against racism on the one hand and for it on the other. . . .

If someone commits violence against us, it is much better—if we can—not to react against the violence, but to react in such a way as to get closer to our goal. People don't like to see a nonviolent movement subjected to violence, and there's a lot of support across the country for nonviolence. That's the key point we have going for us. We can turn the world if we can do it nonviolently.

So, if we can just show people how they can organize nonviolently, we can't fail. It has never failed when it's been tried. If the effort gets out of hand, it's from lack of discipline.

One of the most powerful nonviolent weapons is the economic boycott. Alone, the farm workers have no economic power; but with the help of the public they can develop the economic power to counter that of the growers.

We started the grape boycott helter skelter in October 1965, about a month after the strike started. We had to organize the people first, so they could be more effective and more disciplined. Then, in November, we started putting picket lines wherever the grapes went. We began to send the people to San Francisco and Los Angeles and to have them follow the truckloads of grapes. . . .

To us the boycott of grapes was the most near-perfect of nonviolent struggles, because nonviolence also requires mass involvement. The boycott demonstrated to the whole country, the whole world, what people can do by nonviolent action.

Nonviolence in the abstract is a very difficult thing to comprehend or explain. I'd read a lot, but all of it was in the abstract. It's difficult to carry the message to people who aren't involved. Nonviolence must be explained in context.

People equate nonviolence with inaction—with not doing anything—and it's not that at all. It's exactly the opposite.

In his autobiography, Malcolm X said, "I believe it's a crime for anyone who is being brutalized to continue to accept that brutality without doing something to defend himself. If that's how Christian philosophy is interpreted, if that's what Gandhian philosophy teaches, well then I will call them criminal philosophies."

But Gandhi never said not to do anything. He said exactly the opposite. He said, "Do something! Offer your life!" He said, "If you really want to do something, be willing to die for it." That's asking for the maximum contribution. . . .

Nonviolence is action. Like anything else, though, it's got to be organized. There must be rules. There must be people following.

The whole essence of nonviolent action is getting a lot of people involved, vast numbers doing little things. It's difficult to get people involved in a picket line, because it takes their time. But any time a person can be persuaded not to eat a grape—and we persuaded millions not to eat grapes—that's involvement, that's the most direct action, and it's set up in such a way that everybody can participate.

Nonviolence also has one big demand—the need to be creative, to develop strategy. . . .

Strategy for nonviolence takes a tremendous amount of our time—strategy against the opposition, and strategy to strengthen our support. We can't let people get discouraged. If there's no progress, they say nonviolence doesn't work. They begin to go each and everywhere. And it's only when they are desperate that people think violence is necessary.

Of course, it isn't. If any movement is on the move, violence is the last thing that's wanted.

If we can develop some confidence in an organizer's ability to organize, the organizer's tendency to use violence is much less. Persons who don't have any confidence get discouraged and then get into the trap of thinking that violence is the cure-all. But once that first act of violence is committed, they get on the defensive. And no one wins, that I know of, on the defensive. For example, if they get arrested for violence, then they must redirect their efforts from taking on the opposition to defending themselves.

Many times the leadership, or movements, lose sight of their goal. They are attacked personally and make that the big issue. I've seen the best leaders take off on their own personal problems. It's natural. I don't know how many times I haven't been able to avoid it myself. But we must try, because the people out there are not there because of my problems or because of how I feel, they're there because they want some changes in their lives.

Naturally, nonviolence takes time. but poverty has been with us since the beginning of time. We just have to work for improvement. I despise exploitation and I want change, but I'm willing to pay the price in terms of time. There's a Mexican saying, "Hay más tiempo que vida"—There's more time than life. We've got all the time in the world. . . .

Nonviolence has the power to attract people and to generate power. That's what happened to Gandhi. Besides millions of Indians, he had many Englishmen, both in England and even India siding with him.

By and large, people oppose violence. So when government or growers use violence against us, we strategize around it. We can respond nonviolently, because that swings people to our side, and that gives us our strength.

First, of course, the workers have to understand nonviolence. Gandhi once said he'd rather have a man be violent than be a coward. I agree. If he's a coward, then what good is he for anyone? But it is our job to see he's not a coward. That's really the beginning point of our training.

And while the philosophy of nonviolence covers physical, verbal, and moral behavior, we haven't achieved that goal. If we can achieve it, we're saints—which we're not. We're still working on eliminating physical violence, though that isn't all, by any stretch of the imagination. After workers begin to understand physical nonviolence among people, then we also apply it to property and go on from there.

It's like a leader marching at the head of a column, going up and down hills. Pretty soon there are forks and cross-streets, and the leader can't be followed because they can't see him. They don't know where he went. The important thing is to bring them along. The important thing is not to get lost.

Love is the most important ingredient in nonviolent work—love the opponent—but we really haven't learned yet how to love the growers. I think we've learned how not to hate them, and maybe love comes in stages. If we're full of hatred, we can't really do our work. Hatred saps all that strength and energy we need to plan. Of course, we can learn how to love the growers more easily after they sign contracts.

CÉSAR CHÁVEZ – A SIMULATED INTERVIEW

1. **Why should people commit themselves to fighting for civil rights and human rights?**
   A. People who are outraged at bad conditions should not feel free and happy until they are devoting all their time to making things better. The biggest trap to changing things in the United States is that too many people want to hang on to a good job and a good way of life. They do not want to sacrifice to make things better.
   B. Everyone should be treated with justice, fairness, dignity, and equality. When basic rights are denied, people of conscience should commit themselves to changing conditions. For example, any movement that promotes racism should not be supported.

2. **How are migrant farm workers denied their rights?**
   A. Farm workers are exploited by the growers.
      1. They live in wretched farm camps receiving meager wages for backbreaking work.
      2. They are the victims of racism, and their livelihood is determined by corrupt labor contractors.
      3. They do not have clean drinking water, access to portable toilets, lunch breaks, or short rest breaks.
      4. They are not entitled to the minimum wage, unemployment insurance, adequate housing, or health insurance. Pensions and paid vacations are a dream.
      5. Their children seldom have the chance to finish high school.
      6. They are trapped in a cycle of poverty. They work harder and die younger than any other class of people in the United States.
      7. Growers use pesticides and nitrate-containing fertilizers that cause cancer and kill farm workers and their families. Not only are chemicals sometimes sprayed directly on farm workers, the chemicals leach into the water supply.
   B. Farm workers have very little with which to defend themselves. They do not have the legal right to organize or vote for collective bargaining. A farm worker's union is needed to end the suffering and poverty.

3. **What actions are necessary for the success of a farm workers' union?**
   A. Strikes against growers are necessary even though they may fail. Although farm workers have strength in numbers, they have little money. Growers also replace strikers with imported Mexican workers. These problems, however, should not keep farm workers from going on strike.
   B. Farm workers should take action to win outside help from sympathetic clergy, university students, journalists, and political figures.

C. Farm workers should use nonviolent marches and demonstrations to generate publicity from involving people sympathetic to the farm worker's cause. This publicity will force growers to meet the demands of farm workers. California agribusiness, the largest industry in California, is dependent on Mexican-American workers and can be forced to give in to their demands.

D. The government should pass an Agricultural Labor Relations Act. Government legislation offers the best solution for the problems of farm workers.

E. A farm worker's union should be built in the fields rather than from the work of some remote labor leader.

4. Why is nonviolence the best way to change society?

A. Violence does not help a cause. Violence is a result of desperation and frustration. People who lack confidence and get discouraged start thinking that violence will solve all their problems. If they commit an act of violence, they end up on the defensive. People who are on the defensive cannot win.

B. Nonviolence is the best way to convince people to support a movement for change. People outside a movement do not want violence and can be convinced to support a cause that remains nonviolent. If a nonviolent movement is attacked with violence, the general public will support the nonviolent movement and give it the power it needs for success.

C. Nonviolence forces people to think, to work hard, and to make sacrifices. People who sacrifice for a cause will achieve their goals with longer lasting effects.

D. Nonviolence allows people fighting for a cause to use Gandhi's tactics of moral jujitsu. People should stay true to moral principles while hitting the opposition when it is off balance.

5. What is necessary for the success of a nonviolent movement?

A. The essence of nonviolence is to get a lot of people involved in trying to change unjust conditions. A boycott of grapes is therefore an almost perfect example of nonviolent action.

B. People in a nonviolent movement should understand that nonviolence does not mean inaction. Nonviolence is the opposite of doing nothing. People who use nonviolent tactics must be creative in their strategy.

C. People leading a nonviolent movement should not get discouraged. They should not be concerned with personal attacks or let personal problems get in the way of improving unjust conditions.

D. Love is the most important ingredient in a nonviolent movement. People committed to a cause should learn to love their opponent. Hate only drains the strength and energy needed for other things.

STUDENT ACTIVITIES

Vocabulary
Define the following terms before reading the lesson on Chávez.

1. affluence	7. contempt	13. jujitsu
2. agnostic	8. contract	14. La Raza
3. boycott	9. *dichos*	15. manipulation
4. compensate	10. doctrine	16. picket line
5. comprehend	11. exploitation	17. radicalism
6. *consejos*	12. illiterate	

Review
1. How did Chávez and his family earn a living when he was young?
2. How many elementary schools did Chávez attend?
3. When did Chávez drop out of school?
4. What work did Chávez do for the Community Service Organization?
5. Why did Chávez resign as the national director of the CSO?
6. What was La Huelga?
7. What product was boycotted nationally during La Huelga?
8. What action did Chávez often use as a form of individual sacrifice to bring attention to his cause?
9. What movement, partially inspired by Chávez, created a new consciousness among Mexican-Americans of all classes?
10. What were two reasons Chávez believed farm worker strikes might fail?
11. Why did Chávez believe a boycott of grapes was an almost perfect example of nonviolent action?
12. What did Chávez believe was the most important ingredient in a nonviolent movement?
13. Decide whether the following statements are **True** or **False** according to César Chávez.
    A. Too many Americans are unwilling to sacrifice their jobs or their way of life to make things better.
    B. All people should be treated with justice, fairness, dignity, and equality.
    C. Farm workers live in unjust conditions working for meager wages.
    D. Farm workers need a union to end their suffering and poverty.
    E. Growers use pesticides and nitrate-containing fertilizers that cause cancer and kill farm workers and their families.
    F. Strikes against growers may fail and are therefore unnecessary.
    G. Although agribusiness is the largest industry in California, it can be forced to give in to the demands of farm workers.
    H. Government legislation offers little hope of solving the problems of farm workers.
    I. Nonviolence is the best way to convince people to support a movement for change.

What do you think?
On a scale of one through five, rate your opinion of the following quotations by Chávez. Write a short statement explaining your rating.

1 – You **strongly agree** with the statement *or* you feel the statement is **admirable** considering the historical circumstances surrounding it.
5 – You **strongly disagree** with the statement *or* you feel the statement is **contemptible** considering the historical circumstances surrounding it.

A. *If you're outraged at conditions, then you can't possibly be free or happy until you devote all your time to changing them and do nothing but that.*
B. *The affluence in this country is our biggest trap, because we can't change anything if we want to hold on to a good job, a good way of life, and avoid sacrifice.*
C. *By remaining nonviolent in the face of violence, we win [people outside the movement] to our side, and that's what makes the strength.*
D. *To me, religion is a most beautiful thing. And over the years, I have come to realize that all religions are beautiful.*
E. *I like the whole idea of sacrifice to do things. If they are done that way, they are more lasting. If they cost more, then we will value them more.*
F. *We had a very strong commitment to civil rights. But if we wanted civil rights for us, then we certainly had to respect the rights of blacks, Jews, and other minorities.*
G. *Persons who don't have any confidence get discouraged and then get into the trap of thinking that violence is the cure-all. But once that first act of violence is committed, they get on the defensive. And no one wins, that I know of, on the defensive.*
H. *Love is the most important ingredient in nonviolent work—love the opponent.*
I. *The whole essence of nonviolent action is getting a lot of people involved, vast numbers doing little things.*
J. *I despise exploitation and I want change, but I'm willing to pay the price in terms of time. There's a Mexican saying, "Hay más tiempo que vida."—"There's more time than life."*
K. *No union movement is worth the death of one farm worker or his child or one grower and his child.*
L. *It's tragic that [the growers] have not yet come to understand that we are in a new age, a new era. No longer can a couple of white men sit together and write the destinies of all the Chicanos and the Filipino workers in this valley.*
M. *In the old days, miners would carry birds with them to warn against poison gas. Hopefully, the birds would die before the miners. Farm workers are society's canaries.*

PART 9

PREPARING
FOR A NEW CENTURY

CHAPTER 38

RACHEL CARSON

BACKGROUND

Rachel Carson (1907-1964) grew up in a Pennsylvania family that taught her to love books and nature. As a young woman she went to the Pennsylvania College for Women to study English. She eventually changed her major to biology and at Johns Hopkins University earned a graduate degree in zoology. Her diverse education gave her a background in English and science that later helped her write scientifically accurate books in a literary style.

After her father died in 1935, Carson provided financial support for her mother and the orphaned children of one of her sisters. Working as a biologist for the U.S. Bureau of Fisheries, she wrote conservation bulletins and wildlife booklets for the government. In her spare time she wrote books expressing her strong emotional attachment to the ocean. In 1941 she published *Under the Sea Wind*, the first book in her well-known trilogy about the sea. After her second book *The Sea Around Us* became a bestseller Carson was financially independent and decided to devote herself to writing full time. *The Edge of the Sea*, her last book about the sea, was published in 1955.

In the late 1950s Carson developed an interest in studying the slow disappearance of birds. She discovered that pesticides such as DDT were polluting the air, soil, and water in a way that was not only killing birds, but threatening human beings. This discovery prompted her to spend four years researching and writing *Silent Spring*, a book she finished despite suffering from a cancer that would eventually kill her. When *Silent Spring* was published in 1962 it created an international awareness of the dangers of the uncontrolled use of poisons in the natural environment.

Although *Silent Spring* led to attacks on Carson from the agricultural chemical industry, she eventually received the official endorsement of President Kennedy's Science Advisory Committee. Today, *Silent Spring* is recognized not only as a book that saved birds from extinction, but as a book that energized the modern environmental movement. Quite simply, Rachel Carson introduced the concept of ecology to the general public. Carson died two years after the publication of *Silent Spring*. She did not live to see DDT banned.

RACHEL CARSON – IN HER OWN WORDS

Silent Spring, 1962

There was once a town in the heart of America where all life seemed to live in harmony with its surroundings. The town lay in the midst of a checkerboard of prosperous farms, with fields of grain and hillsides of orchards where, in spring, white clouds of bloom drifted above the green fields. In autumn, oak and maple and birch set up a blaze of color that flamed and flickered across a backdrop of pines. Then foxes barked in the hills and deer silently crossed the fields, half hidden in the mists of the fall mornings.

Along the roads, laurel, viburnum and alder, great ferns and wildflowers delighted the traveler's eye through much of the year. Even in winter the roadsides were places of beauty, where countless birds came to feed on the berries and on the seed heads of the dried weeds rising above the snow. The countryside was, in fact, famous for the abundance and variety of its bird life, and when the flood of migrants was pouring through in spring and fall people traveled from great distances to observe them. Others came to fish the streams, which flowed clear and cold out of the hills and contained shady pools where trout lay. So it had been from the days many years ago when the first settlers raised their houses, sank their wells, and built their barns.

Then a strange blight crept over the area and everything began to change. Some evil spell had settled on the community: mysterious maladies swept the flocks of chickens; the cattle and sheep sickened and died. Everywhere was a shadow of death. The farmers spoke of much illness among their families. In the town the doctors had become more and more puzzled by new kinds of sickness appearing among their patients. There had been several sudden and unexplained deaths, not only among adults but even among children, who would be stricken suddenly while at play and die within a few hours.

There was a strange stillness. The birds, for example—where had they gone? Many people spoke of them, puzzled and disturbed. The feeding stations in the backyards were deserted. The few birds seen anywhere were moribund; they trembled violently and could not fly. It was a spring without voices. On the mornings that had once throbbed with the dawn chorus of robins, catbirds, doves, jays, wrens, and scores of other bird voices there was now no sound; only silence lay over the fields and woods and marsh.

On the farms the hens brooded, but no chicks hatched. The farmers complained that they were unable to raise any pigs—the litters were small and the young survived only a few days. The apple trees were coming into bloom but no bees droned among the blossoms, so there was no pollination and there would be no fruit.

The roadsides, once so attractive, were now lined with browned and withered vegetation as though swept by fire. These, too, were silent, deserted by all living things. Even the streams were now lifeless. Anglers no longer visited them, for all the fish had died.

In the gutters under the eaves and between the shingles of the roofs, a white granular powder still showed a few patches; some weeks before it had fallen like snow upon the roofs and the lawns, the fields and streams.

No witchcraft, no enemy action had silenced the rebirth of new life in this stricken world. The people had done it themselves.

This town does not actually exist, but it might easily have a thousand counterparts in America or elsewhere in the world. I know of no community that has experienced all the misfortunes I describe. Yet every one of these disasters has actually happened somewhere, and many real communities have already suffered a substantial number of them. A grim specter has crept upon us almost unnoticed, and this imagined tragedy may easily become a stark reality we all shall know.

What has already silenced the voices of spring in countless towns in America? This book is an attempt to explain.

The history of life on earth has been a history of interaction between living things and their surroundings. To a large extent, the physical form and the habits of the earth's vegetation and its animal life have been molded by the environment. Considering the whole span of earthly time, the opposite effect, in which life actually modifies its surroundings, has been relatively slight. Only within the moment of time represented by the present century has one species—man—acquired significant power to alter the nature of his world.

During the past quarter century this power has not only increased to one of disturbing magnitude but it has changed in character. The most alarming of all man's assaults upon the environment is the contamination of air, earth, rivers, and sea with dangerous and even lethal materials. This pollution is for the most part irrecoverable; the chain of evil it initiates not only in the world that must support life but in living tissues is for the most part irreversible. In this now universal contamination of the environment, chemicals are the sinister and little-recognized partners of radiation in changing the very nature of the world—the very nature of its life. Strontium 90, released through nuclear explosions into the air, comes to earth in rain or drifts down as fallout, lodges in soil, enters into the grass or corn or wheat grown there, and in time takes up its abode in the bones of a human being, there to remain until his death. Similarly, chemicals sprayed on croplands or forests or gardens lie long in soil, entering into living organisms, passing from one to another in a chain of poisoning and death. Or they pass mysteriously by underground streams until they emerge and, through the alchemy of air and sunlight, combine into new forms that kill vegetation, sicken cattle, and work unknown harm on those who drink from once pure wells. As Albert Schweitzer has said, "Man can hardly even recognize the devils of his own creation."

It took hundreds of millions of years to produce the life that now inhabits the earth—eons of time in which that developing and evolving and diversifying life reached a state of adjustment and balance with its surroundings. The environment, rigorously shaping and directing the life it supported, contained elements that were hostile as well as supporting. . . . Given time—time not in years but in millennia—life adjusts, and a balance has been reached. For time is the essential ingredient; but in the modern world there is no time. . . .

To adjust to these chemicals would require time on the scale that is nature's; it would require not merely the years of a man's life but the life of generations. And even this, were it by some miracle possible, would be futile, for the new chemicals come from our laboratories in an endless stream; almost five hundred annually find their way into actual use in the United States alone. The figure is staggering and its implications are not easily grasped—500 new chemicals to which the bodies of men and animals are required somehow to adapt each year, chemicals totally outside the limits of biologic experience.

Among them are many that are used in man's war against nature. Since the mid-1940's over 200 basic chemicals have been created for use in killing insects, weeds, rodents, and other organisms described in the modern vernacular as "pests"; and they are sold under several thousand different brand names.

These sprays, dusts, and aerosols are now applied almost universally to farms, gardens, forests, and homes—nonselective chemicals that have the power to kill every insect, the "good" and the "bad," to still the song of birds and the leaping of fish in the streams, to coat the leaves with a deadly film, and to linger on in soil—all this though the intended target may be only a few weeds or insects. Can anyone believe it is possible to lay down such a barrage of poisons on the surface of the earth without making it unfit for all life? They should not be called "insecticides," but "biocides."

The whole process of spraying seems caught up in an endless spiral. Since DDT was released for civilian use, a process of escalation has been going on in which ever more toxic materials must be found. This has happened because insects, in a triumphant vindication of Darwin's principle of the survival of the fittest, have evolved super races immune to the particular insecticide used, hence a deadlier one has always to be developed—and then a deadlier one than that. It has happened also because, for reasons to be described later, destructive insects often undergo a "flareback," or resurgence, after spraying, in numbers greater than before. Thus the chemical war is never won, and all life is caught in its violent crossfire.

Along with the possibility of the extinction of mankind by nuclear war, the central problem of our age has therefore become the contamination of man's total environment with such substances of incredible potential for harm—substances that accumulate in the tissues of plants and animals and even penetrate the germ cells to shatter or alter the very material of heredity upon which the shape of the future depends. . . .

It is not my contention that chemical insecticides must never be used. I do contend that we have put poisonous and biologically potent chemicals indiscriminately into the hands of persons largely or wholly ignorant of their potentials for harm. We have subjected enormous numbers of people to contact with these poisons, without their consent and often without their knowledge. If the Bill of Rights contains no guarantee that a citizen shall be secure against lethal poisons distributed either by private individuals or by public officials, it is surely only because our forefathers, despite their considerable wisdom and foresight, could conceive of no such problem.

I contend, furthermore, that we have allowed these chemicals to be used with little or no advance investigation of their effect on soil, water, wildlife, and man himself. Future generations are unlikely to condone our lack of prudent concern for the integrity of the natural world that supports all life.

There is still very limited awareness of the nature of the threat. This is an era of specialists, each of whom sees his own problem and is unaware of or intolerant of the larger frame into which it fits. It is also an era dominated by industry, in which the right to make a dollar at whatever cost is seldom challenged. When the public protests, confronted with some obvious evidence of damaging results of pesticide applications, it is fed little tranquilizing pills of half truth. We urgently need an end to these false assurances, to the sugar coating of unpalatable facts. It is the public that is being asked to assume the risks that the insect controllers calculate. The public must decide whether it wishes to continue on the present road, and it can do so only when in full possession of the facts. In the words of Jean Rostand, "The obligation to endure gives us the right to know." . . .

Water, soil, and the earth's green mantle of plants make up the world that supports the animal life of the earth. Although modern man seldom remembers the fact, he could not exist without the plants that harness the sun's energy and manufacture the basic foodstuffs he depends upon for life. Our attitude toward plants is a singularly narrow one. If we see any immediate utility in a plant we foster it. If for any reason we find its presence undesirable or merely a matter of indifference, we may condemn it to destruction forthwith. Besides the various plants that are poisonous to man or his livestock, or crowd out food plants, many are marked for destruction merely because, according to our narrow view, they happen to be in the wrong place at the wrong time. Many others are destroyed merely because they happen to be associates of the unwanted plants.

The earth's vegetation is part of a web of life in which there are intimate and essential relations between plants and the earth, between plants and other plants, between plants and animals. Sometimes we have no choice but to disturb these relationships, but we should do so thoughtfully, with full awareness that what we do may have consequences remote in time and place. . . .

. . . The balance of nature is not a *status quo*; it is fluid, ever shifting, in a constant state of adjustment. Man, too, is part of this balance. Sometimes the balance is in his favor; sometimes—and all too often through his own activities—it is shifted to his disadvantage.

Two critically important facts have been overlooked in designing the modern insect control programs. The first is that the really effective control of insects is that applied by nature, not by man. Populations are kept in check by something the ecologists call the resistance of the environment, and this has been so since the first life was created. The amount of food available, conditions of weather and climate, the presence of competing or predatory species, all are critically important. . . . Yet most of the chemicals now used kill all insects, our friends and enemies alike.

The second neglected fact is the truly explosive power of a species to reproduce once the resistance of the environment has been weakened. The fecundity of many forms of life is almost beyond our power to imagine, though now and then we have suggestive glimpses. . . .

We stand now where two roads diverge. But unlike the roads in Robert Frost's familiar poem, they are not equally fair. The road we have long been traveling is deceptively easy, a smooth superhighway on which we progress with great speed, but at its end lies disaster. The other fork of the road—the one "less traveled by"—offers our last, our only chance to reach a destination that assures the preservation of our earth.

The choice, after all, is ours to make. If, having endured much, we have at last asserted our "right to know," and if, knowing, we have concluded that we are being asked to take senseless and frightening risks, then we should no longer accept the counsel of those who tell us that we must fill our world with poisonous chemicals; we should look about and see what other course is open to us.

A truly extraordinary variety of alternatives to the chemical control of insects is available. Some are already in use and have achieved brilliant success. Others are in the stage of laboratory testing. Still others are little more than ideas in the minds of imaginative scientists, waiting for the opportunity to put them to the test. All have this in common: they are *biological* solutions, based on understanding of the living organisms they seek to control, and of the whole fabric of life to which these organisms belong. . . .

The current vogue for poisons has failed utterly to take into account these most fundamental considerations. As crude a weapon as the cave man's club, the chemical barrage has been hurled against the fabric of life—a fabric on the one hand delicate and destructible, on the other miraculously tough and resilient, and capable of striking back in unexpected ways. These extraordinary capacities of life have been ignored by the practitioners of chemical control who have brought to their task no "high-minded orientation," no humility before the vast forces with which they tamper.

The "control of nature" is a phrase conceived in arrogance, born of the Neanderthal age of biology and philosophy, when it was supposed that nature exists for the convenience of man. The concepts and practices of applied entomology for the most part date from that Stone Age of science. It is our alarming misfortune that so primitive a science has armed itself with the most modern and terrible weapons, and that in turning them against the insects it has also turned them against the earth.

RACHEL CARSON – A SIMULATED INTERVIEW

1. **What impact does human activity have on the natural environment in modern times?**
    A. Natural change in the environment occurs slowly. However, during the twentieth century human beings have acquired the power to alter the character of the natural world in sudden and drastic ways. The environment is therefore changing with unforeseen and possibly disastrous consequences.
    B. Human beings have contaminated the air, earth, rivers, and seas with dangerous and lethal materials. Human beings have allowed chemicals to pollute the environment with little or no investigation of how the chemicals affect soil, water, wildlife, and people.

2. **Why should human beings care about preserving the natural environment?**
    A. Along with the possibility of extinction by nuclear war, human existence is threatened by the contamination of the environment with toxic chemicals. The central problem of modern times is the contamination of the natural environment with the accumulation of chemical substances in the tissues of plants and animals.
    B. Human beings cannot exist without the plants that harness the sun's energy and manufacture the basic foods needed to stay alive. Plants are being destroyed by human activity.
    C. Polluting the air, water, and soil with chemicals creates a chain of poisoning and death that imperils all life, including human life. Nothing exists alone in nature. Human beings are part of nature and cannot escape the consequences of their actions.
    D. The rapid change inflicted on the environment by humans does not give life time to adjust. It takes hundreds of millions of years for life forms to adjust and reach a balance with the environment. Human beings should therefore take appropriate action to preserve the natural environment.
    E. Natural beauty is necessary to the spiritual development of individuals and society. Whenever human beings destroy something beautiful, they threaten humanity's spiritual growth. All human beings benefit from natural beauty, and no generation has the right to destroy natural beauty, especially to satisfy selfish materialism.

3. **How do pesticides affect the environment?**
    A. The spraying of pesticides upsets the balance of nature. Pesticides pollute the water and soil, damage plants, and kill wildlife. When wildlife is killed, people are also slowly killed. DDT is even found in the fatty tissues of Eskimo who live in areas where DDT has never been sprayed.

B. Insects develop a resistance to pesticides and weaken nature's capacity to balance and control insect populations by the use of pesticides. Human generations, however, come so slowly that it will take hundreds of thousands of years for humans to develop a resistance to pesticides.

C. The intrusion of chemicals into the human body throws the body out of control. Cancer is linked to the man-made substances that are spread throughout nature.

4. What actions should human beings take to preserve the environment?

A. More money should be spent on research. Ignorance about humanity's destructive interaction with the environment might bring disaster. Human beings must therefore gain knowledge and shape their actions accordingly.

B. Human beings should not disturb the essential relations of plants and animals in nature unless the consequences are examined thoughtfully. The earth's vegetation is part of a web of life that cannot be disturbed without consequences.

C. Biological controls of insects should be studied. Natural controls of insects are a positive alternative to pesticides. The vast majority of insects are held in check by natural forces. Human beings possess a right to be free from the lethal poisons that pollute the environment.

D. Pesticides should only be used to kill insects with selective spraying. Specific trees should be targeted and the bases of the trees should be sprayed.

STUDENT ACTIVITIES

Vocabulary
Define the following terms before reading the lesson on Carson.

1. aerosol	10. fallout	19. moribund
2. alchemy	11. fecundity	20. potent
3. alder	12. insecticide	21. prudent
4. biological	13. irrecoverable	22. *status quo*
5. contamination	14. irreversible	23. strontium 90
6. counterpart	15. laurel	24. toxic
7. DDT	16. lethal	25. unpalatable
8. entomology	17. materialism	26. viburnum
9. extinction	18. millennia	

Review

1. What subjects did Rachel Carson study that allowed her to write scientifically accurate books in a literary style?
2. Where did Carson receive her graduate degree?
3. Where did Carson find work as a biologist?
4. What three books comprise Carson's well-known trilogy about the sea?
5. What book by Carson, published in 1962, introduced the concept of ecology to the general public?
6. What did Carson believe was the central problem of modern times?
7. Why did Carson believe nature's ability to control insect populations was weakened by pesticides?
8. What did Carson believe was one of the causes of cancer?
9. Why did Carson believe more money should be spent on research?
10. What did Carson believe was a positive alternative to the use of pesticides?
11. Under what conditions did Carson believe pesticides should be used?
12. Decide whether the following statements are **True** or **False** according to Rachel Carson.
    A. During the twentieth century human beings have acquired the power to alter the character of the natural world in sudden and drastic ways.
    B. Human beings have contaminated the air, earth, rivers, and seas with dangerous and lethal materials.
    C. Human beings are part of nature and cannot escape the consequences of their actions.
    D. All life will adjust to the changes inflicted on the environment by human beings.
    E. The destruction of the natural environment threatens the spiritual development of individuals and society.
    F. No generation has the right to destroy natural beauty.
    G. DDT cannot be found in human beings who live in areas where DDT has never been sprayed.
    H. Human generations come so slowly that it will take hundreds of thousands of years for humans to develop resistance to pesticides.
    I. The earth's vegetation is part of a web of life that cannot be disturbed without consequences.
    J. Human beings possess a right to be free from lethal poisons that pollute the environment.

What do you think?
On a scale of one through five, rate your opinion of the following quotations by Carson. Write a short statement explaining your rating.

1 – You **strongly agree** with the statement *or* you feel the statement is **admirable** considering the historical circumstances surrounding it.
5 – You **strongly disagree** with the statement *or* you feel the statement is **contemptible** considering the historical circumstances surrounding it.

A. *Only within the moment of time represented by the present century has one species—man—acquired significant power to alter the nature of the world.*
B. *The most alarming of all man's assaults upon the environment is the contamination of air, earth, rivers, and sea with dangerous and even lethal materials.*
C. *Given time—time not in years but in millennia—life adjusts, and a balance has been reached. For time is the essential ingredient; but in the modern world there is not time.*
D. *They should not be called "insecticides," but "biocides."*
E. *The chemical war is never won, and all life is caught in its violent crossfire.*
F. *Along with the possibility of the extinction of mankind by nuclear war, the central problem of our age has therefore become the contamination of man's total environment with such substances of incredible potential for harm—substances that accumulate in the tissues of plants and animals and even penetrate the germ cells to shatter or alter the very material of heredity upon which the shape of the future depends.*
G. *If the Bill of Rights contains no guarantee that a citizen shall be secure against lethal poisons distributed either by private individuals or by public officials, it is surely only because our forefathers, despite their considerable wisdom and foresight, could conceive of no such problem.*
H. *This is an era of specialists, each of whom sees his own problems and is unaware of or intolerant of the larger frame into which it fits.*
I. *It is . . . an era dominated by industry, in which the right to make a dollar at whatever cost is seldom challenged.*
J. *The earth's vegetation is part of a web of life in which there are intimate and essential relations between plants and the earth, between plants and other plants, between plants and animals. Sometimes we have no choice but to disturb these relationships, but we should do so thoughtfully, with full awareness that what we do may have consequences remote in time and place.*
K. *The "control of nature" is a phrase conceived in arrogance, born of the Neanderthal age of biology and philosophy, when it was supposed that nature exists for the convenience of man.*

CHAPTER 39

ALVIN TOFFLER

BACKGROUND

Alvin Toffler (1928-), the son of Polish-Jewish immigrants, grew up with his father quizzing him daily on current events from the *New York Times*. Toffler was therefore trained from a young age to think about society and politics. As an adult his interest in current issues continued, and he gained international fame interpreting the dramatic social and technological changes of the late twentieth century.

After earning his college degree in English, Toffler worked for several years as an auto assembly line welder, truck driver, punch press operator, and foundry millwright. He even served for a short time as a private in the United States Army. Eventually, he took a job as a reporter and editor for a trade union publication before becoming a freelance writer and an editor for *Fortune* magazine.

In 1965 Toffler wrote a magazine article in which he coined the term "future shock" to describe the disorientation resulting from too much change in too short a time. After five years of follow-up research Toffler published a book titled *Future Shock*. The book became an international bestseller and popularized a whole new field of research—futurism. As defined by Toffler, futurism was a study of "connections between events, connections that make patterns." In other words futurists make educated assumptions about what the world will be like in the future.

In 1980 Toffler published *The Third Wave* and brought attention to the idea that humanity was entering a third wave of change. He believed the development of agricultural societies was the First Wave of history; industrialization was the Second Wave; the move to an information society was the Third Wave. Toffler argued that America's traditional political and social institutions were becoming obsolete in the Third Wave.

Toffler's message was revitalized in 1994 when Republicans won control of both houses of the United States Congress for the first time in over forty years. When Newt Gingrich became the new Speaker of the House he gave his fellow Republicans a reading list that included *The Federalist Papers*, the Declaration of Independence, and a book by Alvin Toffler. As the twentieth century came to an end Toffler's influence was as significant as ever.

ALVIN TOFFLER – IN HIS OWN WORDS

Future Shock, 1970

In 1965 . . . I coined the term "future shock" to describe the shattering stress and disorientation that we induce in individuals by subjecting them to too much change in too short a time. Fascinated by this concept, I spent the next five years visiting scores of universities, research centers, laboratories, and government agencies, reading countless articles and scientific papers and interviewing literally hundreds of experts on different aspects of change, coping behavior, and the future. . . . I came away from this experience with two disturbing convictions.

First, it became clear that future shock is no longer a distantly potential danger, but a real sickness from which increasingly large numbers already suffer. This psycho-biological condition can be described in medical and psychiatric terms. It is the disease of change.

Second, I gradually came to be appalled by how little is actually known about adaptivity, either by those who call for and create vast changes in our society, or by those who supposedly prepare us to cope with those changes. Earnest intellectuals talk bravely about "educating for change" or "preparing people for the future." But we know virtually nothing about how to do it. In the most rapidly changing environment to which man has ever been exposed, we remain pitifully ignorant of how the human animal copes. . . .

Future shock is a time phenomenon, a product of the greatly accelerated rate of change in society. It arises from the superimposition of a new culture on an old one. It is culture shock in one's own society. But its impact is far worse. . . . Most travelers have the comforting knowledge that the culture they left behind will be there to return to. The victim of future shock does not.

Take an individual out of his own culture and set him down suddenly in an environment sharply different from his own, with a different set of cues to react to—different conceptions of time, space, work, love, religion, sex, and everything else—then cut him off from any hope of retreat to a more familiar social landscape, and the dislocation he suffers is doubly severe. Moreover, if this new culture is itself in constant turmoil, and if—worse yet—its values are incessantly changing, the sense of disorientation will be still further intensified. Given few clues as to what kind of behavior is rational under the radically new circumstances, the victim may well become a hazard to himself and others.

Now imagine not merely an individual but an entire society, an entire generation—including its weakest, least intelligent, and most irrational members—suddenly transported into this new world. The result is mass disorientation, future shock on a grand scale.

. . . If the last 50,000 years of man's existence were divided into lifetimes of approximately sixty-two years each, there have been about 800 such lifetimes. Of these 800, fully 650 were spent in caves.

Only during the last seventy lifetimes has it been possible to communicate effectively from one lifetime to another—as writing made it possible to do. Only during the last six lifetimes did masses of men ever see a printed word. Only during the last four has it been possible to measure time with any precision. Only in the last two has anyone anywhere used an electric motor. And the overwhelming majority of all the material goods we use in daily life today have been developed within the present, the 800th lifetime.

This 800th lifetime marks a sharp break with all past human experience because during this lifetime man's relationship to resources has reversed itself. This is most evident in the field of economic development. Within a single lifetime, agriculture, the original basis of civilization, has lost its dominance in nation after nation. . . .

Moreover, if agriculture is the first stage of economic development and industrialism the second, we can now see that still another stage—the third—has suddenly been reached. . . . Within the same lifetime a society for the first time in human history not only threw off the yoke of agriculture, but managed within a few brief decades to throw off the yoke of manual labor as well. The world's first service economy had been born . . . .

. . . To survive, to avert what we have termed future shock, the individual must become infinitely more adaptable and capable than ever before. He must search out totally new ways to anchor himself, for all the old roots—religion, nation, community, family, or profession—are now shaking under the hurricane impact of the accelerative thrust. Before he can do so, however, he must understand in greater detail how the effects of acceleration penetrate his personal life, creep into his behavior and alter the quality of existence. He must in other words, understand transience. . . .

This massive injection of speed and novelty into the fabric of society will force us not merely to cope more rapidly with familiar situations, events and moral dilemmas, but to cope at a progressively faster rate with situations that are, for us, decidedly unfamiliar, "first-time" situations, strange, irregular, unpredictable.

This will significantly alter the balance that prevails in any society between the familiar and unfamiliar elements in the daily life of its people, between the routine and non-routine, the predictable and the unpredictable. The relationship between these two kinds of daily-life elements can be called the "novelty ratio" of the society, and as the level of newness or novelty rises, less and less of life appears subject to our routine forms of coping behavior. More and more, there is a growing weariness and wariness, a pall of pessimism, a decline in our sense of mastery. More and more, the environment comes to seem chaotic, beyond human control. . . .

Different people react to future shock in different ways. Its symptoms also vary according to the stage and intensity of the disease. These symptoms range all the way from anxiety, hostility to helpful authority, and seemingly senseless violence, to physical illness, depression and apathy. Its victims often manifest erratic swings in interest and life style, followed by an effort to "crawl into their shells" through social, intellectual and emotional withdrawal. They feel continually "bugged" or harassed, and want desperately to reduce the number of decisions they must make. . . .

The striking signs of confusional breakdown we see around us—the spreading use of drugs, the rise of mysticism, the recurrent outbreaks of vandalism and undirected violence, the politics of nihilism and nostalgia, the sick apathy of millions—can all be understood better by recognizing their relationship to future shock. These forms of social irrationality may well reflect the deterioration of individual decision-making under conditions of environmental overstimulation. . . .

Our first and most pressing need, . . . before we can build a humane future, is to halt the runaway acceleration that is subjecting multitudes to the threat of future shock while, at the very same moment, intensifying all the problems they must deal with—war, ecological incursions, racism, the obscene contrast between rich and poor, the revolt of the young, and the rise of a potentially deadly mass irrationalism.

There is no facile way to treat this wild growth, this cancer in history. There is no magic medicine, either, for curing the unprecedented disease it bears in its rushing wake: future shock. I have suggested palliatives for the change-pressed individual and more radically curative procedures for the society— new social services, a future-facing education system, new ways to regulate technology, and a strategy for capturing control of change. Other ways must also be found. Yet the basic thrust of this book is diagnosis. For diagnosis precedes cure, and we cannot begin to help ourselves until we become sensitively conscious of the problem.

The Third Wave, 1980

In a time when terrorists play death-games with hostages, as currencies careen amid rumors of a third World War, as embassies flame and storm troopers lace up their boots in many lands, we stare in horror at the headlines. The price of gold—that sensitive barometer of fear—breaks all records. Banks tremble. Inflation rages out of control. And the governments of the world are reduced to paralysis or imbecility.

Faced with all this, a massed chorus of Cassandras fills the air with doom-song. The proverbial man in the street says the world has "gone mad," while the expert points to all the trends leading toward catastrophe.

This book offers a sharply different view.

It contends that the world has not swerved into lunacy, and that, in fact, beneath the clatter and jangle of seemingly senseless events there lies a startling and potentially hopeful pattern. This book is about that pattern and that hope.

The Third Wave shows . . . that, in the very midst of destruction and decay, we can now find striking evidences of birth and life. It shows clearly and, I think, indisputably, that—with intelligence and a modicum of luck—the emergent civilization can be made more sane, sensible, and sustainable, more decent and more democratic than any we have ever known.

If the main argument of this book is correct, there are powerful reasons for long-range optimism, even if the transitional years immediately ahead are likely to be stormy and crisis-ridden. . . .

. . . This book flows from the assumption that we are the final generation of an old civilization and the first generation of a new one, and that much of our personal confusion, anguish, and disorientation can be traced directly to the conflict within us, and within our political institutions, between the dying Second Wave civilization and the emergent Third Wave civilization that is thundering in to take its place.

When we finally understand this, many seemingly senseless events become suddenly comprehensible. The broad patterns of change begin to emerge clearly. Action for survival becomes possible and plausible again. In short, the revolutionary premise liberates our intellect and our will. . . .

Before the First Wave of change, most humans lived in small, often migratory groups and fed themselves by foraging, fishing, hunting, or herding. At some point, roughly ten millennia ago, the agricultural revolution began, and it crept slowly across the planet spreading villages, settlements, cultivated land, and a new way of life.

This First Wave of change had not yet exhausted itself by the end of the seventeenth century, when the industrial revolution broke over Europe and unleashed the second great wave of planetary change. This new process—industrialization—began moving much more rapidly across nations and continents. Thus two separate and distinct change processes were rolling across the earth simultaneously, at different speeds.

Today the First Wave has virtually subsided. Only a few tiny tribal populations, in South America or Papua New Guinea, for example, remain to be reached by agriculture. But the force of this First Wave has basically been spent.

Meanwhile, the Second Wave, having revolutionized life in Europe, North America, and some other parts of the globe in a few short centuries, continues to spread, as many countries, until now basically agricultural, scramble to build steel mills, auto plants, textile factories, railroads, and food processing plants. The momentum of industrialization is still felt. The Second Wave has not entirely spent in force.

But even as this process continues, another, even more important, has begun, For as the tide of industrialism peaked in the decades after World War II, a little-understood Third Wave began to surge across the earth, transforming everything it touched.

Many countries, therefore, are feeling the simultaneous impact of two, even three, quite different waves of change, all moving at different rates of speed and with different degrees of force behind them.

For the purposes of this book we shall consider the First Wave era to have begun sometime around 8000 B.C. and to have dominated the earth unchallenged until sometime around A.D. 1650-1750. From this moment on, the First Wave lost momentum as the Second Wave picked up steam. Industrial civilization, the product of this Second Wave, then dominated the planet in its turn until it, too, crested. This latest historical turning point arrived in the United States during the decade beginning about 1955—the decade that saw white-collar and service workers outnumber blue-collar workers for the first time. This was the same decade that the Third Wave began to gather its force in the United States. Since then it has arrived—at slightly different dates—in most of the other industrial nations, including Britain, France, Sweden, Germany, the Soviet Union, and Japan. Today all the high technology nations are reeling from the collision between the Third Wave and the obsolete, encrusted economies and institutions of the Second.

Understanding this is the secret to making sense of much of the political and social conflict we see around us. . . .

While the Third Wave carries with it deep challenges for humanity, from ecological threats to the danger of nuclear terrorism and electronic fascism, it is not simply a nightmarish linear extension of industrialism.

We glimpse here instead the emergence of what might be called a "practopia"—neither the best nor the worst of all possible worlds, but one that is both practical and preferable to the one we had. Unlike a utopia, a practopia is not free of disease, political nastiness, and bad manners. Unlike most utopias, it is not static or frozen in unreal perfection. Nor is it reversionary, modeling itself on some imagined ideal of the past.

Conversely, a practopia does not embody the crystallized evil of a utopia turned inside out. It is not ruthlessly antidemocratic. It is not inherently militarist. It does not reduce its citizens to faceless uniformity. It does not destroy its neighbors and degrade its environment.

In short, a practopia offers a positive, even a revolutionary alternative, yet lies within the range of the realistically attainable.

Third Wave civilization, in this sense, is precisely that: a practopian future. One can glimpse in it a civilization that makes allowance for individual difference, and embraces (rather than suppresses) racial, regional, religious, and subcultural variety. A civilization built in considerable measure around the home. A civilization that is not frozen in amber but pulsing with innovation, yet which is also capable of providing enclaves of relative stability for those who need or want them. A civilization no longer required to pour its best energies into marketization. A civilization capable of directing great passion into art. A civilization facing unprecedented historical choices—about genetics and evolution, to choose a single example—and inventing new ethical or moral standards to deal with such complex issues. A civilization, finally, that is at least potentially democratic and humane, in better balance with the biosphere and no longer dangerously dependent on exploitative subsidies from the rest of the world. Hard work to achieve, but not impossible.

Flowing together in grand confluence, today's changes thus point to a workable countercivilization, an alternative to the increasingly obsolete and unworkable industrial system.

They point, in a word, to practopia.

ALVIN TOFFLER – A SIMULATED INTERVIEW

1. **How did the world change in the late twentieth century?**
   A. In the late twentieth century human beings experienced the most extensive and rapid change the world had ever seen. The rapid pace of change was primarily the result of technology feeding upon itself. Technology made more technology possible.
   B. Human beings developed a throw-away mentality that matched their throw-away products. The traditional ideal of building for permanence was lost.
   C. Human relationships became increasingly short-lived. Many people were caught in a process of seeking new friends to replace those no longer present or no longer holding the same interests. Even families became fractured as people turned to serial marriage.
   D. People no longer stayed in one place long enough to acquire distinct regional or local characteristics.
   E. Millions of jobs shifted from factories to homes. A home-centered society began to develop, and every institution, from families to schools to corporations, was transformed.
   F. Human beings faced the paralyzing effect of having too many choices to make, and a condition of "future shock" afflicted society.

2. **What is future shock?**
   A. The term "future shock" describes the stress and disorientation people experience when exposed to too much change in too short a time. Future shock is a real sickness that strikes both individuals and societies forced to operate beyond their ability to adapt to change.
   B. Future shock results when individuals are given few clues to the kind of behavior that is rational. The level of newness and novelty increases while the level of predictability declines. The world seems increasingly chaotic and beyond human control.
   C. Although different people react in different ways, the symptoms of future shock include anxiety, hostility, senseless violence, physical illness, depression, and apathy. People often feel harassed and want desperately to reduce the number of decisions they must make.

3. **How can people cope with future shock?**
   A. Before people can build a humane future they must stop the high speed of change subjecting the masses to future shock. There are limits to the amount of change human beings can absorb, and most people are unprepared to cope with an avalanche of change.
   B. People must develop an awareness of the future. Organizations should be created that are devoted to anticipating probable futures.
   C. Educators must quit thinking of the future as simply an extension of the present. Education should prepare people to adapt to change.

4. **What are the three waves of human history?**
   A. The First Wave began 8,000 to 10,000 years ago when agriculture was invented in the Middle East.
   B. The Second Wave started with the Industrial Revolution beginning in the mid-1700s.
   C. The Third Wave began after World War II with the creation of a society based on tools amplifying the mind rather than muscle. A society was created based on processing information, a society based on the computer, the satellite, and the Internet. Information and imagination emerged as the most important raw materials.

5. **How is the Third Wave changing human life?**
   A. The beginning of the Third Wave is characterized by confusion, anguish, and disorientation. However, the world is not moving toward lunacy. With intelligence and luck people can create a new world that is more sane, sensible, sustainable, decent, and democratic.
   B. People are learning to recognize that industrial civilization is no longer possible for two main reasons:
      1. The natural environment will no longer tolerate an industrial assault. Environmental concerns will shape all future technological advances.
      2. People can no longer rely indefinitely on nonrenewable energy.
   C. People are witnessing changes in economics, family, culture, and politics. The Third Wave gives human beings customized production, micro markets, infinite channels of communication, heterogeneous family styles, and thousands of single issue political groups. The American government is moving toward de-bureaucratization, de-centralization, and a dispersal of power downward.
   D. The process of genetically altering agriculture products is being refined. The problem of world hunger could be solved by the ability to tailor crops to local climate and soil conditions.
   E. People are beginning to face a crisis in eugenics (i.e., the science of controlled breeding). People are searching for guidelines to controlling the biological revolution.

6. **What is a "practopia"?**
   A. A practopia is the type of society emerging in the Third Wave.
   B. Unlike a perfect society, or utopia, a practopia is not free of disease, political problems, or bad behavior. A practopia is not militaristic or antidemocratic. It does not demand the conformity of its citizens.
   C. A practopia offers human beings a civilization that allows individual differences and embraces racial, regional, religious, and subcultural variety.
   D. Human life in a practopia will be centered in the home, and will direct great energy into art, democracy, and environmentalism.

STUDENT ACTIVITIES

Vocabulary
Define the following terms before reading the lesson on Toffler.

1. careen	10. imbecility	19. psychiatric
2. Cassandra	11. migratory	20. superimposition
3. crested	12. millennia	21. symptom
4. curative	13. modicum	22. transience
5. diagnosis	14. nihilism	23. utopia
6. disorientation	15. nostalgia	24. wariness
7. ecological	16. pall	25. weariness
8. facile	17. palliative	26. yoke
9. fascism	18. proverbial	

Review
1. What gave Toffler his interest in current issues when he was young?
2. In what academic area did Toffler earn his college degree?
3. What jobs were held by Toffler before he became a reporter and editor?
4. What term did Toffler first use in 1965 to describe the disorientation resulting from too much change in too short a time?
5. What best-selling book was published by Toffler in 1970?
6. What book was published by Toffler in 1980?
7. What political party won control of both houses of Congress in the 1994 elections for the first time in over forty years?
8. Who became the new Speaker of the House after the 1994 elections?
9. How did the 1994 elections affect Toffler's message?
10. What are the symptoms of future shock?
11. What characterizes each of the three waves of human history?
12. What are the most important raw materials in the Third Wave?
13. What are two reasons industrial civilization is no longer possible?
14. How is the American government changing during the Third Wave?
15. Decide whether the following statements are **True** or **False** according to Alvin Toffler.
    A. America's political and social institutions are becoming obsolete.
    B. The rapid pace of change in the late twentieth century was primarily the result of economic growth.
    C. During the rapid changes of the late twentieth century, families became fractured as people turned to serial marriages.
    D. Future shock is a real sickness striking both individuals and societies.
    E. Most people are unprepared to cope with an avalanche of change.
    F. Education should prepare people to adapt to change.
    G. The world is moving toward lunacy during the Third Wave.
    H. A practopia is a militaristic, anti-democratic society.
    I. Human life in a practopia will be centered in the home.

What do you think?
On a scale of one through five, rate your opinion of the following quotations by Toffler. Write a short statement explaining your rating.

1 – You **strongly agree** with the statement *or* you feel the statement is **admirable** considering the historical circumstances surrounding it.
5 – You **strongly disagree** with the statement *or* you feel the statement is **contemptible** considering the historical circumstances surrounding it.

A. *Take an individual out of his own culture and set him down suddenly in an environment sharply different from his own, with a different set of cues to react to—different conceptions of time, space, work, love, religion, sex, and everything else—then cut him off from any hope of retreat to a more familiar social landscape, and the dislocation he suffers is doubly severe.*
B. *To survive, to avert what we have termed future shock, the individual must become infinitely more adaptable and capable than ever before.*
C. *The old roots—religion, nation, community, family, or profession—are now shaking under the hurricane impact of the accelerative thrust.*
D. *More and more, there is a growing weariness and wariness, a pall of pessimism, a decline in our sense of mastery. More and more, the environment comes to seem chaotic, beyond human control.*
E. *The world has not swerved into lunacy . . . beneath the clatter and jangle of seemingly senseless events there lies a startling and potentially hopeful pattern.*
F. *With intelligence and a modicum of luck—the emergent civilization can be made more sane, sensible, and sustainable, more decent and more democratic than any we have ever known.*
G. *We are the final generation of an old civilization and the first genera- tion of a new one, and . . . much of our personal confusion, anguish, and disorientation can be traced directly to the conflict within us, and within our political institutions.*
H. *One can glimpse in [the Third Wave] a civilization that makes allow- ance for individual difference, and embraces (rather than suppresses) racial, regional, religious, and subcultural variety.*
I. *If we do not learn from history, we shall be compelled to relive it. True. But if we do not change the future, we shall be compelled to endure it. And that could be worse.*
J. *The dark side of the information technology explosion is that it will breed a population that believes nothing and, perhaps even more dangerous, a population ready to believe only one "truth" fanatically and willing to kill for it.*
K. *The illiterate of the 21st century will not be those who cannot read and write, but those who cannot learn, unlearn, and relearn.*

Glossary

A

abhor: to hate; to detest
abridge: diminish; deprive
abstraction: a theory; something difficult to understand
absurd: ridiculous; foolish
abusive: mistreating
accommodation: living space
acculturation: the process of adapting to a different culture or way of life
accumulation: savings; stockpiling of money
acquiescence: agreement without protest
acquisition: gaining possession of
actuate: to put into action
adherence: remaining faithful or attached
adolescent: someone between childhood and maturity
advocate (verb): support; encourage; fight for
advocate (noun): a person who is in favor of an idea
aerosol: a substance dispensed from a pressurized container
aesthetic: having an appreciation of beauty; artistic
affectation: an attempt to assume or exhibit what is not natural
affluence: an abundance of wealth
aggrandize: enrich; strengthen
aggregate: total; the whole sum or amount
aggregation: collection
agitate: to excite; to stir-up
agitation: disturbance
agnostic: someone who does not know whether God exists
alchemy: a process of changing one thing into another
alder: tree or shrub of the birch family
alienation: withdrawing of affections
aliment: food; nutriment
aliquot: fractional; partial
amelioration: improvement
amend: to correct or change
amicable: friendly
amor patriae: love of one's country
analogies: similarities
analogous: similar
anarchy: disorder; confusion; the absence of government; lawlessness

animosity: hostility
annex: attach; to join together
antagonism: opposition; hostility
antagonistic: hostile; conflicting; unfriendly
antecedent: previous; coming before
antidote: something that counteracts the effects of a disease
antipathy: strong dislike; hatred; animosity
apex: the tip; the highest point
apprehend: to grasp the meaning
approbation: approval
arbitrary: decided at random without reason
ardent: enthusiastic
aristocracy: the rich and the well-born
aristoi: the aristocracy
arrogance: feeling of superiority; self-importance
assertion: declaration; statement; allegation
assiduously: energetically; zealously
assimilation: absorption; incorporation
assuage: ease; soften
assumption: guess; theory; speculation
asylum: refuge; safe haven
atone: repent; make amends
augment: increase; make greater
augmentation: increase
augmenting: adding to
autocracy: government by one person having unlimited control
autocratic: like a dictator or tyrant
auxiliary: supporting; providing help
avail: to be of help
avarice: greediness
aversion: dislike
avidity: enthusiasm; eagerness

B

baneful: seriously harmful; causing misery
barbarism: savagery; lack of culture
beacon: guide; signal; light
beget: cause to exist
benefice: the salary of a minister or clergyman
beneficiary: one who receives a benefit or reward
benevolence: kindness
benevolent: kindly
bigotry: narrow-mindedness; intolerance

billow: swell; increase

biological: related to life and living processes

bishopric: the area under the leadership of a bishop

blasphemy: irreverent talk about God or things considered sacred

bombast: pretentious or inflated speech or writing

boon: benefit; blessing; gift

boughs: branches; tree limbs

bounteous: abundant; plentiful

bourgeois: a member of the middle class

bowels: depths; interior

boycott: refusal to buy a product; refusal to do business with someone

breach: the act of breaking; the state of being broken

brethren: brothers

bulwark: protection or defense

buoyancy: lightheartedness; enthusiasm; optimism

buttress: support; prop-up; encourage; strengthen

C

calamity: disaster

canalized: channeled

canker: a sore; an ulcer

canon: a general principle or law

caprice: impulse; whim

careen: to move wildly

Cassandra: one who predicts misfortune or disaster

censor morum: censor of morals

centralization: bringing under the control of one central authority

centralized: brought under the control of one central authority

chastisement: punishment

chauffeur: someone who drives others around in a car

citadel: haven; fortress

civility: good, polite behavior

coerce: force; bully; intimidate

coerced: compelled by threats or force

coercive: forcing; constraining

cognizance: awareness; having knowledge

cognizant: aware; familiar with

cohabit: live together

cohabitation: living together

coincident: occurring at the same time

commensurate: of the same extent; proportionate

commodity: a product for sale

commonwealth: the state or community

compact: an agreement or contract

compatible: capable of existing together

compensate: to make up for something lost or denied

compensation: payment; settlement; profit

competence: skill; ability

competent: having the ability to do what is required

complacency: self-satisfaction accompanied with unawareness of actual dangers; smugness

comprehend: to understand; to grasp the meaning

compulsion: coercion; force

compulsory: required; mandatory

concentration: consolidation; focus

concession: giving up a point in an argument; permitting

concurrence: simultaneous occurrence of events

concurrent: happening at the same time

condemnation: expression of strong disapproval

conduce: to lead to a particular result

conducive: helping to cause or produce

confederacy: a league; an alliance

confederated: associated; brought together

confederation: a uniting in a league or alliance

confidence: trust; a feeling of certainty

confiscation: taking away by force

conflagration: a great and destructive fire

confound: confuse

conjunctures: a combination of circumstances or events usually producing a crisis

consanguinity: a close relationship or connection

conscience: one's sense of right and wrong

conscientious: honest; honorable; moral; ethical

consecrate: make holy; bless; dedicate

consejos: advice

consent: general agreement

conservative: someone who wants to preserve what is established

consilience: coincidence; concurring

consolidation: combination; union

consonant: in agreement; harmonious

consortship: fellowship; partnership

conspicuous: obvious; apparent; plain; noticeable

constituted: formed; made; set up

construe: interpret

consummate: supreme; perfect; excellent

consummated: completed; accomplished; fulfilled

contamination: a process of making impure or unclean

contemner: one who views or treats with contempt

contemplate: gaze at; think about

contemplations: thoughts; ideas

contemporaries: people who live during the same time period

contemporary: belonging to the same time period

contempt: lack of respect; dislike

contemptuous: scornful; arrogant

contract: a binding agreement

contradiction: the opposite of

contradistinction: contrast with something opposite

contrary: opposite

contrivance: a creation; a design

converge: come together; join; meet

countenance: to give approval

counterpart: something that has the same function or characteristics as another

covenant: contract; formal agreement

covert: secret; concealed; hidden; disguised

covetous: desirous of something belonging to another person

crass: insensitive; mean; crude

craven: cowardly

crested: reached a peak or climax

criterion: guideline; standard

curative: something used to cure a disease

D

DDT: a colorless, odorless insecticide that accumulates in ecosystems and has a toxic effect on plants and wildlife

debase: cheapen; degrade

decentralization: distribution of power from a central authority to separate branches

deception: lie; falsehood; something that is not true

declamation: speech

decree: proclamation; command

defective: imperfect

deference: respect

defray: to provide money to pay costs

degeneracy: immorality; depravity

degradation: treatment without dignity; humiliation

de integro: anew; afresh

delinquency: an offense; failure to perform a duty

deluge: flood

demagogue: someone who plays on fear and prejudice to gain power

democracy: government by the people

demoralization: weakening of morale

despotic: like a tyrant

despotism: government by a tyrant

destitute: poor; impoverished; poverty-stricken

dexterity: skill and ease in using the hands

diabolical: fiendishly clever

diagnosis: identifying a disease by studying its symptoms

dialectical: logical; systematic

diatribe: attack with words; abusive criticism

dichos: popular proverbs or sayings

dictum: order; decree; command

diffidence: lack of confidence; timidity

diminish: to make less; to make smaller

diminutive: small; tiny

din: loud noise

dint: force; violence; power exerted

discontented: unhappy; dissatisfied; displeased

discord: conflict

discordant: disagreeing

discretion: ability to make responsible decisions

discretionary: being careful about what one does or says

discrimination: injustice; intolerance; prejudice

disfranchise: deprive of the right to vote

disorientation: state of confusion or disorder

disparity: inequality; difference

dispassionate: calm; impartial

dispensation: distribution

dispose: determine the course of events

disposition: tendency; inclination

disquietude: anxiety; uneasiness

distaff: a stick holding wool for spinning

distilling: extracting; separating

diversification: giving variety to

diversified: different; varied

divine: godlike

docile: humble; obedient; manageable

doctrine: a set of principles, beliefs, or policy

dogmatism: positiveness of opinion; intolerance

dole: a giving of food, money, or clothing to the needy; welfare

domestic: inside one's country; native

domesticity: taking care of home and family

dominant: chief; supreme; controlling; governing

dominion: authority

drone: the lowliest worker; idler; sluggard

dynastic: governed by hereditary rulers

E

ecclesiastical: of the church or religion

ecclesiastics: religious leaders

ecological: concerning the relationship between organisms and the natural environment

edict: law; command

edifice: structure

efficacy: power to produce the desired result

eloquent: speaking fluently and powerfully

embalm: preserve

emigrate: to leave one country to settle in another

eminent: famous; distinguished

emulative: imitative; copying

encroachment: intrusion; trespass

endeavor: attempt; work to achieve something

enervate: to weaken

enfeeble: make weak

engagement: promise; agreement; pledge

enigma: a mystery; something very difficult to understand

ennobling: uplifting; elevating

entomology: the study of insects

enumerated: mentioned one by one; numbered

enumeration: list; numbering

enunciate: announce; proclaim

envenom: to fill with hate; embitter

epoch: a particular period of history; a time period or era

equilibrium: balance

equivocal: open to two or more interpretations

eradicate: remove

eradication: elimination; removal; destruction

erroneous: wrong; false; untrue; mistaken

esteem: respect; admiration

estrangement: a keeping at a distance

eulogy: praise; glorification

evangel: bringer of good news

evince: to show

evitable: capable of being avoided

exclusive: sole; limited to a single individual or group

excommunicate: to eject from a group

execration: a detesting; a curse

exigency: emergency; an urgent need

exorcize: to make free of evil

expedient (adjective): useful or helpful in achieving a goal

expedient (noun): resource; device; method

exploitation: taking advantage of another person for one's own profit

exploited: taken advantage of; misused

exploiter: one who takes advantage of another

extemporary: happening suddenly and unexpectedly

extensible: capable of being extended

extinction: elimination from existence

extirpate: to root out and destroy completely

extort: to obtain something from a person by force

exuberance: enthusiasm; cheerfulness

F

facile: easy to understand; easy to accomplish

facilitation: making easier; simplification

faction: a group that is often self-interested

faculties: abilities; gifts; talents; skills

fallacy: misconception; untruth

fallible: liable to make mistakes

fallout: radioactive particles descending through the atmosphere from a nuclear explosion

fascism: system of government characterized by rigid one-party dictatorship

fawning: groveling

fealty: loyalty

fecundity: fruitfulness; fertility

felicity: happiness

feminine: having the qualities, appearance, and character of women

ferocious: savage

fetid: stinking; foul; rotten

fetters: chains; things that confine

firmament: the sky; the heavens

flagrant: outrageous; disgraceful; shameless

fornicator: one who has sex outside of marriage

fraternal: brotherly

fraud: dishonesty; faking

fraudulent: dishonest; unlawful

frivolous: unimportant

frugal: economical; penny-pinching; thrifty

G

generic: common; collective

glaciation: covering with ice

gluttony: overeating: greed

graduated: divided into graded sections

grandeur: excellence; splendor

gratitude: appreciation

gratuitously: uncalled for; unnecessary

grievance: a cause of distress; injury; injustice; unfairness

H

habeas corpus: a written command ordering an accused person to be brought into court

hallow: to honor as holy

harbinger: forerunner; messenger; a sign or omen

headsmen: executioners; hangmen

hereditary: passed from one generation to another

heretic: nonconformist; freethinker; nonbeliever

heterogeneous: not alike

hobgoblin: a mischievous or evil spirit

homage: respect; honor; devotion

homogeneous: of the same kind

hypocrite: someone who pretends to be good or virtuous; a phony

hypocritical: two-faced; dishonest; phony

I

idealistic: noble; having high ideals; visionary

ideological: pertaining to the ideas that form the basis of an economic or political theory

idolater: one who worships idols or false gods

ignominy: deep humiliation or disgrace

illicit: unlawful

illiterate: lacking education; unable to read or write

imbecile: fool

imbecility: mental deficiency

immortality: lasting fame; unending existence

immunity: exemption; privilege

immutable: unchangeable

impartiality: fairness

impede: stand in the way of

impediment: something in the way of achieving a goal

impetus: incentive; motive

impiety: ungodliness; disrespect

impious: wicked

implacable: unforgiving; merciless

inalienable: not to be given or taken away

incarnation: form; substance; a deity in an earthly embodiment

incite: urge; encourage; stimulate

inconsistent: contradictory; illogical

incontestable: undeniable; indisputable

incorporate: combine; unite

incriminate: accuse

indemnity: exemption from penalty

indifference: unconcern; disinterest

indiscriminate: random; casual; haphazard

indispensable: essential; irreplaceable

indivisible: cannot be divided

indolence: inactivity; laziness

indolent: lazy

indomitable: courageous; firm; persistent

induce: persuade

inducement: persuasion

inefficient: ineffective; weak; inadequate; incompetent

inequitable: unfair; unjust

inestimable: too great to be estimated

inexplicable: unable to be explained

infamous: having a reputation of the worst kind; dishonorable

inference: conclusion; assumption

infringe: trespass; to violate the rights of another

iniquitous: sinful; wicked

iniquity: evilness; sinfulness

injurious: harmful; damaging

inordinate: excessive; unreasonable

inquisition: investigation

insatiable: endless; unlimited

insecticide: chemical that destroys insects

insidious: underhanded

insolent: arrogant

integrity: honor; honesty; uprightness

intemperance: extremism; excessiveness

intercourse: communication

intermeddle: to interfere in a disrespectful way

intermittent: occurring at intervals

interpose: interfere; intrude; to stand in the way

interposition: intervention by a state between its citizens and the federal government

intestine: internal; domestic

intolerance: narrow-mindedness; prejudice; one-sidedness

intricacy: complexity

intrigue: conspiracy; plot

intrinsically: naturally; essentially; inherently

inveterate: customary; deep-rooted

invidiously: resentfully; spitefully

irrecoverable: not capable of being repaired or recovered

irreversible: not capable of being turned back or reversed

irrevocably: unalterably

J

judicature: the administration of justice

judicial: of judges; law courts; or their functions

judicious: wise; sensible; just

jujitsu: an ancient Japanese method of fighting without weapons, using holds, throws, and paralyzing blows to disable an opponent

jurisdiction: the authority to govern or legislate

juvenile: someone who is underage or too young to be held responsible for his actions

K

kindred: one's relatives

knave: villain; scoundrel

Know-Nothing: an 1850s political organization that was anti-Catholic and anti-immigrant

L

laity: church members who are not clergy

La Raza: "la raza" refers to "the people" or "the race;" *La Raza Unida* (Mexican-Americans United) was established in 1970 to seek an end to discrimination against Chicanos (Mexican-Americans)

latent: hidden

latter: more recent; the one mentioned second of two

latterly: recently; lately

laurel: a type of tree or shrub with small flowers and berries

lavished: wasted; poured out

legatee: a person who receives an inheritance

lethal: capable of causing death

lethargy: apathy; indifference

libertine: a person who lives an immoral life

licentiousness: disregard for accepted rules of conduct

lineaments: distinguishing features

lisping: speaking like a child

lunatic: insane person; foolish person

lust: an intense desire for something

M

machination: clever manipulation; scheming; plotting

magistrate: a judge or city official

magnanimous: generous; noble

maladjustment: failure to adjust to the conditions of one's life

malady: illness

malice: spite; ill will; hatred; hostility

manifest: clear; plain

manifested: displayed; shown; expressed

manipulation: controlling someone or something through artful or unfair methods for one's own advantage

manorial: of a large mansion with servants and acres of land

martyr: one who dies or suffers in support of a belief, a cause, or a principle

materialism: a preoccupation with material things rather than intellectual or spiritual things

maternal: motherly

maudlin: sentimental; mushy; emotional

maxim: a saying; a belief

mean: a middle point between two extremes

melancholy: depressing; sad

menial: humble; degrading; unskilled; tedious

mercenaries: people who serve only for money; those who are greedy or materialistic

middling: moderately good

migratory: wandering; roving

militantly: in an aggressive or warlike manner

militia: a civilian military force

millennia: periods of a thousand years

mischief: harmful actions

mitigate: make less intense or severe

mitigating: moderating; making less severe

modicum: a small portion; a limited quantity

molestation: harassment; mistreatment

monarchy: rule by one person who rules by hereditary right

mongrelize: to mix together different types of persons or things

monopoly: sole possession or control

moraine: a mass of debris carried down and deposited by a glacier

mores: customs; traditions; standards

moribund: dying

mortify: to punish; humiliate

multitude: crowd; a large number

mundane: dull; routine; ordinary

munition: weapon; ammunition

mutual: shared; common; similar

mutuality: sharing in common

myriad: numberless; can't be counted

mystique: the mysterious or special skills essential in a calling or activity

N

naturalization: granting of citizenship

negligence: carelessness; thoughtlessness

negligent: careless; thoughtless

niggardly: stingy; cheap; miserly; ungenerous

nihilism: an idea that traditional beliefs are groundless and that life is senseless

nodal: pertaining to the point where a leaf or bud grows out

nostalgia: a yearning for the past

nugatory: worthless; inoperative

null and void: having no force or validity

nullification: invalidation

O

obeisance: respect; courtesy

obligatory: necessary

obstinacy: stubbornness

obstinate: stubborn

obviate: prevent; avoid

odious: disgusting; hateful

odium: disgust; hatred

oligarchical: having the form of government in which power is in the hands of a few people for selfish purposes

oligarchy: a form of government in which power is in the hands of a few people for selfish purposes

ominous: threatening; sinister

omnipotence: very great or unlimited power

oppressive: tyrannical; dictatorial

opulence: prosperity; riches; abundance

ordination: decree; installation; appointment

originative: creative

P

pacific: peaceful

pall: something producing gloom

palliative: something that lessens the intensity of a disease and hopelessness

palpitation: beat; pulse

panacea: a cure-all; a remedy for all kinds of diseases and troubles

parable: a story told to illustrate a moral or spiritual truth

paradox: contradiction; inconsistency

paramount: highest; of main importance

parish: an area with its own church and clergyman or minister

parochial: showing interest in a limited area

partiality: preference; favoritism

passion: emotion; enthusiasm

paternal: fatherly

patrician: aristocrat; nobleman

pauper: beggar; someone living in poverty

pecuniary: financial: commercial; economic

penury: poverty

periphery: border; perimeter

permissiveness: allowance of too much freedom

perpetuate: continue; preserve

perpetuation: continuing; prolonging; sustaining

perplexing: confusing; puzzling

persecute: to subject to constant hostility or cruel treatment because of one's beliefs; to oppress, abuse, or harass

persecution: oppression; abuse; harassment

persevere: persist

perversions: the opposite of what is right, expected, or desired perverted: corrupted; distorted

petted: treated with particular affection or indulgence; spoiled

philanthropy: charity; generosity; trying to promote human welfare

phraseology: the way something is worded

picket line: a line of people protesting against a business, organization, or institution

piety: extreme devoutness

pilgrimage: a religious journey

plausibility: something seeming to be reasonable, though not proven

plebeian: common person

plutocracy: a nation ruled by the rich

polarize: to set apart at opposite extremes of opinion

posse comitatus: local body of armed men; sheriff's posse

posterity: the future

postulate: to assume a thing to be true

potent: powerful or effective

practicable: able to be done

precarious: unstable; uncertain; unsafe; insecure

precariousness: danger; lack of security

precipitate: to bring about abruptly

predatory: exploiting others; thieving

predecessor; the former holder of an office or position

predispose: to bring about in advance

predominant: having control

predominate: to have control

preeminence: condition of being outstanding; of higher importance

prepossession: an attitude formed beforehand; bias

prerogative: a right or privilege

presumption: acting without authority

presumptuous: arrogant; smart-alecky

pretension: a claim to a right or honor of doubtful validity

pretext: excuse

prevalence: widespread existence

prima facie: at first sight; first impression

privation: lack of the necessaries of life; poverty; hardship

proclivity: tendency: leaning toward

prodigious: huge; immense; vast

progressive: proceeding steadily at different steps or speeds

proletariat: the working class

promiscuous: not restricted to one class, sort, or person; diverse

promptitude: being on time

promulgate: make known; proclaim

proneness: inclination to do something

propaganda: spreading of ideas or information that will persuade or convince others

propensity: bias; tendency

propriety: decency; uprightness

prostitution: selling oneself for unworthy purposes

proverbial: having become commonly used

providence: God's care and protection

proximate: near; close

prudence: carefulness; reasonableness

prudent: cautious; careful; sensible; levelheaded

prudential: careful

psychiatric: related to the scientific study of mental, emotional, or behavioral disorders

pursuance: performance; carrying out

Q

quixotic: unrealistic; fantastic

R

rabble: disorganized or disorderly mob

radicalism: extremism in one's beliefs or actions

rampant: widespread; excessive

ransack: search; plunder

rebuke: scold

reciprocal: interchangeable; shared by both sides

reconciliation: bringing into harmony when there is conflict

redress: set right; repair; correct; repay

refractory: resisting control or authority

reminiscence: reflection; recalling past experiences

remuneration: pay; reward; profit

remunerative: profitable

renunciation: giving up the right to something

repose: rest; sleep; calm

repression: domination; holding down

republican: of a government in which the people express their will through elected representatives

repugnant: distasteful; disgusting

repulsive: offensive; disgusting; distasteful; hateful

requisite: necessary for success

resentment: anger; outrage; bitterness

respective: relating to each one separately
retard: slow down
retinue: followers
reverence: respect
rogue: criminal; scoundrel; good-for-nothing
roguery: dishonest practices

S

sanction: give approval or permission
sanctuary: a safe place; shelter; refuge
schizophrenic: having a disease characterized by hallucinations
score: a group of twenty
scourged: punished; plagued; cursed
segregation: the separation of individuals from a larger group
segregationist: one who believes in separating a minority from the larger group
self-aggrandizement: an increase in one's own wealth, power, or rank
self-exalted: being the author of one's own glorification
self-incrimination: answering questions that would cause one to be charged with a crime
servile: slavish
shiftless: lazy; incompetent; unreliable; undependable
sibling: brother or sister
slavish: showing no originality or independence
slovenly: untidy; sloppy; messy; unclean
smite: to hit
smugness: self-satisfaction; conceit
socialization: government ownership
solicitude: concern about a person's welfare or comfort
solidity: soundness and reliability
solitude: privacy; seclusion; aloneness
sovereignty: supreme power
spectre: any object of fear or dread
speculative: theoretical; not practical
staple: regularly produced; used by many
status quo: the existing state of affairs
statute: a law passed by a governing body
stereotyped: standardized; lacking originality
stifle: repress; discourage
stigma: blemish; disgrace
stipulation: agreement; contract
strontium 90: radioactive substance present in nuclear fallout
stultify: obstruct; frustrate

subjection: bringing under control of a superior
subjugate: enslave; put down; crush
sublime: glorious; magnificent
subordination: subjection; submission; obedience
subsequent: following; next
subsistence: means of support or livelihood
subversion: attempt to overthrow or ruin
subvert: overthrow; destroy
succession: act of coming after
successive: continuous
suffrage: the right to vote
sullen: depressed; brooding
superfluity: that which is unnecessary
superfluous: unnecessary
superimposition: placing over or above something
superstructure: a structure that rests on something else
supplant: replace; substitute for
sustenance: nourishment; livelihood; support
sympathetic: feeling pity or tenderness for one who is hurt or in trouble
symptom: condition that indicates a disease
synonymous: equivalent in meaning

T

tabula rasa: clean slate; blank mind
taint: contaminate
tare: bad seed
taunt: insult; put down; ridicule; mock
tedious: boring; dull
temperateness: moderation; reasonableness; sensibility
tenement: slum apartment
testament: a will
theology: the study of God or religion
thither: there
thriven: developed well; prosperous
tillage: cultivated land
tithe: one-tenth of a year's income donated to the church
totalitarian: having absolute or total government control; no personal freedom
toxic: poisonous
tranquility: peacefulness; calm
transgress: to break a rule or a law; to sin
transgression: going beyond the limits
transgressor: one who sins or breaks the law
transience: state of being temporary
transmit: pass on

transmute: to cause a thing to change
treachery: betrayal; an act of disloyalty
tribunal: court; decision-makers
trite: hackneyed; stale
trust: an association of business firms formed to reduce or defeat competition
tumult: noise and confusion
tutelary: having the guardianship of a person or thing
tyranny: rule by a person with absolute power
tyrant: one who insists on absolute obedience; dictator; bully

U

umbrage: resentment; anger
unalienable: not to be given or taken away
unequivocal: plain; clear; unmistakable
unfeigned: genuine
uniformity: sameness
unimpaired: unharmed; unhurt; intact; strong
unpalatable: distasteful; unpleasant; disagreeable
unscrupulous: dishonest; corrupt; unjust
usufruct: use and enjoyment without waste or destruction
usurer: a person who lends money at an unusually high interest rate
usurp: to take wrongfully by force
usurpation: taking or seizing in a wrongful manner
utilitarianism: doing something practical or useful
utopia: an ideal society

V

vacillation: shifting back and forth; wavering; fluctuating
vagabond: beggar; tramp; vagrant
vagrant: a person without a home; a person without employment
vanity: conceit; arrogance
vantage: superior position
vengeance: revenge
venison: deer meat
vested: fixed; settled; not in a state of contingency
vesture: a covering garment
viburnum: shrub or tree of the honeysuckle family
vicinage: vicinity; neighborhood
vindicate: to justify by evidence or results

virtue: goodness; honor; integrity

W

wanton: immoral
wantonly: senselessly; uncalled for; playfully mean or cruel
wariness: state of being cautious or prudent
wary: cautious; careful
weariness: state of exhaustion
weal: well-being
weariness: state of exhaustion
wrath: extreme anger
wretched: very unfortunate; miserable
wretchedness: a state of poverty, hopelessness, or misery
writ of assistance: a general search warrant

Y

yoke: restraint

Z

zeal: enthusiasm; ambition

Bibliography

Abraham Lincoln: A Documentary Portrait Through His Speeches and Writings, ed. Don E. Fehrenbacher (Stanford, Calif.: Stanford University Press, 1964)

American Issues: A Documentary Reader, eds. Charles Dollar and Gary Reichard (New York: Random House, 1988)

American Political Thought, ed. Kenneth Dolbeare (Monterey, Calif.: Duxbury Press, 1981)

An American Primer, ed. Daniel J. Boorstin (New York: Meridian Books, 1966)

The American Reader, ed. Diane Ravitch (New York: Harper Perennial, 1990)

The Annals of America (Chicago: Encyclopedia Britannica, 1968)

Anti-Federalist Papers and the Constitutional Convention, ed. Ralph Ketcham (New York: Penguin Group, 1986)

Axelrod, Alan and Charles Phillips, *What Every American Should Know About American History* (Holbrook, Mass.: Bob Adams, Inc., 1992)

Bailyn, Bernard, *Debate on the Constitution* (New York: The Library of America, 1993)

The Basic Works of Aristotle, ed. Richard McKeon (New York: Random House, 1941)

Berkin, Carol et al., *American Voices: A History of the United States* (Glenview, Ill.: Scott Foresman and Company, 1992)

Bosmajian, Haig, *Justice Douglas and Freedom of Speech* (Metuchen, N.J.: Scarecrow Press, 1980)

Braeman, John, *Wilson* (Englewood Cliffs, N.J.: Prentice-Hall, Inc., 1972)

Brogan, Hugh, *Tocqueville* (Bungay, Suffolk, Great Britain: Collins/Fontana, 1973)

Capers, Gerald M., *John C. Calhoun—Opportunist: A Reappraisal* (Gainesville, Fla: University of Florida Press, 1960)

Carson, Rachel. *Silent Spring* (Boston: Houghton Mifflin, 1962)

Chupack, Henry, *Roger Williams* (New York: Twayne Publishers, Inc., 1969)

Civil Rights Leaders, ed. Richard Rennert (New York: Chelsea House Publishers, 1993)

Classics of Moral and Political Theory, ed. Michael Morgan (Indianapolis: Hachett Publishing Co., 1992)

The Complete Madison: His Basic Writings, ed. Saul K. Padover (Norwalk, Conn., The Easton Press, 1953)

Countryman, Vern, *The Judicial Record of Justice William O. Douglas* (Cambridge, Mass.: Harvard University Press, 1974)

Current, Richard et al., *American History: A Survey* (New York: Alfred A. Knopf, 1979)

Currie, Harold W., *Eugene Debs* (Boston: Twayne Publishers, 1976)

Danzer, Gerald et al., *The Americans* (Evanston, Ill.: McDougal Littell, 1998)

Davis, Kenneth C., *Don't Know Much About History* (New York: Crown Publishers, 1990)

Debs, ed. Ronald Radosh (Englewood Cliffs, N.J.: Prentice-Hall, 1971)

Debs, Eugene V., *Walls and Bars* (Chicago: Charles H. Kerr & Company, 1927)

Degregorio, William A., *The Complete Book of U.S. Presidents* (New York: Wings Books, 1993)

The Democracy Reader, eds. Diane Ravitch and Abigail Thernstrom (New York: Harper Collins Publishers, 1992)

Douglas, William O., *An Almanac of Liberty* (Garden City, N.Y.: Doubleday and Company, 1954)

Douglas, William O., *The Court Years* (New York: Random House, 1980)

Douglas, William O. *Points of Rebellion* (New York: Vintage Books, 1970)

Dowd, Douglas F., *Thorstein Veblen* (New York: Washington Square Press, 1966)

DuBois, Ellen Carol, *Elizabeth Cady Stanton/Susan B. Anthony: Correspondence, Writings, Speeches* (New York: Schocken Books, 1981)

Elkins, Stanley and Eric McKitrick, *The Age of Federalism: The Early American Republic, 1788-1800* (New York: Oxford University Press, 1993)

The Essential Adam Smith, ed. Robert Heilbroner (New York: W. W. Norton & Company, 1986)

The Essential Franklin Delano Roosevelt, ed. John Gabriel Hunt (Avenel, N.J.: Portland House, 1996)

Essential Writings of Karl Marx, ed. David Caute (New York: Simon and Schuster, 1972)

Fehrenbacher, Don E., *Lincoln in Text and Context: Collected Essays* (Stanford, Calif.: Stanford University Press, 1964)

Ferriss, Susan and Ricardo Sandoval. *The Fight in the Fields: Cesar Chavez and the Farmworkers Movement* (New York: Harcourt Brace & Company, 1997)

Frederick Douglass, ed. Benjamin Quarles (Englewood Cliffs, N.J.: Prentice-Hall, Inc., 1968)

Friedan, Betty, *The Feminine Mystique* (New York: W.W. Norton & Company, Inc, 1963)

Friedan, Betty, *It Changed My Life: Writings on the Women's Movement* (New York: Signet, 1993)

Friedan, Betty, *Our American Sisters* (Boston: Allyn and Bacon, Inc., 1976)

Friedan, Betty, *The Second Stage* (New York: Summit Books, 1981)

Garraty, John A., *The American Nation: A History of the United States* (New York: Harper Collins College Publishers, 1995)

Gartner, Carol B. *Rachel Carson* (New York: Frederick Ungar Publishing Co., 1983)

George, Henry, *Progress and Poverty* (New York: AMS Press, 1973)

George Washington: A Collection, ed. W.B. Allen (Indianapolis: Liberty Classics, 1988)

Goldman, Peter, *The Death and Life of Malcolm X* (New York: Ballantine Books, 1964)

Great Documents in American Indian History, ed. Wayne Moquin (New York: Da Capo Press, 1995)

The Great Thoughts, ed. George Seldes (New York: Ballantine Books, 1985)

Hakim, Joy, *The New Nation* (New York: Oxford University Press, 1993)

Haley, Alex, *The Autobiography of Malcolm X* (New York: Ballantine Books, 1964)

Hamilton, Alexander, James Madison, and John Jay, *The Federalist Papers,* ed. Clinton Rossiter (New York: Penguin Group, 1961)

Hamilton, ed. Milton Cantor (Englewood Cliffs, N.J.: Prentice-Hall, 1971)

Hart, Michael H., *The 100: A Ranking of the Most Influential Persons in History* (New York: Carol Publishing Group, 1995)

Heilbroner, Robert, *The Worldly Philosophers* (New York: Simon and Schuster, 1972)

Hirschfelder, Arlene, *Native Heritage: Personal Accounts by American Indians, 1790 to the Present* (New York: MacMillan, 1995)

Hobson, Charles F., *The Great Chief Justice: John Marshall and the Rule of Law* (Lawrence, Kans.: University Press of Kansas, 1996)

Hochman, Stanley and Eleanor, *A Dictionary of Contemporary American History* (New York: Signet, 1993)

Hofstadter, Richard, *The American Political Tradition* (New York: Vintage Books, 1948)

Holland, Michele, " . . . *And Many a Rebel Made by that Short Pause." Feminism, Domesticity, and the Political Rhetoric of Harriet Beecher Stowe, Helen Hunt Jackson, and Elizabeth Cady Stanton* (Las Cruces, N. Mex.: New Mexico State University, 1994)

Huggins, Nathan Irvin, *Slave and Citizen: The Life of Frederick Douglass* (Boston: Little, Brown, and Company, 1980)

John C. Calhoun, ed. Margaret L. Coit (Englewood Cliffs, N.J.: Prentice Hall, Inc., 1970)

John Marshall, ed. Stanley I. Kutler (Englewood Cliffs, N.J.: Prentice-Hall, Inc., 1972)

Karl Marx: Selected Writings, ed. David McLellan (Oxford, England: Oxford University Press)

Keynes, John Maynard, *The Collected Works of John Maynard Keynes, Volume VII—The General Theory of Employment, Interest, and Money* (Cambridge, England: MacMillan St. Martin's Press, 1936)

Lerna, Gerda, *The Woman in American History* (Menlo Park, Calif.: Addison-Wesley Publishing Company, 1971)

Levy, Jacques E. *Cesar Chavez: Autobiography of La Causa* (New York: W. W. Norton & Company, 1975)

Link, Arthur S., *The Higher Realism of Woodrow Wilson and Other Essays* (Nashville: Vanderbilt University Press, 1971)

McCoy, Drew, *The Last of the Fathers: James Madison and the Republican Legacy* (Cambridge, Mass.: Cambridge University Press, 1989)

McGraw-Hill Encyclopedia of World Biography (New York/San Francisco/St. Louis: McGraw-Hill Book Company, 1973)

McKay, Mary A. *Rachel Carson* (New York: Twayne Publishers, 1993)

Miller, Perry, *Roger Williams: His Contributions to the American Tradition* (Indianapolis: The Bobbs-Merrill Company, Inc., 1953)

Morgan, Edmund, *Roger Williams: The Church and the State* (New York: Harcourt, Brace & World, Inc., 1967)

Moritz, Charles, ed. *Current Biography, 1975* (New York: The H. H. Wilson Company, 1975)

The Morrow Book of Quotations in American History, ed. Joseph Conlin (New York: William Morrow and Company, 1984)

The New York Times Biographical Service (New York: The New York Times Company)

Norman, Geoffrey. "The Flight of Rachel Carson" (*Esquire*: December 1983)

Novas, Himilce. *Everything You Need to Know About Latino History* (New York: Penguin Books USA, 1994)

Novas, Himilce. *The Hispanic 100: A Ranking of the Latino Men and Women Who Have Most Influenced American Thought and Culture* (New York: Citadel Press, 1995)

Oser, Jacob, *Henry George* (New York: Twayne Publishers, 1974)

Pancake, John S., *Thomas Jefferson and Alexander Hamilton* (Woodbury, New York: Barron's Educational Series, Inc., 1974)

The Papers of Alexander Hamilton, ed. Harold C. Syrett (New York: Columbia University Press, 1961)

The Portable Thomas Jefferson, ed. Merrill D. Peterson (New York: Penguin Books, 1975)

Power Quotes, ed. Daniel B. Baker (Detroit: Visible Ink Press, 1992)

President Reagan's Quotations: Inaugural Edition, ed. Clark Cassell (Washington, D.C.: Braddock Publications, 1984)

Rakove, Jack N., "The Madisonian Theory of Rights" (*William and Mary Law Review*, Volume 3, Number 2, Winter 1990)

Rakove, Jack N., *Original Meanings: Politics and Ideas in the Making of the Constitution* (New York: Alfred A. Knopf, 1966)

The Readers Companion to American History, eds. Eric Foner and John A. Garraty (Boston: Houghton Mifflin, Co., 1991)

Reagan, Ronald, *The Creative Society* (New York: Devin-Adair Company, 1968)

Reagan, Ronald, *Speaking My Mind* (New York: Simon and Schuster, 1989)

Reagan, Ronald, *A Time for Choosing: The Speeches of Ronald Reagan, 1961-82* (Chicago: Regnery Gateway, 1983)

Scruton, Roger, *Dictionary of Political Thought* (New York: Hill and Wang, 1982)

Sochen, June, *Herstory: A Woman's View of American History* (New York: Alfred Publishing Co., 1974)

Social Darwinism: Selected Essays of William Graham Sumner, ed. Stow Persons (Englewood Cliffs, NJ: Prentice-Hall, 1963)

Stone, John and Stephen Mennell, *Alexis de Tocqueville on Democracy, Revolution, and Society* (Chicago: The University of Chicago Press, 1980)

Sumner Today: Selected Essays of William Graham Sumner with Comments by American Leaders, ed. Maurice R. Davie (New Haven, CT: Yale University Press, 1940)

Sumner, William Graham, *What Social Classes Owe to Each Other* (Caldwell, ID: The Caxton Printers, 1966)

Teluja, Tad, *American History in 100 Nutshells* (New York: Ballantine Books, 1992)

A Testament of Hope: The Essential Writings of Martin Luther King, Jr., ed. James Melvin Washington (San Francisco: Harper & Row, 1986)

Thoreau: The Major Essays, ed. Jeffrey L. Duncan (New York: E. P. Dutton & Co., 1972)

Tocqueville, Alexis de, *Democracy in America, Volumes I and II* (New York: D. Appleton and Company, 1899)

Toffler, Alvin. *Future Shock* (New York: Bantam Books, 1970)

Toffler, Alvin. *The Third Wave* (New York: Bantam Books, 1980)

The Turner Thesis: Concerning the Role of the Frontier in American History ed. George Rogers Taylor (Boston: D.C. Heath and Company, 1956)

Veblen, Thorstein, *The Theory of Business Enterprise* (New Brunswick, NJ: Transaction Publishers, 1996)

Veblen, Thorstein, *The Theory of the Leisure Class* (New Brunswick, NJ: Transaction Publishers, 1992)

Weibe, Robert H., *The Search for Order, 1877-1920* (New York, Hill and Wang, 1967)

Winthrop, Robert C., *Life and Letters of John Winthrop* (Boston: Ticknor and Fields, 1867)

The Wisdom of Martin Luther King, Jr., ed. Alex Ayres (New York: Meridian Books, 1993)

The Writings of George Washington, ed. John Fitzpatrick (Washington, D.C.: U.S. Government Printing Office, 1931-44)

NOTES